A Practical Guide to Teaching History in the Secondary School

A Practical Guide to Teaching History in the Secondary School offers comprehensive advice, inspiration and a wide range of tried and tested approaches to help you find success in the secondary history classroom. Covering all aspects of history teaching, it is designed for you to dip in and out of and to enable you to focus on specific areas of teaching, your programme or pupils' learning.

This completely revised edition has been rewritten with new chapters reflecting recent work into curriculum thought, different types of historical knowledge, designing enquiry questions and decolonising the curriculum. Emphasising the importance of pedagogy, detailed subject knowledge, a well-informed and diverse curriculum, evidence-informed practice and a focus on building long-term student understanding in the subject, the chapters cover:

- Curriculum design
- Teaching causation and consequence
- Teaching interpretation and significance
- Using evidence
- Delivering a more inclusive and representative history curriculum
- Progress and assessment

Packed with ideas, resources and practical teaching activities and underpinned by the latest research, this is an essential companion for all training and early career history teachers.

Dan Keates is Deputy Head Teacher at Framingham Earl High School in Norfolk.

Matt Stanford is National Lead for History for Astrea Academy Trust.

Corinne Goullée taught history for eight years at Cottenham Village College in Cambridgeshire.

Routledge Teaching Guides

Series Editors: Susan Capel and Marilyn Leask

Other titles in the series:

A Practical Guide to Teaching Design and Technology in the Secondary School
Edited by Gwyneth Owen-Jackson

A Practical Guide to Teaching Citizenship in the Secondary School
Edited by Liam Gearon

A Practical Guide to Teaching ICT in the Secondary School
Edited by Steve Kennewell, Andrew Connell, Anthony Edwards, Michael Hammond and Cathy Wickens

A Practical Guide to Teaching Computing and ICT in the Secondary School
Andrew Connell and Anthony Edwards with Alison Hramiak, Gavin Rhodes and Neil Stanley

A Practical Guide to Teaching Mathematics in the Secondary School, 2nd Edition
Edited by Clare Lee and Robert Ward-Penny

A Practical Guide to Teaching Physical Education in the Secondary School, 3rd Edition
Edited by Susan Capel, Joanne Cliffe and Julia Lawrence

A Practical Guide to Teaching English in the Secondary School, 2nd Edition
Annabel Watson and Ruth Newman

A Practical Guide to Teaching Music in the Secondary School, 2nd Edition
Edited by Carolyn Cooke and Chris Philpott

A Practical Guide to Teaching Science in the Secondary School, 2nd Edition
Douglas P. Newton

A Practical Guide to Teaching Foreign Languages in the Secondary School, 3rd Edition
Edited by Norbert Pachler & Ana Redondo

A Practical Guide to Teaching Art and Design in the Secondary School
Edited by Andy Ash & Peter Carr

A Practical Guide to Teaching History in the Secondary School, 2nd Edition
Edited by Dan Keates, Matt Stanford and Corinne Goullée

These Practical Guides have been designed as companions to **Learning to Teach X Subject in the Secondary School**. For information on the Routledge Teaching Guides series please visit our website at www.routledge.com/education.

A Practical Guide to Teaching History in the Secondary School

Second Edition

Edited by
**Dan Keates,
Matt Stanford
and
Corinne Goullée**

LONDON AND NEW YORK

Designed cover image: JingJongArt

Second edition published 2025
by Routledge
4 Park Square, Milton Park, Abingdon, Oxon, OX14 4RN

and by Routledge
605 Third Avenue, New York, NY 10158

Routledge is an imprint of the Taylor & Francis Group, an informa business

© 2025 selection and editorial matter, Dan Keates, Matt Stanford and Corinne Goullée; individual chapters, the contributors

The right of Dan Keates, Matt Stanford and Corinne Goullée to be identified as the authors of the editorial material, and of the authors for their individual chapters, has been asserted in accordance with sections 77 and 78 of the Copyright, Designs and Patents Act 1988.

All rights reserved. No part of this book may be reprinted or reproduced or utilised in any form or by any electronic, mechanical, or other means, now known or hereafter invented, including photocopying and recording, or in any information storage or retrieval system, without permission in writing from the publishers.

Trademark notice: Product or corporate names may be trademarks or registered trademarks, and are used only for identification and explanation without intent to infringe.

First edition published by Routledge 2007

British Library Cataloguing-in-Publication Data
A catalogue record for this book is available from the British Library

ISBN: 978-1-032-39355-1 (hbk)
ISBN: 978-1-032-39354-4 (pbk)
ISBN: 978-1-003-34936-5 (ebk)

DOI: 10.4324/9781003349365

Typeset in Palatino
by KnowledgeWorks Global Ltd.

This book is dedicated to Helen Snelson.

We want to be more like her.

We want to be as kind and welcoming, as brilliant, as clever, as open and as thoughtful.

As three individuals, we didn't know Helen well, but we all spent time with her as part of our role as history teachers and educators. She had many gifts, but we recall her kindness and her commitment to making other people better for the sake of the pupils they would teach.

In this book, we hope to welcome teachers into the 'history teaching community'. No-one did that better than Helen, and thousands upon thousands of children have benefited, directly and indirectly, from her work, her brilliance and her generosity.

Contents

List of Contributors	ix
1 Introduction Matt Stanford, Corinne Goullée and Dan Keates	1
2 Curriculum Design in History Will Bailey-Watson	4
3 Planning Enquiries in History Paula Worth	16
4 Substantive and Disciplinary Knowledge Michael Fordham	32
5 Change and Continuity Matt Stanford	43
6 Teaching Causal Reasoning Laura London	57
7 Teaching Consequence Molly-Ann Navey	72
8 Teaching Similarity/Difference and Historical Perspective Jacob Olivey	90
9 Interpretations Dan Keates	104
10 Historical Significance Helen Snelson	118

CONTENTS

11	**Sources and Evidence** *Alex Ford*	135
12	**'Decolonising' the History Curriculum in Schools** *Dan Lyndon-Cohen and Josh Preye Garry*	157
13	**Progress and Assessment in History** *Victoria Barnett*	169
14	**Teaching Extended Writing in History** *Jim Carroll*	183
15	**Teaching Using Historical Scholarship** *Victoria Crooks*	202
16	**Teaching Local History** *Luke Mayhew*	219
	Index	*228*

List of Contributors

Will Bailey-Watson is the Subject Leader of a History Initial Teacher Education programme. After working as a history teacher and Head of History, he has written about, and presented on, a range of issues related to history curriculum design. Among his activities to make history curriculum design ambitious and expansive, Will has created a popular website called 'meanwhile, elsewhere', curated the *Curricularium* – an influential set of talks on curriculum thinking and co-authored the successful *Changing Histories* textbook series.

Victoria Barnett is Head of History and Classics at an 11–18 school in Norwich and a former Local Research Lead at Norwich Research School. She has written blogs on the role of cognitive science in the classroom and has given talks at ResearchEd Rugby and Ipswich on such topics. She delivers lectures on Cognitive Load Theory to secondary PGCE students and has been a PGCE and SCITT History mentor throughout her career.

Jim Carroll is Departmental Lecturer in History Education at the University of Oxford. Prior to this, he worked as a history teacher for eight years. He has a PhD in Education from the Institute of Education, University College London, where his thesis was on literacy in history teaching. He has published articles on history pupils' extended writing in *Teaching History, The Curriculum Journal, The Journal of Curriculum Studies* and *The History Education Research Journal*. He has presented on the topic of extended historical writing at several history education conferences and at INSET for a variety of schools, networks and trusts.

Victoria Crooks is Associate Professor in History Education at the University of Nottingham, where she is the subject lead for the history PGCE. Her current research work focuses on the subject-specific mentoring of beginning history teachers. Prior to working in initial teacher education, Victoria was Head of Sixth Form and a history and humanities teacher in schools in the East Midlands. She is an Honorary Fellow of the Historical Association and Co-Chair of the History Teacher Educators Network.

Alex Ford is a PGCE History Tutor at Leeds Trinity University and a Fellow of the Schools History Project. He was formerly a Head of History in a large comprehensive school in Leeds. Alex has delivered educational training on curriculum, planning, assessment and progression for Teach First, SSAT, the Historical

LIST OF CONTRIBUTORS

Association and the Schools History Project. He is also part of the Ofsted subject working group for History.

Michael Fordham is Principal at Thetford Academy. Previously, he worked as a history teacher and head of department in schools in Cambridgeshire, Inspiration Trust's Director of Initial Teacher Training and Assistant Head Teacher at the West London Free School. He has completed a PhD in the field of history education and was a Senior Teaching Associate at the University of Cambridge where he worked on education development projects in Kazakhstan. He was the Outstanding-Educator-in-Residence to the Singapore Ministry of Education in 2014 and is an Honorary Fellow of the Historical Association following eight years as an editor of the Teaching History journal. He has written widely in the fields of history education and the philosophy of education and has presented his research at a variety of national and international conferences.

Corinne Goullée taught history for eight years at Cottenham Village College in Cambridgeshire. During that time, she mentored PGCE history trainees for the University of Cambridge and delivered workshops on aspects of history teaching for the Schools History Project and West London Free School Conference.

Dan Keates is Deputy Head Teacher at Framingham Earl High School in Norfolk, where previously he was Head of History for eight years. He has presented workshops at the Schools History Project Conference, including on the teaching of the GCSE thematic unit looking at migration to Britain through time. He wrote an article on effective teaching of historical interpretations, and this was published in Teaching History magazine in 2020. An experienced history mentor, he has presented at UEA to the History PGCE cohort on different topics over several years.

Laura London is a Lecturer in Education in the School of Education and Lifelong Learning at the University of East Anglia. She began her career as a history teacher and worked for 15 years in 11–18 secondary schools in East Anglia. At the UEA, she has led workshops on trainee feedback and sequencing the ITE curriculum at both the 2019 and 2020 UEA Professional Tutor and Mentor Conferences. In addition, she has presented her work on trainee feedback and school visits to UCET. As well as being part of the Historical Association she is also a branch member of the Norfolk and Norwich Committee.

Dan Lyndon-Cohen has been teaching History in London schools for over 25 years. He has also published many books on multicultural British history for KS2, KS3 and KS4. Dan collaborated on the specification for the OCR GCSE History of migration courses, co-authoring GCSE textbooks on the topic and working as an exam constructor for 5 years. He is Honorary Fellow of the Schools History Project and consultant for the Colonial Countryside Project.

Luke Mayhew has been working in secondary schools for 15 years and in that time has been both a history teacher and head of department. He has played a full part in his professional community delivering training and workshops at the SHP Conference, to UEA trainees and local subject networks. He has been published in Teaching History sharing best practice in teaching local history enquiries and is a regional SHP advisor in the East of England.

Molly-Ann Navey is a History Teacher in East Sussex. She has been published in the Historical Association's journal Teaching History and has also presented workshops for the Historical Association and at the Cambridge Festival. She currently mentors trainee PGCE History teachers at the University of Sussex, as well as leading taught sessions for Sussex History trainees across a variety of areas, including historical consequence.

Jacob Olivey teaches history at Ark Soane Academy in London. He has written articles in Teaching History about bringing cultural history into Key Stage 3, planning a more diverse and coherent Year 7 curriculum and planning for progression in pupils understanding of 'historical perspective'. Jacob has also led workshops about teaching cultural history at the Schools History Project and the Historical Association's annual conferences. Previously, he mentored trainee PGCE History teachers at the University of Cambridge.

Josh Preye Garry is a Deputy Head of Department at an inner-city London school, who is due to start an MA in Black British History at Goldsmiths University. He has co-authored the new Pearson Migration GCSE textbook and collaborated with Miranda Kaufmann to create resources for her Black Tudors book. He is also an examiner for Pearson and is a member of the BeBold Network which aims to provide free CPD for History teachers. He has presented at various conferences for both the Schools Historical Project and Historical Association. He has a Fellowship with the Historical Association for a scheme of work which focuses on the Kingdom of Benin and works as a consultant for ACLS. His work centres around the decolonisation of the school curriculum to ensure that the voices silenced from the past are heard.

Helen Snelson was a history teacher for over twenty years in secondary schools in the UK. The history department she led had the Historical Association Gold Quality Mark and she was a Chartered History Teacher. She was recently the Curriculum Area Leader for the History PGCE at the University of York. Helen regularly contributed to webinars, conferences, online materials and textbooks relating to history teaching in the UK and beyond. She wrote several articles, including for Teaching History. Helen was a Fellow of the Historical Association and a EuroClio ambassador.

Matt Stanford is currently National Lead for History for Astrea Academy Trust. Prior to that, he was Director of the Schools History Project and a head of department in a comprehensive school in Cambridgeshire. He has written about and delivered workshops on various aspects of history teaching to a wide variety of audiences.

Paula Worth has taught History in state and independent schools for over a decade. She is an Associate Lecturer on the History PGCE course at the University of Bristol and an Honorary Fellow of the Historical Association. She has supervised masters' students at the University of Cambridge and has been an associate editor for the journal Teaching History for several years. She has written several articles for Teaching History and is an author for a series of textbooks at Key Stage 3.

Chapter 1 Introduction

Matt Stanford, Corinne Goullée and Dan Keates

WELCOME

One aim of this book is to welcome new teachers into the community of history teachers, outlining much of the best thinking and writing that has been done by history teachers and offer practical suggestions as to how this wisdom might wash up in our classrooms. The chapters in this book follow a similar format: they all explore an issue around the teaching of history, they all make reference to academic and professional scholarship, and they all contain practical activities that will help you think about how you can implement these ideas in your classroom. However, the authors of the chapters don't all give the same weight to each of these elements. The chapters don't all sound the same.

We make no apology for that inconsistency.

They are different because they are written by different experts, with different experiences and different perspectives. This means that some chapters may be more to your tastes than others, some lay more emphasis on the theoretical, some on the practical. This also reflects one of the glorious things about being a *history* teacher in Britain today: by joining this profession, you are joining the most engaged, vibrant and supportive community of teachers in the country. Perhaps more than for any other subject, it is history teachers with chalk on their shoulders (whiteboard pen on their fingers? green pens in their pocket?) from across the country, from across the Key Stages, who are the ones who shape the debate about what should be taught and how it should be taught. Perhaps more than in any other subject, it is teachers themselves who are theorising and experimenting and then talking and publishing about the nature of our subject, about the goals we are seeking to achieve and about how to deliver these for the benefit of our pupils.

By being a history teacher, you are part of that community and you can look to that community for advice and support in a number of ways. Not least through this book, but also through established organisations such as the Schools History Project and the Historical Association, through exam boards, the Be Bold Network, the History Teacher Book Club, Teach Meets, social media and many other places.

Is this community perfect? No. There is always room for more voices and fresh perspectives and we all, always, need to be mindful of whose voices get amplified, but we firmly believe that there is space for everyone and that you too can make a contribution to that community, shape its debates, refine its ideas and open its eyes. After all, the expert contributors to this book are also, for the most part, practising history teachers. While we find ourselves in awe of their range of knowledge about history and pedagogy, they also know about assemblies, uniform policies and parents' evenings. They might be thinking deeply about the ideas of Marc Bloch but they may well be doing it on break duty outside the music block. They might be asking themselves about the theoretical underpinnings of the subject discipline but they are also asking Year 8 pupils to tuck in their shirts.

And so, we welcome you to this book and hope that you find its contents both inspiring and useful. However, while we heartily recommend the ideas and strategies outlined here, we also invite you to approach them with a critical eye: Where are the gaps? What are the short-comings? What could still be better? Because without that critical engagement, we, as a professional community, cannot move forward. Without the contributions of people like you to the discussions and debates about what and how we should teach and assess, we cannot fully serve the young people entrusted to our care.

THE CHAPTERS

In some ways, Michael Fordham's chapter addresses some of the most fundamental questions in history teaching: What does it mean to know something in history? What different types of knowledge are there and for how long do we want pupils to know what has been taught? His incredibly clear-sighted chapter outlines these issues, making simple what can often feel like a complicated mess of ideas.

How we turn this into a history curriculum that can be taught is a problem that Will Bailey-Watson addresses in his chapter. He takes us on a tour of the ways in which this thorny problem has been approached by thoughtful practitioners in our community over the last quarter of a century. While Bailey-Watson doesn't claim to have the perfect answer, the way he articulates these issues helps us to find the starting points from which we can begin this tricky work.

For all of the approaches that Will Bailey-Watson outlines, enquiry questions are at the heart of them. In her chapter, Paula Worth walks us through what a good enquiry question is, how it can be used to shape a sequence of lessons, and provides us with eight principles to guide us as we try and create our own. Worth illustrates these principles, and inspires us, with a wide variety of examples from other people's practice, but also with her thoughtful and deeply honest reflection on her own trials and tribulations.

As Worth reminds us, a good enquiry question is based around a second-order concept (also referred to as a disciplinary concept) to foreground a certain aspect of historical thinking. The chapters by Matt Stanford (change and continuity), Laura London (causation), Molly-Ann Navey (consequences) and Dan Keates (interpretations) outline the professional and academic literature behind these ideas and offer practical examples as to how you can teach these effectively in your classroom. As upholders of the enquiry question, they also provide a more detailed outline of an enquiry governed by each of these second-order concepts. Similarly, Helen Snelson carefully unpacks the complexities behind the frequently misunderstood concept of historical significance, while offering useful examples to follow.

When it comes to similarity and difference, Jacob Olivey not only gives us an overview of how we teach this concept; he goes further and makes a much bolder case. He argues that we can illuminate the complexity of the past by basing our enquiries around the work of cultural historians and histories 'from the inside' and 'from below'. He reframes similarity and difference as 'historical perspective' – an attempt to help pupils understand the different meanings people in the past attached to ideas, institutions and events.

Alex Ford, when writing on the use of evidence, offers an overview of the concept and makes a case that we need to think carefully about the language we use so that we can help pupils really understand how historians make and support claims about the past, while avoiding the formulaic and reductivist approaches to 'sources' and 'reliability' that many of us experienced in our own education.

Beyond the second-order concepts, Dan Lydon-Cohen and Josh Garry help us understand what has been meant by 'decolonisation,' make a passionate call for that to shape our curricular choices and share their approaches to amplify voices that have been marginalised or silenced. Similarly, Luke Mayhew makes a compelling case for the importance of local history in our curricula and gives suggestions as to how this can be achieved.

Both Victoria Crooks and Jim Carroll make a strong case for how we can stay true to the discipline of history in our teaching. Crooks outlines three principles as she argues for the place of historical scholarship in the history classroom, both for teachers in their planning and to bring pupils closer to the interpretative nature of the discipline. Crooks isn't the only exponent of this though as many of the chapters give examples of enquiries built around the work of historians. Meanwhile, Carroll explains the importance of extended writing in allowing pupils to engage with the argument of history. Recognising the difficulty of this, he offers his wisdom for supporting pupils in both structuring an argument into paragraphs and crafting it at the sentence level.

Then, importantly, Victoria Barnett reflects on how we can tell whether our pupils have actually learned the things we are teaching them and what tools might help us do this. She offers examples of both formative and summative assessments and brings us back to the questions of how this might affect both our enquiry and curriculum planning.

CONCLUSION

The contributors to this book and its editors hope that you find it useful and inspiring. That it provides an entry into the discussions and debates around history teaching, and at the same time practical strategies that influence what happens in your classroom next week. All the chapter authors, whose work this book is, were once at the start of their careers. Through engagement with the professional literature and debate, and reflection on their classroom experiences, they have added to the collective wisdom of the history teaching community. We hope that in the future, when the next editions come out, they will contain revisions, improvements and fresh perspectives from people like you, who are perhaps now, just at the start of their careers.

Chapter 2 Curriculum Design in History

Will Bailey-Watson

BACKGROUND

It is common for any history teacher involved in curriculum design to flit between inspiration and despair. It can feel ever-changing and never-ending. Unsurprisingly for such a complex activity, pinning down a definitive summary of how to *do* curriculum design has, thus far, proved elusive. Instead, history teachers have regularly turned to metaphors to convey what it *feels* like to design a history curriculum. While no one has conceived a metaphor that captures the full range and complexity of the many facets of curriculum design, when these metaphors are considered together, they do conjure up an assortment of appropriate images. This is fitting, because at different times, in different contexts, when facing different challenges, history teachers will relate more closely with different metaphors. One day a *gardener* might be apt; another day it's a *pugilist*. The next term, the idea of a *cartographer* feels right, but soon it becomes a *wrestling* match. My argument is that through these metaphors, we can build up a coherent picture of not only how to design a history curriculum, but how it feels to do so.

THE HISTORY CURRICULUM DESIGNER AS A *GARDENER*

At the turn of the 21st century, Michael Riley used the metaphor of a gardener to capture the positive opportunity that awaited history teachers. Riley (2000) argued that the recently published 2000 National Curriculum afforded history teachers the chance to revisit their department's Key Stage 3 curriculum. Or as he put it, they could seize this moment to produce some 'pedagogical and horticultural wizardry in the Key Stage 3 history garden'. Under the guise of 'gardeners', Riley encouraged history teachers to be creative and start with updating content choices and how they were taught ('weeding and planting'). However, if the 'gardener' wasn't ready to get their hands dirty just yet, Riley also suggested this might be the time to stand on the patio, take a deep breath and survey the landscape: the new National Curriculum, with a noticeable absence of curricular diktats, challenged teachers to audit and reflect on their curriculum. Such a perspective might encourage a 'radical replanting of the whole ... history garden in order to create stronger themes, deeper understanding and greater overall appeal'.

Riley's starting point for such a comprehensive review of curriculum design was to begin with how the content was framed. Like the 'gardener', decisions are not made randomly; through structure comes beauty. In Riley's view, curriculum designers should start with carefully crafted enquiry questions to frame a sequence of lessons. History *is* argument and pupils deserve a chance to participate in contested debates; therefore, breaking a curriculum down into a series of rigorous, challenging and intriguing questions is both appropriate and rewarding (see Chapter 3 by Worth for more on this). While enquiry questions might be the most effective way to arrange the curriculum, the designer must not lose sight of both how these questions work individually and collectively as part of a whole. The components of the curriculum, like the garden, must sit in harmony.

Taking the questions individually, Riley suggested a three-step set of criteria for curriculum designers. They must plan questions that capture interest, place an aspect of historical thinking at the forefront of pupils' minds and result in a 'tangible, lively, substantial, enjoyable outcome activity'. For each enquiry question, it must be asked: 'What part do they play in making sure that different types of progression will happen across the key stage?' A garden requires constant attention, and each question requires on-going consideration, with pruning and renourishment required. The metaphor of the garden shows that curriculum design involves very precise and deliberate thought about the here and now, as well as the long-term picture. Perhaps most strikingly, tending to one's garden is a pleasurable pursuit; the ultimate outcome is satisfying and uplifting. For Riley, gardening is to be enjoyed. As he concludes, 'whatever the weather in the Key Stage 3 history garden … enjoy your planning'.

Activity 2.1

Reflecting on Riley's ideas

- Reflect on the curriculum in your school. Which sequences of lessons are framed around meaningful enquiry questions? Which of these questions would pass the 'three-step criteria for curriculum designers'?
- How do the sequences of lessons fit together? Take a few of the sequences and reflect on Riley's question: 'What part do they play in making sure that different types of progression will happen across the key stage?'

THE HISTORY CURRICULUM DESIGNER AS A *PROFESSIONAL WRESTLER*

Riley is not alone in ascribing living and breathing characteristics to a history curriculum. History teachers' on-going attempts to harness and control what the pupils learn about the past makes the curriculum itself feel alive. Not all visions are as tranquil as a garden, however. Writing in 2019 (Bailey-Watson, 2019), I outlined my own perceived loss of control after discovering pupils' reflections on their history curriculum. This article explained how the history curriculum is a natural phenomenon to be navigated, for '[it] runs and flows; it is fluid, gushing and meandering; it is a translucent structure with wobbly parameters, that can be breached and redirected'. Here, the curriculum designer's challenge is to tame their curriculum through constant attention and enormous effort. Soon after writing a textbook on the British Empire, Byrom and Riley (2003) felt compelled to develop Riley's gardening metaphor to account for this sense of struggle. To them, the endeavour had felt akin to professional wrestling.

Byrom and Riley's experience had highlighted that planning a history curriculum is 'rarely straightforward'. Crucially, and at the heart of any serious conversation about history curriculum design, Byrom and Riley recognise that history itself is complicated and the teaching of the subject defies simplistic planning. This leads to the constant need for resolving tensions, often at the same time, be they schemes of work, lesson plans or activities. To set out their case as professional wrestlers, the authors pose a series of questions (a selection of which are shown below) that they feel they regularly ask themselves and their departments and which are common across all schools:

- *Why are we asking them to study this topic?*
- *What do we really want the pupils to get better at here?*
- *How on earth do we decide what to leave out?*
- *Yes, but can we really leave that bit out?*
- *This is difficult but important – how do we make it accessible?*
- *This is important but boring – how can we make it enjoyable?*
- *How does this work build on earlier work?*
- *How does this work prepare for later work?*
- *Are we asking enough of them?*
- *Are we asking too much of them?*
- *We know exactly where they will go wrong here – but what can we do about it?*

Byrom and Riley continue the wrestling metaphor by framing their most pressing conflicts to be resolved as four rounds in the ring.

> **Round One:** curriculum designers must 'wrestle with content'. To demonstrate the scale of this challenge, they show a range of possible topics they *could* have taught about India under British rule. Every potential pathway could lead to a valid, interesting and worthwhile history, but there isn't time for all of them. The curriculum designer needs to hold on to some while discarding others, for now. All the while, Byrom and Riley refuse to overlook how their choices might change depending on the historical concept they want to emphasise and the overall takeaways they want **from their history curriculum**.
>
> **Round Two:** curriculum designers must 'wrestle with outline and depth'. Heavily influenced by Byrom and Riley, Banham (2000) developed the interplay of breadth and depth across a curriculum. To Banham, a curriculum that focuses on only depth studies is too episodic, while a curriculum that skips along the surface in the pursuit of coverage is too superficial. Using King John as a case study, Banham shows how curriculum designers could choose to home in on very particular topics and explore them in rich detail, without losing sight of the bigger picture. In his curriculum, Banham saw that the development of a keen sense of period and place through this depth study on King John accelerated subsequent breadth studies, particularly of the Middle Ages, as the pupils had a more profound historical understanding. The balance of depth to breadth, and which focus to be applied to each topic, remains up to the individual wrestler though.
>
> **Round Three:** curriculum designers must 'wrestle with the enquiry'. Nearly two decades after Riley set out his principles for effective enquiry questions, Worth (2018) provided a case study of the impact that can be achieved if curriculum designers invest effort in wrestling with the questions that pupils

will ultimately answer. Worth's experience was that a lot of attention goes into how history teachers *started* lessons, but not so much with how they *concluded* them. As Worth posited different considerations for concluding a lesson, she kept finding herself drawn back to the questions that she was asking her pupils in the first place. If pupils are to think meaningfully about complex historical objectives, Worth argues that the question they are attempting to answer must be worth wrestling with. Worth brings this back to the role of the teacher, who must spend time wrestling with their questions to ensure they serve the purpose for which they are intended. Within the enquiry that Worth focuses on in her article, she changed lesson questions like 'What was the liturgical year?' in order to give them greater analytical thrust; in this case the lesson became 'Why did the liturgical year matter to medieval English men and women?' Such a shift of emphasis opened up new possibilities for both Worth and her pupils, specifically by allowing critical engagement with similarity and difference. Worth drew upon historical scholarship for guidance, ultimately settling on an overarching enquiry question of 'To what extent did the Church shape medieval "rhythms of life"?' Her wrestling had been worth it: the question ensured that there was sufficient puzzle and intrigue, and it could be reviewed throughout the sequence of lessons. Following Byrom and Riley, Worth argues that to 'wrestle with a conclusion is to wrestle with the whole enquiry'.

Round Four: curriculum designers must 'wrestle with a … learning activity'. As can, and will, be seen in each of the discussed metaphors, planning can only achieve so much: implementation defines how effective the curriculum will be. It goes without saying, but: teaching matters. Byrom and Riley argue that curriculum designers must be precise in identifying learning objectives for lessons, creative in how they 'sell' activities to pupils, and inclusive, ensuring that every pupil has access to appropriate support. To conclude the metaphor, they surmise that 'quality medium-term planning can stun our opponent but only carefully crafted short-term planning and imaginative teaching can bring him down'. Similarly to Riley's gardener, the wrestler metaphor affords the curriculum designer a satisfying, albeit brief, moment when they can feel pride and pleasure in what has been achieved. However, the curriculum designer doesn't claim the spoils. The winners are 'without doubt the pupils'.

Activity 2.2

Reflecting on Byrom and Riley's ideas

Think about a sequence of lessons in your current curriculum. Ask yourself the questions that Byrom and Riley asked themselves.

THE HISTORY CURRICULUM DESIGNER AS A *PUGILIST*

While Riley, and Byrom and Riley's metaphors set out generic principles, they operate in a value-free space. What motivates the gardener? What fires-up the wrestler? Mohamud and Whitburn (2016) carried the metaphor of curriculum design being a fight, but also argued that more attention needed to be paid to *why* they were fighting and *who* they were fighting against. Mohamud and Whitburn were arguing in the shadow of Michael Gove's influential tenure as Conservative Secretary of State for Education. In 2013, Gove floated a draft Key Stage 3 National Curriculum that was radically different from the 2000 National Curriculum that Riley had seen as an opportunity for curriculum development and teacher initiative. The 2013 draft National Curriculum specified 'heroes' of the British Empire who would be taught as such, including Robert Clive, a historical actor who wasn't even considered a 'hero' in his own lifetime, let alone by historians. History teachers and historians campaigned to ensure this draft curriculum never made it into the classroom, but it had a lasting impact: many history teachers felt they were under pressure to produce history curricula that continued traditional hierarchies of whose histories mattered most and assumed master narratives that historians had spent decades trying to unpick. See Chapter 12 for a perspective on decolonising the curriculum from Dan Lyndon-Cohen and Josh Garry.

Writing specifically about including Black history, from the perspective of those Black historical actors involved in the events being studied, Mohamud and Whitburn (2016) called for curriculum design to include *pugilists*, *diggers* and *choreographers*. The diggers' role was to research and uncover powerful and meaningful stories to teach pupils. The choreographers' job was to turn ideas and content into something attractive, coherent and engaging through their thoughtful and creative pedagogies – two traits needed in any curriculum. However, it was the metaphor of pugilists which really stood out when it came to thinking about history curriculum design. All history teachers have questions to answer: How far, and for which battles, are you prepared to be a pugilist?

For Mohamud and Whitburn, these pugilists 'fight for greater justice in history education and for inclusive, diverse curricula in schools'. While Byrom and Riley were satisfied that it was hard enough to wrestle with the vastness and complexity of history itself, Mohamud and Whitburn argue that the fight must be taken into the real world. Traille (2007) has shown that some Black pupils in England have been made to feel ashamed of the stories of their ancestors told in classrooms, often through the lens of slavery. Commonly in these lessons, Black pupils encountered people of colour for the first time as enslaved people who were brutally repressed, before studying how they were emancipated by White campaigners. Reflecting on the absence of 'authentic history', that which rejects out of hand the 'inferiority … of people of African descent', Mohamud and Whitburn insist that curriculum designers need to take the fight to senior leadership teams and their departments, and beyond if required.

Pugilists regularly appear within the history-teaching community. Assuming the identity awarded them by Mohamud and Whitburn, they are willing to fight against established, entrenched narratives and assumed hierarchies in order to give different minoritised groups a representative and 'authentic' role in the history curriculum. Boyd (2019) sets out a model of progression when integrating women throughout a history curriculum, moving from exceptional women, like Queen Elizabeth I, to inclusive history where all narratives inherently accept that women were involved, their actions mattered, and their lives are revealing. Snelson and Lingard (2018) have similarly fought for the status of disabled people through history, while Austin and Harris (2021) insist that curriculum designers owe it to their pupils to include past stories of LGBTQ communities. Through collaborative initiatives and academic guidance, it seems that by the time this book is published, the history-teaching community will have found pugilists to fight for the place of climate, environment and sustainability education within their curricula (Bailey-Watson, 2023; Hawkey, 2023).

There is a caveat, of course: fighting is exhausting. Fighting can leave bruises. Fighting can distract from other things. Curriculum designers might be forgiven for deciding that it is sufficient, practical and sensible to focus on wrestling with traditional content. However, when given the chance, history teachers have shown there is an appetite for pugilism. In 2020, at the heart of the first nationwide lockdown, over 1,500 history teachers and school leaders watched the *Curricularium*, a series of online videos by teachers that focused on aspects of curriculum design that required pugilists. Hannah Cusworth, a history teacher in London, argued curriculum designers must put the 'black in the Union Jack', while Claire Holliss, a history teacher in Surrey, argued curriculum designers must find ways to represent women both routinely and deeply across their curriculum. The *Curricularium* showed that, when given space to think about what sort of curriculum designer they want to be, history teachers were willing to be pugilists. As Mohamud and Whitburn conclude, pugilists will likely fail if they fight alone; they need to engage with other pugilists across their professional community in order to win.

> **Activity 2.3**
>
> **Reflecting on Mohamud and Whitburn's ideas**
>
> Write a definition of the three terms that Mohamud and Whitburn say are needed for curriculum design: 'diggers', 'pugilists' and 'choreographers'.
> Whose history might a 'pugilist' fight to include?

THE HISTORY CURRICULUM DESIGNER AS AN *ARCHITECT*

Some metaphors for curriculum design are present in the language used in schools every day. Such is the language around curriculum designers as *architects*. They *build*, they *scaffold*, they *structure* and they *construct*, as do curriculum designers. In 2012, the editors of *Teaching History*, the Historical Association's professional journal, decided to respond to 'strange distortions of the press', accusing history teaching of not thinking hard about their curriculum choices. They centred the edition around curriculum architecture (the Editorial Board, 2012).

History teachers as architects proves a compelling metaphor. Different curricula, like different buildings, are made for different purposes. Different curricula, like different buildings, are made up of different materials; even if they weren't, the materials would likely be positioned differently. Different curricula, like different buildings, have an altered appearance when viewed on a micro and on a macro level. Crucially, this doesn't make them any better or any worse than any other, but the architect must know what they are aiming for and why. The Editorial Board (2012) argued that 'history teachers think very hard about those content choices, seeking different forms of coherence and rigour, different forms of responding to up-to-date scholarship or different ways of enabling more pupils to get the history bug'.

An architect must also think carefully about where to begin: What will be the foundations of their history curriculum? For Mohamud and Whitburn (2020), this basic question has been underexplored with many curriculum designers. The history that pupils encounter at the beginning of Key Stage 3 can have a lasting impact on what they perceive history to be and the significance of what should be learnt in history lessons. If a curriculum begins with a generic 'What is history?' module looking at modes of historical thinking, it could appear that knowledge isn't particularly important. If a curriculum begins with a high political and military study of 'How William became the Conqueror' it could appear that the most important meta-narrative in history is to establish why and how elite men assume dominance over other men. Mohamud and Whitburn wanted to suggest a way of overcoming these objections. They present a curriculum that begins in Year 7 by anchoring a 'What is history?' module within the context of African history. They argue that this would still achieve the aim of introducing historical thinking but very explicitly attached to substantive knowledge of a particular place and time. Furthermore, their starting point disrupts pupils' assumptions about where matters in history, and introduces a source base that gives pupils a much wider perspective of how historians make arguments about the past. Like the architect, as long as the curriculum design proposes a structure that achieves ambitious aims and is fit for purpose, these could legitimately be laid as the foundations.

The process of sequencing content has been further explored since the metaphor of curriculum designers as *architects* was introduced. As part of a comprehensive curriculum review, we hypothesised that our department's strict chronological sequencing might actually be hindering our pupils' historical understanding (Bailey-Watson 2019). Analysis of pupils' emerging understanding of history as a discipline revealed that when structured in a strictly chronological way, pupils saw the distant past as flatter, more remote and ultimately harder from which to discern meaning. Therefore, despite sticking with a largely chronological curriculum, our department decided to introduce a short module on family history in the first term of Year 7. Pupils had to challenge assumptions they had of their own background by using different historical methodologies. It proved revelatory for the pupils, not just for their own identities but also about what history was. Afterwards, pupils commented on how they couldn't believe that William the Conqueror and their grandfather both had a place in the discipline of history. The concluding argument is that curriculum designers should structure the topics and desired outcomes to elicit powerful revelations.

Ultimately, the metaphor of architect operates differently in different contexts. An architect can be given licence to show creativity, without constraints; they can produce wildly different structures, which reflect the vision of their creator. However, sometimes architects must also operate under rigid regulations, with a predetermined template, a lack of resources and a general lack of incentive to innovate. Curriculum designers might experience both sets of conditions, perhaps even within the same curriculum. Whether they innovate or comply, the building still needs to be used for its intended purpose.

THE HISTORY CURRICULUM DESIGNER AS A *CONDUCTOR*

In 2018, Ford and Kennett had become frustrated by the increasingly narrow definitions of what it meant to be 'knowledge-rich' in schools. These two history teachers felt that the role of curriculum designer was being undermined, as bloggers and school leaders encouraged generic implementation of cognitive science at the expense of pedagogies that allowed curriculum aims to be achieved. Ford and Kennett (2018) make a compelling case that it isn't just the designing of the curriculum that matters; the role of the classroom teacher is absolutely vital. To make this argument they use the metaphor of the history teacher as one who *conducts* an orchestra in order to find harmony and beauty. Similarly to Mohamud and Whitburn's vision of a choreographer, they argue that every curriculum needs somebody to interpret and tell their own stories to capture the imaginations of the particular pupils in front of them.

The conductor may or may not have been directly involved with the genesis and composition of the score, but it is nothing without them. The notes sit on a page, silent and lifeless. There can be an absence of joy in something that is designed to be appreciated in action, being implemented without careful consideration. If the audience are to feel differently about themselves and the world around them, then the notes need the conductor as much as the conductor needs the notes. In a tightly argued case, Ford and Kennett draw explicit links to the history classroom:

> In our experience we have found that the best teachers act like historical conductors, helping their students appreciate the beauty of a symphony of knowledge-rich learning. Such teachers choose their scores carefully, keep the flow, sustain the rhythm and, at the right times, emphasise particular instruments or passages that they think are powerful. Students are therefore able to listen to and appreciate the unfolding symphony of the past.

Of particular importance to the authors, as they set out to challenge generic pedagogies as a basis for effective history teaching, is the idea that knowledge should be made memorable. Like the conductor who recognises their own performance as a means to excite an audience and identifies sections of a score to bring the house down, the teacher needs to think carefully about what needs to be remembered and how the past can be made to stick in pupils' minds.

To achieve this ambition, they argue that stories need to be used to bring coherence and meaning to pupils. Here they combine metaphors as the teacher is both *composer* and *conductor*. The composer chooses the notes for how they sound together and in sequence, the melody for how it rises and falls, and the volume and pace to affect desired emotions. Teachers can achieve this through choosing where to start and end their stories of the past, which actors to spotlight, and how to create drama, tension, sorrow and profundity.

Canning (2020) has developed her own metaphor to capture the importance of sequencing knowledge in a way that is memorable for her pupils. As Canning thought carefully about what knowledge pupils needed to revisit throughout a topic, so it was at their fingertips when they needed it, she felt akin to a *TV producer*. Canning happened to be watching the British television crime series *Luther* as she planned her Year 10 curriculum on the Cold War. At the beginning of each episode, the producers had selected content to revisit that not only drew upon the previous episode, but sometimes from much earlier on in the series, if that prior knowledge might allow an accelerated engagement with the new content to be covered. Canning noted how she could learn from this. Similarly to *Luther*, the big story that Canning wanted to tell through her curriculum was 'complex, interwoven and intricate ... with multiple characters and storylines'. Through careful planning, Canning argues that the curriculum designer needs to take 'deliberate steps to stimulate and strengthen the essential information in the narrative that the pupils have been following'.

Whether they see themselves as composers or TV producers, Ford and Kennett argue that curriculum designers need pupils to *want* to know their curriculum. They draw upon Phillips' (2001) seminal argument for content to be introduced in intriguing ways, eliciting curiosity in their pupils and generating questions that drive the momentum of the curriculum. Bateman (2018), writing at the same time as Kennett and Ford, experienced a similar sensation as she wrestled with the balance of generic and bespoke pedagogies. Bateman noticed that lots of thought had gone into designing the history curriculum, but that unless the classroom teacher commits themselves to orchestrating the knowledge effectively, the pupils are not excited to learn more. Her pupils were learning and could recall lots of acquired knowledge, but Bateman found there was something missing. The pupils didn't feel they needed, or even wanted, to know what happened next.

To counter this Bateman looked at the curriculum aims for that term: to develop an understanding of what it was like to live in the Middle Ages, and how different people experienced life differently at different times. Bateman decided to plan a sequence of lessons where the pupils would write their own works of historical fiction about life in the Middle Ages. They were given scaffolds for story writing and clear assessment criteria. They were taught certain features of medieval life and offered possible routes to take. As the pupils' stories started to develop, so did their attitudes towards knowledge. No longer was the curriculum something that they were dictated and tested on; the curriculum was something of which they needed more in order to develop their own personal understanding. There is no argument by Bateman, or Ford and Kennett, that such a radical approach would be needed often; however, there is a consensus that the curriculum designer needs to think before commencing about what exactly is going to motivate the pupils. The curriculum designer needs to think like the conductor: What will make the audience want to take up their seats and fully engage in the performance? More than anything else, the metaphor of a conductor places heart and soul at the centre of the conversation about what it means to not just design but to implement a curriculum.

> **Activity 2.4**
>
> **Reflecting on Ford and Kennett's ideas**
>
> What do Ford and Kennett mean by describing teachers as 'conductors'? What implications does this have for the delivery of a curriculum?

THE CURRICULUM DESIGNER AS *A GLOBAL CARTOGRAPHER*

It does not feel controversial to argue that a significant number of history teachers have become increasingly ambitious in deciding the scope and aims of their curricula. Even with squeezed resources, shortened Key Stage 3 and increased exam content, curriculum designers often want to further their pupils' horizons. There is no better example of this desire than the popularity of 'Meanwhile, Elsewhere' resources. These worksheets, to be completed in class or at home, allow pupils to learn about historical people and societies that are contemporaneous to the enquiry they are currently studying in their taught curriculum. The teacher uses this knowledge to draw comparisons and contrasts, provide perspective, challenge assumptions and ultimately provide a hinterland knowledge that improves their overall understanding of the period. Bailey-Watson and Kennett (2019) wrote about how a Tweet turned into a website and how many teachers began to expand their curriculum in this way.

There is a strong case that history curriculum designers need to respond to historiographical trends and initiatives. As discussed with the need for pugilists, historians are not asking the same questions as they were 50 years ago. The proliferation of evidential approaches, combined with the desire to ask questions that reflect our present-day priorities, means that new histories are being written every day. While it is unrealistic, and undesirable, to chase every new development, Bailey-Watson and Kennett (2019) both drew upon their experience as Heads of History in secondary schools, to suggest that curriculum designers regularly revisit the boundaries of their curricula. To this end, they drew upon the metaphor of a global cartographer:

> World maps have always been about the world, but crucially they are also of their world: they are products of their cartographer and reflect the time and place in which they are created. The creation of world maps involves conscious processes of selection and omission, and as a result maps offer a proposal of the world as they hope others may come to conceptualise it. For example, while there are legitimate reasons for placing the United Kingdom in the middle of a map, cartographers need to have a clear rationale for doing so. World maps do not offer handy guides for where to go but instead prompt broader questions about orientation and perspective. The parallels are unmissable. Designing a world map really has a lot in common with designing a history curriculum.

Like a map, a curriculum is an interpretation. To my mind, the most important aspiration of any history curriculum is to understand history as an interpretative discipline. Husbands (1996) made the case that this was central to the purpose of teaching history in schools. Pupils make progress by increasing their understanding of the shifting, restless, subjective nature of the decisions made by those arguing about the past. The editors of *Teaching History* (2019) state that there is an 'extraordinarily rich tradition of practice, debate and research' of deconstructing and critiquing interpretations, and every curriculum teacher has the responsibility to 'protect and renew' this (the Editorial Board, 2019). Once curriculum designers have mapped out their curriculum, 'Meanwhile, Elsewhere' resources enable teachers to explicitly show that a curriculum is full of choices about what to foreground, what to touch upon and what to ignore. By seeing curriculum design as that of a cartographer, ever making choices that should be subject to scrutiny, history teachers can redefine the limits of their pupils' imaginations and engage them in an active process of interpretation.

Activity 2.5

Reflecting on curriculum designers as a 'global cartographer'

Think about your current curriculum. What is the geographical spread of the topics that are taught? What stories are not told by your curriculum? How were these decisions made? Are you happy with this?

THE *EMOTIVE AND ENDLESS* WORK OF THE HISTORY CURRICULUM DESIGNER

None of these metaphors are perfect. Many of them contain interchangeable features and none of them have been explored in their entirety here. Perhaps there is an emotional pull to the particular one that a history teacher may associate with. Writing at a time when historical horizons felt like they were being narrowed, Mohamud and Whitburn *felt* like pugilists; yet, when writing at a time when a lot of history teachers wanted to be more ambitious and adventurous, Bailey-Watson and Kennett *felt* like cartographers. As Riley surveyed a new landscape of possibilities and challenges, he *felt* like he was seeing his garden in a new light.

It is incumbent to select which metaphor is most fitting to the individual curriculum designer at a particular moment. It is clear from the associated verbs of each metaphor that this little pattern relates to the endeavour of curriculum design. Just a sample shows: gardeners sow, plant, tend and prune; wrestlers grapple, struggle and wrestle; pugilists fight, attack, bruise, recover and scrap; architects design, innovate, build, structure and scaffold; conductors interpret, synthesise, curate and perform; and cartographers map, position, space and explore. Each of these verbs has its place in the lexicon of curriculum design. What is important is that history teachers are aware of the metaphor that fits what they are seeking to achieve. There is no need to find the ultimate, definitive metaphor; however, it won't stop history teachers continuing to find new metaphors to capture the joy, complexity, challenges and emotional toll of designing a history curriculum.

> **Activity 2.6**
>
> This chapter does not give you a list of things to do, or a recipe to follow. Which of the metaphors most appeals to you?
> What practical steps could you take to implement some of the ideas about curriculum design that Bailey-Watson outlines?

SUMMARY OF KEY POINTS

- Designing a history curriculum is complicated and many authors have tried to pin down what it feels like to design a curriculum.
- In expressing themselves, these authors have drawn upon a wide range of metaphors which resonate with different history teachers at different times.
- The metaphors reveal the extent to which curriculum design can be an emotive process; with teachers experiencing joy, triumph, beauty, bruises, despair and frustration.
- There are different levels of curriculum design, such as conception, implementation and reflection, but they all operate in a co-dependent ecosystem.
- At the crux of all these metaphors, curriculum design involves choices. History teachers must try to embrace the professional agency and responsibility afforded by the wealth of choices available to them.
- Finally, no history curriculum is, or will ever be, perfect. The pleasure comes with the journey, the struggle and the little wins along the way.

RESOURCES AND FURTHER READING

Austin, Amy, & Harris, Rebecca. 'Putting the 'T' into LGBT history' [Paper Presentation], Historical Association Conference, (2021).

Bailey-Watson, Will. 'To Think That These Things Did Actually happen…': Structuring a History Curriculum for Powerful Revelations' in Teaching History, 174, Structure Edition, (2019): 53–61. London: Historical Association.

Bailey-Watson, Will. 'One Year of Embedding Climate and Sustainability Education in Our History PGCE' [Blog Post], One Big History Department, (2023). https://shorturl.at/fvPW7

Bailey-Watson, Will, & Kennett, Richard. 'Meanwhile, elsewhere …': Harnessing the Power of Community to Expand students' Historical horizons' in Teaching History, 176, Widening Vistas Edition, (2019): 36–43. London: Historical Association.

Banham, Dale. 'The Return of King John: Using Depth to Strengthen Overview in the Teaching of Political Change' in Teaching History, 99, Curriculum Planning Edition, (2000): London: Historical Association.

Bateman, Chloe. 'I Need to know …': Creating the Conditions That Make Students Want knowledge' in Teaching History, 173' in Opening Doors Edition, (2018): 32–40. London: Historical Association.

Boyd, Susanna. 'From Great Women to an Inclusive Curriculum: How Should Women Be Included at Key Stage 3? in Teaching History, 175, Listening to Diverse Voices Edition, (2019): 16–23. London: Historical Association.

Byrom, Jamie, & Riley, Michael. 'Professional Wrestling in the History Department: a Case Study in Planning the Teaching of the British Empire at Key Stage 3' in Teaching History, 112, Empire Edition, (2003): 6–14. London: Historical Association.

Canning, Pam. 'Cunning Plan: Using TV producers' Techniques to Make the Most Effective Use of Retrieval practice' in Teaching History, 179, Culture in Conversation Edition, (2020): 66–69. London: Historical Association.

Ford, Alex, & Kennett, Richard. 'Conducting the Orchestra to Allow Our Students to Hear the symphony' in Teaching History, 171, Knowledge Edition, (2018): 8–16. London: Historical Association.

Hawkey, Kate. History and the Climate Crisis: Environmental History in the Classroom. London: UCL Press 2023.

Husbands, Chris. What Is History Teaching? Language, Ideas and Meaning in Learning About the Past. London: Open University Press 1996.

Snelson, Helen, & Lingard, Ruth. 'Hidden in Plain Sight: Bringing the Past of People With Disabilities into the History classroom' in Teaching History, 173, Opening Doors Edition, (2018): 24–29. London: Historical Association.

Mohamud, Abdul, & Whitburn, Robin. Doing Justice to History: Transforming Black History in Secondary Schools. Stoke-on-Trent: Trentham Books 2016.

Mohamud, Abdul, & Whitburn, Robin. 'What Is History?' Africa and the Excitement of Sources With Year 7' in Teaching History, 181, Handling Sources Edition, (2020): 17–25. London: Historical Association.

Phillips, Robert. 'Making History Curious: Using Initial Stimulus Material (ISM) to Promote Enquiry, Thinking and literacy' in Teaching History, 105, Talking History Edition, (2001): 19–25. London: Historical Association.

Riley, Michael. 'Into the Key Stage 3 History Garden: Choosing and Planting Your Enquiry questions' in Teaching History, 99, Curriculum Planning Edition, (2000): 8–13. London: Historical Association.

The Editorial Board. 'Editorial' in Teaching History, 147, Curriculum Architecture Edition, (2012): 2–3. London: Historical Association.

The Editorial Board. 'What's the Wisdom On … Interpretations of the Past?' in Teaching History, 177, Building Knowledge Edition, (2019): 23–27. London: Historical Association.

Traille, Kay. 'You Should Be Proud About Your History. They Made Me Feel Ashamed: Teaching History hurts' in Teaching History, 127, Sense and Sensitivity Edition, (2007): 31–37. London: Historical Association.

Worth, Paula. 'Here Ends the Lesson: Shaping Lesson Conclusions as an Iterative Process in Improving Historical enquiries' in Teaching History, 173, Opening Doors Edition, (2018): 58–67. London: Historical Association.

Chapter 3 Planning Enquiries in History

Paula Worth

BACKGROUND

The construction of historical 'enquiries' is a cornerstone in history teaching in England. Planning an historical 'enquiry' ensures that history lessons are purposeful. First, the process of planning enquiries requires history teachers to think carefully about the substantive and disciplinary concepts that they want pupils to engage with. Second, the process of wrestling with the wording of an enquiry question requires history teachers to create a real and engaging puzzle that pupils will *want* to answer at the end of the lesson sequence. Third, by using the enquiry question to drive each lesson within the enquiry, pupils will be able to build knowledge systematically and cumulatively in order to answer the enquiry question at the end.

Imagine that you have already done some macro-planning of your curriculum: engaging in the sort of professional wrestling of curricular content that was discussed in Chapter 2. After carefully considering the needs of your pupils, community and department, you decide that you want to plan a series of lessons for Year 8 about the Industrial Revolution in Britain. You might decide that you want to teach pupils about some of the important changes that took place during the revolution. First, you might consider the importance of coal (to power steam engines and to create iron, for example); second, new transport methods (canals and railways); and, third, new ways of working (in textile mills and coal mines). These three 'big changes' could form your three lessons on the Industrial Revolution and allow you to skip merrily onto your next lesson sequence.

The problem with this approach, however, is that it does not lead anywhere. At the end, the pupils will have learnt some facts about trains, mills and mines, but several golden opportunities will have been missed. You might have used this series of lessons to help pupils to do much more than learn a few facts. You could help pupils to make progress in their understanding of the substantive concept of 'revolution'. You could help pupils to make progress in their understanding of the concept of causation by asking them to wrestle with the causes of the Industrial Revolution or encourage them to consider change and continuity across the eighteenth and nineteenth centuries in Britain. You could use your lessons on the Industrial Revolution to prepare pupils for later studies of migration or Chartism. Whatever you decide, creating a purposeful and engaging enquiry provides you and your department with a wealth of opportunities to excite pupils about history, to enable pupils to engage with intriguing historical questions that historians are asking and answering, and to help pupils make progress in their understanding of substantive and disciplinary concepts.

It is important to note that the curricular tradition of creating and employing historical 'enquiries' is very different from the idea of 'enquiry' as independent discovery learning. For example, if I had asked Year 8 to research the 'key changes of the Industrial Revolution' on the internet, some educators would call this 'independent discovery learning' because pupils would have 'found out the facts out for themselves'. The Historical Association recently made a public statement distinguishing between using 'enquiry' in the general pedagogic-sense (meaning pupils discovering things for themselves), and the history-specific tradition of 'enquiry', meaning a sequence of lessons geared toward a single, open-ended enquiry question (Sullivan, 2018).

This chapter outlines eight principles that can help history teachers to create and shape successful enquiries. I will use several examples of successful enquiries and enquiry questions to illustrate these principles, including an exciting new enquiry about the Industrial Revolution that I have crafted with the help of the historian Emma Griffin.

Activity 3.1

Which of the enquiry questions below are designed to help pupils develop their understanding of which second-order concepts?

Some of the answers are straightforward, other questions could, perhaps, be used to address more than one second-order concept depending on the content of the actual lessons.

Possible Enquiry Questions on the Industrial Revolution	Second-Order Concepts (Disciplinary Knowledge)
• What can diaries tell us about how working-class people felt about the Industrial Revolution? • What allowed Emma Griffin to write a 'people's history' of the Industrial Revolution? • How 'revolutionary' was the Industrial Revolution? • Why did the Industrial Revolution start in c.18th Britain? • Did the Industrial Revolution change life for people in South Yorkshire more than in South Cambridgeshire? • What did it mean to people to be 'working class' in the Industrial Revolution?	• Causation • Consequence • Change and continuity • Similarity and difference • Historical significance • Use of evidence • Interpretations

PRINCIPLE 1: USE ENQUIRY QUESTIONS TO DIRECT LEARNING ACROSS A SEQUENCE OF LESSONS

In my school, I only see Year 7 once a week, so it is tempting to treat each weekly lesson as a discrete whole. The problem with planning each lesson individually on a Sunday evening for a Monday morning, however, is that the lessons become disconnected and inconclusive. If I spend time crafting a sequence of four or five lessons together, however, I can make each lesson more purposeful: each lesson in the sequence builds to the point where pupils can answer the enquiry question. For an example of the Year 7 enquiries that form the basis of the Year 7 curriculum at my school, see Table 3.1. The need to produce an answer at the end of each enquiry in

Table 3.1 An outline of our Year 7 curriculum

1	What can a journey along the Silk Roads tell us about the world in c.1000 AD?
2	What drove Baghdad's thirst for knowledge?
3	What light can one saint's story shed on western Christian worlds?
4	How disruptive were the Normans?
5	Why do historians tell different stories about the Crusades?
6	What does Mansa Musa's story reveal about Medieval Africa?
7	How did one village respond to the Black Death?
8	Why did the peasants revolt in 1381?
9	How do historians use sources to study the Inkas?

Many of these enquiries and enquiry questions are based directly on the Hodder textbook series *Changing Histories* (Counsell et al., 2024), which I have co-authored with several other history educators.

our Year 7 curriculum makes clear to pupils the value of the knowledge that they are developing.

To illustrate the enquiry planning process, let us return to my lesson sequence on the Industrial Revolution. Instead, of planning each lesson individually on a different 'change', where pupils learn a series of loosely connected facts, I decided to construct an enquiry of four lessons for a new Key Stage 3 textbook series edited by Counsell et al. (2024). Before writing my new enquiry, however, I decided to update my subject knowledge about the Industrial Revolution. I therefore set about reading the highly celebrated book *Liberty's Dawn* by Emma Griffin (2014). I was not disappointed.

> **Activity 3.2**
>
> Choose one of the possible enquiry questions on the Industrial Revolution from Activity 3.1.
>
> - Write a list of the things that a Year 8 pupil would need to know in order to answer that question.
> - How might you sequence the teaching of those things?
> - Number the points on your list in a sequence that would allow Year 8 pupils to build their knowledge so that, by the end, they could answer the question.

PRINCIPLE 2: BASE YOUR ENQUIRIES ON HISTORICAL SCHOLARSHIP

Griffin's history of the Industrial Revolution is based on over 350 autobiographies of working people. Griffin used these sources to establish evidence of the huge changes brought about by the Industrial Revolution to the lives of working-class people. I was fascinated by Griffin's fresh approach to studying the Industrial Revolution, and I was excited about using extracts from working people's autobiographies in class with Year 8. Griffin's work is fresh and exciting because it challenges two stereotypes: first, that the voice of the working class in early 19th-century Britain is completely lost and unheard, and second that the Industrial Revolution was a period of unending misery. I thought that Year 8 would be galvanised by Griffin's determination to hear the voices of working people: by the hours she spent in the dark and dusty vaults of local record offices, carefully turning over the leaves of ripped and torn autobiographies.

Trying to find out about the experiences of working people during the Industrial Revolution, to find out how those people saw their industrial worlds, is a real and engaging problem. It was problematical for Griffin and would provide a fascinating puzzle for my pupils. Perhaps the biggest challenge is to find out about the experiences of women and children, whose literacy rates were the lowest. Asking pupils what workers' autobiographies can reveal about their world of 19th-century Industrial Britain would give them a focused objective. Sometimes pupils would have to hunt through extracts from men's autobiographies to hear the voices of their wives and children. The need to discover a working class 'voice' would give my pupils a *reason* to identify and record new knowledge about experiences of the Industrial Revolution. Eventually, after a great deal of wrestling with other history educators, I came up with the enquiry question: **'What do the voices of the working class reveal about their industrial worlds?'** (The whole enquiry is available in the *Changing Histories* textbook edited by Counsell et al. (2024).)

My new enquiry, based on Griffin's use of autobiographies that reveal a fresh perspective on the Industrial Revolution, gives pupils a reason to retain knowledge beyond a simple, uninspiring directive that 'you just need to know this', which might be given in an exam specification. In contrast, constructing a purposeful enquiry requires pupils to carry forward knowledge from one lesson to the next, and encourages them to connect new information to their existing knowledge.

Throughout the enquiry pupils use a data-catcher to record what extracts from workers' autobiographies reveal about the lives of working people during the Industrial Revolution in Britain (see Table 3.2). For each autobiography they study pupils are required to describe basic details about the individual's work before

Table 3.2 A data-catcher for Year 8 pupils to complete as they progress through their enquiry about the Industrial Revolution

Enquiry Question: What can historians infer about industrial worlds from working peoples' voices?			
Source	What can we infer about the industrial worlds of working **men**?	What can we infer about the industrial worlds of working **children**?	What can we infer about the industrial worlds of working **women**?
Life's Battles by Thomas Whittaker	The work Thomas did was hard, as shown when he… Thomas earnt enough money to…		
Family Records by Benjamin Shaw	Benjamin Shaw earnt… Benjamin's job was to… When he moved to Preston, Benjamin found it easy to …		
True Stories of Durham Pit Life by George Parkinson	The work in mines was dangerous because …	George began work aged … In the mine, George had to…	
Yesterday by Bessie Walker			Women's work involved looking after their husbands, by …

making wider inferences about the experiences of working men, women and children to record in their table. Furthermore, as they read and infer evidence from each new source, pupils will have the opportunity to connect their new knowledge about using workers' autobiographies as sources to previous source analysis. The teacher can make this explicit, for example by commenting: Do you remember, Year 8, when you analysed physical artefacts and Spanish chronicles in order to infer evidence about the Inka empire back in Year 7? In our new enquiry we are also using sources, a different but equally exciting type of source. The historian Emma Griffin had to be very determined to find these sources – many of the autobiographies have been gathering dust in the vaults of record offices …

In summary, reading Griffin's research provided me with a wealth of opportunities to construct a purposeful and rigorous enquiry. Indeed, there is a well-established tradition of basing historical enquiries on historical scholarship, and you can read more about the exciting ways in which history teachers are bringing historical scholarship meaningfully into the classroom in Chapter 15.

When history educators Richard Kerridge and Helen Snelson (2022) began designing a new lesson sequence to support the teaching of Gypsy, Roma and Traveller (GRT) histories, they began by consulting GRT community groups and the work of academic historians. This enabled Kerridge and Snelson to develop a lesson sequence that focused on how Gypsy and Traveller life changed in Britain in the period 1753–1914. Using the scholarship of Professor Becky Taylor (2014) was vital in enabling Kerridge and Snelson to create an enquiry that helped Gypsy, Roma and Traveller children feel 'seen' in the history classroom. Taylor's scholarship helped Kerridge and Snelson to develop an enquiry that gave agency to Gypsy and Traveller people, 'as a part of British society affected by events and changes'.

It would be unrealistic for teachers to keep track of every new debate, or to read every new history book that hit the shelves of the local bookshop, but there are some useful strategies to ensure that teachers remain connected with their subject community. Teachers could begin planning their enquiries by reading one or two recent works of historical scholarship, but if time is limited there are other very helpful opportunities for teachers to base their enquiries around historical scholarship:

- **Teachers could use the feature 'Polychronicon' in the journal *Teaching History*.** Recently renamed 'What have historians been arguing about …', this feature aims to help history teachers update their subject knowledge, with special emphasis on recent historiography and changing interpretations. A recent 'Polychronicon' about the English Reformation (Sangha, 2022), for example, outlines the latest debates in assessing the course and impact of the Reformation. The feature ends by encouraging teachers to consider the enquiry question, 'How have historians changed the way they write the history of the English Reformation?'.
- **Teachers could join the BeBold History Network:** a group of history teachers who facilitate connections between university academics and history teachers, by hosting and broadcasting one-hour webinars based on the latest historical research. For example, in one webinar Dr Sarah Longair presented her research into the history of the British Empire in East Africa and the Indian Ocean. In the webinar, history teachers had the opportunity to ask Dr Longair questions about her research methods and the sources she studied. After the webinar, several history teachers decided to use Longair's research to create a new enquiry based on the use of artefacts to tell rich stories about the past.

- **Teachers could use existing textbook enquiries that are explicitly based on historical scholarship.** For example, history teacher Emmy Quinn (2023) rooted her textbook enquiry question 'What did colonisation mean for the Irish?' in a work of scholarship by the historian Jane Ohlmeyer (2005). In her chapter *A Laboratory for Empire? Early Modern Ireland and English Imperialism*, Ohlmeyer argues that Ireland was a laboratory for **English imperialism**. Quinn used the scholarship to shape her enquiry, which is outlined in full in the textbook.

> **Activity 3.3**
>
> Reflect on a piece of historical scholarship you have read, listened to or watched recently.
>
> - What question had the historian set themselves?
> - What second-order concept does this focus on?
> - What would be the opportunities and challenges of presenting (a version of) that same question to a Key Stage 3 class?
> - Would a Key Stage 3 class be interested in how and why the historian put together that book, podcast, radio show, TV programme? In other words, is there material for an interpretation enquiry there? If not, why not? (See Chapter 9 for more on the teaching of historical interpretations.)

PRINCIPLE 3: CREATE ENQUIRIES THAT RESPOND TO THE NEEDS OF YOUR SCHOOL COMMUNITY

It is vital to pay attention to the needs and interests of your pupils and community when planning the enquiries in your curriculum, as discussed in Chapter 2. A good example of this is shown in the work of teachers Nathanael Davies and Taslima Rakib at Oaklands Second School in Bethnal Green in London (Davies, Rakib & Zakaria, 2022). Davies and Rakib decided to create a new enquiry on the history of Bangladesh to respond to the needs of their school community. As Davies explains:

> Over three-quarters of the students in my school were British Bangladeshi. While 'Bengal' was named in one [existing] enquiry, it served merely as a backdrop for the British Empire's expansion. Not only was there no mention of the history of Bangladesh in the curriculum that I taught, I also failed to find any examples of it being taught meaningfully in other secondary school history departments in the borough.

Davies's new enquiry about the history of Bangladesh was therefore rooted in the needs of his school community. Historical scholarship was still important to the construction of this enquiry, however, as Davies explains:

> I knew very little about the creation of Bangladesh. Neither did my department.

> Educated in England, we had been taught to 'look away' from the Indian subcontinent (and from much else besides) after 1947.

Even after a year of reading historical scholarship and talking to members of his school community, however, Davies's first attempt at an enquiry on the creation of Bangladesh felt 'dry' and 'lacklustre'. It was not until he read Anam Zakaria's book, *1971*, on what the Year 1971 meant for Bangladesh, Pakistan and India, that Davies arrived at the concept that would eventually lay at the heart of the enquiry: historical interpretations. It then took Davies three attempts to come up with the precise wording for his enquiry question; precision matters when planning enquiries. Davies's eventual enquiry question was: **'Why have some stories of 1971 been so difficult to tell?'**.

In summary, Davies's use of Zakaria's scholarship enabled him to construct a purposeful and rigorous enquiry about the events of 1971 in Bangladesh, which was centred on the concept of historical interpretations. My own use of Griffin's scholarship enabled me to create an engaging enquiry about the Industrial Revolution, which was centred on the concept of inferring evidence from sources. Centring an enquiry around one particular concept leads me onto my next principle.

> **Activity 3.4**
>
> Reflect on the community that your school serves. Are the stories that have shaped that community told in your curriculum?
>   Draft an enquiry question that would meet any unmet needs.

PRINCIPLE 4: PLACE A SUBSTANTIVE OR DISCIPLINARY CONCEPT AT THE HEART OF YOUR ENQUIRIES

Planning enquiries is vital at all key stages; do not allow the demands of GCSE and A-Level specifications to prevent you from planning purposeful, engaging enquiries that place substantive or disciplinary concepts at their heart. Resist the temptation to plan individual, disconnected lessons that seek to meet a bullet point on an examination specification, and no more! Continuing to plan exciting enquiries at Key Stage 4 and Key Stage 5 will ensure that your pupils continue to make progress in concepts such as change, continuity and inferring evidence from sources.

I have made the mistake of failing to plan enquiries at A-Level myself (Worth, 2018). A few years ago, I began teaching a new AQA A-Level Course about religious change in c.1529–1570. The A-Level specification demands that pupils learn about 'popular piety and the Church's spiritual role'. Flicking through the AQA-approved textbook one Sunday evening, I quickly learnt that people's lives in the Tudor era were structured around the liturgical year, including Feast Days, Eastertide and Advent. I therefore created the enquiry question 'What was the liturgical year?' and designed several activities to help pupils answer this question, including creating a calendar of the Church Year and matching paintings of holy days to their descriptions.

When I taught the lesson on the Monday, it was catastrophically boring. A few watery smiles and an unenthusiastic 'see you on Thursday then, Miss' at the end of the lesson were enough to tell me that I had failed to engage my pupils with the topic. The problem was obvious: my enquiry question made few conceptual demands on my pupils beyond the substantive. My enquiry question was asking for pupils to learn some facts about medieval socio-religious customs. There was no puzzle for pupils to unpick.

My enquiry question on the medieval liturgical year, I now recognised, was not driven by a second-order concept such as change, causation or significance. In a seminal article on creating enquiry questions, the history educator Michael Riley (2000) encourages teachers to place disciplinary concepts at the heart of historical enquiries: The enquiry question should capture the interest and imagination of pupils *and* the question should place an aspect of historical thinking, concept or process at the forefront of their minds.

Following Riley's advice, I considered changing the enquiry question to, 'Why did the liturgical year matter to medieval Englishmen and women?' This question was more rigorous in that it would allow me to organise pupils' problem-solving around the concept of similarity and difference: the liturgical year mattered in differing ways across society. I could also help prepare my pupils for the eventual exam because a practice essay has been given by the AQA exam board on the question of why the Church was important in the lives of both the rich and poor.

But the question still seemed rather boring. Remember how Davies was also left uninspired after his initial stab at creating an enquiry about the creation of Bangladesh? It was the same for me with the English Reformation. So, just like Davies, I reached for the bookshelves again.

Activity 3.5

How can enquiry questions continue to be a useful planning tool at Key Stage 4 and Key Stage 5?

Find the specification for any GCSE or A-Level courses that you teach, some of them may already be framed around enquiry questions, others may be framed around topics.

Can you devise enquiry questions that would deliver the desired content but might interest and intrigue pupils and develop the rigorous thinking that these qualifications require?

PRINCIPLE 5: DRIVE YOUR ENQUIRIES WITH AN ENGAGING PUZZLE

After some more unpromising false starts, I eventually took down a book by the historian Eamon Duffy (2005), called *The Stripping of the Altars*. In his illustration of how life in medieval villages and towns was dominated by a liturgical calendar, outlining the numerous feast days when work was not permitted, Duffy wrote that 'for townsmen and countrymen alike, the rhythms of the liturgy on the eve of the Reformation remained the rhythms of life itself'.

I was puzzled, and I shared my puzzlement with the other history teachers in my department. My questions were as follows:

What did Duffy mean by 'rhythms of life?' Did he mean smaller elements of life such as breakfasts, playtimes and bedtimes, or did he mean larger 'rhythms' such as how work was structured across the year or important events such as marriage and death? What does it mean to have a 'rhythm' to one's life, and would those rhythms have been more pronounced in medieval England than those experienced in the twenty-first century? Did religion shape those rhythms with its liturgical year of ritual and piety, or were economic imperatives actually more important, but shrouded from the gaze of subsequent historians by the pious language of the past? **To what extent did the Church shape medieval 'rhythms of life'?**

This final question (in bold) became my new enquiry question. I was puzzled, I was challenged, I was curious. My intention was not to make the enquiry question gimmicky; instead, I wanted to create a genuine puzzle, making it possible for every teacher in my department to 'reiterate it with passion and mystery, lesson by lesson, as they lead pupils towards its resolution' as Riley (2000) had envisioned. When I taught my new enquiry question the following year, my pupils were also enthusiastic, discussing the rhythms of their own lives, and who or what guided those rhythms. The time spent wrestling with my new enquiry question was worth it, and this leads me onto my next principle.

PRINCIPLE 6: WORK WITH OTHERS TO REFINE YOUR ENQUIRIES AND ENQUIRY QUESTIONS

I was very lucky to have some thoughtful colleagues who helped me wrestle with my new enquiry about the liturgical year. There are many different ways to characterise the process of planning enquiries. The term 'intellectual wrestling' has become a popular and useful way to describe the way that teachers work thoughtfully and collaboratively to arrive at the best enquiry question to guide a lesson sequence (Byrom and Riley, 2003). History teachers Mohamud and Whitburn have come up with the analogy of a builder working with a spirit level to discuss the precision required in arriving at the final wording of an enquiry question. Byrom and Riley outline the many questions that history teachers could ask themselves as they begin planning a new enquiry. Their questions are adapted in Table 3.3 and discussed further in Chapter 2.

Table 3.3 is a long list of questions; Byrom and Riley point out that 'planning history is intellectually exhausting'. Getting the enquiry question right can be particularly exhausting. Enquiry questions should be framed carefully to make it clear to pupils what they are trying to do. For example, are they inferring evidence from sources, which is made clear in my Griffin-inspired enquiry question: 'What do the voices of the working class reveal about their industrial worlds?'. Or are they analysing patterns of similarity and difference, which is incorporated into my Duffy-inspired enquiry question: 'To what extent did the Church shape medieval "rhythms of life"?'

Let us look at another example of collaborative planning. In the process of planning a new enquiry about Mughal India, I needed a great deal of help to get my enquiry question right. I began planning my new enquiry by **thinking carefully about my rationale** for inserting a new study of the Mughals into an already-crowded Year 8 history curriculum (Question 1, Table 3.3). Beyond ensuring that my curriculum was broad, with a diverse range of enquiries, I had other powerful reasons to study the Mughals. A study of the Mughal Empire would **allow me to build on previous enquiries** about the empires of Mali, the Mongols and the Inkas, which pupils studied in Year 7, helping pupils to **improve their understanding of 'empire'** by studying the concept in different contexts (Questions 2 and 4). A new

Table 3.3 Example questions that teachers could ask themselves when designing a new enquiry, adapted from Byrom and Riley, 2003

1. Why are we asking pupils to study this topic?
2. How does our new enquiry allow pupils to build on earlier learning?
3. How does our new enquiry prepare pupils to access later learning?
4. What substantive 'takeaways' (substantive content such as 'empire' or 'nobility') do we want to plan for?
5. How does our department's reading of historical scholarship help us to decide about the substantive or disciplinary concept that should sit at the heart of the enquiry?
6. How can we create a rigorous, genuinely puzzling and engaging enquiry question to govern the lesson sequence?
7. How many lessons should the enquiry take?
8. How can we ensure pupils' learning builds cumulatively across the enquiry?
9. What can we ask pupils to do to show the progress they have made in their learning?
10. What is the outcome activity (or 'end product')? How does engaging in this activity allow pupils to answer the enquiry question?

enquiry on the Mughals would also help **prepare my pupils to access a later study** on the East India Company (EIC) and the British Empire in India (Question 3). When I tackled the EIC in the Spring Term of Year 8, I wanted to plan for instant resonance: of location, place and culture.

The Mughal Empire is a vast historical topic. Many books have been written about the Mughals, and it was easy to become overwhelmed in researching the new enquiry. I began by reading the chapters about Mughal India in a sweeping historical overview by historian John Keay called India: A History (2001). I grew fascinated by the Great Mughal Emperors' interest in Art and Architecture. Mughal Emperor Jahangir, for example, used to spend hours watching Portuguese artists paint. The paintings created during Jahangir's rule (1605–1627) offered a fascinating source base to study the Mughal Empire. A **first reading of the scholarship suggested that sources could form the disciplinary heart of my enquiry** (Question 4, Table 3.3).

Mughal paintings are beautiful, of course (see Figure 3.1 for an example), and reveal many aspects of life in Mughal India, such as the way court ceremonies were conducted, but there was not yet a genuine puzzle for pupils to solve. It was when I came across a recent work of scholarship by historian Ruby Lal (2018) that I became really excited about a genuine historical puzzle. When Lal declared that she was going to write a history of the twentieth wife of Jahangir, Nur Jahan (shown in the painting in Figure 3.1), her colleagues were incredulous: 'How are you going to write a history of Mughal women?', they asked. 'There are no sources for it!'.

But Lal was determined. 'I dived deeply into the court records', she explains. 'Nur is there, it turns out; all we have to do is look for her. You have to peer around the towering figures of men'. Here was a puzzle that would engage and excite my pupils, and I was excited about using Nur's story as a window into the Mughal world, helping pupils to understand how the Mughal Empire worked and the reasons for its expansion and success. I immediately created the enquiry question: 'What can one woman tell us about the Mughal world?'.

Excitedly, I spoke to Christine Counsell about the enquiry, with whom I was working on a new Year 8 textbook (Counsell et al., 2024). Christine pointed out that this question does not focus on Ruby Lal's methods to use sources to infer evidence about Nur's life. Why base the enquiry on Ruby's scholarship if we do not focus on her determination to solve the puzzle of finding out about Mughal women, who were often hidden from public life? I then suggested, 'Why do historians think Nur Jahan is so special?' but Christine and I then agreed that question placed emphasis on historical significance, which would certainly work as an enquiry question, but would guide pupils towards discussing Nur Jahan only, rather than guiding them towards my overall purpose: to build pupils' knowledge about the Mughal Empire.

Eventually, after several Zoom conversations and emails, Christine and I settled on an engaging and puzzling enquiry question (Question 6, Table 3.3): **'How can we tell the story of Nur Jahan?'**. This gloriously open enquiry question would do several things:

1. Guide pupils towards discussing the *challenges* in telling a story about a Mughal woman (giving emphasis to the 'How' part of the question);
2. Encourage pupils to explore and discuss the way in which the historian Ruby Lal used sources constructively to *'tell'* her story (i.e. create her interpretation) of Nur Jahan;
3. Allow pupils to 'tell' their *own* stories about Nur Jahan and what she reveals about the Mughal world in an outcome activity (Question 10, Table 3.3).

Figure 3.1 A painting commissioned by Mughal Emperor in c.1640–50 in Jahangir. It shows Emperor Jahangir and Prince Khurram entertained by Nur Jahan.

My eventual lesson sequence (see Table 3.4) placed sources at the heart of the enquiry. In their outcome activity, my pupils create a story about Nur for children, explaining how historians like Ruby Lal use sources to tell stories, and coming up with their own story. The need for a clear focus does not mean that teachers must deal with one single second-order concept, however. Look back at the list of enquiry questions in Table 3.1. The seventh enquiry question, created by Rachel Foster, is: 'How did one village respond to the Black Death?'. This question focuses primarily on change and continuity within the village of Walsham in the fourteenth century, but the question also provides scope for pupils to consider similarities and differences between the village of Walsham and the experience of other villages during the fourteenth century. Avoid encompassing every second-order concept in an enquiry question, however, in order to retain conceptual clarity.

PRINCIPLE 7: ASSESS THE PRECISION AND RIGOUR OF YOUR ENQUIRY QUESTION

A great deal of time and effort was spent in getting the enquiry question about Mughal India exactly right. A useful way to test the rigour of an enquiry question is to play the 'Dodgy Questions game' as presented by Christine Counsell and included in Michael Riley's seminal article on enquiry questions (2000). This 'game' or process of 'sniffing out' weak questions is fundamental to creating a rigorous history curriculum:

So often, when an enquiry question loses focus or fails to require genuine historical reasoning, it turns out that it was impossible to attach a second-order concept to it. For example, the question 'How should we remember the First World War?' is a moral question, rather than an historical one. Another 'dodgy' question is 'What was life like in medieval towns?' This question contains no imperative for any type of analysis; it is purely descriptive. A further problematical question is 'Who should be king?' This question is fine for an activity inviting in-period reconstruction of the past from the point of view of past actors but does not, in itself, engender a rigorous historical argument about the past such as an enquiry question would command.

Activity 3.6

Sloppy wording in an enquiry question can derail the whole enquiry. See if you can spot the problems with these three enquiry questions about Mughal India by playing the 'Dodgy enquiry questions' game yourself:

- What was it like to be a woman in Mughal India?
- Why was life so unfair for Mughal women?
- Was Jahangir a hero or a villain?

I planned for my enquiry on Mughal India to take four lessons (see Table 3.4 for the overview of this enquiry). Enquiry questions should be designed to govern a series of lessons (or 'lesson sequence'); there is no need to create separate enquiry questions for every lesson. The same question, 'How can we tell the story of Nur Jahan?' governs all four lessons within the enquiry.

Table 3.4 Overview of my enquiry about Mughal India

Enquiry Question:	How can we tell the story of Nur Jahan?
Lesson 1	**Begin** the lesson by telling the story of Mihr's birth in 1577 (Nur Jahan's original name was Mihr) on the Silk Roads, and her family's journey from Persia to the India of the Great Mughals; build the world of the Mughal Empire by doing some guided reading with pupils that recount the sights, smells and sounds of Mughal India **Continue** the lesson by asking pupils to create a map of Mughal India, including Akbar's court; physical features such as the Indus River and Himalayas; the towns/ cities of Dehli, Lahore and Agra; and finally the regions of Bengal, Kashmir and Malwa (which are mentioned in the narrative) **Read** more of Mihr's (Nur's) story with pupils, asking them to analyse paintings of Akbar's and Jahangir's court as you read. Continue the story up to the marriage of Jahangir and the naming of Mihr as 'Nur Jahan' **Finish** the lesson by asking pupils what the story of Nur Jahan reveals about Mughal India so far. Pupils record this in a table using three columns: The role of women; Mughal kingship and government; Mughal wealth.
Lesson 2	**Begin** the lesson by providing pupils with a blank outline map of India and asking them to write down everything they remember about Mughal India **Continue** the lesson by asking pupils to create a parallel timeline at the side of their map, recording the reigns of Akbar and Jahangir on one side, and the reigns of Elizabeth I, James I and Charles I on the other side **Read** more of Mihr's (Nur's) story with pupils, asking them to analyse paintings of Jahangir and Nur Jahan as you read. Continue the story up to Nur's famous hunting expedition, in which she kills four tigers in 1617. Ask pupils to re-read the story and add more details to their table about the role of women in the Mughal empire, Mughal kingship and government, and Mughal wealth **Read** the final part of Nur's story, including her actions as co-sovereign of the Mughal empire, her famous rescue of Jahangir in 1626, the death of Jahangir, and the accession of Shah Jahan **Finish** the lesson by asking pupils to add some final details to their table. Ask pupils: what makes Nur Jahan's story so remarkable? Why tell her story?
Lesson 3	**Begin** the lesson by studying a painting of Nur Jahan holding a musket. Ask pupils: what does the painting reveal about Nur? Why might historians be surprised by this painting? Why is this source so special? **Continue** the lesson by introducing the historian Ruby Lal and the challenges she faced in finding sources to tell the story of Nur Jahan's life **Study** four important sources that Ruby Lal used to establish evidence about the life of Nur Jahan: Nur's imperial orders, the coins that Nur commissioned, Mughal paintings, and Jahangir's diary (the Jahangirnama). Ask pupils to make a new table. In the first column, ask pupils to write down the sources that Ruby Lal used to create her story. In the second column, ask pupils to write down how Lal used the sources to establish evidence about Nur Jahan's life. **Finish** the lesson by asking pupils to put a selection of sources in chronological order to tell the story of Nur Jahan's life. Ask pupils which sources are the most revealing for historians interested in Nur's life and how they help tell her story.
Lesson 4	**Begin** the lesson with a quiz of ten questions about Mughal India and Nur Jahan in order to recap and consolidate pupils' knowledge **Show** a video clip of Ruby Lal discussing her research methods and motives; while watching the clip, ask pupils to identify two challenges that Ruby faced in writing her story about Nur Jahan and two sources that she used to overcome those challenges **Introduce** the outcome activity: pupils will be asked to plan and write a story about Nur Jahan for Year 5 pupils attending a local primary school. Give pupils guidance and scaffolds, as appropriate, on how to plan and write their stories. **Monitor** pupils as they write their stories (consider asking them to finish their stories for homework) **Finish** the lesson by asking pupils to answer the enquiry question orally; guide pupils towards different ways of answering the question, including the challenges involved in telling Nur's story as a *female* Mughal leader, and Ruby Lal's motives to write Nur's story.

PRINCIPLE 8: USE ENQUIRY QUESTIONS TO MAP THE WHOLE CURRICULUM

So far, we have looked at planning one enquiry at a time, but a history curriculum will encompass a series of enquiry questions (as discussed in Chapter 2). When creating my Mughals enquiry for Year 8, you will have seen that I considered enquiries that preceded and connected to the new Mughals enquiry (such as those on the empires of Mali and the Inkas in Year 7) and subsequent enquiries (like that on the East India Company later in Year 8). I did not plan my new Mughals enquiry in isolation; the rationale for studying the Mughals (Question 1, Table 3.3) draws power from the relationship that the Mughals enquiry has to previous and later enquiries. The Mughals enquiry was created to become part of a coherent curriculum. When planning all enquires, I have to make careful and considered decisions about how the enquiry fits within my overall curriculum plan.

Planning enquiries therefore provides a golden opportunity to consider how pupils make progress across a whole key stage, first in terms of their progress in understanding disciplinary concepts such as 'evidence', and second in terms of their progress in understanding substantive concepts such as 'empire'. Carefully considering the placement of enquiry questions within a curriculum is a well-established tradition in history education: Riley (2000) uses the analogy of carefully planting a 'garden' of enquiry questions so that pupils' progress blossoms. This planting process is crucial, as discussed in *Teaching History's* 'What's the Wisdom on Enquiry Questions' (2020):

> Because the careful crafting of an enquiry question compels teachers to identify *both* the essential second order [*disciplinary*] concept(s) with which each lesson sequence is concerned *and* the substantive knowledge required to answer the question, the process of drafting and mapping enquiry questions across a key stage allows teachers to plan for progression in *both* dimensions.

Let's look first at the disciplinary concepts. If we return to my enquiry about the Industrial Revolution, you will have noticed that I explicitly sought to connect Year 8's use of sources (working class autobiographies) to study the Industrial Revolution with a previous enquiry in Year 7, when pupils used physical artefacts to study the Inkas. By mapping the places where pupils encounter concepts such as 'evidence', 'change' or 'empire' across the curriculum, I was able to create patterns of reinforcement in pupils' historical thinking. This will ensure that 'questions of the same type resonate over time, enabling pupils to consolidate and build on previous understandings'.

Activity 3.7

To reflect further on the mapping of disciplinary concepts across the curriculum, either:

- Look back again at Table 3.1. Can you spot patterns where pupils will encounter the concepts of causation and change at different times in the curriculum, allowing pupils to make progress in their understanding of those concepts?
- For a different example of how history teachers map pupils' opportunities to make progress in their understanding of disciplinary concepts, you can read about how history teacher Matt Stanford (2019) planned for pupils to use increasingly complex models of causation over the whole of Key Stage 3 in his *Teaching History* article, 'Did the Bretons break?'.

The same principles of reinforcing pupils' understanding across a curriculum apply to pupils' *substantive* knowledge. This time, let us return to my new A-Level enquiry, 'To what extent did the Church shape medieval "rhythms of life"?'. The 'Church' will make little sense if my pupils did not understand the concept of the 'Church' beyond a physical building with a pointy spike on top. My pupils would not have been able to answer the question meaningfully if they did not understand that the 'Church' was a term that encompassed a great deal more than a building: parishes and parish churches, yes, but also bishops and archbishops with a political and religious role; abbeys, priories and nunneries with connections to their centres on the continent; also, before the Break with Rome, the 'Church' included the Papacy in Rome, cardinals and legates in England, and so on. Considering what comes before and after each enquiry is therefore vital to plan for pupils to access the substantive content in each topic.

Sometimes, of course, the substantive concept will live at the heart of the enquiry, such as in Quinn's enquiry (2023), 'What did colonisation mean for the Irish?' Quinn's enquiry question is brilliantly worded because it acts as an impetus for pupils to do several things:

1. Improve their understanding of 'colonisation' by studying this substantive concept in the context of the British colonisation of Ireland;
2. Identify the methods used by the British to colonise Ireland, which will prepare pupils to compare and contrast those methods with colonisation in other territories within the British Empire;
3. Consider the perspective of people living in Ireland during the period of British colonisation: How did Irish contemporaries see, make sense of, and challenge British 'colonisation'? (For more discussion of the concept of 'historical perspective', see Chapter 8).

Planning enquiries can be time-consuming, but the process is also intellectually stimulating and extremely rewarding. Take a look at the example enquiry questions discussed in other chapters, such as Laura London's discussion of rigorous enquiry questions that can help pupils wrestle with the concept of causation in Chapter 6, or Helen Snelson's discussion of enquiry question stems that are useful for discussing historical significance in Chapter 10.

You can use your best enquiries year after year, and you do not plan every single enquiry from scratch: there are so many superb enquiries already crafted, some of which I have discussed in this chapter. On the other hand, planning enquiries is not like cooking: the enquiries you will enjoy teaching the most will nearly always be the ones that you have crafted yourself.

SUMMARY OF KEY POINTS

- Use enquiry questions to direct learning across a sequence of lessons.
- Base your enquiries on historical scholarship.
- Create enquiries that respond to the needs of your school community.
- Place a substantive or disciplinary concept at the heart of your enquiries.
- Drive your enquiries with an engaging puzzle.
- Work with others to refine your enquiries and enquiry questions.
- Assess the precision and rigour of your enquiry question.
- Use enquiry questions to map the whole curriculum.

RESOURCES AND FURTHER READING

Byrom, Jamie, & Riley, Michael. 'Professional Wrestling in the History Department: a Case Study in Planning the Teaching of the British Empire at Key Stage 3' in Teaching History, 112, Empire Edition, (2003): 6–14. London: Historical Association.

Counsell, Christine, Foster, Rachel, & Kinloch, Nicolas (eds.). Changing Histories for KS3: Connected Worlds c.1000-c.1600. London: Hodder Education 2024.

Davies, Nathanael, Rakib, Taslima, & Zakaria, Anam. 'Telling Difficult Stories About the Creation of Bangladesh' in Teaching History, 188, Representing History Edition, (2022): 28–39. London: Historical Association.

Dawson, Ian. 'Enquiry: Developing Puzzling, Enjoyable' in Effective Historical Investigations' in Primary History, 70, (2015): 8–14. London: Historical Association.

Duffy, Eamon. The Stripping of the Altars: Traditional Religion in England, 1400-1580. London: Yale University Press 2005.

Griffin, Emma. Liberty's Dawn: A People's History of the Industrial Revolution. London: Yale University Press 2014.

Keay, John. India: A History. New York: Grove Press 2001.

Kerridge, Richard, & Snelson, Helen. "We Are Invisible!' Ensuring Gypsy, Roma and Traveller Children Do Not Feel Unseen in the History classroom' in Teaching History, 188, Representing History Edition, (2022): 10–17. London: Historical Association.

Lal, Ruby. Empress: The Astonishing Reign of Nur Jahan. New York: Norton & Company 2018.

Mohamud, Abdul, & Whitburn, Robin. 'Anatomy of Enquiry: Deconstructing an Approach to History Curriculum Planning' in Teaching History, 177, Building Knowledge Edition, (2019): 28–41. London: Historical Association.

Ohlmeyer, Jane. H. 'A Laboratory for Empire?: Early Modern Ireland and English Imperialism' in Kenny, Kevin (ed.). Ireland and the British Empire. Oxford: Oxford University Press 2005: 26–59.

Quinn, Emmy et al. A New Focus On … The British Empire c. 1500-Present. Hodder, 2023.

Riley, Michael. 'Into the Key Stage 3 History Garden: Choosing and Planting Your Enquiry questions' in Teaching History, 99, Curriculum Planning Edition, (2000): 8–13. London: Historical Association.

Sangha, Laura. 'What Have Historians Been Arguing About… the Impact of the English Reformation' in Teaching History, 188, Representing History Edition, (2022): 62–65. London: Historical Association.

Stanford, Matthew. 'Did the Bretons Break? Planning Increasingly Complex Causal Models at Key Stage 3' in Teaching History, 175, Listening to Diverse Voices Edition, (2019): 8–15. London: Historical Association.

Sullivan, Rebecca. 'DfE Clarifies Reference to Enquiry-Based Learning' [press release], Historical Association, (2018). https://www.history.org.uk/ha-news/categories/455/news/3613/dfe-clarifies-reference-to-enquiry-based-learning. Accessed 06/01/23

Taylor, Becky. Another Darkness, Another Dawn: A History of Gypsies, Roma and Travellers. London: Reaktion Books 2014.

The Editorial Board. 'What's the Wisdom On… Enquiry Questions?' in Teaching History, 178, Constructing Accounts Edition, (2020): 16–19. London: Historical Association.

Worth, Paula. 'Here Ends the Lesson: Shaping Lesson Conclusions as an Iterative Process in Improving Historical enquiries' in Teaching History, 173, Opening Doors Edition, (2018): 58–67. London: Historical Association.

Chapter 4   Substantive and Disciplinary Knowledge

Michael Fordham

BACKGROUND

What do we need to know to be good historians? You can line up to offer your glib answers to this question: 'a lot', 'never enough' and 'not as much as you might expect' come to mind. But for us as history teachers, this is one of the most crucial questions we need to ask ourselves. We set so many educational goals for our pupils, and we boldly proclaim that we are teaching them objectives such as analysing the impact of British rule on Indian society. But what does an 11-year-old or 17-year-old need to know in order to do the things we want them to do?

Hammond (2014) wrote about this challenge extensively. For Hammond, a pupil's ability to complete a task to a high standard will depend on the layers of knowledge they already have. In analysing the written work of her GCSE pupils, she realised that what distinguished the highest quality causal analysis was an ability to draw on substantive knowledge on three scales: topic knowledge (in this case Nazi Germany), period knowledge (20th-century Europe) and wider historical knowledge. The best essays on Hitler's rise to power not only deployed topic knowledge of Nazi propaganda but were able to draw implicitly on wider historical knowledge of elections and democratic government to 'flavour' their claims. We also know, thanks to the psychologists, that we cannot take on lots of new information in one go, and so our ability to read, interpret and understand a text is going to be highly dependent on what we already know (Willingham, 2009).

Activity 4.1

Consider the following extract from David Olusoga's *Black and British* (2017). It is the kind of thing that we might reasonably expect a 14-year-old, at the end of their compulsory history education, to understand, possibly with some support from their teacher.

> The London of 1948, to which the Empire Windrush brought those early settlers, was busily preparing to host another Olympics. A month and a week

after the Windrush docked at Tilbury, the 1948 games got underway in London's old Wembley Stadium, a relic of the 1924 British Empire Exhibition. The opening ceremony began with the traditional parade of the teams from each competing country. The athletes then were mainly male and the audience that cheered them on almost entirely white, as was the case when Arthur Wint, the six-foot-four-inch black Jamaican sprinter, won the 400 metres. Wint took the podium to receive Jamaica's first ever Olympic gold medal to the strains of 'God Save the King', as Jamaica was then a British Crown Colony so had no national anthem of her own. Like half of the men who arrived in London on the Empire Windrush, Arthur Wint had served in the Second World War. Having trained in Canada he became a Spitfire pilot for the RAF, rising to become Flight Lieutenant Wint. Fittingly, it was the band of the RAF that played the national anthem as the gold medal was hung around his neck.

In her article, 'The knowledge that "flavours" a claim', Hammond (2014) posits three categories of knowledge that she found in her pupils' work and three 'scales' at which these were manifest.

Knowledge of the characteristics of ...	In this topic	In this period	Generally in history
... people's ideas and thinking.			
... political and economic systems.			
... social and cultural systems.			

Draw a table like the one above and have a go at filling it in with the kinds of things pupils would need to know in order to understand what the text is saying.

This little exercise is one of the most powerful things we can do as history teachers to plan our enquiries with pupils. If we sit down and take the time to work out what we want pupils to be able to do (write an essay, analyse a text, give an oral presentation, and so on), then we can unpack what prior knowledge those pupils are going to need to have, and we can then work out how best to teach that.

This chapter will be one that risks being too philosophical and one you may feel tempted to skip. What I hope to show in this chapter is that questions about knowledge and the forms knowledge take in history are central to what we do as history teachers and that, with a few conceptual tools, we can navigate a way through the debates in a way that helps us plan, teach and assess pupils in history more meaningfully than we would otherwise be able to do.

DEFINING SOME KEY IDEAS

All of the following are contested ideas and there will be as many people who disagree with my interpretation of them here as there are those who agree. I have found the following interpretations of the ideas helpful, but clearly if you are interested in the philosophy that sits behind these ideas then there is a world of reading awaiting you.

Propositional and Procedural Knowledge

Propositional knowledge is knowledge that can be expressed in a proposition. For example:

- 'The Battle of Lepanto was in 1571'.
- 'The concept of liberty was important in the American Revolution'.
- 'Very few texts survive from fifth-century Britain'.
- 'Edward Gibbon's interpretation of the collapse of the Roman Empire is not widely accepted by historians in the 21st century'.

All these propositions are things that we might write or talk about as historians, and indeed, all are things of which we might (with varying degrees of success) dispute the truth. But the fact that truth claims can be contested does not make these claims unimportant to the historian: to the contrary, claims to truth, expressed in propositional form, are the fibres from which history in all its forms is built. Unsurprisingly, deciding what propositional knowledge we want pupils to learn is at the heart of the curriculum planning process.

Although there is a great deal of philosophical scholarly debate about this, a distinction is often drawn between 'propositional' and 'procedural' knowledge or, to use a more straightforward term 'know that' versus 'know how'. I have procedural knowledge if I know how to do something. You might know how to ride a bike or play a saxophone. There is some overlap here with the concept of 'ability', but they are probably not quite the same thing. For example, we might say that a baby is able to breathe, but it would not make sense to say a baby 'knows how to breathe'. I find it easiest to think of procedural knowledge as 'something you have learnt to do'.

There are lots of things we want pupils to know how to do in history, which might include:

- How to write an essay
- How to construct a causal argument
- How to read a source 'against the grain'
- How to reference an interpretation

The nature of these things is that they are likely to be common to almost any bit of history that we choose to study – unlike the examples of propositional knowledge given previously, which are likely to be relevant only if you are studying the periods in question, historians of all times, places and things need to critique, argue and write. This is probably why there has been a strong temptation to classify these things as 'the skills' or 'the craft' of the historian and, once this is done, it is not too big a logical jump to say that these are the things that should be prioritised in a history education. In my view this is partly correct but also more complex than it first appears, but before I get to that part of my argument, I have a further distinction I would like you to understand: substantive and disciplinary knowledge.

Substantive and Disciplinary Knowledge

In history education, we often draw a distinction between 'substantive' and 'disciplinary' knowledge. Substantive knowledge is typically understood in history education to mean 'knowledge of the past', whereas as disciplinary knowledge refers to 'knowledge of the discipline'.

You may be tempted to do what many others have done in the past, which is to assume that 'substantive' knowledge is the same as 'propositional' knowledge

Table 4.1 *A matrix of different types of historical knowledge.*

	Substantive	Disciplinary
Propositional	Truth claims about the past, such as 'the concept of liberty was important in the American Revolution'.	Truth claims about the practice of history, such as 'Gibbon's interpretation of the fall of Rome is not widely accepted today'.
Procedural	Knowing how something was done in the past, such as practising swordsmanship techniques from a renaissance fencing manual.	Knowing how something is done in the practice of history, such as structuring a causal argument.

and that 'disciplinary knowledge' is the same as 'procedural knowledge'. But let's remind ourselves of our examples of propositional knowledge:

- 'The Battle of Lepanto was in 1571'.
- 'The concept of liberty was important in the American Revolution'.
- 'Very few texts survive from fifth-century Britain'.
- 'Edward Gibbon's interpretation of the collapse of the Roman Empire is not widely accepted by historians in the 21st century'.

The first two propositions here are quite clearly knowledge *of* the past – there is an attempt in each proposition to make a truth claim about (respectively) the 16th and 18th centuries. But consider the second two: these are not claims about the fifth and sixth centuries. These are rather claims that we need to know to understand the construction of knowledge of those periods. A historian of late antiquity would clearly need to know that few texts survive from fifth-century Britain and that Gibbon's interpretation is not widely accepted, but this is not the same as making a claim about the periods in question. These are therefore the kinds of things I have in mind when I talk about 'propositional disciplinary' knowledge: it is a mistake to equate the procedural and the disciplinary (or the propositional and the substantive). Instead, we might think of it more as a matrix, as shown in Table 4.1.

I think the propositional row in this matrix will make sense to most, as will the category of 'procedural disciplinary' knowledge. There might be a case for arguing that procedural substantive knowledge is not a thing, but I have spent too long talking to people who take historical re-enactment very seriously to dismiss this completely. Knowing how to fence with a 14th-century longsword is not the same as being able to describe the process in propositions, and learning to do something as (we believe) it was done in the past can provide insights that we cannot otherwise attain.

Activity 4.2

Based on this section, write your own definition of the following terms:

- Propositional knowledge
- Procedural knowledge
- Substantive knowledge
- Disciplinary knowledge

Then choose a period of history you know well and create your own matrix, as shown in Table 4.1, with an example of each type of knowledge.

SOME FORMS OF SUBSTANTIVE KNOWLEDGE

Having drawn some hopefully not too tentative distinctions between propositional and procedural knowledge and substantive and disciplinary knowledge, the hope might be that we now have all the tools we need to get to grips with the dauting task ahead of us. I am however going to push us further now and break the categories of substantive and disciplinary knowledge down. As we go, the grey areas and overlaps will naturally increase and it does not do to be dogmatic about these, but I have found these useful ways of thinking about what we are doing in history education.

Simple Facts

Simple facts are just that: ideas that can easily be conveyed in a proposition. To return to our example, 'the Battle of Lepanto was in 1571' would be a simple fact. Few forms of knowledge have suffered so much at the hands of critics than simple facts, and indeed, it is nearly a century now since the most amusing critique of simple facts in history was made by Sellar and Yeatman (1930) in their classic satire *1066 and all that*. Much ink has been spilt on this matter, often by well-meaning educationalists and other commentators looking to avoid history being a dull diet of 'drill and kill'. Surely, the argument runs, we do not need children learning simple facts: after all, if they need to know something, they can just look it up.

Well, yes and no. All historians look things up. I have had to look up lots of things when writing this chapter – sometimes it is for a more substantial thing I need to know ('what exactly did this person say about this?'), but sometimes it really is for something simple ('what year was that paper published?'). Those who go 'historian spotting' in university libraries will have noticed the behaviour of these creatures in the wild: constantly referring back to texts, grabbing books to check references and revisiting an extract to make sure they have got it right. Looking things up is so central to a historian's craft that it would make no sense at all to say that history is the preserve only of those with photographic memories.

The problem arises when you have to look up a lot of things. In even a simple school essay, there will be a very large number of simple facts being used. We have all felt that feeling (which some psychologists call 'cognitive overload') of trying to hold too many things in our consciousness at once, and that overwhelmed feeling will be all too familiar to those of us who have spent time teaching children to do a complex task like writing an essay. If you cannot remember whether Alfred was the King of Wessex or Northumbria, then you are probably not ready to write a book on ninth-century state formation.

So learning simple facts would seem important. We do not need to know everything – our historians in the wild are proof of that – but we do need to know *enough* to avoid being overwhelmed. I find the concept of 'critical mass' useful here: for any given historical topic, there will be very few individual simple facts which are utterly essential for us to know, but we need to have enough of these facts in place to ensure we can look up the things we need to look up in a meaningful and efficient manner.

Does this mean 'drill and kill'? Well, it might mean drill, and we as teachers might identify some simple facts we think might serve a purpose if learnt by heart. But this again is where some of the psychology can be useful: we know from our psychologist colleagues that we are most likely to remember simple facts when those facts are meaningful and tied to other things that we know. Knowledge is, to use Counsell's (2017) phrase, 'sticky'. And some of the stickiest forms of substantive knowledge are not simple facts, but other things to which we shall now turn.

Narratives and Stories

Humans seem to have some predilection for narratives. If you give someone a list of bios of people then they may struggle to remember them all, but make those people characters in a story and suddenly they come to life and we remember them far more easily. Narratives and stories achieve this by creating meaning through connections: those connections can be temporal (one thing precedes or follows another) and social (one person has a connection to another person), but perhaps most importantly they play on our own humanity.

Narratives and stories can be handled in classrooms in quite distinct ways. Storytelling is something that historians and history teachers alike are very good at, and whether it is a spoken tale or a written story, there are few things as likely to capture the long-term attention of a class than a ripping yarn. But we can also do more structural things around narratives: we can make timelines from them, we can sequence events, and we can draw maps that make clear the connections between people. So knowing a narrative might mean being able to re-tell a story you have heard, but it also encompasses a range of tasks that will be well-known to history teachers.

Sense of Period

Spotting and challenging anachronism has long been a task of the history teacher, and, certainly in a primary school setting, these might be fairly straightforward things to correct – no mobile phones in Mughal India, no televisions in Tenochtitlan, and that sort of thing. Although these things still come up in secondary schools, the kinds of anachronism we face are often more subtle. Consider for example the following sentences written by a Year 7 pupil:

> King John signed Magna Carta because he was worried that public opinion might turn against him if he did not agree to it. The barons were angry that John was abusing human rights by locking people up without a fair trial.

There is a great deal wrong in these sentences (John did not 'sign' anything), but the things that will jump out to a medievalist will be some key anachronistic ideas: the concepts of 'public opinion' and 'human rights' are used here in a very modern sense.

But consider now how you would explain to this child that 'public opinion' and 'human rights' are not the right concepts to use here. This is not a simple factual correction – rather, it reflects a fairly significant misunderstanding of the period in question. This is I think what Hammond (2014) was getting at when she described her second and third layers of substantive knowledge. These things could perhaps be reduced to simple propositions of a more general nature ('people in this period normally believed ...') but I am not convinced that this broad sense of period comes about through learning such propositions. This wider sense of period is even more subject to the 'collectively sufficient rather than individually necessary' framing I identified when discussing simple facts, and is perhaps most clearly seen when we think about substantive concepts.

Substantive Concepts

Substantive concepts have in history education typically been distinguished from their 'second-order' variety. Whereas we talk of second-order concepts such as 'cause' and 'change', we talk of substantive concepts as things like 'empire', 'social class' and 'liberty'.

These terms are very difficult for novices learning history because their meaning cannot be reduced to a definition. The Roman Empire was very different in form from the Portuguese Empire, and yet we feel the word 'empire' is useful for conveying some kind of commonality between the two. The enslavement of black Africans in North America in the 18th-century Caribbean differed in all sorts of meaningful ways from the enslavement of the Laconian helots in sixth-century B.C. Sparta, yet we find a concept such as 'slavery' used to describe both. While we could construct a working definition of empire or slavery for children to use, it would have to be so general in form that it would lose much of its explanatory power.

This is why I would agree with Counsell (2017) that our best approach to learning substantive concepts in history classrooms is by learning instantiations: a concept such as 'middle class' is one that we need to return to time and again, showing children how the concept has been used in different historical contexts to mean different things. The more examples of 'middle class' or 'revolution' that pupils encounter, the more complex their understanding of these terms will become. These are not just 'Tier 3 vocabulary': they each represent a central nexus of historical meaning, and building up knowledge of these concepts is not something that can be done quickly or easily. But it is also in this complexity that we find their curricular power. If we decide in advance a set of core substantive concepts we want pupils to master, then we can design our curriculum over several years to create the opportunities to revisit these concepts and to make them more complex in the minds of our pupils.

> **Activity 4.3**
>
> Choose a topic you are currently teaching. Create a list of the substantive knowledge pupils need to know in order to successfully complete the outcome task. Use Fordham's categories of substantive knowledge to help you:
>
> - Simple facts
> - Narratives and stories
> - Sense of period
> - Substantive concepts

DISCIPLINARY KNOWLEDGE

Disciplinary knowledge is a phrase that has turned up in history education only in recent years, in part as a response to an attempt by the government in England in the 2010s to characterise the work of history education as being 'skills-based' rather than 'knowledge-based'. 'Not so', the history teachers responded, and a significant amount of time was spent over the subsequent decade re-asserting that history teachers reject a 'knowledge-skills' dichotomy. The idea of 'disciplinary knowledge' did I think emerge as a challenge to that.

It is however a bit of a clunky term, not least because the distinction between 'propositional' and 'procedural' disciplinary knowledge creates plenty of scope for confusion, and indeed, there is sufficient grey areas between the two to give fuel to the argument that maybe it is not a helpful distinction. Despite this possible critique, I find the distinction is a useful one in helping to make sense of what we do as history teachers, but it is important not to be dogmatic by trying to make things simple that are in reality complex.

Second-order Concepts

The first port of call when thinking about disciplinary knowledge is likely to be second-order concepts. Not least because much of the literature on history education produced in England in the latter part of the 20th century and the first part of the 21st has been structured around the idea. Writing in 1998, Counsell referred to the second-order concepts in the 1995 National Curriculum – there known as the 'key elements' – as the only thing over which she would chain herself to the railings (Counsell, 1998).

You will have seen elsewhere in this volume that second-order concepts are very powerful for teachers. As shown in Chapter 3, they help us design enquiry questions which give direction to the work we want pupils to do. They help us understand what makes our work distinctively 'historical', rather than English Literature, or psychology, or geography. There is no single universal model of second-order concepts, and that alone should warn you that such models are abstractions of reality. In the English National Curriculum (which has been shaped by and influenced the thinking of history teachers in England over the last thirty years), the second-order concepts have been identified as:

- Cause and consequence
- Change and continuity
- Similarity and difference ('diversity' in 2008)
- Significance
- Evidence
- Interpretations

Contrast this with the model of Seixas and Morton (2013) which has been influential in Canada, and which offers:

- Historical significance
- Primary sources
- Continuity and change
- Cause and consequence
- Historical perspectives
- Ethical dimensions

When you get down into the detail of what different people have meant by these ideas, then there is a lot of commonality. For example, the English curricular concept of 'interpretations' has been heavily worked on by history teachers, and encompasses much of what Seixas means by 'historical perspective' and 'ethical dimensions', but there are a lot of nuances within that.

To my mind, the power of second-order concepts lies in their ability to help us form meaningful historical questions and to identify the kinds of analysis we might need to answer those questions. For example, a pupil who knows a little about 'causation' will recognise a causal question when they see one, and immediately start to think about the forms of argument that might answer the question. This might, for example, involve knowing that causal arguments can be structured into 'long-term' and 'short-term' causes, or perhaps that an argument needs to be thematic and weigh up different 'factors'. It might involve knowing what a counter-factual is, and how a counter-factual argument could be deployed to give analytical weight to an argument.

Causation is just one second-order concept, and all of the ones listed have been unpacked extensively by history teachers and others to help us make sense of what we need to do with these concepts. Rather than cover this in more detail here, a good starting point would be Chapters 5 through to 11 in this volume, which each explore a different second-order concept and how to incorporate them into a history curriculum.

Historians' Methods and Historiography

A second component of disciplinary knowledge is knowledge of the methods that historians use. History is a very diverse discipline and its methods are often fairly intuitive: there are relatively few academic history papers, for example, that contain a discrete 'methodology' section. Much history is based on the interpretation of the written record, and as such, reading strategies are fairly high up the list of techniques that one needs to learn as one progresses through the discipline. There are specific techniques that one can learn: Wineburg and his colleagues at Stanford have, for example, done a great deal of recent work on how to read online texts, and have identified a number of very specific techniques that experts use to establish how confident they are in what that text tells them (Caulfield & Wineburg, 2023).

So-called 'source analysis' has been a longstanding component of history curricula, and in one form or another the idea that there are source analysis techniques that can be identified, broken down and taught has been embedded in every version of the English National Curriculum, and exam board assessment criteria still lean heavily on the idea. Space here prevents a full critique of this position and, although now somewhat dated, the arguments made by McAleavy (1998) a quarter of a century ago still provide a helpful critique of what goes wrong when we attempt to teach 'source analysis' as a decontextualised set of techniques.

My advice here is to focus on introducing pupils to lots of different kinds of sources, and to show how those sources have been used by historians to reach conclusions. At its most powerful, this approach might involve taking a source and showing pupils how different historians have reached different conclusions by using the source in a different way. Foster's (2011) work on this is still the best starting point. See also Chapter 11 for the many ways in which history teachers can use sources in the classroom, and how pupils can use sources as evidence to make their own claims about the past.

We may also want pupils to develop knowledge of what is sometimes called 'historiography', which encompasses both the published record of historians (and others) on a particular topic, and the theories of how history works that have been developed by historians (and others) over the years. A great deal has been written in recent years on bringing historians into the classroom and there are some wonderful case studies over the pages of *Teaching History* that show how historiography might be introduced to pupils: take, for example, Holliss's (2014) work that took Christopher Clark's book 'The Sleepwalkers' and placed it at the heart of a sequence of lessons for pupils. See Chapter 15 for further examples of how history teachers have introduced historical scholarship to allow pupils to see the interpretation at the heart of history.

PRACTICAL IMPLICATIONS

Much of what you have read here is fairly philosophical in character, and in some ways that is part of what makes history teaching such an intellectual challenge. The thing we are teaching children is not easy, and the more we think about it, the more complex it becomes. But you are not reading this book because you want to learn to be a philosopher of history or history education, where these debates can be left abstract and contested. As a history teacher, you need to make it real: 9x3 will be there on Friday afternoon regardless of whether you have come to firm conclusions about the nature of history as a discipline. In this last part of the chapter, therefore, I want to offer a set of questions that you might consider in the planning process which allows you to draw on what you have learnt from this chapter in a way that has immediate practical application for the task in front of you. I have phrased this as a series of steps which will relate to what you have read elsewhere in this volume about the planning process.

What Is the Nature of the Task You Want Pupils to Complete?

In the thousands of history lessons I have taught, and hundreds I have seen other people teach, I would say this is always the thing that most seems to cause a problem: the teacher (usually me) not being sufficiently clear about *what* we want the pupils to do.

What Knowledge of the Past Do They Need to Complete the Task?

You cannot ever predict what children will bring to the table, and one of the joys of being a teacher is those surprising moments when a pupil draws something from their knowledge to help do what you have asked them to do that was completely unexpected. Overall, however, you will be the one who provides them with much of what they need, and so a good step is to map out what you think a pupil would need to know – both in terms of substantive and disciplinary knowledge – to complete the task at hand.

What Should They Already Know, and Do They Know It?

Hopefully, if you have a well-planned curriculum, pupils will already know a lot of what you need them to know, but there will be gaps in their knowledge, for a variety of reasons, and this is what makes ongoing assessment so important – do not be afraid to stop and re-teach something if it's what needs to be done.

Structure That Knowledge Over Time

Finally, structure things over time. There will be thousands of possible ways of structuring what you need them to know over a sequence of lessons, so look for the kinds of internal logic that will give you a sense of direction. Chronology, for example, is probably the default position, where we use chronological frameworks to structure knowledge over time, but there are other ways of achieving the same end.

And, finally, good luck. The intellectual hoops we jump through as history teachers are remarkable, and, although at times frustrating, this is part of what attracts so many of us to the profession.

SUMMARY OF KEY POINTS

- The following ideas are useful when considering historical knowledge: propositional versus procedural knowledge, and substantive versus disciplinary knowledge.
- Propositional knowledge ('know that') refers to knowledge which can be summarised in a proposition, while procedural knowledge ('know how') is best understood as something you have learnt how to do.

- Substantive knowledge is typically understood to be 'knowledge of the past', while disciplinary knowledge is 'knowledge of the discipline' (how knowledge of the past is constructed).
- It is too simple to equate propositional knowledge with substantive knowledge, and procedural knowledge with disciplinary knowledge, as you can have propositional knowledge of both the past and the discipline of history.
- When considering what substantive knowledge your pupils need, it is helpful to think in terms of: simple facts, narrative and stories, sense of period and substantive concepts.
- Disciplinary knowledge involves both second-order concepts, which are powerful for shaping meaningful historical questions for pupils to answer, and a knowledge of the methods a historian uses to reach their conclusions.
- It is our role as teachers to work out what we want our pupils to be able to do, and the substantive and the disciplinary knowledge they need to achieve it.

RESOURCES AND FURTHER READING

Caulfield, Mike, & Wineburg, Sam. Verified: How to Think Straight, Get Duped Less, and Make Better Decisions About What to Believe Online. Chicago: University of Chicago Press 2023.

Counsell, Christine. 'Editorial' in Teaching History, 91, Evidence and Interpretation Edition, (1998): 2. London: Historical Association.

Counsell, Christine. 'The Fertility of Substantive Knowledge: in Search of Its Hidden Generative power' in Davies, Ian (ed.). Debates in History Teaching. Oxon: Routledge 2017: 80–99.

Foster, Rachel. 'Passive Receivers or Constructive Readers? Pupil's Experiences of an Encounter With Academic history' in Teaching History, 142, Experiencing History Edition, (2011): 4–13. London: Historical Association.

Hammond, Kate. 'The Knowledge That 'flavours' a Claim: Towards Building and Assessing Historical Knowledge on Three scales' in Teaching History, 157, Assessment Edition, (2014): 18–25. London: Historical Association.

Holliss, Claire. 'Waking up to Complexity: Using Christopher Clark's The Sleepwalkers to Challenge Over-Determined Causal explanations' in Teaching History, 154, A Sense of History Edition, (2014): 48–54. London: Historical Association.

McAleavy, Tony. 'The Use of Sources in School History 1910–1998: a Critical perspective' in Teaching History, 91, Evidence and Interpretation Edition, (1998): 10–16. London: Historical Association.

Olusoga, David. Black and British: A Forgotten History. London: Pan Books 2017: 522.

Seixas, Peter, & Morton, Tom. The Big Six: Historical Thinking Concepts. Nelson Education 2013: 10–11. Also available at: https://historicalthinking.ca/sites/default/files/files/docs/Guideposts.pdf

Sellar, W.C., & Yeatman, R.J. 1066 and All That: English History Served up a La Carte: A Unique and Hilarious Spoof. Malton: Methuen & Co 1930.

Willingham, Daniel T. Why Don't Students Like School? A Cognitive Scientist Answers Questions About How the Mind Works and What It Means for the Classroom. San Francisco: Wiley 2009.

Chapter 5 Change and Continuity

Matt Stanford

BACKGROUND

Christine Counsell opens her chapter on change and continuity in *Debates in History Teaching* with the words, 'Change and continuity are elusive prey' (Counsell, 2011). The reason for this is that things changing is of relevance to many of the second-order concepts and so when we are thinking about change and continuity we can get confused between the wood and the trees.

This second-order concept is also intricate because it asks pupils to think about things that did happen (change) and things that didn't happen (continuity). Asking pupils to find continuities as well as changes can prove more tricky. Like the curious incident of the dog that didn't bark in the night-time, noticing something that didn't happen is often more difficult than noticing something that did, even though it may be of greater importance.

In this chapter, we will consider what change and continuity means in the history classroom, in distinction from related and similar second-order concepts, and how we can help pupils to make and support meaningful judgements about change and continuity in response to genuine historical questions.

CHANGE AND CONTINUITY IS NOT CAUSATION

One of the most important things to say about change and continuity as a second-order concept might also seem to be one of the simplest: change it is, not causation. In an enquiry on causes (as discussed by Laura London in Chapter 6), we will ask pupils to analyse *why* events in history happened. A change and continuity enquiry is asking them to make and support a judgement about the change brought about by that event. The focus is *the change itself*. Or, indeed, the lack thereof.

A causation question might ask pupils to justify an argument about the interrelation or relative importance of the causes of the Reformation, while a change and continuity question will ask them to describe the changes wrought by the Reformation.

> **Activity 5.1**
>
> All the questions in the list below could make for decent enquiry questions. Which of them are focused on the second-order concept of change and continuity and which on causation? Are there any which might reasonably be used to address either depending on the content of the lessons themselves?
>
> - Why did William win the Battle of Hastings?
> - What was the impact of the Norman Conquest on Yorkshire?
> - Why did the peasants revolt in 1381?
> - How did the Reformation change Europe?
> - How revolutionary was revolutionary France?
> - Why did the Industrial Revolution begin in Britain?
> - Did the Sixties really swing?

CHANGE AND CONTINUITY IS NOT CONSEQUENCE

Although there may be some ambiguity in some of the questions above, things get more complicated when we think about causation running in the other direction. If we ask pupils to make a judgement about the *consequences* of an event, it can be more difficult to separate this from a change and continuity question. After all, if one were to ask pupils to explain the consequences of, say, the Second World War on British society, we would hope that they would talk about things that had changed. That there was no National Health Service on VJ Day in 1945, but there was one by the end of July 1948 is quite certainly a change, and the creation of this National Health Service is, undeniably, a consequence of the Second World War, and it would be remiss of any teacher asking pupils about the consequences of the war on British society not to mention one of the most characteristic features of post-war British society. A pupil asked something like, 'How much did British society change after the Second World War?' would also definitely need to include the NHS. However, the difference is what we are asking our pupils to *do with the fact of* the creation of the NHS. In the consequences enquiry, we would be getting pupils to look for roots of the change – what was it about the Second World War that made the creation of the NHS possible? In the change enquiry we want pupils to think about how different the creation of the NHS made British society. What is the difference between a society where healthcare is restricted to many, particularly the poorest, women and children, and a society where healthcare is free at the point of use? What is the difference between a society that sees the health of the citizen as, almost entirely, the responsibility of the citizen, and a welfare state? As Navey explains in Chapter 7 on Teaching Consequence, historians analysing consequence focus on the out-workings of an event, as distinct from analysing the process of change over time.

THE CHANGE IS THE THING

This is challenging for pupils as thinking about change requires them to engage at an abstract level. We do want pupils to be able to recall chronological lists of facts that we deem important enough to fill their precious lesson time, but those lists are a minimum. Even if pupils can reel them off with confidence in a low-stakes retrieval quiz, they are still items on a list. The 'changes' that these events engendered or represent is an abstraction created by the historian. It is a colligation of ideas about the world before the events, the nature of the events, and the world after. It is not items on a list, it is the list itself. It is not the itinerary but the journey.

Let's stay with this metaphor of a journey for a little while. If I were to leave my house where I am writing this and travel to the village's war memorial I will pass my daughter's friend's house, the graveyard, the Hoops, the barbers, Book Café, the Spar ... until I arrive at the war memorial. This list of things I pass you might call my itinerary. However, in my *journey* I will have travelled 0.9 miles, climbed 13ft and descended 3ft. I might have done this journey in a car or on foot. I might have run the first bit and then walked because my knee is crocked. I might have travelled pleasantly admiring the view over to the neolithic long barrows of the Heath. It might be good that I went. It might be better if I had gone somewhere else ...

By making a colligation, by sweeping up all the places passed and all the footsteps and the rest and putting them in a linguistic bag labelled 'journey', we can talk about my movement through the village in lots of different ways. How was my journey? Short, slow, faster at the end, interrupted, worthwhile, wet ...? All of these could be valid descriptions of the total of the events that I have bundled into the word 'journey'.

When we talk about 'the change in British society' in the post-war period or 'the Industrial Revolution' we are talking in the abstract. Both of these are colligations, rag-bags of different events, facts and ideas, created by historians.

Forgive me if this seems either a pompous pseudo-intellectual distinction or, on the other hand, something from the Institute of the Blindingly Obvious, but I feel it's worth pointing out because for us, who have read, watched and listened to history, dealing with these abstractions is so normal as to not be noticeable. However, this may not be the case for our pupils and we need to make sure that we are clear in our own heads what we are asking them to do. Are they clear, for example, about the ontological difference between the events and the changes? Do they know that 'the NHS' is a different *order of thing* to 'changes in British society'? Do they know that we want them to use the one to talk about the other?

This idea that pupils should be asked to engage with the change itself was first articulated by Denis Shemilt (1980) in his work on the early Schools Council History Project. It was added to by Peter Lee (see *Teaching History's* 'What's the Wisdom on Change and Continuity?' (The Editorial Board 2020), for more details) giving us these aspects of change for pupils to analyse:

- pace or rate of change
- degree or extent of change
- nature or type of change
- the process of change

While these ideas can, and often do, overlap, it is important for a history teacher to be clear in their own minds which of these ideas they want their pupils to engage with.

Activity 5.2

Which of the above ideas about change might you want pupils to engage with in the following enquiry questions?

- Why did Islam spread so far and so fast?
- How much did enclosure change the English countryside?
- Which of the American, French and Haitian Revolutions was the most revolutionary?
- In what ways did the Reformation change English society?

DEVISING A CHANGE AND CONTINUITY ENQUIRY QUESTION

As Worth explains in Chapter 3, an enquiry question can give shape and purpose to a sequence of lessons by foregrounding a particular disciplinary concept. In the case of a change and continuity enquiry, careful thought needs to be given to the wording of the question so that it focuses pupils' analysis on the process or journey of change, as opposed to the causes or consequences of the event these changes are part of (as highlighted in Activity 5.1). Historical scholarship, such as the following quote by Simon Schama, is a very good place to start.

> [T]here are moments when history is unsubtle; when change arrives in a violent rush, decisive, bloody, traumatic; as a truck-load of trouble, wiping out everything that gives a culture its bearings – custom, law and loyalty.
> *(Schama, 2009)*

Using a historian's work as a way of finding a good change and continuity enquiry question brings all the benefits that Victoria Crooks talks about in Chapter 15 on using historical scholarship. Simon Schama's description of the impact of the Norman Conquest is used as a stimulus or starting point in many, many British schools. (I am sure that many people, beguiled by Schama's style, had the idea at the same time but the first person I saw using his work in a classroom was Michael Fordham.)

If you want to help pupils make a good assessment of the changes wrought by the Norman Conquest, breaking down those changes into the categories offered by Schama gives a useful direction to a scheme of work. How far did 'custom' change? How far did 'law' change? What about 'loyalty'? Were they 'wiped out'? What changes and what continues? Obviously, it takes care and attention to help pupils understand what things those categories might entail but it is eminently do-able.

Alternatively, you could ask pupils whether Schama's characterisation of the changes being 'a violent rush, decisive, bloody and traumatic' is accurate. You could help pupils make a judgement about whether the changes brought about by the Conquest were 'violent'? Were they 'decisive'?

For another example of a change and continuity enquiry on the Norman Conquest, directly built upon historical scholarship, see Eve Hackett's (2020) work in *Teaching History* where she describes using Marc Morris's metaphor of England as a tree reshaped by the Norman Conquest. Hackett took this idea and asked her pupils to use the same metaphor to describe the changes brought by the Conquest.

Corinne Goullée has also used historical scholarship as the basis for her enquiry, 'In what ways did the Reformation matter to ordinary people?', a version of which is available from the Oak National Academy website (Goullée, 2020). This scheme of work seeks to show the effects of sixteenth century religious change by focusing, not on the high politics of the Tudor court, or the theological arguments, but on the way it shaped ordinary people's lives. This carefully constructed enquiry was based on the work of Steve Mastin (Mastin & Counsell, 2015), which was inspired by Eamon Duffy's *The Voices of Morebath* which asks:

> The fifty years between 1530 and 1580, England moved from being one of the most lavishly Catholic countries in Europe to being a Protestant nation, a land of whitewashed churches and anti-papal preaching. What was the impact of this religious change in the countryside? And how did country people feel about the revolutionary upheavals that transformed their mental and material worlds under Henry VIII and his three children?
> *(Duffy, 2001)*

In the classroom, Mastin and Goullée both used an extended society game where pupils are given information, derived from Duffy's book, about real people who lived in the Devon village before the Reformation. Armed with their own historical character, pupils can see what the local church meant to the villagers on the eve of the Reformation and how central it was to village life. As subsequent lessons reveal the religious policies of each Tudor monarch, pupils reflect on how their church and their characters' daily lives have changed, as well as how they might have felt about this. How do the local craftsmen react to the destruction of their precious statues of saints in the reign of King Edward VI? What about the villagers who had devoted their time to raise money for these statues? How does this affect the priest Sir Christopher Trychay? What happens when four of the young men join the Prayer Book Rebellion in 1549? The story of Morebath Church paints a vivid picture of the English Reformation and allows pupils to see how the religious changes might have been experienced by individuals. When pupils share their thoughts and reflections on their individual character's experience with the rest of the class, a diversity of experiences can be seen from which they can draw conclusions about the changes in different areas of life. Whose economic position changed? Whose social status changed? Who might have been most emotionally affected? In this way, the complex changes of the Reformation become more concrete without being oversimplified to 'Protestants liked plain churches' and 'Catholics liked beautiful churches'.

In 2024, Steve Mastin updated his work in a chapter for the Key Stage 3 textbook 'Connected Worlds' on this topic using the question 'What changed in the village of Morebath between 1520 and 1574?' (Counsell et. al, 2024).

Example Enquiry: Was There More Continuity than Change in British–Jamaican Relations between 1760 and 1870?

In his article *Staying with the shot*, Nathanael Davies (2020) shows how the powerful question to be asking pupils about the abolition of slavery is how far it *changed* the lives of people living in the Americas. Traditionally many departments have focused more on the causes of abolition, failing to continue to look at the lives of formerly enslaved people after 1833. Davies talks about how he wants to 'keep the camera rolling' and 'stay with the shot' to really help pupils understand how far the lives of people on Jamaica did or did not change beyond the traditional cut-off points of the abolition of the slave trade in 1807 and the abolition of slavery across the British Empire in 1833. This enquiry has been hugely influential for not just being an excellent example of a change and continuity enquiry, but also for tackling the topics of empire and slavery from the perspective of the colonised and enslaved (see Chapter 12 for more on what it means to decolonise a history curriculum). Davies directs his pupils to look at this period of history through a series of lenses, including the lenses of resistance to British rule and the living conditions of black Jamaicans (see the overview of the enquiry in Table 5.1). Indeed, the enquiry is book ended by two revolts against British rule. As pupils begin the enquiry by learning about both Tacky's Revolt of 1760 and the Morant Bay Rebellion of 1865, they are well-placed to discuss how much has really changed for black Jamaicans. The enquiry is designed to be taught as part of an A Level coursework module, but it could be adapted for younger years by reducing the level of detail and historiography.

Table 5.1 Overview of the enquiry: Was there more continuity than change in British–Jamaican relations between 1760 and 1870? (Davies, 2020)

Lesson	Lesson Title	Lesson Summary
1	Was there more continuity than change in British–Jamaican relations between 1760 and 1870?	In this lynchpin lesson, students encounter the enquiry question by juxtaposing the revolts of 1760 and 1870. Students are introduced to the different lenses they will be asked to consider in the coming lessons.
2	Did Britain really engage in an 'inglorious crusade' against slavery?	After introducing W.E.H. Lecky's famous (1869) declaration of Britain's steadfast 'inglorious crusade' against slavery, students consider if such continuity in public attitudes existed throughout our period of study. We also consider Hochschild's (2012) concept of a 'tipping point'. Using the timeline and sources, students then track British public opinion during and after abolition. Students find evidence to decide whether Lecky (1869) was right to imply continuity in public attitudes.
3	Did the 'West Indian' economy face an 'uninterrupted decline' after 1776?	In approaching such a complex topic, students draw upon research by Katie Donington (2019) on the Hibbert family in order to gain an understanding of why slavery in Jamaica was so profitable. They then follow the Hibbert family in ascertaining whether Eric Williams (1994) was right to assert that it was 'uninterrupted decline' for the West Indian economy after American Independence.
4	Did 'the monster' really die in 1838?	Students assess how far Knibb's famous 1838 description of the 'monster' being killed on Emancipation Day matched the experiences of the Afro-Jamaican worker. Students consider the evidential problem at the heart of such a question and the techniques historians from below must use in order to make inferences from sources available in the archive.
5	Were the 1790s a turning point for the organised resistance of the enslaved of Jamaica?	Using historian Eugene Genovese's (1979) contentious interpretation that the revolutions in France and St Domingue brought a 'turning point' in the resistance of enslaved workers across the Americas, students use sources (together with their timeline) to assess whether Genovese's thesis applies to Jamaica. Students again consider the evidential problem at the heart of writing any history of resistance.
6	How did the racism of British rule in Jamaica develop between 1760 and 1870?	Drawing on recent historical scholarship on race, students assess how ideas of race developed over the period. Students use a selection of sources from across the period to identify evidence of religious, cultural or biological constructions of race. Students consider the incomplete and contested nature of racial ideas and the ambiguity that this presents to the historian.
7	Was there more continuity than change in British– Jamaican relations between 1760 and 1870?	Finally, students draw together what they have learned in previous lessons on the changes and continuities in British rule in Caribbean, considering each of the lenses they have studied (British public opinion, economic relations, experiences of the Afro-Jamaican worker, enslaved resistance and the development of racism). Students now construct a detailed essay plan with a clear answer to the enquiry question.

ACTIVITIES FOR HELPING PUPILS ANALYSE CHANGE AND CONTINUITY

Having designed a suitable enquiry question, the following activities could be used to support pupils in analysing change and continuity. Some are more useful for analysing the extent or pace of change, while others help pupils characterise the nature of change that took place.

Graphs and the Rate of Change

Using graphs is a powerful way to help pupils see change. Either as your pupils work their way through an enquiry, or as a way of refreshing their knowledge at the end of an enquiry, asking them to plot events on a graph where the x-axis is 'time' will allow them to visualise the information they have learned in a different way.

> **Activity 5.3**
>
> Take one of the following topics and try this for yourself:
>
> - Weimar Germany – plot the important events 1918–1933 with a y-axis that runs from 'chaos' to 'stability'. When Germany is most stable, mark your points high up the y-axis, where there is uncertainty or turmoil, plot events low down. How might this help pupils see how Germany changed in this period?
> - Medicine Through Time – plot the important events in the development of surgery with a y-axis of 'painful' to 'painless'. Using a different colour create a second y-axis that runs from 'certain death' to 'certain survival', and then plot the course of this aspect of surgery. How might a graph like this help pupils with their understanding of how medicine changed over time?

As our colleagues in the science and maths departments will tell us, we need to make sure that we take care to interpret graphs correctly. (Indeed, it might even be worth popping into those departments to check that you are not going to use any terminology that will be actively unhelpful to their teaching. Biscuits often help at this point!) We need to help pupils to understand that 'change' isn't when the line on the graph is high or low, but when the line moves. A very wobbly line or a sharp incline or decline marks a period of change, a steady line, continuity.

By asking pupils to describe the graph, we are asking them to describe the change in a period of history: how far the line travels up and down is an indicator of the extent of change and continuity while the shape of the line (steep or gradual inclines, for example) allows us to see the rate of change.

Living Graphs

Graphs on paper are only one way of helping pupils visualise information about change over time. If you are interested in the ways 'living graphs' (i.e. graphs made by pupils arranging themselves in lines) can be used, there are a wealth of examples to be found at Ian Dawson's *Thinking History* website (Dawson, n.d.).

Using Metaphor and the Nature of Change

Historians' work is often redolent with metaphor and this is often a fruitful tool in the classroom. The classic example of the use of metaphor to help pupils make and support claims about change was written by Rachel Foster in 2008 where she used the extended metaphor of a road trip to describe the changes wrought by the Civil Rights Movement in the USA (Foster, 2008). One example of where I have used visual metaphor to help pupils to describe change was with the question: 'How did British politics change over the 19th century?'. (Note, the question is not, 'How *much* did British politics change…?' what we are concerned with is the nature of the change rather than simply the extent of change suggested by the second question.)

Why are car insurance companies so keen for you to get chips in your windscreen fixed? Because a small chip can quickly lead to fundamental cracks. A glancing blow from a tiny loose pebble can weaken the integrity of the plate of glass and cause the whole windscreen to shatter. The dink caused by the pebble is a tiny change in the glass but without it, the catastrophic failure is very unlikely.

To what extent is that a good metaphor for the effect the Great Reform Act had on British politics? While it did not enfranchise many, and, of those, none were working class men let alone women, did it undermine the fundamental argument that the natural evolution of the British parliamentary system was its strength? Did that small chip, lead to the spreading cracks until the whole system had to be punched out by the 1918 Representation of the People Act?

Or, should the change be understood to be more steady than that? Is it more like a staircase where each step moved Britain closer to a more representative democracy?

Or, was it more like a skate-boarder standing at the top of a quarter-pipe? The act of tipping the skateboard's nose over the edge is in itself a small action, but once the board is gone, once gravity takes over, it is only going to get faster. Is this what happened after 1832?

Or, should we think about nineteenth century political reform as an aeroplane taking off? Yes, the Great Reform Act meant that reform gathered speed. Yes, the 1867 Reform Act made it go faster. But, when the Secret Ballot Act was passed in 1872, was that the point where the wheels left the ground? The plane is still getting faster but something is now different, it is now flying. Was 1872 a point where the quality of democracy changed in Britain?

Once pupils had been taught about the political changes in the 19th century, they were asked to select visual metaphors such as these from images on a board to help them bring together what they had learned and to articulate their view on the nature or character of change. This simple addition to the end of the enquiry provoked more sophisticated and nuanced discussion about the nature of change than my previous attempts had achieved.

Vocabulary

Similarly to the use of metaphor, the introduction of vocabulary can enhance pupils' historical analysis. As Woodcock's seminal article (2005) showed, an explicit focus on vocabulary not only provides pupils with more advanced ways of expressing themselves, but unlocks more sophisticated and nuanced analysis. Woodcock's work focused specifically on vocabulary for analysing causation (see Chapter 6 for examples of this), but the same is true for analysing change and continuity. Activity 5.4 provides some vocabulary which could be used to support pupils in analysing different aspects of change, although care would need to be taken when choosing which words to use and when.

> **Activity 5.4**
>
> Below are a list of adjectives that describe change. What are the differences between them? Which are about the pace or rate of change, extent of change, the nature of change or the process of change? Which are more than one?
>
> - acceleration, apocalyptic, cataclysmic, catastrophic, complete, decline, development, eruption, evolutionary, glacial, gradual, imperceptible, inconsistent, irregular, irreversible, partial, positive, radical, revolution, revolutionary, slide, step-wise, violent.

DEFINING AN ERA

Historians loved to define eras. Ever since the 14th-century scholars decided that the times they were living in were the 'the middle ages' between antiquity and a brighter future (Rubin, 2014). The imposition of chronological categories by historians is all to do with change. By saying that something is 'ancient' or 'early modern' historians are using a short-hand to generalise about periods. Whether they see the beginning or end points as being to do with political power, ruling dynasties, invasion or climate change, periodisation requires there to be things that were different then.

Of course, it would take a historian fewer than ten seconds to point out the constructed and artificial nature of such categorisation, offer exceptions, caveats and apologies but the tool of periodisation is so useful because it helps in the quest to move from the specific to the general, from the concrete to the abstract, to derive patterns from the chaos that separates history from chronicle or story-telling.

By saying 'the medieval period ran from … to …' what a historian is really saying is, 'the world was like this, then it changed'. By asking pupils to think about the nature of historical periods, you are really asking them about change. This could be done for vast swathes of history or over short periods.

When Did the Third Reich Begin?

> This book is the first of three on the history of the Third Reich … Its central theme is how the Nazis managed to establish a one-party dictatorship in Germany within a very short space of time, and with seemingly little real resistance from the German people. A second book will deal with the development of the Third Reich from 1933 to 1939.
>
> *(Evans, 2004)*

Richard J. Evans' excellent series on the Third Reich could provide an interesting opportunity for pupils to think about what might characterise one period rather than another. Evans' first book is called 'The Coming of the Third Reich' and his second, 'The Third Reich In Power'. Obviously, by entitling his books in this way, Evans sees a point at which Germany stops being 'the Weimar Republic' and starts being 'the Third Reich'. The point at which the first book ends and the second begins is, for Evans, a point at which Germany has changed. Using this as a framing device ('So, Year 10, when should Evans end his first book and when should he begin his second?') as pupils are taught about the Nazis' election successes, Hitler's appointment to the chancellorship and his subsequent consolidation of power, would ask them to think about the differences between the Weimar Republic and the Third Reich.

Does, for example, the Third Reich begin with Hitler's chancellorship or, at that point, is Hitler just the latest von Schleicher or von Papen? Another right-wing popinjay who only governs by the whims of the Republic's President? Does the Third Reich begin with the death of Hindenburg? Or when Hitler declares himself Führer? Or, had Hitler arrogated to himself enough power that Weimar democracy was already beyond redemption? Perhaps the Third Reich had already begun with the Reichstag Fire Decree? Perhaps it was the Enabling Act?

In a sense, it doesn't matter what conclusion pupils come to in this discussion, its purpose is to make them think carefully about the nature of democracy and dictatorship and use their recall of events to support their claims. Knowing that this periodisation is a real concern for historians, and being able to see Evans' argument about his decision to end his first book, is a powerful way of showing that these aren't idle parlour games.

Who Should Be in a *Horrible History* of the Enlightenment?

> [A] small army of researchers furnished [Terry Deary, the author of Horrible Histories] with truckloads of facts, anecdotes and stories, and the author, having established his 'over-arching narrative' for the period, picked those that told it best, including 'the hardest-hitting facts'.
>
> *(Henley, 2012)*

One way of assessing whether pupils have understood the characteristics of a period of time, and, therefore, implicitly, how that period is different from what went before or came afterwards, is to ask them for an event, person or idea that best 'sums up' that period.

If you introduced pupils to the methods of the *Horrible Histories* franchise, you could show them that the characters and events that appear in the books, songs and sketches are not just chosen at random but do try and educate the viewer about the nature of the period from which they are taken. If you helped them understand the characteristics of a historical period such as the Enlightenment, then you could ask them to construct a sketch or song that would foreground a person or event that best summarises the ideas that (historians have said) represent that period. Discussing with Year 8 whether Denis Diderot or Mary Wollstonecraft should be parodied in a *Horrible Histories*-style sketch is a way of asking them to reflect upon the nature of the Enlightenment and, as mentioned above, the ways in which it was different to prior and subsequent periods.

Activity 5.5

Any time a historian declares the existence of a time period, they are asserting a claim about its nature and distinction from what went before and came after. Because they are constructs of the historian, (no-one woke up in 1485 and said, 'Oooh, I feel early-modern this morning...') they are, by definition, contestable and therefore ripe for turning into enquiry questions.

> Try writing an enquiry question based around a historical period. Your question might accept the period and ask something about its start or end. Alternatively, you could ask pupils to question whether the characterisation applied by the historian was correct.
>
> Some time periods are suggested for you below for inspiration:
>
> - The 'Dark Ages',
> - The 'Islamic Golden Age',
> - The 'Long 19th Century',
> - The 'Swinging '60s",
> - The 'American Century',
> - The 'Anthropocene Epoch'.

THEMATIC STUDIES AT GCSE

One of the many revolutionary things about the work of the Schools Council History Project (SCHP, later the Schools History Project, SHP) in the 1970s was the decision to include a 'study in development'. 'The primary aim of this study is to help pupils understand the processes by which change takes place in human affairs and continuities of the past survive' (Schools Council History Project, 1976). What was revolutionary about this was the chronological scale with which pupils were asked to engage. Instead of a topic that might cover a few decades, the SCHP's first topic, the now ubiquitous history of medicine, covered thousands of years.

As with many things that that SCHP/SHP did, it is sometimes difficult to see how radical their work was given that so much of it has been taken up by others and become mainstream. In the 2014 GCSE reforms, there was, for the first time, a requirement for GCSE specifications to include a 'thematic study' in the style of the SHP studies in development.

'Thematic studies should require students to understand change and continuity across a long sweep of history, including the most significant characteristics of different ages. They should reveal wider changes in aspects of society over the centuries and allow comparisons to be made between different periods of history. These aspects should include (but are not restricted to) some or all of the following: culture, economics, politics, religion, science, technology and war' (Department for Education, 2014).

While this requirement to include a thematic study is surely to be welcomed, teaching these specifications can prove challenging: the broad chronology can make it challenging for pupils to keep the 'story' in sight. Because the elements of the course are necessarily of the same type (i.e. they are all developments in medicine, groups of migrants, changes to the structure of political power etc.) these courses can easily feel like 'one thing after another'.

Concrete Examples: Great Stories and Resonant Places

One way to avoid this list-ification is to make sure that the abstract changes are illuminated by great stories about interesting people or resonant places.

One great example of this for a thematic study on migration to Britain is the way in which the rather bluntly named Jew's House in Lincoln illuminates the paradoxical experiences of many Jewish people in medieval England. Asking pupils to reflect on this place will give them a peg on which they can hang their learning about one of the groups that came to England in the medieval period.

At the point that I showed pupils an image of Jew's House, they were already able to infer that the rounded arches suggested a Romanesque style which, in turn, would suggest a 12th-century date. That it is a solid stone building near the heart of the city would suggest that it belonged to a wealthy person – we are a long way from the wattle-and-daub of most peasants' homes. It is just up the hill from a very similar building that was thought to have been owned by Aaron of Lincoln, the wealthiest man in England in the 1100s. A Jewish man so wealthy that he could not only lend Henry II more than £600, but could also fund the building of the cathedral, a hundred-or-so yards away. All of this should lead Year 10 to the conclusion that Jewish people's experience was positive as it was possible to make money and live close to the sources of political and religious power. Indeed, Jews in England enjoyed the personal protection of the monarch.

However, this protection was because of their legal status as property of the monarch. This allows us to explain the particular position of Jewish people in English society – they could make money as lenders who were needed by the monarchs and the Church but were reviled for it at the same time because of the Church's ban on usury. When Aaron died, he wasn't able to pass his assets on to his children, the money that was owed to him was now owed to the monarch and a separate division of the exchequer was needed to deal with the £7,500 that was now owed to the king.

We can see this paradoxical status by looking again at the house – why is it here? Why hasn't the owner built a country manor to show their wealth? Why is it a townhouse? Because Jewish people weren't allowed to own land. The traditional markers of status and wealth were barred to them. Why also might it be so heavily built? The front windows are not from the 12th century – there were no downstairs windows. Why? This is a defensive structure as well as a home.

Standing outside Jew's House, you can see the spire of Lincoln Cathedral – built with Aaron's money. It is the site of a shrine to 'Little Saint Hugh', a boy whose death sparked a blood-libel pogrom against Jewish people who had gathered to celebrate the wedding of a woman called Bellaset who was staying in Jew's House. This culminated in around 90 Jewish people being hanged by a royal court.

The last record we have of Bellaset herself is the record of her execution for coin-clipping. This allows us to examine the wave of antisemitic laws that were introduced that pushed Jewish people further and further to the edges of society before their final expulsion by Edward I in 1290. Was the charge against Bellaset an antisemitic slander or was it the act of a desperate person whose ability to live within the law had been taken from under her?

The fabric of the building, its location and the associated stories give weight to the otherwise rather dry 'list' of groups that came to Britain in the middle ages, and helps them see how the experiences of one group changed across this period.

Activity 5.6

If you teach a GCSE course, what is the thematic study?

Choose a period from that study. What person, event or place most embodies the changes that occurred during that period? Write an intriguing story about that person that will grab pupils' attention and, at the same time, allow them to see how those changes are embodied in that example.

SUMMARY OF KEY POINTS

- Change and continuity is not causation; what we want pupils to think and write about is not the reasons for change but the change itself.
- Historical scholarship is a rich vein for finding good enquiry questions for analysing change and continuity.
- You need to be clear in your own head about whether you want pupils to engage with pace or rate, degree or extent, nature or type, or the process of change.
- Graphs are a powerful tool for helping pupils plot change over time, and analyse the degree and pace of that change.
- Metaphors can be incredibly useful for helping pupils make and support claims about the nature of change.
- Questions about periodisation or 'sense of period' can be framed as questions about change.
- Well-chosen concrete examples can help pupils make meaning of change, especially over a broader sweep of time.

RESOURCES AND FURTHER READING

Counsell, Christine. 'What Do We Want Students to Do With Historical Change and Continuity?' in Davies, Ian (ed.). Debates in History Teaching. Routledge 2011: 109.

Counsell, Christine, Foster, Rachel, & Kinloch, Nicolas (eds.). Changing Histories for KS3: Connected Worlds c.1000-c.1600. London: Hodder Education 2024.

Davies, Nathanael. 'Staying With the Shot: Shaping the Question, Lengthening the Narrative and Broadening the Meaning of Transatlantic slavery' in Teaching History, 180, How History Works Edition, (2020): 21–31. London: Historical Association.

Dawson, Ian. 'Chronological Knowledge and Understanding' [Blog Post], Thinking History, (n.d.). https://thinkinghistory.co.uk/chronology/index.htm

Department for Education. History GCSE Subject Content. Department for Education 2014: 4. https://www.gov.uk/government/publications/gcse-history

Donington, Katie. The Bonds of Family: Slavery, Commerce and Culture in the British Atlantic World. Manchester: Manchester University Press 2019.

Duffy, Eamon. The Voices of Morebath: Reformation and Rebellion in an English Village. London: Yale University Press 2001: sleeve notes.

Evans, Richard J. The Coming of the Third Reich: How the Nazis Destroyed Democracy and Seized Power in Germany. London: Penguin 2004: xv.

Foster, Rachel. 'Speed Cameras, Dead Ends, Drivers and Diversions: Year 9 Use a 'road map' to Problematise Change and continuity' in Teaching History, 131, Assessing Differently Edition, (2008): 4–8. London: Historical Association.

Genovese, Eugene D. From Rebellion to Revolution: Afro-American Slave Revolts in the Making of the Modern World. Louisiana: Louisiana State University Press 1979.

Goullée, Corinne. 'Key Stage 3, History, In What Ways Did the Reformation Matter to Ordinary People?' [Online Resources], Oak National Academy, (2020). https://classroom.thenational.academy/units/in-what-ways-did-the-reformation-matter-to-ordinary-people-96c9

Hackett, Eve. 'Cunning Plan: How Far Did Anglo-Saxon England Survive the Norman Conquest?' in Teaching History, 178, Constructing Accounts Edition, (2020): 28–31. London: Historical Association.

Henley, Jon. 'Terry Deary: The man behind the Horrible Histories', [Newspaper Article], The Guardian, (2012). https://www.theguardian.com/lifeandstyle/2012/jul/14/terry-deary-horrible-histories

Hochschild, Adam. Bury the Chains: The British Struggle to Abolish Slavery. London: Pan Macmillan 2012.

Lecky, William Edward Hartpole. A History of European Morals from Augustus to Charlemagne. New York: D. Appleton and Company 1869.

Mastin, Steve, & Counsell, Christine. 'Narrating Continuity: Investigating Knowledge and Narrative in a Lower Secondary School Study of Sixteenth Century Change' in Chapman, Arthur, & Wilschut, Arie (eds.). Joined-up History: New Directions in History Education Research. Charlotte, NC: Information Age Publishing 2015: 317–350.

Rubin, Miri. The Middle Ages: A Very Short Introduction. Oxford: Oxford University Press 2014.

Schama, Simon. A History of Britain: At the Edge of the World? 3000BC-AD1603. London: Bodley Head 2009: 63.

Schools Council History Project. A New Look at History, Schools Council History 13 - 16 Project. Glasgow: Holmes McDougall 1976: 43.

Shemilt, Denis. History 13–16 Evaluation Study: Schools Council History 13–16 Project. Glasgow: Holmes McDougall 1980.

The Editorial Board. 'What's the Wisdom on Change and Continuity?' in Teaching History, 179: Culture in Conversation Edition, (2020): 50–53. London: Historical Association.

Williams, Eric. Capitalism & Slavery. North Carolina: University North Carolina Press 1994.

Woodcock, James. 'Does the Linguistic Release the Conceptual? Helping Year 10 to Improve Their Causal reasoning' in Teaching History, 119, Language Edition, (2005): 5–23. London: Historical Association.

Chapter 6 Teaching Causal Reasoning

Laura London

BACKGROUND

It is not unusual, when writing about causal reasoning, for writers to start with E. H. Carr's famous quote (1961) that 'the study of history is a study of causes'. While there are a great many historians and history teachers who would disagree, at least in part, with this, it is generally acknowledged that causation is one of the most frequently taught disciplinary (or second-order) concepts. It would be unusual to pick up a GCSE, A Level or undergraduate examination paper and not find at least one question, asking in one form or another, 'why' an event or situation in history occurred. Fundamentally, human beings are curious creatures, who are averse to uncertainty, and this curiosity sends us in search of answers to the 'why' questions. We want our pupils to wonder at these questions, before meaningfully tackling them, while also understanding that they will not always find the clear-cut answers that they might like. Cultivating this historical thinking is challenging and requires careful curriculum planning so that pupils can 'get better' at causal reasoning or argument. When historians are explaining why something happened, they are at the same time building a causal argument. And when pupils are learning about causation, they are also learning how to construct a certain type of historical argument. Indeed, as *Teaching History's* 'What's the wisdom on causation' (2019) points out, 'In history, causal explanation and causal argument are the same thing'.

This chapter will start with the big picture by reflecting on what forms of causal reasoning we want pupils to encounter across the curriculum, before considering enquiry questions and zooming in on lesson activities that will promote this form of historical thinking.

WHAT SHOULD PUPILS LEARN ABOUT CAUSAL REASONING?

Historical events and their causes are unique. The causes of the Peasants' Revolt are very different from the causes of the First World War, which are very different again from the reasons why Apartheid in South Africa ended. Causes of events might share common features, but the interplay between them is always different. This seems like an obvious point to make but it is an important reminder of the link between the substantive and the conceptual. Any history curriculum should be underpinned by robust, carefully selected substantive knowledge. Pupils need this substantive knowledge to be able to engage in causal analysis. This also reminds us that pupils' understanding of causation (like all the disciplinary concepts) is built over time as they work their way through the curriculum. As Lee and Shemilt (2003) explain, 'it is a mistake to try to bundle progression in different concepts together' and you need to be clear about what you want pupils to understand about causation at the end of each key stage. It is also useful to think of pupils developing 'knowledge takeaways' (Dawson, n.d.) in relation to causal reasoning where knowledge is disciplinary. This disciplinary knowledge can be articulated in different ways; Seixas and Morton (2013) outline 'guideposts' to historical thinking for cause and consequence, such as events having multiple causes, which vary in their importance. These are usefully developed by Alex Ford (2014) who identifies 'signposts' for developing pupils' thinking about historical concepts. For causation these include: causal webs; varying influence of factors; personal and contextual factors and unintended consequences. These signposts are not intended to be seen as some sort of linear assessment framework or to be tackled in turn, but instead were developed to address pupils' genuine historical misconceptions and inform curriculum planning over time.

No one enquiry question will allow you to consider causation from every angle; instead, it is important to explore different aspects of causation across the whole curriculum. As Burnham and Brown illustrate (2009), it is valuable for departments to stand back and think big and discuss as a department what it means to get better at causal reasoning, before using these ideas to design their curriculum. The questions in Activity 6.1 provide a practical starting point for these discussions and will also allow you to explore pupils' prior knowledge and understanding of causal reasoning.

Activity 6.1 The big picture: Standing back to decide what it means to get better at causal reasoning

Reflect individually or as a department.
How does the curriculum in your department allow pupils to:

- Recognise that events have more than one cause and that events occur for multiple reasons? And understand that these reasons are often overlapping and linked?
- Recognise that some causes are more influential and important than others?
- Explore different ways to categorise causal factors? (Time, importance, theme, role, agency)
- Understand that there are different types of causation questions and that they need different 'patterns' of thinking to answer them?
- Understand that causes 'are related to, but distinguishable from, motivations (or intentions) of any group or individual'? (Seixas, 2008)
- Allow pupils to engage in 'possibility thinking'? (Lee & Shemilt, 2003) This involves pupils asking 'what if' questions.

HOW CAN YOU DESIGN 'GOOD' CAUSATION ENQUIRY QUESTIONS?

In Chapter 3, Paula Worth describes the use of historical enquiries as a 'cornerstone in history teaching in England' established by Riley (2000), before explaining eight principles to support teachers in crafting successful enquiry questions that engage pupils in meaningful and historically rigorous ways of thinking. Placing causal reasoning at the heart of an enquiry or series of enquiries will provide an opportunity to develop pupils' disciplinary thinking about causation. By using each lesson to serve the enquiry question, and get a bit closer to answering it, pupils' understanding of causation will develop over a sequence of lessons, as outlined by *Teaching History's* 'What's the wisdom on causation' (2019). Enquiry questions that produce a 'tangible outcome', as advocated by Riley (2000), also provide pupils with an opportunity to practise their own extended, analytic argument. Different causation questions will also prompt a different 'type' of response, depending on the substantive knowledge underpinning the question. Using enquiry questions can help to mitigate some of the misconceptions that pupils encounter when thinking about causation – for example, pupils, who like many of us dislike ambiguity or uncertainty, often feel that the events of the past were inevitable or were just one thing after another (Chapman, 2017).

Furthermore, it is possible to plan for progression in the teaching of causation across the curriculum, through carefully sequenced enquiry questions. In his article for *Teaching History* 175 Matt Stanford (2019) outlines how his department planned their curriculum to support pupils to understand increasingly complex causal models. This involved considering how to best develop pupils' substantive knowledge *and* disciplinary thinking, in this case causal reasoning. As a result, the department made the decision to move away from the more complicated Year 7 enquiry 'Why did William win the Battle of Hastings' to 'Why did the Peasants' revolt in 1381?', which lends itself to a 'relatively simple causal model' that is 'uni-directional (only events that made the revolt more likely are included in the model)' with 'largely independent causes'. In Year 8, pupils work on the enquiry question 'Why did the Civil War break out in 1642?'. There are now two actors (the King and Parliament), and the enquiry is more complex as causal factors are interrelated. In Year 9, pupils work to answer the enquiry question 'What caused the First World War?'; pupils are now considering multiple actors, interrelated factors and follow a multi-directional approach. In this way, choices about substantive content support pupils to make progress in their understanding of causation.

Table 6.1 provides some examples of enquiries that involve causal reasoning and explores how changes to the focus of questions can encourage different types of response and ways of thinking about causation. Some of the questions are more obviously 'complex' than others. This is followed by Activity 6.2, which provides an opportunity to reflect on how to develop and design enquiry questions rooted in causal reasoning.

> **Activity 6.2 Reflection: How does your curriculum develop pupils' understanding of causation?**
>
> i. Consider a sequence of lessons that you have taught or an enquiry from your scheme of work that involves causal reasoning. Reflect on the enquiry question to consider:
>
>   - The complexity of the causal model required to answer the enquiry question.
>   - How many 'actors' are involved?
>   - How are factors interrelated?
>   - What sort of understanding of causation does the question develop?
>
> ii. Next time you plan an enquiry around causation what are the considerations that you will make?

Table 6.1 Example causation enquiry questions

Example Enquiry Question	Type of Causation Response	What Sort of Understanding Will This Develop	Potential Tangible Outcome
Why did some women get the vote in 1918?	This is a more open question that could bring in multiple factors including the role of suffragist campaigners, militant tactics, and the First World War.	Many types of causal argument could work. Pupils could, for example, categorise causes by content, but also see how causes overlap and are linked together. Pupils could also temporally categorise the causes (long term/ short term) or consider a hierarchy of causation.	Many options for example extended writing in the form of an essay, website entry or letter to an historian.
Did militancy help or hinder the granting of suffrage for women?	This question requires a more direct focus on the militant tactics and the role of these tactics in the campaign for suffrage.	Pupils are explicitly asked to consider the *role* that the militant tactics played. The question more directly captures some of the more recent debate between historians (Purvis, 2019). It also requires pupils to weigh up the different arguments to come to an overall conclusion.	A speech for a class debate.
Why did revolution happen in Iran in 1979?	This question asks pupils to think about determining causal relationships to consider what factors determined where and when the revolution happened.	Pupils are asked to focus on the nature of society and religion in Iran and how this meant revolution happened there and not elsewhere in the Middle East. Pupils will also consider the timing of the Revolt, for example, 'Did Ayatollah Khomeini dictate the timing of the revolution?'	Entry for a recent textbook about the history of the Middle East.
Why were families fighting against each other in Spain in the 1930s?	This question requires a greater focus on individual personal motivations. It emphasises individual stories and begins to capture some of the political division that currently exists within Spain.	Pupils are required to locate individual perspectives within broader political, social economic and religious factors.	Article for a Spanish newspaper or magazine.

TEACHING CAUSAL REASONING

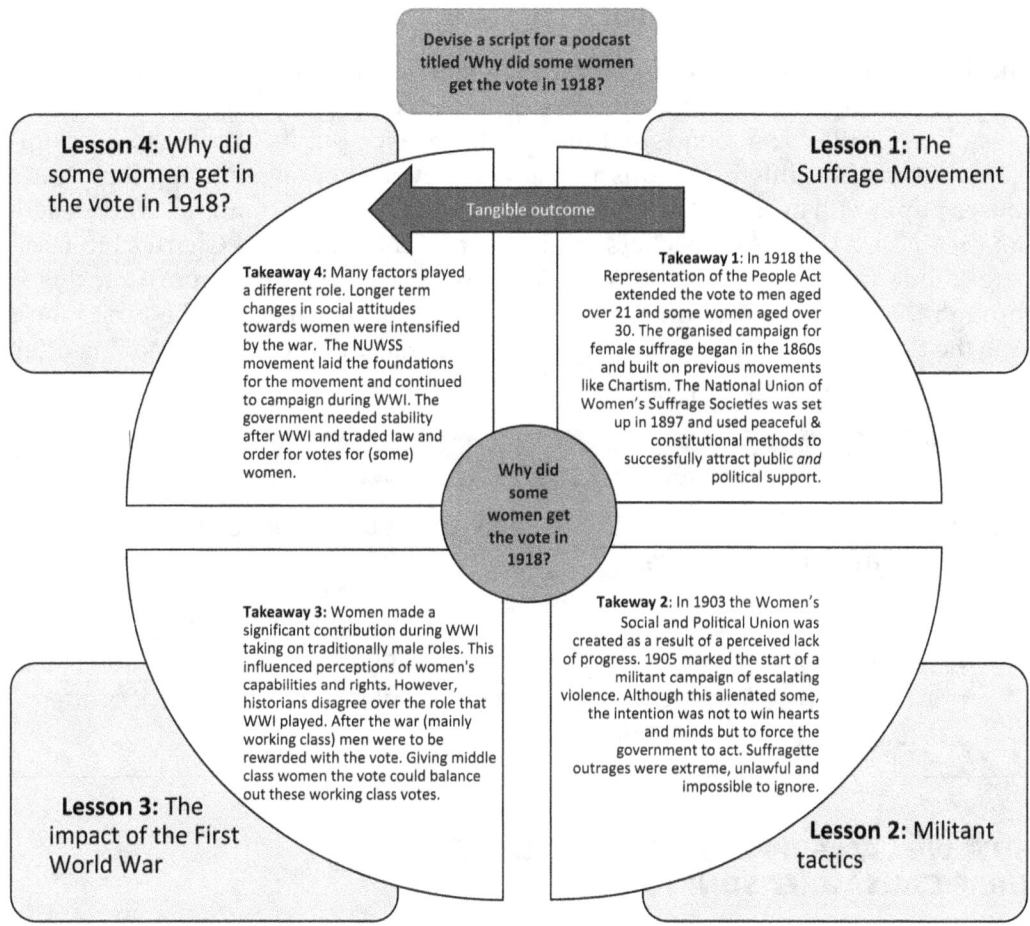

Figure 6.1 Enquiry overview: Why did some women get the vote in 1918?

An Example Causation Enquiry: 'Why Did Some Women Get the Vote in 1918?

Within this enquiry (shown in **Figure 6.1**), each lesson is designed to serve the enquiry question 'Why did some women get the vote in 1918?' The timing of the end of the First World War and the Representation of the People Act of 1918 means that it is easy to assume that women's contribution to the war effort was the deciding factor. However, this overlooks the role of the women's suffrage movement before and during the war, and the fact that it was mainly middle-class women who received the vote in 1918. This enquiry is designed to explore the role and timing of the different factors that meant that some women got the vote in 1918, so that pupils can construct their own historical argument in response to the enquiry question.

The enquiry has been designed and presented using a circular planning method as explained by Crooks and London (2023). This places the enquiry question at the centre of the planning process. Teachers then work 'outwards' to decide on the knowledge takeaways for each lesson, before devising lesson titles and objectives and selecting activities. This supports teachers to plan lessons to serve, and ultimately answer, the enquiry question by asking pupils to complete a tangible outcome activity.

Beginning an Enquiry with a Puzzle to Solve

Like E. H. Carr we want our pupils to be the kind of thinkers who ask the question 'why' and *want* to find out the answers. *Teaching History's* 'What's the wisdom on causation' (2019) recommends setting up a puzzle for pupils to solve to 'leap forward in time and interest pupils in the war, revolution, event, situation whose causes pupils will eventually build into an explanation'. For example, when teaching the English Civil War teachers might start with the death of Charles I to fascinate pupils in the story of the war's origins. Another way to approach this is through the enquiry question itself. When teaching the causes of the First World War the enquiry question 'How did one bullet lead to 20 million dead?' is often used to create an intriguing puzzle.

> **Activity 6.3 Department discussion**
>
> Consider the questions below. Discuss how you could introduce each of these questions as a puzzle to solve.
>
> - Why was the crusader army defeated at the Battle of Hattin, 1187?
> - Why did the Mongols destroy Baghdad in 1258?
> - Why was there European colonisation and settlement in the Americas after 1492?

HOW WE CAN SUPPORT PUPILS TO DEVELOP THEIR CAUSAL REASONING

As Carr (1961) points out you can know that the Second World War occurred because Hitler wanted a war, but that this also 'explains nothing'. Similarly, pupils might know that the Holocaust occurred because Hitler hated the Jews, but this is a very long way from a real understanding of why the Holocaust happened. It is important to move pupils beyond monocausal explanations of events, to start to see that the historian deals in a 'multiplicity of causes'. And yet, there is also a huge difference between identifying a list of causal factors and understanding the relationship between them and their relative importance. This section provides a number of practical activities which can be used in the classroom to help pupils explore the multiplicity, importance and interrelationship of an event's causes.

Using Diagrams to Understand Causation

In her *Teaching History* article, Rachael Cook (2018) considers what it means for her pupils to make progress with causal reasoning. Cook wants her pupils 'to understand that causation is not a simple, linear process, but that causation is more of a web of interlinking factors'. Cook also recognises that pupils' progress with this concept is not linear either and more like a web 'that grows increasingly intricate as time goes on'. One way to do this is to encourage pupils to start thinking of causes in patterns or shapes. Using diagrams is one practical way to do this.

Placing an event at the centre of a mind map (see Figure 6.2) and adding different causal factors, with clusters of causes to show categories, allows pupils to see

TEACHING CAUSAL REASONING

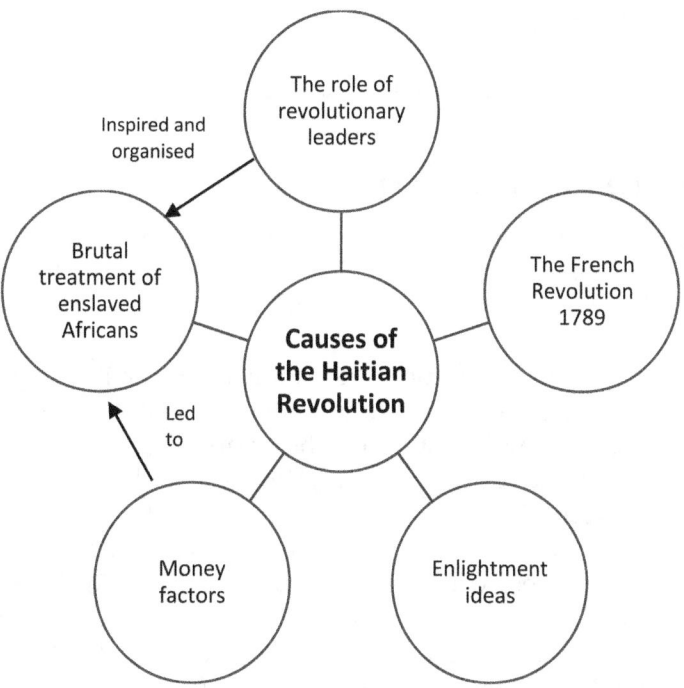

Figure 6.2 A mind map of the causes of the Haitian Revolution.

patterns and links between causal factors. Pupils can also shade different boxes according to categories and add arrows and comments between them to show the relationship between causes. A diagram using hexagons to connect causal factors can also work well to show links between them.

Showing Relative Importance

When we want pupils to understand hierarchies of causes, diagrams can also be used to show their relative importance. For example, a pyramid or a diamond nine activity allows pupils to position those causes they believe to be more important in causing an event at the top. Another alternative is to use a Venn diagram where one factor's relative importance is shown by its size on the page (see Figure 6.3). Venn diagrams are also very useful for showing overlap or links between causes.

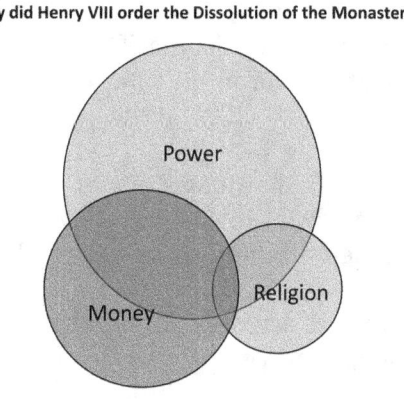

Figure 6.3 A Venn diagram on the dissolution of the monasteries.

Some evidence may not fit comfortably inside the diagram and pupils will need some support to decide if this means the evidence is outside the 'zone of relevance' (Counsell, 2004) or a new pattern or diagram is needed.

When to Introduce Causal Diagrams

A mind map or diagram can be helpful for capturing how pupils' understanding develops over the course of an enquiry (Worth, 2018). This could be completed at the end of each lesson in the enquiry as pupils make new links and connections between factors.

Alternatively, these diagrams provide useful tools for revising the causes of events. As pupils become more used to different types of diagrams, they can start to select the diagram that will best reflect their pattern of causes. Another way to use causal diagrams to support pupils' revision and independent thinking is by using a post-it note game.

For example, organise Year 10 pupils into groups and ask them the causation question 'Explain why there was a revolution in Russia in 1917'. Ask each group to write down as many points as they can, with each point on a separate post-it note. You can make a competition out of this as pupils recall all their knowledge. Once they have filled in as many points as they can (or time allows) you can begin the questioning phase of the activity. With all these activities, it is important for teachers to use questioning to probe pupils' historical thinking. It can help to plan your questions in advance. For this activity you could ask your pupils to look for potential patterns within the post-it notes by asking questions like:

- How could you organise these into groups?
- Do some groups have more post-it notes than others?
- What headings could you give each group?
- Do some points link together? Which ones? How?
- Are there any points or ideas that are less relevant and don't need to be included?
- How will you finally organise the points to answer the question?

Using Card Sorts to Develop Causal Reasoning

Card-sorting activities are a valuable tool for developing pupils' causal reasoning. A cleverly designed card sort allows pupils to see that history is complex, and messy, and perhaps most importantly, that accounts of history are not fixed but are constructed and very much up for debate. The cards can be organised flexibly to show different patterns of causation. In Chapter 2 of the brilliant *History and Literacy in Year 7*, Christine Counsell (2004) writes:

> The beauty of card-sorting is that it sets out assumptions in a graphic, visual way. Pupils are then very clear about what they are arguing about. They can 'see' the proposed argument in the form of a very physical device.

The chapter outlines a range of activities for organising cards containing the various causes into different shapes and categories as pupils wrestle with the question 'Why did Henry and Becket's quarrel turn bitter and fatal?' There is guidance for how these cards can be used to develop pupils' extended writing as they identify 'big points' from the cards and hunt for 'little points' to support these.

In a recent blog post Jonathan Grande (2022) provides very helpful and practical advice for how to make a card sort activity 'fly' in the classroom. Suggestions include ensuring that pupils have 'lots and lots of knowledge before they are allowed anywhere near the cards' and 'explicitly and deliberately teaching pupils how to cut out the cards in the most efficient way possible'. Numbering the cards is another excellent tip for when you would rather not get out the scissors! I highly recommend the whole blog for further practical tips, a fuller understanding of the rationale behind card sorts and more practical examples.

Example Card Sort: Why Was a New Israeli State Declared on 14 May 1948?

The following card sort (Table 6.2) is designed to be used with a Year 12 class to support their understanding of how a new Israeli state came to be declared in 1948 and is designed to help pupils understand the failures of British policy, against a backdrop of increasing violence in the region.

The cards can be categorised in different ways:

- Chronologically—to secure the timeline of events or as a living graph to demonstrate escalating violence or the build-up of tension
- By content categories (British Policy/World War II/Zionism) or time categories (long term/short term/trigger)
- Zone of relevance (Counsell, 2004) or relative importance
- For possibility thinking. For example, by asking is there one card that you could remove that would have stopped the declaration of an Israeli state? Or if you removed card number 16 what difference would this have made?

Table 6.2 Example card sort: Why was a new Israeli state declared on 14 May 1948?

1. The British Army had withdrawn from Palestine by the morning of 14th May.	2. In February 1947, Britain decided to hand over control of Palestine to the United Nations.	3. In 1896, Theodor Herzl published the book *Der Judenstaat* (The Jewish State) calling for a Jewish national home.
4. In 1920, Britain were given a mandate (the authority) to govern Palestine. This was not meant to be permanent.	5. From the late 19th century, Zionism (the idea of a Jewish homeland) received increasing support from Jewish people living around the world.	6. In 1917, the British government declared their support for a Jewish homeland, this was called the Balfour Declaration.
7. In 1933, Adolf Hitler came to power in Germany and Nazi anti-Semitism drove many Jews abroad.	8. By 1919, there were 60,000 Jewish people living in Palestine, this increased to 430,000 by 1939.	9. In 1908, the Jewish Agency was created.
10. In 1937, the British planned to partition (divide up) Palestine.	11. Between 1936 and 1939, the Arab Rebellion took place. This is also called the First Intifada. The British government responded brutally.	12. The British government issued a White Paper (a proposal) in 1939 restricting Jewish immigration to Palestine.

(Continued)

Table 6.2 Example card sort: Why was a new Israeli state declared on 14 May 1948? (Continued)

13. The Arab Higher Committee was formed in 1938 to resist the British administration in Palestine.	14. In the First World War, the Turkish army was defeated by Britain and her allies. Britain and France agreed to divide land in the Middle East between themselves.	15. During the Second World War (1939–45), 6 million Jews were killed in the Holocaust.
16. In 1947, US President Truman declared support for partition in Palestine.	17. After the Holocaust, some American Jewish people put pressure on their politicians to support a Jewish state in Palestine. 4.5 million Jewish people were living in the USA.	18. After World War II, the USA emerged as one of two superpowers (the other being the Soviet Union).
19. In 1947, the British authorities prevented the Exodus, a ship carrying refugees from Europe, from landing in Palestine. There was a huge public outcry.	20. There was a Civil War in Palestine after the United Nations announced the partition plan.	21. In November 1947, the United Nations voted to partition Palestine. This divided Palestine into a Jewish and an Arab State. Jerusalem was an international zone.
22. The Arab Higher Committee rejected the UN's Partition Plan.	23. In the week before May 1948, some of the bloodiest fighting took place around Jerusalem.	24. By 14 May 1948, over 300,000 Palestinian Arabs had fled, or were forced from, Palestine.
25. In April 1948, Irgun (Jewish fighters) attacked the village of Deir Yassin in Arab territory. 245 inhabitants were killed.	26. Jewish people had lived in the land of Palestine from about 1500BC.	27. In AD70 and AD135, Jewish people living in Palestine were expelled by the Roman rulers. This created the diaspora (the dispersal) of Jewish people to different parts of the world.
28 Before 1914, the Ottoman Empire (Turkish) ruled over what is now Iraq, Lebanon, Syria, Palestine, Israel, Jordan and parts of Saudi Arabia.	29 The Ottomans did not consider Palestine to be a clearly defined area. By 1914, the Ottoman Empire had been in decline for decades.	30 The Middle East was strategically important to the British government – for example, they needed to maintain their access to the Suez Canal.

The Role of Analogies

In his seminal *Teaching History* article 'Camels, diamonds and counterfactuals: a model for teaching causal reasoning', Arthur Chapman introduces us to his now famous Alphonse the Camel analogy (Chapman, 2003). In the analogy, Alphonse is subject to all manner of indignities before the 'straw that breaks the camel's back'. This analogy powerfully demonstrates how more concrete analogies can unlock pupils' ability to think about different types of causes and how they link together. By comparing the familiar with the unfamiliar, it is possible to make abstract or complex ideas easier to understand. Many departments explore this analogy with their pupils as an introduction to causal reasoning (Cook 2018; Grande, 2022).

There are numerous ways to practically use analogies to teach causation. You could ask pupils to examine an everyday occurrence for its possible causes. This could be a car accident, being late for work or getting the sack. There are many possible choices, but as you make your decision think about the number of variables involved, the different types of cause (e.g., long term, short term, trigger), their relative importance, and perhaps most importantly, the extent that the analogy will engage the pupils. It must be a familiar example – there is no point using the analogy of a car engine if pupils have no understanding of how a car engine actually works. Really great analogies will also include factors that are coincidental to help pupils spot the difference between causation and correlation and prove the point that just because two things occurred together does not mean that one caused the other.

As an alternative, ask pupils to vote on the best analogy to capture the causes of an event. If you were asking pupils about the causes of the First World War, the choices could include a fire about to be lit, the loading of a gun, a match to a powder keg, a fight in the playground or even a sleepwalker about to fall. By the end of Year 9 or 10, when pupils are more accustomed to using analogies, you could ask pupils to design their own.

Analytic Vocabulary

Pupils need to be taught explicitly how to build a causal argument and given opportunities to practise this. Causation is a slippery concept and to be able to think and write effectively about causation pupils need precise vocabulary. James Woodcock (2005) outlined the 'clumsiness' of the word cause in the context of appeasement, revealing just how vague and inappropriate the use of the word cause can be. He goes on to assert:

> 'Ultimately, if pupils have a refined and diverse vocabulary, and develop expertise and confidence in its use, they will be able to think and communicate in a more sophisticated manner, and that can only make them better historians'.

The analytical vocabulary in Table 6.3 could be used to support pupils to construct causal arguments orally and in writing. It has been divided into descriptive categories, helping pupils to categorise different kinds of causes, and explanatory categories, to help pupils explain the role of a particular cause (Chapman, 2017).

This analytical vocabulary, used on its own, is very unlikely to be meaningfully deployed by pupils. It cannot simply be bolted on to pupils understanding and is most effectively used in the context of specific enquiries (Carroll, 2022). Used thoughtfully it does have practical uses for developing pupils' 'expertise and confidence' as they begin to construct their own causal arguments.

A teacher could:

- Ask pupils to use the vocabulary mat to label the links between their causes on a causal diagram.
- Integrate the explanatory categories into a card sort as additional cards to link different factors together.
- Ask pupils to use this vocabulary to analyse and unpick an analogy or metaphor in class.
- Provide opportunities for using this vocabulary when pupils rehearse their arguments orally. For example, 'Did X make Y happen? Or did X just make Y possible?' or 'Why did X happen then and not before?'

Alternatively, teachers could use the different categories as a department to unpick the causal reasoning within an enquiry question. For example, an enquiry

Table 6.3 Analytical vocabulary to support the construction of causal arguments

	Vocabulary for...					
Descriptive categories	Categorising causes by subject matter					
	Social	Economic	Political	Religious	Cultural	Technological
	Military	Imperial	Environmental*			
	Categorising causes by timescale					
	Long term	Medium term	Short term	Immediate		
Explanatory categories	Explaining the role of different causes					
	More likely	Probable	Possible	Contextual	Bring about	Enabled
	Necessary	Sufficient	Compelled	Nurtured	Undermined	Eroded
	Deepening	Worsening	Exacerbating	Speeding up	Contributing	Intensified
	Underlying	Underpinning	Foundation	Inherent	Precondition	Latent
	Incite	Trigger	Spark	Erupt	Provoke	Inflame
	Explaining the relative importance of causes					
	Fundamental	Crucial	Essential	Vital	Decisive	Driving factor
	Less relevant	Acted as a deterrent	Extraneous	Proved unimportant	Less significant	Marginal
	Analysing the role of individuals					
	Individual actions	Motive	Agency	Lack of independence	Autonomy	Unintentional

*In *History and the Climate Crisis* (2023), Kate Hawkey powerfully asserts that one important step that teachers can take towards including climate history in their teaching is to include environmental factors in causal arguments, in order to move away from an 'exclusively human-centric focus'. Chapter 7 of Hawkey's book is also very useful for considering the concept of origins as distinct from causation.

into Hitler's appointment as Chancellor in 1933 might be more influenced by an analysis of the roles of the individuals, whereas an analysis of the causes of the Spanish Civil War might be more focussed on the role of enabling factors.

Importantly, pupils need to see this vocabulary in use in historical scholarship to use it in their own writing. It is helpful for pupils to be exposed to different examples of historians' causal arguments, and to unpick these to understand how a causal argument is constructed. Figure 6.4 provides one example of how you might approach this with your pupils. See Chapter 14 by Jim Carroll for further

The Causes of the Spanish Civil War

Read this excerpt from *The Spanish Civil War* by Helen Graham explaining the causes of the military coup of 18th July 1936 that marked the beginning of the Spanish Civil War.

1. Highlight the key words that relate to causes in the following categories:
   - Content (Social/economic/political etc)
   - Time (long term/ short term)
   - Explanatory categories (importance/ role)
2. Explain your choices in the margins.
3. Make a note of any words you don't understand or questions you still have.

Content		Explanatory
	'So historians are required to explore what this violence meant and how it related to the pre-war domestic environment. Three factors were crucial here. First, the extremely uneven levels of development obtained inside Spain by the 1930s. This meant that the military coup unleashed what was in effect a series of culture wars: urban	Means important- couldn't happen without
Social	culture and cosmopolitan lifestyles versus rural tradition; secular	
Religious	against religious; authoritarianism against liberal political cultures;	Set off/ triggered- these things were bottled up- war unleashed- 'bomb'
Political	centre versus periphery; traditional gender roles versus the 'new	
Gender	woman'; even youth against age since generational conflicts were also present. Second the force with which the opposing elements clashed owed more than a little to the cultural influence of a Manichaean	
??????	brand of Catholicism that still predominated in Spain, affecting even many of those who had consciously rejected religious belief and the authority of the Church. Third since the detonator of events was a military coup, we must also examine the role played by Spain's army	Again, comparison to bomb going off
Military	and, in particular, the emergence of a rigid and intolerant political culture in its officer corps during the early decades of the 20th	Showing importance again- does this sit below other factors or make them worse? Can't all be crucial!
Empire- loss contributing to all these problems	century. Crucial to all these factors but especially the military was Spain's final loss of empire in 1898. This deprived the country of its protected external markets and in doing so kickstarted an intermittent and acrimonious debate over how Spain should modernise itself economically and who should bear the cost.'	
Economic	Graham, H. (2005) *The Spanish Civil War: A Very Short Introduction*. Oxford: Oxford University Press.	Speeding up
Time		
Long term causes- building up	Short term	Trigger

Figure 6.4 An activity analysing historian Helen Graham's (2005) argument on the causes of the Spanish Civil War.

examples of using the work of historians to support the development of pupils' extended writing in history.

SUMMARY OF KEY POINTS

- Pupils need to be prepared to tackle enquiry questions that involve causal reasoning, and our curriculum should be designed so that pupils can 'get better' at causal reasoning. This takes time and is not a linear process.
- Any causation enquiry should be underpinned by robust, carefully selected, substantive knowledge. Pupils need sufficient substantive knowledge to be able to engage in causal analysis.
- One way to bring together substantive and disciplinary knowledge is by planning using enquiry questions and a range of enquiry questions are outlined in this chapter.
- Causal diagrams, card sorts and analogies can help pupils to identify patterns of causation and to make links between causal factors.
- Analytical vocabulary and historical scholarship are also useful for supporting pupils to develop their causal arguments.
- Exposing pupils to examples of historians' causal arguments can support pupils to understand how to construct causal arguments more effectively.

RESOURCES AND FURTHER READING

Burnham, Sally, & Brown, Geraint. 'Assessment Without Level descriptions' in Teaching History, 115, Assessment without Levels? Edition, (2009): 5–15. London: Historical Association.

Carr, E. H. What Is History? London: Macmillan 1961: 37.

Carroll, James Edward. 'Terms and Conditions: Using Metaphor to Highlight Causal Processes With Year 13' in Teaching History, 187, Widening the World Lens Edition, (2022): 40–49. London: Historical Association.

Chapman, Arthur. 'Camels, Diamonds and Counterfactuals: a Model for Teaching Causal reasoning' in Teaching History, 112, Empire Edition, (2003): 46–53. London: Historical Association.

Chapman, Arthur. 'Causal Explanation' in Davies, Ian (ed.). Debates in History Teaching. Oxon: Routledge 2017: 130–143.

Cook, Rachael. 'From Flight Paths to spiders' Webs: Developing a Progression Model for Key Stage 3' in Teaching History, 172, Cause and Consequence Edition, (2018): 64–70. London: Historical Association.

Counsell, Christine. History and Literacy in Year 7: Building the Lesson Around the Text. London: Hodder Murray 2004: 45.

Crooks, Victoria, & London, Laura. 'Chapter 4: Helping Beginning History Teachers to Plan, Deliver and Evaluate lessons' in Crooks, Victoria, & London, Laura, & Haydn, Terry, (eds.). Mentoring History Teachers in the Secondary School. Oxon: Taylor & Francis 2023.

Dawson, Ian. 'Takeaways and their central role in planning KS3 courses', [Blog Post], Thinking History, (n.d.). http://thinkinghistory.co.uk/Issues/Takeaways.html

Ford, Alex. 'Setting Us Free? Building Meaningful Models of Progression for a 'post-levels' world' in Teaching History, 157, Assessment Edition, (2014): 28–41. London: Historical Association.

Graham, Helen. The Spanish Civil War: A Very Short Introduction. Oxford: Oxford University Press 2005.

Grande, Jonathan. 'This week, in history…how I use card sorts (and why I've fallen back in love with them)', (2022). https://curricularpasts.wordpress.com/2022/01/22/3-this-week-in-history-how-i-use-card-sorts-and-why-ive-fallen-back-in-love-with-them/

Hawkey, Kate. History and the Climate Crisis (2023) Available as a free open access PDF from UCL Press: www.uclpress.co.uk/products/191132

Haydn, Terry, & Stephen, Alison. Learning to Teach History in the Secondary School: A Companion to School Experience (5th ed.). Oxon: Routledge 2021: 160–162.

Lee, Peter, & Shemilt, Dennis. 'A Scaffold Not a Cage: Progression and Progression Models in history' in Teaching History, 113, Creating Progress Edition, (2003): 13–23. London: Historical Association.

Purvis, June. 'Did Militancy Help or Hinder the Granting of women's Suffrage in Britain?' in Women's History Review, 28(7), (2019): 1200–1234.

Riley, Michael. 'Into the Key Stage 3 History Garden: Choosing and Planting Your Enquiry questions' in Teaching History, 99, Curriculum Planning Edition, (2000): 8–13. London: Historical Association.

Seixas, Peter. "Scaling Up" the Benchmarks of Historical Thinking: A Report on the Vancouver Meetings. University of British Columbia 2008: 8. Also available at: https://historicalthinking.ca/sites/default/files/files/docs/Scaling%20Up%20Meeting%20Report.pdf

Seixas, Peter, & Morton, Tom. The Big Six: Historical Thinking Concepts. Nelson Education 2013: 10–11. Also available at: https://historicalthinking.ca/sites/default/files/files/docs/Guideposts.pdf

Stanford, Matthew. 'Did the Bretons Break? Planning Increasingly Complex Causal Models at Key Stage 3' in Teaching History, 175, Listening to Diverse Voices Edition, (2019): 8–15. London: Historical Association.

The Editorial Board. 'What's the Wisdom on…Causation' in Teaching History, 175, Listening to Diverse Voices Edition, (2019): 24–27. London: Historical Association.

Woodcock, James. 'Does the Linguistic Release the Conceptual? Helping Year 10 to Improve Their Causal reasoning' in Teaching History, 119, Language Edition, (2005): 5–23. London: Historical Association.

Worth, Paula. 'Here Ends the Lesson: Shaping Lesson Conclusions as an Iterative Process in Improving Historical enquiries' in Teaching History, 173, Opening Doors Edition, (2018): 58–67. London: Historical Association.

Chapter 7

Teaching Consequence

Molly-Ann Navey

BACKGROUND

Despite being a consistent focus of the argumentation of historians, within school history, consequence is a messy second-order concept. At various times, consequence has been bound with causation, significance, and change and continuity, as opposed to being viewed as a stand-alone concept. Despite this, consequence has become increasingly a focus of pupils' historical argumentation at Key Stage 4 and Key Stage 5 and, in recent years, consequence enquiries have become more common at Key Stage 3 too.

This chapter will explore how historians have grappled with the concept of historical consequence and argue for its importance as a distinct line of historical thinking, separate to causation, significance, or change and continuity. It will discuss how we might define historical consequence at a school history level and the different ways that we might want pupils to argue about consequence in its own right. Once this has been established, the second part will suggest practical strategies to support pupils in effectively developing their own arguments around consequence and how historical enquiries and pupil activities can be created to secure pupils' knowledge and understanding of the concept.

WHAT DO HISTORIANS ACTUALLY DO WITH HISTORICAL CONSEQUENCE?

Regardless of the area, time period or types of history that they research, historians often study the consequences of historical events in their work. These historians seem to develop their arguments around a range of different themes when focused on historical consequence, and these themes appear to be common regardless of the historical events and the substantive knowledge that the historians are relying upon.

For example, Cat Jarman's *River Kings* (2021) focused on the Vikings and David Reynold's *The Long Shadow* (2013) centred around the First World War and both elicit similar key themes and areas of argumentation, despite their very different temporal, spatial and thematic frames.

These historians and others appear to focus on three key areas:

1. **Defining the relationship between an event and its subsequent consequences**
2. **Developing their analysis through colligatory generalisations**
3. **Characterising consequences with a clear focus on relative importance**

Defining the Relationship between an Event and Its Subsequent Consequences

Often, when historians focus on the relationship between an event and its subsequent outworkings, they tend to analyse the **direct** and **indirect** nature of these consequences. For example, David Reynolds (2013) argued that 'As the direct impacts of 1914–1918 diminished after 1945, the cult of memory did become more important, but remembrance was constantly shaped by contemporary concerns'. This historian explores the direct consequences of the First World War on geography, empire, economy and democracy yet also the indirect consequences as collective memory was shifted and attitudes to conflict changed as a result of the Great War.

Through such analyses of the relationship between events and their consequences, historians also focus on the **immediate** and **long-term** impact of particular events. This is the case in Cat Jarman's *River Kings* (2021) where she argues that there was an 'enormous human cost' of the Viking invasion in the immediate term, such as the monks at Lindisfarne, but also the long-term consequence of evolving cultural identities as the Viking migrants and locals interacted.

Activity 7.1

Thinking about direct and indirect, immediate and long-term consequences.

- David Reynolds argues that there were 'direct' and 'indirect' consequences of the Great War. What is the difference between these two types of consequence? Can you write a definition of 'direct' and 'indirect' consequences of a historical event?
- Cat Jarman makes a distinction between 'immediate' and 'long-term' consequences of Viking invasion. What are the differences between these two ideas? Can you write a definition of each?

Developing Their Analysis through Colligatory Generalisations

Historians also use colligatory generalisations or concepts (as discussed by James Carroll, 2016) in order to create meaningful generalisations from multiple different consequences. Rather than listing each consequence in turn, historians synthesise their arguments by combining the collective effects of particular developments together. For example, Reynolds' title *Long Shadow* is used to meaningfully capture the consequences of the First World War on a range of areas such as geography, democracy and memory, while Cat Jarman (2021) uses the term 'globalisation' to collectively refer to the technological, ecological and trading developments that spread across the world following Viking migration. Through this thematic organisation and generalisation, we are able to develop our sense of the interconnections between individual consequences and their collective effect.

> **Activity 7.2**
>
> Thinking about colligatory generalisations.
>
> 'Colligation' comes from the Latin words for 'binding' (like 'ligature' and 'ligament') and 'connection' (like 'collect'). Therefore 'colligatory concepts' are just concepts that are made up of other ideas 'bound together'.
>
> Historians use colligatory concepts all the time. In the sentence, 'Persistent belief in the four humours made the development of new ideas about disease difficult'. The colligatory concept is, 'Persistent belief in the four humours'. This is a colligation of many things: (a) the theory of humours, (b) the assumption that there was a commonality of belief amongst medical practitioners, and (c) the fact that the theory had been around for a long time. When these three ideas are 'bound together' into one 'colligatory concept', that concept can be used as shorthand by the historian.
>
> If you build an aeroplane out of Lego bricks, you can say, 'My aeroplane landed in the jelly', rather than, '"A red brick, three blue ones, a yellow one and the triangular-shaped flat ones that used to be white that have been stuck together" landed in the jelly'. It is not just shorter, but more useful. If we think of the blocks as having been bound together into 'an aeroplane', it might make more sense for the reader to trying to understand why the blocks might have been 'flying' and 'landed' in someone's dessert. In other words, the consequence, the spilt jelly mess, is easier to explain.
>
> Have a look at some common colligations below. What ideas and concepts are bound up in these short phrases?
>
> - 'British foreign policy in the 1930s'
> - 'Resentment at the imposition of the Statute of Labourers of 1351'
> - 'New ideas from the Arab world'
> - 'Stalin's paranoia'
> - 'Aboriginal ideas about land'
> - 'The First World War'

Characterising Consequences with a Clear Focus on Relative Importance

Historians also use a language of consequential reasoning in order to develop their arguments about the character and relative importance of particular consequences. This is, at times, through a focus on the cumulative impact and, at other times, through a focus on the significance of consequences and, by extension, the event from which these out-workings stemmed. Both Jarman and Reynolds consider the different kinds of effects and the relative importance of consequences in their interpretations. Jarman (2021) purports that the Viking impact on Britain was **profound** and '**affected everything** from the developments of towns to the currency, culture, language and art'. Jarman is judging the Scandinavian migration to Britain as significant to all areas of British life in the mid-eleventh century. Also reflecting on the broadness of impact, Reynolds (2013) refers to the **turbulence** of the century following the First World War and the **big bang** of democracy, demonstrating his judgement that the consequences were particularly politically significant.

Thus, when historians are arguing about consequences, they appear to be doing something distinct. Historians of consequences appear to focus their arguments around one particular event and its various out-workings, as opposed to a process of change over time or the significance of a particular event or the reasons for it occurring.

HOW DOES CONSEQUENCE DIFFER TO OTHER HISTORICAL CONCEPTS?

What Makes Historical Consequence Different to Historical Change?

The key distinction between historical consequence and historical change lies in what historians are arguing about when they focus on each concept. For change, historians' arguments are primarily focused on characterising a process, experience or development across a temporal scale. This results in historians problematising the nature, speed or extent of that process. By contrast, historians' consequential arguments are more concerned with identifying, characterising and interrelating the out-workings of a particular event, action or happening.

As a result of these key differences, historians ask very different questions depending on whether they are focused on change or consequence. Change questions will always consider a process over time, while consequence questions will focus on a particular event and its out-workings. For example, the historian Emma Griffin writes about changes to the lives of working-class people during the Industrial Revolution in her book *Liberty's Dawn* (2014). She might ask the question 'How did the experiences of working-class men change during the Industrial Revolution?'. This historian's focus is on change as a process, considering how experiences developed across this period compared to life prior to the Industrial Revolution.

By contrast, the historian David Reynolds (2013) is focused on the consequences of the First World War. He might ask the question 'How did the First World War change American politics?'. Although this historian is also asking about change, Reynolds is focused on a particular event (the First World War) and its out-workings (American politics) rather than a process of change over time.

What Makes Historical Consequence Different to Historical Significance?

Another complication for history teachers is where historical consequences are bound with the concept of historical significance. If historical significance is about what gets remembered, valued, ignored and forgotten from the past, as discussed by Helen Snelson in Chapter 10, it is easy to see how events with multiple and enduring consequences are therefore judged to be historically significant by pupils. However, the judgements that we are making are different. With consequence, we are asking pupils to form a judgement about the nature of the out-workings, while with significance we are asking pupils to judge the meaning given to particular events, or even consequences, at different time periods and by different people. For more on historical significance, see Chapter 10, which explains the importance of pupils recognising that significance is not simply inherent to the event, but is attributed in different ways by different people, and also how we might support pupils in analysing historical significance in this way.

What Makes Historical Consequence Separate to Causation?

Teaching History's 'What's the Wisdom on Consequence' (2021) notes clearly the parallels between causal reasoning and consequential reasoning, as both involve identification and classification in some form and focus around one particular event. For example, we might look at the causes of the English Civil War for a causation question and the out-workings of this same event for a consequence question. However, causal questions are focused on why an event or situation happened and analysing the patterns and nature of particular causes (as explained in Teaching History's 'What's the Wisdom on Causation', 2019). This is separate to consequence questions where the event itself forms the starting point. While learning both the causes and consequences of an event might be important for pupils' substantive knowledge, avoiding questions that cover both is essential to stop pupils falling into the trap of oversimplified conceptual judgements. See Chapter 6 by Laura London for more on teaching historical causation.

> **Activity 7.3**
>
> Sum up the difference between historical consequence and the following second-order concepts:
>
> - historical change;
> - historical significance; and
> - causation.

A WORKING DEFINITION

Historical consequence has been part of the National Curriculum for history since its first iteration in 1991, combined in a pair as 'cause and consequence'. Since then, each updated National Curriculum for history has focused on this pair through describing and explaining 'reasons for, and results of', particular historical events. There was some early non-statutory guidance for teachers on what this might include: the 1991 Attainment Target 1 Knowledge and understanding of history suggested that pupils' knowledge of cause and consequence should include the ability to 'identify types' and 'recognise that causes and consequences can vary in importance', for example. This guidance also specifically noted that a focus on 'short-term consequences' and 'consequences which are limited in their scope' would help develop pupils' arguments (Department of Education and Science, 1991). However, as with other concepts, clarity of what pupils should do with the concept has been difficult to cement.

The most recent National Curriculum for history in England (Department for Education, 2013) states that all pupils should 'understand historical concepts such as … cause and consequence … and use them to make connections, draw contrasts, analyse trends, frame historically-valid questions and create their own structured accounts, including written narratives and analyses'. This iteration also refers to specific examples such as 'The Black Death and its social and economic impact', 'Britain as the first industrial nation- the impact on society' and states pupils should study 'an aspect of social history, such as the impact through time of migration of people to, from and within the British Isles'. While the examples provide a sense of what substantive knowledge teachers might focus on within their curriculum, the specificity of what argumentation around each concept might look like is still left open to interpretation.

Since this, however, the OFSTED Research Review Series of 2021 has sought to offer further clarification on what pupils might do with historical consequence and the challenges of analysis. This review provides a useful starting point to explore the concept in relation to others' concepts too, noting that formulating a hypothesis about the impact of a major event might form a useful starting point before specific characterisation or classification of consequences. This review also helpfully discerns the importance of distinct consequence enquiries entirely separate from questions focused on causation, noting that the types of analyses are different.

Amongst history teacher educators and history education researchers, historical consequence remains relatively untheorised. However, Teaching History's 'What's the Wisdom on Consequence?' (2021) feature provides a useful summary of the thinking around consequence in the context of school history in England to date. This review considers the complications and pitfalls, as well as effective ways, to develop consequential arguments within the classroom and would enable teachers to engage with the complexity of the concept more readily. Given the limited theorisation of consequences, there is still much room for teachers to join and shape the debate of what this concept should mean within school history.

Based on the model of academic historians and current theorisation of consequences for school history, historical consequence is about the study of one historical event and the multiple out-workings of this event. Pupils need to learn how to analyse historical consequences according to the areas outlined from historians: the relationship between the event and its subsequent consequences, colligatory generalisations and characterisation of consequences, with a clear focus on their relative importance.

PRACTICAL STRATEGIES FOR THE HISTORY CLASSROOM

If we are to be able to support our pupils to meaningfully engage with the concept of historical consequence, history teachers need to ensure that they have absolute clarity of what it means to analyse historical consequence and how we can help pupils achieve this for themselves. This is not to suggest that there is a hierarchical structure of 'getting better' at consequences but rather that there are a range of areas where pupils can be supported to develop their judgements.

What Types of Questions Would Help Pupils Engage with Historical Consequences?

For teachers to ensure they are able to help pupils develop their own judgements, they need to pre-plan questions that encourage consequential thinking. The following questions will provide a helpful starting point to use within individual lessons:

- What were the consequences of X?
- Were the consequences of X short term, medium term or long term? (temporal)
- How quickly did the consequences of X spread to Y? (temporal)
- Which place/country was most affected by X? (spatial)
- How far spread were the consequences of X? (spatial)
- In what direction did the consequences of X travel? (spatial)
- Why were the consequences of X so different in Y and Z? (spatial)
- Were the consequences of X social/political/economic/religious/military/cultural/environmental/emotional/physical/psychological? (thematic)
- Were the political consequences or social consequences more important to Y? (thematic)
- Who was affected by the consequences of X? (thematic)
- How were people affected by the consequences of X? (thematic)

- Which person/people/group were most affected by X? (thematic)
- How did X physically affect Y? (physical)
- Which consequence of X was most important?
- Why did people experience the consequences of X in different ways?
- Were the consequences of X direct or indirect?
- What would the consequences of X look like?

Considering a range of these questions during medium-term planning of a consequence enquiry and within individual lessons will help to ensure that pupils are explicitly directed to develop their consequential thinking.

> **Activity 7.4**
>
> Using the list of example consequence questions, try replacing 'X' with some of the events that are currently in your school's Key Stage 3. Do different questions lend themselves better to some events over others? Why is that?

How Can Using the Language of Historical Consequences Help to Develop Pupils' Analysis?

If teachers seek for pupils to be familiar and versed in the language of historical consequence, they need to use this language consistently and explicitly themselves within both lesson planning and verbal discussion in class. For example, categorising consequences as direct or indirect, short term or long term, substantial or limited. After careful and deliberate modelling, pupils should then be encouraged to use consequential language themselves in their discussions and writing. Table 7.1 is based on the work of Paula Worth (2017) and includes some examples of language teachers may find it useful to incorporate into their own explanations and models to pupils as well for pupils to use themselves.

How Can Using Visual Models Help to Develop Pupils' Analysis?

Visual models can support pupils to identify the relationship between a particular event and its out-workings, as well as the nature of consequences. If pupils are well supported to map the interconnectedness and scale of consequences through visual diagrams, this can provide a useful first step for pupils to identify the different areas that they may wish to analyse further. Figure 7.1 (also based on the work of Worth, 2017) includes some examples of images teachers may find useful to share with pupils to support their visualisation of the scale of consequences.

> **Activity 7.5**
>
> With the questions that you wrote in Activity 7.4, which of the suggested language in Table 7.1 would you use to describe the consequences of the event you have chosen? Can you draw an appropriate visual metaphor for the consequences of the events (see Figure 7.1 for ideas)?

Table 7.1 Suggested language that teachers may wish to use with pupils when arguing about historical consequences, based on the work of Paula Worth (2017)

Describing the Nature (Types) of Consequences

strengthening	imperceptible	serious	adverse	immediate	direct	unforeseen	profound
severe	violent	damaging	extreme	mild	fatal	lasting	enduring
direct	indirect	unanticipated	necessary	subtle	radical	positive	negative
short-term	medium-term	long-term	physical	emotional		psychological	

Describing the scale (sizes and shapes) of consequences

smooth	jagged	multi-dimensional	uniform	varied	clearly defined	enduring	even
uneven	wide	narrow	large	small	monumental		hazy

Describing the relative importance of consequences

transformative	ground breaking	pivotal	revolutionary	significant	most	least	quite

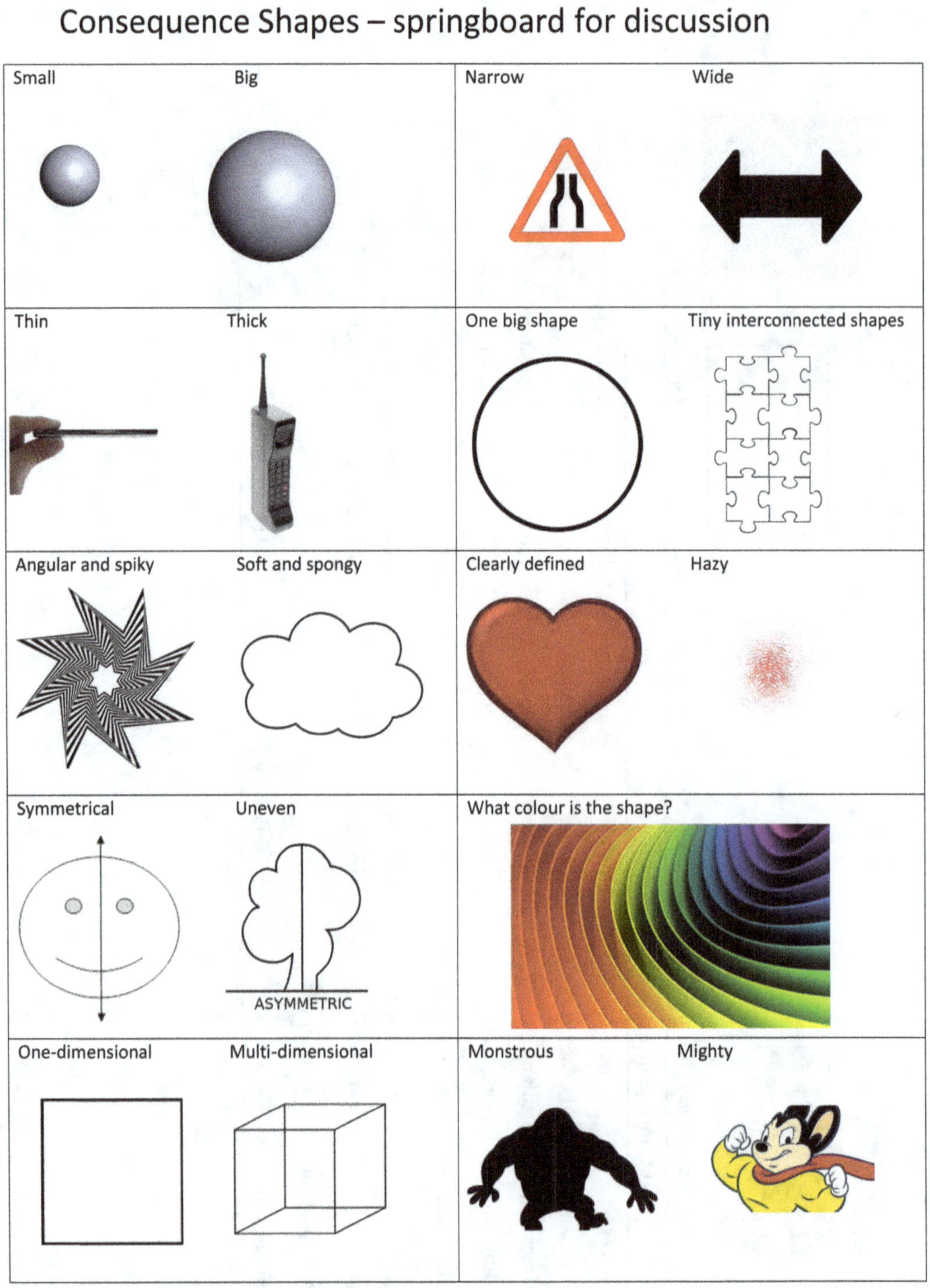

Consequence Shapes – springboard for discussion

Small	Big	Narrow	Wide
Thin	Thick	One big shape	Tiny interconnected shapes
Angular and spiky	Soft and spongy	Clearly defined	Hazy
Symmetrical	Uneven	What colour is the shape?	
One-dimensional	Multi-dimensional	Monstrous	Mighty

Figure 7.1 Suggested images that teachers may wish to use with pupils when arguing about the shape of historical consequences, based on the work of Paula Worth (2017).

CONSEQUENCE ENQUIRY QUESTIONS

In order for pupils to become secure in analysing historical consequence, teachers need to ensure that the concept is revisited across a range of different time periods and substantive topics throughout Key Stage 3. An effective way to achieve this is for pupils to encounter an array of historical enquiry questions, which enable them to grapple with the consequences of past events across a sequence of lessons.

Chapter 3 from Paula Worth demonstrates the importance of this approach to school history, drawing upon the seminal work of Riley (2000) and others, and outlines eight principles for developing an effective enquiry.

Examples of enquiry questions with a specific focus on the concept of historical consequence include the following:

- Why were the consequences of the fall of the Roman Empire so varied?
- What were the consequences of the Black Death for the medieval peasantry?
- How did the Black Death shape the future of medieval towns?
- What were the long-term consequences of the fall of Constantinople?
- What did the Columbian Exchange create and destroy?
- How did the events of 1517 in Germany travel across early-modern Europe?
- What did the American Revolution achieve for the Thirteen Colonies?
- In what directions did the consequences of the American Revolution travel?
- How far reaching were the consequences of the French Revolution?
- What *Long Shadows* did the First World War cast on 20th-century Europe?
- What happened when capitalism went bust in 1920s America?
- How did the Great Depression shape the future of 20th-century Germany?
- How did the Second World War change Indian attitudes to independence?
- How did September 2001 shape the nature of conflict in the 21st-century?

An Example of a Consequence Enquiry

Consequence enquiries can be framed in a range of different ways. Some might focus on one area of consequential thinking: short term or long term, economic or political, for example. Others will seek to incorporate a range of analyses, such as characterisation of consequences and helpful colligatory generalisations. This example will seek to demonstrate how a range of consequential thinking can be incorporated into one enquiry. However, this should only be attempted once pupils have become more familiar with the concept of consequence over time and have sufficient knowledge to make meaningful analyses. The question that frames the enquiry is the following: What *Long Shadows* did the First World War cast on 20th-century Europe?

This enquiry is based around the different consequences that David Reynolds identifies in his 2013 book *The Long Shadow: The Great War and the Twentieth Century*. Focused on Reynolds' three themes of public memory of war, the birth of mass democracy and the rise of extremism, the enquiry invites pupils to consider the scale and cumulative impact of consequences. Pupils begin with a focus on shapes as a visual model before considering the overlap and interconnections between consequences. See Table 7.2 for an overview of the enquiry in full and Table 7.3 and Figure 7.2 for example resources used during this enquiry.

Throughout each lesson, pupils are introduced to the arguments that David Reynolds makes about the consequences of the First World War before drawing shapes as a visual model of these consequences. At the beginning of lesson one, pupils are asked to draw upon their prior knowledge of the First World War to draw and label a shape that represents their understanding of the consequences. They are given no guidance on how to do this to elicit ideas from their own memory: some pupils draw a poppy, reflecting their own participation in collective memory, while others draw symbols of the violence of war such as barbed wire or guns. After this point, pupils are then introduced to a range of images to support them in developing their future drawings, based on the work of Worth, as shown in Figure 7.1 earlier in this chapter. At this stage, clear criteria are established to

Table 7.2 Overview scheme of work for a year 9 enquiry 'What long shadows did the First World War cast on 20th century Europe?'

Lesson focus:	EQ: 'What *Long Shadows* did the First World War cast on 20th century Europe?'
L1: … on collective remembrance?	**Intro/ISM:** • Pupils draw the shape that immediately comes to mind when they think of the consequences of the FWW (previously studied in Y8). • Pupils introduced to Reynolds' title with a blank for 'Long Shadow' and consider what the gap might be. • Pupils introduced to title 'Long Shadow'. Hypothesise what Reynolds might argue. • Pupils read edited extract from Reynolds' book/BBC documentary for idea of 'mentally stuck in trenches' and memory 'shifting repeatedly over time'. **Main sequence of learning:** • Pupils introduced to Reynolds' arguments about memory of FWW in Britain and Germany from 1918 to present day. • Pupils watch/listen to a range of British and German popular representations of the FWW. E.g. 1919 Cenotaph, 1930 All Quiet on the Western Front and 2019 '1917'. Pupils focus on feelings/tone/story created in each representation. • Pupils note how the representations confirm/challenge Reynolds' argument. **Plenary:** • Pupils draw and label two shapes to represent public memory of FWW in Britain and Germany, respectively. They label these shapes to explain their decision-making. Language and shape suggestions provided.
L2: … on politics and ideologies?	**Intro/ISM:** • Pupils shown images of political events from Russia, Britain, America and Italy in the post-war period. Pupils choose a word to describe the events happening in each picture. See Figure 7.2. • Events of each photograph revealed to pupils; see Figure 7.3. Explanation that each event was key to the country's journey to or away from democracy. • Pupils read edited extract from Reynolds' book/BBC documentary for idea of 'turbulent age of mass democracy' and 'three very different visions' of post-war politics. **Main sequence of learning:** • Political spectrum reminder for pupils from extreme left to right wing. • Keywords related to politics reminder for pupils. E.g. Republicanism, Fascism and Ideologies • Pupils read about post-war politics in the USA, Russia/USSR, Britain and Italy. Pupils annotate the four places on a map, noting how democracy was introduced/whether democracy was stable and the key event that made democracy stable or turbulent. • Pupils return to Reynolds' extract and consider whether he was right to argue that FWW was 'birth to a turbulent age of mass democracy'. **Plenary:** • Pupils draw and label four shapes to represent changing democracy across the four countries. They label these shapes to explain their decision-making. Language and shape suggestions provided.

(Continued)

Table 7.2 Overview scheme of work for a year 9 enquiry 'What long shadows did the First World War cast on 20th century Europe?' (Continued)

Lesson focus:	EQ: 'What *Long Shadows* did the First World War cast on 20th century Europe?'
L3: 'What *Long Shadows* did the First World War cast on 20th century Europe?'	**Intro:** • Pupils complete a quiz of ten questions about David Reynolds' arguments in order to recap and consolidate their knowledge. **Main sequence of learning:** • Pupils introduced to the outcome activity: pupils analyse the consequences for memory, democracy and extremism across Britain, the USA, Germany, Russia/USSR and Italy. Pupils pick out the nature, scale and cumulative impact and relative importance of the consequences. • Pupils spend the majority of the lesson completing their EQ overview sheet. **Plenary:** • Pupils return to Reynolds' arguments for a final time and consider the 'long shadows' of war across the different countries studied. • Pupils answer the EQ orally: paired and whole class discussion of the nature of consequences across Europe and the USA.

Table 7.3 *Extracts from David Reynolds' Long Shadow (2013) used with students throughout the enquiry*

Lesson 1: From the theatre of war to the theatre of memory, along the old front to the now familiar monuments of the dead of 1914–1918. Every year we observe solemn and moving rituals. But for those of us now who didn't live through the Great War, what are we remembering? A terrible sacrifice, and for what? In Britain the usual answer is nothing. We tend to think of the Great War as pointless slaughter, mud and blood, the carnage illuminated only by poignant war poetry. But I think mentally we have become stuck in the trenches. Our view of 1914–1918 is now a caricature.

This deadlocked war unleashed huge dynamic forces that have pummelled and shaped the whole century since 1914. One of our biggest legacies is the memory of the Great War, the story we tell ourselves about it. This isn't something fixed in stone, it shifted repeatedly over time. Different countries remember the Great War in different ways. The Great War has cast shadows over the whole century since 1914 and equally important is how the events of that turbulent century have cast **long shadows** over the way we remember the Great War.

Lesson 2: One paradox of the war is that it wasn't caused by profound political or ideological divisions, but it did create them in its wake. The war made politics red-hot, it gave birth to a **turbulent age of mass democracy** with the vote extended to ordinary men and women.

Today we take democracy for granted, elections are familiar, even boring. But a century ago democracy hit Europe like a big bang. In the aftermath of the war the old order was blown apart and ordinary people rose up. Three leaders offered three very different visions for harnessing and directing this people power. Three ideologies that would convulse the world. First Lenin and the Bolsheviks seized control in Russia and established a one-party **communist** state. Second Woodrow Wilson, the American President, championed **liberty** and **republicanism** with no place for monarchs or aristocrats. Finally, a third leader, Benito Mussolini, in Italy smashed communism and rejected liberal democracy to pioneer a new militaristic ideology, **fascism**.

Figure 7.2 The beginning of Lesson 2 where pupils are invited to consider politics in post-First World War Europe and the USA.

support judgements about size and scale to encourage pupils to create shapes that are comparable and tightly focused on Reynolds' argument.

Once pupils have drawn their shapes, they are encouraged to move beyond this level of abstraction by beginning to consider and explain reasons for differences in their visual representations. Careful questioning here is important. For example, why might their model for Britain look so different to their model for Germany? Why have you drawn multiple little shapes? Why have you used this particular colour? Pupils are encouraged to compare their shapes to others to really question and critique their own judgements. This helps to ensure that pupils have thought really clearly about their choices and that their shapes start to hold real meaning in the context of historical consequences. Guided discussion in the second lesson, focused on multiple countries, also ensures pupils start to explain the interconnectedness of the consequences across countries but also the distinctive experiences of the same event too. In the case of public memory, the success versus defeat significantly shapes the experiences of Britain and Germany, for example.

After pupils have developed their judgements throughout the enquiry, the enquiry outcome then invites them to consider the range of consequences collectively based on Reynolds' interpretation. See Figure 7.4 for the worksheet used during the outcome activity.

By ending the enquiry with pupils analysing the nature, relative importance and scale and cumulative impact of consequences across different countries, they are asked to demonstrate their broader knowledge of the interconnections of the *Long Shadows* of war, as well as the distinct nature of the consequences across each

TEACHING CONSEQUENCE

Figure 7.3 Later in Lesson 2 the event descriptions are revealed to students to help them build their understanding of the nature of the event and its impact on that country.

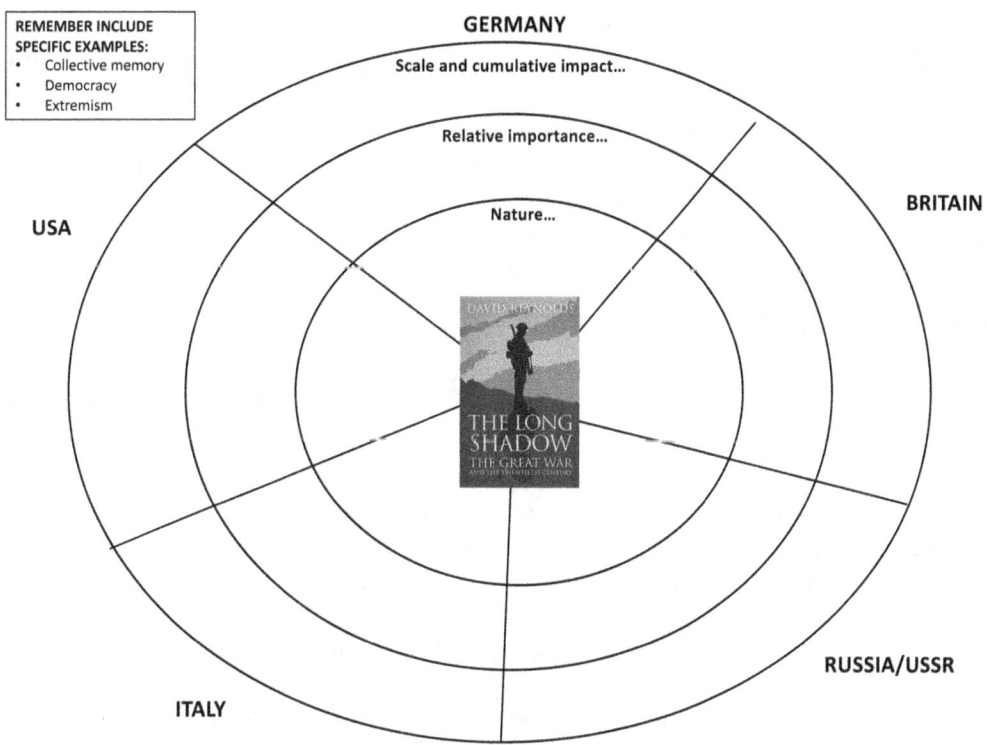

Figure 7.4 The outcome activity completed at the end of the *Long Shadows* enquiry.

country. Pupils are expected to add a judgement in each area, using their labelled visual models as a guide. They then shade in each segment to analyse the *'shadow'* cast by the First World War with a darker colour suggesting a more significant impact.

By the end of this enquiry, pupils have wrestled and engaged with consequence across a range of different parameters. However, building up pupils' experience through a range of different activities and encounters with consequence is essential before engaging with consequence at this level.

> **Activity 7.6**
>
> In the scheme of work in Table 7.2 that is further exemplified in Table 7.3, Figure 7.2 and Figure 7.3, in which lessons and activities does the concept of the 'long shadow' come up? What does this allow the pupils to do as the sequence progresses? Write down how the pupils' understanding of this idea would be different between the first lesson and the outcome activity.

PUPIL ACTIVITIES

There are a range of activities that could be used across different enquiries and key stages to support pupils to analyse historical consequences. As noted throughout this chapter, for these activities to be successful, teachers must have a strong understanding of the concept themselves and also a strong sense of how each activity links to their objectives for the lesson and enquiry.

Hypothesising Consequences

Once pupils have strong substantive knowledge of a historical event, teachers might wish for pupils to hypothesise what consequences this event might have for themselves. For example, after studying the English Civil War and the execution of King Charles I, pupils might be invited to consider how this affected politics or radicalism in England. This can then be used as a basis of discussion throughout lessons and as a puzzle to be tested throughout an enquiry. A word of caution for such activities is to provide a clear criterion or area of focus and to ensure that these hypotheses are grounded in the history being studied.

Classification or Categorisation Card Sorts

Similar to activities that pupils may undertake for causal analysis, pupils can be given a range of cards depicting different consequences, which they then categorise according to pre-arranged themes or classify for themselves. For example, a teacher might ask pupils to arrange the consequences of the Black Death according to economic, political and social themes. Alternatively, a teacher might encourage pupils to develop their own categories. This activity works well to develop pupils' awareness of the interconnectedness of consequences. This can be pushed even further by asking pupils to sort consequences into a Venn diagram where they consider the overlapping consequences and those that are more fixed.

Card sorts can also provide a good opportunity for pupils to consider the relative importance of individual consequences, creating a line from most important to least important consequences. These can be developed further with pupils considering which themes appear in their lines. For example, are most of their economic consequences towards the top of their line or does there appear to be a mix across different themes?

Creating 'Best Patterns' of Consequences

Building upon these classification activities, Paula Worth (2023) has recently written about her use of visual images to support pupils in creating patterns of consequence across a variety of different frameworks. Worth encouraged her pupils to consider a range of different consequences of Mary I's reign based on temporal, spatial, thematic, size and physical impact. Through this, she demonstrated to pupils that consequences are not fixed and have multifaceted dimensions. For this activity, pupils are expected to classify different consequences according to each focus area. This ensures that pupils are aware that there are consequences that overlap across themes, time and space, while others appear to sit in more fixed boundaries.

Zones of Relevance

Pupils can also be encouraged to track different consequences into 'zones of relevance' based on temporal, spatial and thematic dimensions. Through placing consequences along diagrams that cover multiple different time periods, countries or themes, pupils may consider the relative importance of consequences based on a particular area of focus. Figure 7.5 provides an example of what this activity might look like.

Teachers may wish for pupils to place numbers along the line where there is overlap. Alternatively, teachers might wish for pupils to form a judgement of the relative importance of each consequence by creating a numerical scale along the different zones. This activity supports pupil knowledge of the varied effects of consequences based on the area historians have chosen to focus on. Good substantive knowledge is absolutely key to success when pupils engage in activities such as this.

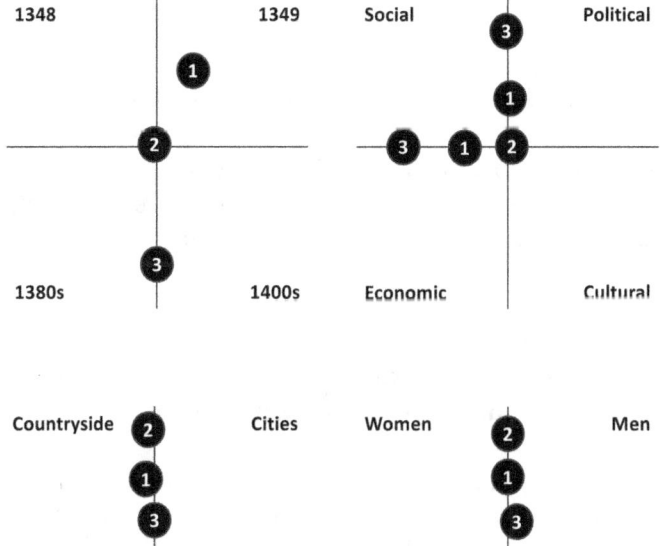

1. The Ordinance of Labourers (1349) fixed wages, imposed price controls and required under 60s to work.	2. 40% to 60% of the population of Europe, the Middle East and North Africa were killed.
3. The 1381 Great Revolt was unsuccessful but showed that survivors would rebel if restricted.	4. Plague returned to England again in the 1350s and 1360s.
5. Entire villages disappeared, such as Wharram Percy.	6. Women begun to take on more roles such as running workshops and training as apprentices.
7. By the 1370s, more people were working in towns and fewer people were working in farming.	8. People's attitude to death changed and art such as 'the Dance of Death' became more commonplace.

Figure 7.5 An example pupil activity where consequences of the Black Death are placed into zones of relevance.

Drawing Visual Models

As noted in the example enquiry, pupils can create their own drawings of particular consequences in order to consider the size and scale of the consequences. By drawing multiple different models, pupils can be supported to compare consequences on a temporal scale (drawing shapes for immediate, short term, medium term and long term), a spatial scale (comparing based on geographical difference) and a thematic scale too.

Engaging with the Language Used by Historians

Ensuring that pupils have a good grasp of consequential language is essential to helping them form their own arguments about historical consequences. One way that pupils can begin to see the importance of language is by focusing on what historians themselves have actually argued about historical consequence. Introducing pupils to an extract by a historian and asking them to zoom in on the adjectives and adverbs used, as well as how the meaning of the extract changes if these adverbs or adjectives are changed, is a good place to start. This will enable pupils to see how language is key to argumentation and allow them to trial this for themselves before writing more extended pieces on historical consequence.

Exploring the Relationship between Consequences and Significance

Once pupils are confident and competent in their analyses of historical consequences, teachers may wish to support pupils in considering why some historical events have been ascribed significance on the basis of their consequences. Worth (2023) encouraged her pupils to consider the source record used to find out about the impact of Mary I, for example, and noted that our knowledge of 'hearts and minds' from contemporaries has been largely silenced due to a lack of records for historians to work from. Encouraging pupils to engage with these questions and ideas can push them to see that consequences are not fixed and our understanding of these may shift and develop further as historians encounter new evidence and continue to acknowledge where stories of the past have been silenced.

SUMMARY OF KEY POINTS

- Historical consequence is a second-order concept and is a curricular entitlement in school history.
- Historical consequence is under-theorised and history teachers should continue to debate and develop their professional thinking around this concept.
- The work of historians should be used to identify the particular consequential problem to be puzzled with.
- Teachers should plan for pupils to grapple with historical consequence through the use of enquiry questions.
- Teachers should decide the temporal, spatial and thematic parameters of the consequential thinking they want pupils to engage with before they begin their enquiries.
- Pupils should not be expected to engage with all areas of consequential reasoning at once. Zooming in on one area can help to elicit more complex and developed arguments.
- Pupils should be supported to analyse historical consequences through the use of visual models and consequential language.

RESOURCES AND FURTHER READING

Carroll, James Edward. 'The Whole Point of the Thing: How Nominalisation Might Develop students' Written Causal arguments' in Teaching History, 162, Scales of Planning Edition, (2016): 16–25. London: Historical Association.

Department for Education. History Programmes of Study: Key Stage 3, National Curriculum in England. 2013: 1, 3–5. It is available here: https://assets.publishing.service.gov.uk/media/5a7c66d740f0b626628abcdd/SECONDARY_national_curriculum_-_History.pdf

Department of Education and Science. History in the National Curriculum. 1991.

Griffin, Emma. Liberty's Dawn: A People's History of the Industrial Revolution. New Haven and London: Yale University Press 2014.

Jarman, Cat. River Kings: The Vikings from Scandinavia to the Silk Roads. London: Harper Collins 2021: 16, 284–289.

Navey, Molly-Ann. 'Dealing With the Consequences: What Do We Want Students to Do With Consequence in History?' in Teaching History, 172, Cause and Consequence Edition, (2018): 40–49. London: Historical Association.

OFSTED. Research Review Series: History. 2021. It is available here: https://www.gov.uk/government/publications/research-review-series-history/research-review-series-history

Reynolds, David. The Long Shadow: The Great War and the Twentieth Century. Simon and Schuster 2013: xxii, 40–83.

Riley, Michael. 'Into the Key Stage 3 History Garden: Choosing and Planting Your Enquiry questions' in Teaching History, 99, Curriculum Planning Edition, (2000): 8–13. London: Historical Association.

The Editorial Board. 'What's the Wisdom on ... Causation' in Teaching History, 175, Listening to Diverse Voices Edition, (2019): 24–27. London: Historical Association.

The Editorial Board. 'What's the Wisdom On… Consequence' in Teaching History, 182, A Sense of Period Edition, (2021): 50–55. London: Historical Association.

Worth, Paula. '"It's like this big, black hole, Miss, that's dragging everything into it". Year 9 consider the impact of the World War I on Russia by playing with the idea of consequence 'shapes'' [Blog Post], Lobworth, (2017). https://lobworth.com/2017/09/24/its-like-this-big-black-hole-miss-thats-dragging-everything-into-it-year-9-consider-the-impact-of-world-war-i-on-russia-by-playing-with-the-idea-of-consequence-shapes/

Worth, Paula. 'Problems, patterns, playing with words: tackling 'historical consequence'' [Blog Post], Lobworth, (2023). https://lobworth.com/2023/05/01/problems-patterns-playing-with-words-tackling-consequences-in-essays/

Chapter 8

Teaching Similarity/Difference and Historical Perspective

Jacob Olivey

BACKGROUND

On 16 June 1858, temperatures in London reached 38°C. The heat was unbearable, but the stench was worse. Day after day, gallons of industrial waste and raw sewage flowed into the Thames. The river became a blackish-green sludge, boiling and bubbling in the sun; its foul odours left passersby choking and retching. The smell was so bad; it even forced laissez-faire politicians to improve London's sanitation.

In *One Hot Summer* (2017), the historian Rosemary Ashton traces how three Londoners – Darwin, Dickens and Disraeli – suffered through the 'Great Stink' of 1858. Versions of this story, often accompanied by *Punch* cartoons projected onto the board, are also told by history teachers across the country. Now, of course, classroom tales cannot match the detail found in a work of scholarship such as *One Hot Summer*. But these different historical accounts do have something in common: they contain generalisations. In her opening chapter, Ashton (2017) argues that 'for ordinary people, and for the rich, the famous, and the powerful, the summer of 1858 was in one way or another a summer of consequence'. Even in a work of microhistory, focused on a few people for a short period of time, we find generalisations about the experiences of 'ordinary people' and 'the rich'. This observation is not, however, a criticism of Ashton's work: the past is too complicated, the traces of it that survive are too incomplete, and books are too short for us to 'make' history without making some generalisations.

Historians need to make generalisations – but some generalisations are better than others. History teachers know this all too well; according to some pupils, 'medieval people' were stupid and, according to others, 'the Victorians' were posh. Thankfully, history teachers have found ways to help pupils notice bad generalisations such as these and make better ones. This work comes under the second-order concept of similarity/difference: teaching pupils to see the *similarities* and the *differences* that existed *within* groups and *between* groups of people in the past. *Teaching History's* 'What's the wisdom on … similarity and difference' (2020) explains that the aims of this second-order concept include leaving pupils with a

Table 8.1 Some of Ian Luff's fictional character cards, taken from Luff (2000)

Sidney Spot Clerk for Fraser's feed business	**George Mainbearing** Bank Manager	**Seth Hovell** Agricultural labourer. Father of seven.	**Bessie Hovell** Wife of an agricultural labourer. Mother of seven.	**Eleanor Shade** Unmarried mother of a nine-month-old baby.
Harold Scrubb Unemployed father of ten. Able-bodied.	**Lillie Scrubb** Barmaid. Walks the streets at night.	**William Good** Disabled in a factory accident. Widower. Father of eight.	**Reverend Aves** Rector of the church on the Earl's estate.	**Gladys Bleach** Workhouse matron.

'disposition to question labels, categories, and generalisations' and 'an expectation of complexity'.

This chapter will begin by outlining some activities that can be used for teaching similarity/difference so that pupils see the complexity in the past. It will then introduce a new second-order concept, historical perspective, which aims to help pupils study history 'from the inside' by exploring how people from the past saw themselves and their world.

TEACHING SIMILARITY/DIFFERENCE

One very powerful classroom activity for teaching similarity/difference is Ian Luff's 'society line'. Writing over 20 years ago, Luff (2000) was concerned that 'the subtle gradations of status in society are frequently bulldozed by over-simplistic textbooks'. To combat this, Luff gave each pupil in his class a fictional 'character card' (see Table 8.1) and asked them to sort themselves into a line from 'most important' to 'least important'. As Luff explained, the discussions that followed helped pupils to realise that 'relative status and rank always contain grey areas'. In a similar vein, Christine Counsell's (2009) 'generalisation game' makes it easier for pupils to see a more complicated past. At the end of an enquiry on medieval life, Counsell read a series of generalisations to her class, such as 'all medieval people lived in mud huts' and 'life was hard in the fourteenth century'. She encouraged pupils to shout out 'too simple' when they heard a statement that was, well, too simple – and to explain why said generalisation does not stand up to scrutiny. Afterwards, Counsell helped her pupils to construct their own, better and more nuanced generalisations about medieval life (see Activity 8.1).

In addition to one-off classroom activities, however, history teachers have used enquiry questions that ask pupils to think about problems of similarity/difference over a sequence of lessons. Read Chapter 3 on Planning Enquiries for how enquiry questions can be used to frame a sequence of lessons around a disciplinary concept such as similarity/difference. Some enquiry questions, such as 'Who supported the Nazis?', encourage pupils to see the diversity *within* one group of people from the past. Others, such as 'How similar was fascism in Germany and Italy?', ask pupils to judge the extent of similarity/difference *across* two or more groups. The most striking similarity/difference enquiry is undoubtedly Elizabeth Carr's (2012) 'How Victorian were the Victorians?'. Over a sequence of six lessons, Carr's pupils studied stereotypical notions of what made someone or something Victorian – and then decided how appropriate this label is for describing different people from the nineteenth century.

> **Activity 8.1 Counsell's generalisation game**
>
> Here is an example of a 'dodgy generalisation' that Counsell (2009) gave to her Year 7 pupils: 'Villagers in the early 14th century were told how much firewood they could collect'. Counsell then asked her pupils to explain *why* this generalisation was too simple. She provided the following words and phrases to help pupils be more tentative in their descriptions of medieval village life:
>
> - Some villagers …
> - Some groups …
> - In some places …
> - Sometimes …
> - One exception …
>
> Now think about your curriculum. When do you teach pupils to use tentative language like this? Why would these words and phrases help pupils make better generalisations about the past?

So far, we have established that making generalisations is an essential part of history-making – and that classroom activities and enquiry questions focused on similarity/difference can teach pupils to make better generalisations about groups such as 'medieval peasants'. But is this enough? Does similarity/difference help pupils understand *what* mattered to 'medieval peasants' (or *that* these people mattered)? Perhaps not. Here, it is useful to consider a distinction Chris Husbands (1996) draws between history 'from the outside' and history 'from the inside'. Similarity/difference enquiries ask pupils to challenge bad and make better generalisations *about the past* – to approach history 'from the outside'. They rarely require pupils to consider the ideas and beliefs *of people in the past* – to approach history 'from the inside'. As Husbands argues, history 'from the inside' has a marginal place in most English schools; the following section will consider why this is the case.

THE RISE OF CULTURAL HISTORY AND THE DEMISE OF EMPATHY

Though history 'from the inside' seldom features in most English school curricula, it has become commonplace in academic circles. The 'cultural turn' that began in the 1970s has made the 'subjective' perspectives of people from the past a valid object of study – alongside more 'objective' political and social structures (Burke, 2013). But what differentiates cultural history from other forms of history writing? In *What is Cultural History*, Peter Burke (2013) concludes that 'the common ground of cultural historians might be defined as a concern with the symbolic and its interpretation'. As fellow cultural historian Miri Rubin (2002) explains, many scholars now ask not only 'how it really was' but also 'how was it for him, or her, or them'. In the words of David Reynolds (2006), their focus has shifted 'from causes to meanings'. Even academics who do not call themselves cultural historians have been influenced by these trends; in *One Hot Summer*, for example, Ashton (2017) is less concerned with *why* the Great Stink happened than she is with what it *meant* to those who suffered through it.

Interestingly, history 'from the inside' used to enjoy far more prominence in English schools. When the second-order concepts were first theorised by members of the Schools Council History Project in the early 1970s, they included the now-shunned concept of 'empathy' (Sylvester, 1976). Some of the project's members were interested in early French cultural historians' efforts to read sources 'against the grain' to reconstruct the mentalités of individuals and groups (Keating & Sheldon, 2011). Empathy was supposed to bring this new way of looking at the past into the classroom. Initially, it proved popular with history teachers; empathy questions even featured in the first GCSE examinations in 1988 (Simkin, 1986). But there were problems with how this concept was being taught in some schools. As Peter Lee and Denis Shemilt (2011) explained, empathy was not supposed to be an 'unfettered exercise of historical imagination' and 'literary invention', with pupils trying to invent the feelings of fictitious characters ('You are a passenger on the Titanic. It is sinking. How do you feel?'). Instead, the aim of empathy was to use *sources* to 'reconstruct people's beliefs and values in ways that make actions and social practices intelligible'. Sadly, it was the ahistorical 'Imagine that you are X!' and 'How would Y have felt?' questions that came to characterise the teaching of empathy. Denis Shemilt recalled that, in the 1980s, pupils at a girls' grammar school in Kent wrote coursework 'imagining that they were kitchen maids' in stately homes, complete with 'torrid stuff about having affairs with young masters' (Keating & Sheldon, 2011). A year later, pupils at the same school were imagining that they were kitchen utensils.

The lack of history 'from the inside' being taught in most English schools today can, in part, be explained by the backlash against the teaching of empathy in the 1980s. Perhaps unsurprisingly, empathy was ridiculed by Conservative politicians and the right-wing press. *Daily Mail* articles warned that 'history teachers are undermining children's knowledge and respect for our heritage' by replacing 'knowledge of historical events' with 'the bogus skills of empathy learning' (Bates, 1989). Critics of empathy complained that 'instead of understanding the significance of the Battle of Agincourt', pupils were 'being told to imagine how English troops felt about taking part in it' (Bates, 1989). By the time the first National Curriculum was published in 1991, this backlash had made empathy too toxic to be included as a second-order concept. Its place in history classrooms in England has been marginal ever since this omission.

THE EMERGENCE OF HISTORICAL PERSPECTIVE

With the demise of empathy, none of the second-order concepts in England's National Curriculum focus on history 'from the inside' – on how people in the past saw themselves and their world. While the demise of bogus 'empathy' tasks outlined in the previous section should not be regretted, denying pupils a chance to think about how the past was experienced by individuals seems to run contrary to what historians are doing following the 'cultural turn'. As we shall see, some history teachers have tried to bring history 'from the inside' into the classroom via the existing second-order concepts. Others have proposed a more radical solution in the form of a new second-order concept: historical perspective.

When Rachel Foster (2014) planned an enquiry about the cultural legacies of the First World War, she experimented with a second-order focus on significance ('What was shocking about the Great War?') and change/continuity ('Did the Great War really end civilisation?'). Though Foster was 'convinced of the inherent value in teaching cultural history', she found it difficult to identify a second-order concept that captured its methods and concerns. Other teachers have encountered the same problem. When Kathryn Elsdon and Hannah Howard (2019) used an example of material culture – a nineteenth-century spice box – to teach pupils about the British Empire, they could not find a second-order concept that foregrounded what objects meant to people in the past.

Like Foster and Elsdon and Howard, when I planned an enquiry about what being 'working class' meant to people in nineteenth-century Britain, I also struggled to identify a second-order concept that captured cultural history's exploration of meaning. Eventually, I focused my enquiry on similarity/difference, since this second-order concept can help pupils make better use of labels such as 'working class'. Looking at the *objective* similarities and differences within a group such as 'working-class men' certainly helped my pupils use more tentative language and make better generalisations. But it also seemed to encourage pupils to dismiss the *subjective* ideas that people in the past had about being working class – on the basis that they were 'wrong' or 'too simple' (Olivey, 2019). In sum, the second-order concepts in England's current National Curriculum seem ill-suited to approaching history 'from the inside'. It is difficult to teach cultural history without having a second-order concept that is explicitly focused on the perspectives of people from the past.

This problem led Alexander Benger (2020) to propose a radical solution: a new second-order concept. Initially, Benger reasoned that the best way to 'teach Year 9 to argue like cultural historians' would be through an enquiry focused on empathy; after all, this second-order concept was partially inspired by the work of early cultural historians in the 1970s. Drawing on over one hundred letters written by his great-grandfather during the First World War, Benger planned an enquiry asking pupils 'What did the Great War mean to Theo Reid?'.

Midway through teaching, however, Benger noticed that his pupils seemed unclear about his enquiry's conceptual focus. Reflecting on his lessons, Benger concluded that the word 'empathy' was the problem – because the word 'did not directly link to the historical product that pupils were engaged in creating'. When teaching enquiries focused on other second-order concepts, a teacher can ask 'What caused X?' and 'To what extent did Y change?'. The word 'empathy' cannot be used in this way. Instead, Benger found himself using the word 'perspective', given that 'the historical task pupils were engaged in was the construction of an historical perspective'. This, Benger concluded, should be its own second-order concept. Interestingly, 'historical perspective' was already included in Canada's 'Big Six' historical thinking concepts (Seixas and Morton, 2013), which is why I have described history 'from the inside' as having a marginal place in *English* history education.

Since Benger's article was published in 2020, other history teachers have built upon his ideas about historical perspective. Sarah Jackson-Buckley (2022) planned a local study of a single street in Cambridge. Jackson-Buckley built her enquiry, 'What did it mean to belong in Mill Road, 1962-1988?', around interviews with people who lived there. Her pupils were able to see how Mill Road's residents' ideas about 'belonging' were shaped and reshaped by migration, gentrification and other socio-economic shifts. Focusing on the Middle Ages, Jessica Philips (2022) has argued that confronting 'presentism' can help pupils make sense of ways of seeing the world which are very different from their own. Phillips read her pupils part of *The Vita of Catherine of Genoa*, which describes how God instructed the future saint to eat lice (to rid herself of the revulsion she felt when treating the sick). After her pupils had got past their initial reaction of shock and disgust, Phillips helped them to understand what this source meant at the time and why Saint Catherine's actions made sense to medieval Christians. Both of these historical perspective enquiries attempt to 'reconstruct the perspective of people (individuals or groups) from the past' by 'analysing historical sources to try to work out what their world meant to them' (Benger, 2020).

> **Activity 8.2 Reflect on the following questions**
>
> 1. What is the difference between history 'from the outside' and history 'from the inside'? Can you think of some examples?
> 2. Why was the teaching of 'empathy' criticised in the 1980s? What was the main problem with how this second-order concept was interpreted by history teachers?
> 3. How would you define 'historical perspective'? How does it differ from the 'Imagine you are X!' and 'How would Y have felt?' empathy activities of old?

THREE PRINCIPLES FOR TEACHING THESE SECOND-ORDER CONCEPTS

The first half of this chapter made four main arguments: that it is impossible to make history without making some generalisations, that teaching similarity/difference can help pupils make better generalisations about the past, that the current second-order concepts in England's National Curriculum make it difficult to teach cultural history and that teaching historical perspective can help pupils see history 'from the inside'. The second half of this chapter puts forward three principles for planning and teaching enquiries about similarity/difference and historical perspective:

1. Read histories 'from below' and use them to shape your enquiries
2. Teach pupils how historians use sources to reconstruct the perspectives of people from the past
3. Fill your lessons with extraordinary stories about ordinary people

To make these principles more concrete, they also 'tell the story' of how I planned a new historical perspective enquiry about working-class political culture in nineteenth-century Britain.

PRINCIPLE 1. READ HISTORIES 'FROM BELOW' AND USE THEM TO SHAPE YOUR ENQUIRIES

When he wrote *The Making of the English Working Class*, E.P. Thompson's aim was to rescue ordinary people from 'the enormous condescension of posterity' (Thompson, 1991). In the 1960s, Thompson was part of a movement to write 'history from below'; he wanted to study the lives of ordinary people, not just the rich and powerful (Rediker, 2022). Today, if you go into the history section of any bookshop, you will find examples of 'history from below'; take Julia Boyd's *A Village in the Third Reich* (2023), which traces what life was like for ordinary Germans in one village between 1933 and 1945. This first principle is very simple: if you want to plan similarity/difference enquiries that challenge stereotypes about ordinary people, or historical perspective enquiries that explore how ordinary people saw themselves and their worlds, then you should read histories 'from below' and use them to shape your enquiries. As Paula Worth explained in Chapter 3, all the 'raw materials' needed to plan a new enquiry – interesting sources, small stories and a sense of 'where the debate is' on the given topic – can often be found in one book. What follows is an example of how I used Malcom Chase's *Chartism* (2007) to shape a new enquiry about working-class political culture in the 1800s.

In *Chartism*, Chase asks why, between 1838 and 1848, millions of ordinary men and women across Britain started to call themselves Chartists. He explains how the Chartists used petitions, public meetings and, occasionally, violence to fight for a vote for all adult men (and the five other political reforms included on their 'People's Charter'). Chase explains that the earlier historiography of Chartism was focused on its ultimate failure to secure parliamentary reform (after politicians rejected a third national petition in 1848, the movement faded away). There is certainly a debate to be had here. Did disagreements between different Chartist leaders over the use of 'physical force' weaken the movement? Or was Chartism really an example of 'hunger politics' that simply petered out as Britain became more prosperous? Consequently, when Chartism is taught in schools, enquiry questions often focus on causation (asking 'Why did Chartism fail?' or something similar). Initially, I thought about having causation as the conceptual focus for my enquiry.

As I read more of *Chartism*, however, I realised that there might be more interesting questions to ask: questions that foreground the Chartists themselves, as opposed to their movement's 'failure' to achieve its aims. Chase's narrative is punctuated by short chapters about lesser-known Chartists. One tells the story of William Cuffay, the mixed-race, disabled tailor who was transported to Tasmania for plotting revolution in 1848. Very quickly, I was struck by the diversity of the Chartists. I thought about using these short chapters to plan a similarity/difference enquiry, asking 'Who were the Chartists?' (see Table 8.2 for an overview of this enquiry).

Yet, once I had finished *Chartism*, I concluded that a focus on similarity/difference might not be the most interesting angle to approach this topic. Chase was not simply arguing that the Chartists came from different backgrounds; rather, he was arguing that they also had different ideas about 'what' they were trying to change. Some Chartists were solely focused on securing political power for working-class men: through enormous national petitions, strikes and the ill-fated Newport Rising. Other Chartists wanted wider-reaching social changes: there were Knowledge Chartists (who promoted working-class education), Church Chartists (who aimed to make religion more relevant to ordinary people), and Teetotal Chartists (who argued that alcohol always leads to poverty and vice). With this in mind, I eventually settled on an enquiry question that focused on the perspectives of the Chartists, asking 'What did the Chartists want to change?' (see Table 8.3 for an overview of this historical perspective enquiry).

Chase's history of Chartism 'from below' helped me to find an enquiry question that foregrounded the ideas of ordinary people. When planning a new similarity/difference or historical perspective enquiry, it is worth reading history books that approach the past in this way. This will allow you to see 'where the debate is' and work out what might make for an interesting question.

Activity 8.3 Coming up with your own enquiry questions

This is the publisher's description of Julia Boyd's *A Village in the Third Reich* (2023). Consider how Boyd's work could be used to plan (1) a similarity/difference enquiry and (2) a historical perspective enquiry.

Oberstdorf is a beautiful village high up in the Bavarian Alps, a place where for hundreds of years ordinary people lived simple lives while history was made elsewhere. Yet even here, in the farthest corner of Germany, National Socialism sought to control not only people's lives but also their minds.

Table 8.2 Who were the Chartists?

Lesson 1.	**Substantive knowledge:**
The People's Charter	• Reasons Chartism emerged in the 1830s (dire poverty, appalling working conditions and the lack of any political representation for ordinary people) • The six political reforms that the Chartists demanded in their People's Charter **Disciplinary focus:** • Introducing 'the Chartists' as a seemingly homogenous, monolithic group (and then suggesting that this might be too simple…)
Lesson 2.	**Substantive knowledge:**
Moral force and physical force Chartists	• The disagreement between the leading Chartists over whether it was legitimate for the movement to threaten to use violence if MPs rejected their national petition • The main differences between William Lovett (a key moral force Chartist) and Feargus O'Connor (a key physical force Chartist) **Disciplinary focus:** • Showing that it is difficult to generalise about 'the Chartists' tactics, given their disagreements about the use of violence
Lesson 3.	**Substantive knowledge:**
Female Chartists	• The role that over 100 women-only Chartist groups played in gathering signatures for the national petition • The story of Anne Knight, the anti-slavery campaigner who organised Britain's first women's suffrage society **Disciplinary focus:** • Showing that, even though the People's Charter only called for votes for working-class men, women played a major role in Chartism
Lesson 4.	**Substantive knowledge:**
Chartist children	• The different forms of activity that included children, including Chartist bands, Chartist schools and Chartist churches. • The story of Ann Dawson, the six-year-old girl who sewed a sampler dedicated to Feargus O'Connor **Disciplinary focus:** • Showing that being a Chartist was an identity that mattered to many ordinary people, including very young children
Lesson 5.	**Substantive knowledge:**
The faces in the crowd	• Recap of Lessons 1 to 4 • The story of William Cuffay and the demise of Chartism after 1848 **Disciplinary focus:** • Writing a short essay that answers the enquiry question

Overview of a similarity/difference enquiry.

> *By putting one village under the microscope, this book evocatively portrays the momentous period of Nazism in Germany. Why did Germans respond to Hitler in the manner that they did? How did their attitudes change as the war progressed? And when all hope was gone and their country lay in ruins, how did they pick themselves up and start again?*
>
> *Drawing on archive material, letters, interviews and memoirs,* A Village in the Third Reich *is an extraordinarily intimate portrait of Germany under Hitler, of the descent into totalitarianism and of the tragedies that befell all of those touched by Nazism. In its pages we meet the Jews who survived - and those who didn't; the Nazi mayor who tried to shield those persecuted by the regime; and a blind boy whose life was thought 'not worth living'. It is a tale of conflicting loyalties and desires, of shattered dreams, despair and destruction. But if this is primarily a tale of political tragedy, it is also one in which human resilience triumphs. These are the stories of ordinary lives at the crossroads of history.*

PRINCIPLE 2. TEACH PUPILS HOW HISTORIANS USE SOURCES TO RECONSTRUCT THE PERSPECTIVES OF PEOPLE FROM THE PAST

When cultural historians make claims about what things meant to people in the past, their claims are supported by the sources that they have studied. The main problem with the way empathy was often taught in the 1980s was that this focus on sources was missing; pupils were asked to 'Imagine they were X' and 'How would Y have felt?' without being given any sources to inform their ideas. This second principle is very simple: we should teach pupils how historians use sources to reconstruct the perspectives of people from the past. In *Chartism*, Chase makes use of a range of archival materials, from the *Northern Star* and other Chartist newspapers to the hymns that were sung in Chartist churches. Following Chase's lead, I used these sources to teach pupils that being a Chartist was an identity that mattered to many working-class people: they prayed in Chartist churches, played in Chartist bands and drank in Chartist pubs. Hundreds even named their children after William Lovett and Feargus O'Connor.

In Lesson 4 of 'What did the Chartists want to change?' (see Table 8.3), I introduced pupils to Chartist poetry. One of these poems came from an advert in the *Northern Star*, promoting the Chartist Cooperative Land Company. This scheme, launched by Feargus O'Connor in 1846, promised to resettle urban workers on small farms in the countryside. The poem offers a vision of rural paradise (see Figure 8.1). Moreover, closely analysing its lines makes it clear the kinds of social

> Come let us leave the murky gloom,
> The narrow crowded street:
> The bustle, noise, the smoke and din,
> To breathe the air that's sweet.
> We'll leave the gorgeous palaces
> To those miscalled great;
> To spend a day of pleasure on
> The People's First Estate

Figure 8.1 A Chartist poem, published in 1847 in the *Northern Star.*

Table 8.3 What did the Chartists want to change? Overview of a historical perspective enquiry

Lesson 1. **Life in Industrial Britain**	**Substantive knowledge:** • Reasons Chartism emerged in the 1830s (dire poverty, appalling working conditions and the lack of any political representation for ordinary people) **Disciplinary focus:** • Ensuring that pupils understand why so many people were demanding reform in the 1830s
Lesson 2. **The People's Charter**	**Substantive knowledge:** • The story of the meeting in Glasgow that launched Chartism in 1838 • The six political reforms that the Chartists demanded in their People's Charter • The early disagreements between William Lovett and Feargus O'Connor over the use of physical force **Disciplinary focus:** • Showing that the Chartists wanted political changes
Lesson 3. **Moral force and physical force**	**Substantive knowledge:** • The Chartist's first national petition, which MPs rejected in 1839 (the failure of moral force) • Violent episodes that followed the rejection of the first national petition, including the Newport Rising (the failure of physical force) • The imprisonment of William Lovett, Feargus O'Connor and other leading Chartists **Disciplinary focus:** • Showing that the Chartists disagreed about how best to secure political changes
Lesson 4. **Shifting to social reform**	**Substantive knowledge:** • William Lovett's efforts to promote 'Knowledge Chartism' and working-class education after his release from prison • Feargus O'Connor's Chartist Land Company, a scheme that aimed to resettle urban workers on small farms • The story of Ann Dawson, the six-year-old girl who sewed a sampler dedicated to Feargus O'Connor **Disciplinary focus:** • Showing that, after the rejection of the national petition, some Chartists started to focus on securing social changes
Lesson 5. **The end of Chartism**	**Substantive knowledge:** • Recap of Lessons 1-4 • The story of William Cuffay and the demise of Chartism after 1848 **Disciplinary focus:** • Writing a short essay that answers the enquiry question

> We can picture Ann embroidering by the window (maybe helped by sister Betty or the lodgers Catherine or Martha) then tidying her work away as the daylight fades. A carder's cough is heard in the unlit street outside. A mother slips to a neighbour's to share news about exclusive dealing. Men talk volubly of Feargus's latest letter 'to the fustian jackets' on their way to the Chartist rooms in nearby Edward Street. All too often the intimate and the personal evade the historian's gaze. We see through a glass darkly; yet whoever Ann was her sampler affords us a glimpse of Chartism at its 'grassroots'. And what we see is not mere hunger politics but an endeavour to improve every dimension of human life.
> Chase, Malcolm. Chartism (2007), p. 270.

Figure 8.2 Historian Malcom Chase concludes his chapter about Ann Dawson's sampler, taken from Chase (2007).

changes its author was promising. First, the poem conveys the urban misery of many workers, living in 'the murky gloom', 'the narrow crowded street', and 'the bustle, noise, the smoke and din'. It also offers a vision of rural paradise, where workers can 'breathe the air that's sweet' and 'spend a day of pleasure'. This only formed a short activity in a lesson, but it provided pupils with a tangible example of how historians can use sources to see the world as people in the past saw it.

The best example I found of Chase (2007) using one unique source to reconstruct the perspective of an individual was that of Ann Dawson. Ann was from a family of low-paid textile workers from Droylsden. In 1847, they scraped together enough money to subscribe to the Chartist Cooperative Land Company. The Dawsons prayed that they would be one of the lucky few chosen, at random, to start a new life in a community of small farms (which came to be known as O'Connorville). Like many Victorian girls, Ann sewed samplers. Amazingly, one of her samplers still survives. It depicts an idyllic scene of O'Connorville's schoolhouse, surrounded by songbirds and flowers. Ann's sampler also includes a short poem about 'O'Connor the brave'. Its last line is 'the Charter and no surrender'. Chase wrote an entire chapter, reconstructing the world that Ann Dawson was born into, and what would have mattered to her and her family. He concludes that her needlework sampler 'is a vivid reminder that Chartism embraced men, women, and all ages, and at its heart was a profound commitment to education and self-improvement'. I discussed this quote and other extracts from the chapter with pupils, as they provided a perfect example of how historians use sources to reconstruct the perspectives of people from the past. I also shared this excerpt, where Chase describes how Ann's family would have lived (see Figure 8.2).

PRINCIPLE 3. FILL YOUR LESSONS WITH EXTRAORDINARY STORIES ABOUT ORDINARY PEOPLE

In some ways, it was difficult to write a chapter about two second-order concepts. But similarity/difference and historical perspectives do have something important in common: both concepts are about people from the past. With similarity/difference, the emphasis is on what *we* (historians writing in the present) can say about them (people from the past). With historical perspective, the emphasis is on what *they* (people from the past) thought about themselves and their world. Therefore, the third and final principle is that, when teaching about similarity/difference or historical perspective, you should fill your lessons with extraordinary stories about ordinary people.

TEACHING SIMILARITY/DIFFERENCE AND HISTORICAL PERSPECTIVE

> In November 1839, 5,000 troops shivered in the rain. They were waiting outside the Welsh town of Newport. Some prayed quietly, others drank beer. One fired his pistol into the night. But these troops had not been sent by the government. They were miners, ironworkers, ordinary men...
>
> ...these troops were Chartists.
>
> Their leader, John Frost, had a daring plan. Secret preparations had been underway for months. Frost's troops would free fellow Chartists who had been imprisoned in the Westgate Hotel. Armed with pikes and guns, they would take Newport by force.
>
> At dawn, Frost's Chartist troops marched. But they were marching into a trap. Waiting inside the Westgate Hotel were infantrymen, armed with rifles by the local authorities.
>
> People watched in horror as a 'dreadful scene' unfolded. The road became 'ankle deep with gore'. The infantrymen killed 22 Chartists. Frost's Newport Rising had failed.

Figure 8.3 My account of John Frost's Newport Rising.

In Malcom Chase's *Chartism*, I came across the story of John Frost and his failed Newport Rising. I wrote my own version of this dramatic story, which I then read aloud to pupils (see Figure 8.3). For leading an armed rebellion against the government, Frost was found guilty of high treason. Initially, Frost was sentenced to be hanged, drawn and quartered; after a public outcry, however, he was instead transported to Tasmania for 16 years. I came across another fantastic story in Paul Pickering's (1986) article on 'symbolic communication' in the Chartist movement. When the Chartist firebrand Feargus O'Connor was released from York Castle in 1841, he was greeted by a grand carriage shaped like a conch shell that was drawn by six white stallions (see Figure 8.4). Stories such as these helped me to show that individual Chartists were real people, not faceless members of a failed political movement.

Both similarity/difference and historical perspective enquiries can provide pupils with a richer and more complicated picture of the past. Extraordinary stories about ordinary people, such as John Frost and Feargus O'Connor, can help teachers make this picture more vivid.

> On the morning of the great day the streets of York began to fill with crowds of onlookers and Chartists, who had been arriving steadily throughout the previous day. According to the *Northern Star*, some Chartists had 'walked forty miles to hail the release of their beloved friend'. During the morning people began to converge on York Castle.
>
> One o'clock saw the arrival of the elaborate triumphal car that had been constructed specially for the occasion. This carriage of pink and green velvet was formed in the shape of a conch-shell and drawn by six white stallions. The postilions and attendants were costumed in green jackets and hats and white breeches. Some, commented the *Northern Star*, considered it one of the finest carriages ever seen. O'Connor was quickly at its side and greeted by thunderous cheering.
>
> Pickering, Paul A. Class Without Words (1986), p. 157.

Figure 8.4 Paul Pickering's account of Feargus O'Connor's release from prison, taken from Pickering (1986).

SUMMARY OF KEY POINTS

- Historians need to make generalisations – but some generalisations are better than others. Activities and enquiry questions focused on the second-order concept of similarity/difference can help pupils make better generalisations about the past.
- Similarity/difference is a second-order concept that is well-suited to questions about how people in the present should describe people in the past (history 'from the outside'); it is ill-suited to exploring how people in the past saw themselves and their world (history 'from the inside').
- While cultural history has grown in popularity in university history, its focus on meaning has had a marginal place in school history in England ever since the demise of empathy as a second-order concept in the 1980s.
- The second-order concept of historical perspective offers a way to bring history 'from the inside' into the classroom, using sources to reconstruct how people in the past saw themselves and their world.
- If you want to plan new similarity/difference or historical perspective enquiries, you should read histories 'from below' and use them to shape your enquiries, teach pupils how historians use sources to reconstruct the perspectives of people from the past, and fill your lessons with extraordinary stories about ordinary people.

RESOURCES AND FURTHER READING

Ashton, Rosemary. One Hot Summer: Dickens, Darwin, Disraeli, and the Great Stink of 1858. New Haven and London: Yale University Press 2017: 8.

Bates, Stephen. 'History teachers who tamper with the past' in *Daily Mail*, 3 January 1989.

Benger, Alexander. 'Teaching Year 9 to Argue Like Cultural Historians: Recasting the Concept of Empathy as Historical perspective' in Teaching History, 179, Culture in Conversation Edition, (2020): 24–35. London: Historical Association.

Boyd, Julia, & Patel, Angelika. A Village in the Third Reich: How Ordinary Lives Were Transformed by the Rise of Fascism. New York and London: Pegasus Books 2023.

Burke, Peter. What Is Cultural History? Cambridge: Polity Press 2013: 3.

Carr, Elizabeth. 'How Victorian Were the Victorians? Developing Year 8 Students' Conceptual Thinking About Diversity in Victorian Society' in Teaching History, 146, Teacher Knowledge Edition, (2012): 9–17. London: Historical Association.

Chase, Malcolm. Chartism: A New History. Manchester: Manchester University Press 2007: 261, 270.

Counsell, Christine. 'Cunning Plan: The Generalisation Game - Challenging Generalisations' in Teaching History, 135, To They or Not to They Edition, (2009): 13–15. London: Historical Association.

Foster, Rachel. 'A World Turned Molten: Helping Year 9 to Explore the Cultural Legacies of the First World War' in Teaching History, 155, Teaching about the First World War Edition, (2014): 8–19. London: Historical Association.

Elsdon, Kathryn, & Howard, Hannah. 'Triumphs Show: Spicing It up: Using Material Culture as a Means to Generate an Enquiry on the British Empire' in Teaching History, 176, Widening Vistas Edition, (2019): 44–47. London: Historical Association.

Husbands, Chris. What Is History Teaching?: Language, Ideas, and Meaning in Learning About the Past. Buckingham and Philadelphia: Open University Press 1996: 60.

Jackson-Buckley, Sarah. 'What Did It Mean to Belong in Mill Road 1962–1988?' [Teaching Unit], Historical Association Teacher Fellowship Programme (2021–22). https://www.history.org.uk/secondary/categories/872/module/8741/teacher-fellowship-programme-local-history/11682/what-did-it-mean-to-belong-in-mill-road-19621988

Keating, Jenny, & Sheldon, Nicola. 'Interview with Denis Shemilt, 3 July 2009' [Spoken Interview], History in Education Project, (2011). https://archives.history.ac.uk/history-in-education/browse/interviews/interview-denis-shemilt-3-july-2009.html

Lee, Peter, & Shemilt, Denis. 'The Concept That Dares Not Speak Its Name: Should Empathy Come Out of the Closet?' in Teaching History, 143, Constructing Claims Edition, (2011): 39–49. London: Historical Association.

Luff, Ian. "I've Been in the Reichstag': Rethinking roleplay' in Teaching History, 100, Thinking and Feeling Edition, (2000). London: Historical Association.

Olivey, Jacob. 'What Did 'class' Mean to a Chartist? Teaching Year 8 Pupils to Take Seriously the Ideas of Ordinary People from the past' in Teaching History, 176, Widening Vistas Edition, (2019): 60–71. London: Historical Association.

Philips, Jessica. "Alluringly Strange, Discomfortingly familiar': Using the Present to Construct a Meaningful Picture of the Medieval past' in Teaching History, 188, Representing History Edition, (2022): 66–75. London: Historical Association.

Pickering, Paul A. 'Class Without Words: Symbolic Communication in the Chartist movement' in Past & Present, 112(1), (1986): 144–162.

Rediker, Marcus. 'Reflections on History from Below' in Trashumante Revista Americana De Historia Social, 20, (2022): 296–299. Medellín: Universidad de Antioquia.

Reynolds, David. 'International History, the Cultural Turn and the Diplomatic Twitch' in Cultural and Social History, 3(1), (2006): 75–91.

Rubin, Miri. 'What Is Cultural History now' in Cannadine, David (ed.). What Is History Now?. Basingstoke: Palgrave Macmillan 2002: 81.

Seixas, Peter, & Morton, Tom. The Big Six: Historical Thinking Concepts. Nelson Education 2013: 10–11.

Simkin, John. Modern World History Evidence and Empathy: Hitler's Germany. Brighton: Spartacus Educational 1986.

Sylvester, David (ed.). A New Look at History, Schools Council History 13 - 16 Project. Edinburgh: Holmes McDougall 1976.

The Editorial Board. 'What's the Wisdom On…Similarity and difference' in Teaching History, 180, How History Works Edition, (2020): 52–56. London: Historical Association.

Thompson, E. P. The Making of the English Working Class. London: Penguin 1991: 12.

Chapter 9 Interpretations

Dan Keates

BACKGROUND

Historical interpretations is the study of how and why the past has been constructed by others, and the processes by which this happens. When we refer to interpretations, we are referring to the material output created after the events being studied. This material is always created to show aspects of the past in a particular way and always involves an element of selection and omission. Thus, we are really working to get to the heart of how history is constructed. In the UCL publication *Knowing History in Schools*, Harris (2021) makes the case that 'students need to understand that the past is a construct, and so should appreciate the process by which our understanding of the past is put together'. In some ways, interpretations lie at the heart of the study of the discipline of history, as the majority of our study of the past is reliant on the interpretations of others. Chapman (2017) states that 'there is no alternative to studying historical interpretation, if we want to help pupils think reflectively and critically about a key dimension of their humanity, and about the ubiquitous and often competing history stories and memory practices that clamour for attention in the present'. If we accept Chapman's assertion that we are teaching an understanding of the process of history, not just history itself, then the real question is not whether to study interpretations, but how well we do it.

WHAT IS THE STUDY OF HISTORICAL INTERPRETATIONS?

Historical interpretations can frequently mean understanding the arguments of historians. However, we must remember that claims about the past also come in other forms. This includes films, children's books, museum exhibits, TV adverts, computer games, paintings and music, to mention a handful. These are all rich seams to mine in our study of interpretations. They can help to build the understanding in young people that the past is always with us and we have to pay close attention to the choices and selections made in presenting it. A more comprehensive list of interpretations is provided in Figure 9.1, originally developed by McAleavy (1993) in his influential article on interpretations, and then added to and developed by subsequent history teachers and educators. It broadens out the sense of where we might look for representations of the past to use in the classroom.

A selection of interpretation types commonly examined by history teachers between 1991 and 2004	
Academic • Books, journals, papers by professional historians • Scholarly lectures • Excavation reports	**Fictional/semi-fictional** • Novels, paintings, plays • Films • TV drama/comedy
Educational • Textbooks • Museums and sites • Reconstructions • TV documentaries/news • CDs, websites, Internet discussions, podcasts, blogs	**Popular and/or political** • Folk wisdom/ personal reflection • Theme parks/souvenirs • Paintings of earlier periods • Monuments/ceremonies/protests • Advertising • Websites, magazines • Political speeches or arguments that invoke the past in some way

Figure 9.1 A selection of interpretations, taken from 'What's the Wisdom On ... Interpretations of the past?' in Teaching History, 177, and based on the 2004 HMI Conference on interpretations, Bristol.

While many history teachers have always taught pupils about interpretations of the past, particularly those teachers connected to the Schools History Project, the entitlement of historical interpretations first appeared officially in the National Curriculum 1991. This was then built upon by the work of McAleavy (1993), where he makes the case for the study of how 'events have subsequently been presented', crucially cementing the place of interpretations in history teaching in England. This work has been developed over time by history teachers and educators, and the National Curriculum of 2013 laid out that pupils had to 'understand the methods of historical enquiry, including how evidence is used rigorously to make historical claims, and discern how and why contrasting arguments and interpretations of the past have been constructed'. It seems the study of historical interpretations is here to stay, but it is easy to miss the mark in the classroom when we are attempting to teach pupils in this area.

WHAT ISN'T THE STUDY OF HISTORICAL INTERPRETATIONS?

First, it is important to recognise that the study of historical interpretations is not asking pupils to produce their own interpretations. While this may be a valid classroom activity, it is distinct from the curricular entitlement of interpretations. Enquiry questions like, 'Was Haig really the "Butcher of the Somme"?' and 'Was Cromwell a hero or a villain?' fail to engage pupils with the how and why of interpretation construction. As I hope to demonstrate, the study of interpretations in the classroom can be fascinating for pupils, and immensely valuable for them to really look behind the curtain of how events in the past are being presented. This may be by working through enquiry questions, as laid out by Riley (2000) all those years ago, or it may be interpretations are woven throughout an enquiry that has a different overall focus.

Second, and connected to the first point, the study of historical interpretations is asking pupils to analyse and understand interpretations, where they have come from and how and why they have been constructed. There is important work to be done weighing the relative merit of different claims, particularly if those claims are created to further the historical argument. However, many popular interpretations have different intentions: to entertain or advertise. As such interpretations work here would not usefully ask pupils to evaluate the interpretations or judge them for accuracy. This may be part of understanding the choices which have been made in the construction, but it is not the main objective of an interpretations enquiry: to judge accuracy or validity of material which does not have accuracy or validity as the primary concern of its creator. Spotting anachronisms in *Horrible Histories* does little to help build an understanding of how the past has been constructed. Considering which information has been selected and the choices that have been made in the construction, and the reasons for those choices, does more to build this understanding.

Third, although closely related, the study of historical interpretations is distinct from the study of historical significance. In Chapter 10, Snelson outlines the difference between these two historical concepts. While significance is concerned with the meaning attributed by people to events in the past, the study of historical interpretations is focused on the **material outcomes** of that meaning. As Card (2023) illustrates so well in her article discussing the relationship between the two concepts, 'events considered "significant" form the raw material or building blocks for the construction of "historical interpretations"'. Interpretations are created about events and people that are considered to be significant. Clearly, the two concepts are closely connected, but the role of the history educator is to hold this distinction in mind when constructing enquiries and activities for pupils to engage with. For example, the poet T.S. Eliot (1935) considered the story of the murder of Thomas Becket in 1170 to be particularly significant in the febrile atmosphere of the 1930s: the story of one man standing up against tyranny. The interpretation he created, *Murder in the Cathedral*, is the material outcome of that. A significance enquiry, 'Why is Thomas Becket so significant?' would chart his changing significance over time, and the ways in which his story has resonated with others. Through the lessons of the enquiry, many interpretations could be studied, as a means to explore Becket's significance at different moments in time. By contrast, an interpretations enquiry would place the emphasis on the construction of certain interpretations and might ask why T.S. Eliot, writing in 1935, portrayed Becket as he did in *Murder in the Cathedral* or why Becket has been portrayed in different ways at different times. Both could be valid forms of study, but a teacher needs to be aware of what conceptual lens they are asking pupils to employ.

HAZARDS AROUND TEACHING HISTORICAL INTERPRETATIONS

Many history teachers have written about the hazards and pitfalls that can occur along the way to constructing successful interpretations enquiries. As Coffin (2009) has argued, working critically with historical interpretations to unpick them and understand their construction is not a skill which is 'easily and naturally acquired in everyday interaction'. The good news is that we can learn from these lessons to ensure we don't make the same mistakes.

Hazard One: Challenging Texts

As historical interpretations have made their way increasingly into exam specifications, it is good to bear in mind that when delivered as brief quotes out of context, or without adequate time and preparation, work can fall flat. Lee and Shemilt (2004) laid out many of the misconceptions and misunderstandings which can develop in pupils' understanding of historical accounts. At times the interpretations in front of pupils can contain complex or unfamiliar language. However, this is not a

Vocabulary
Most academic texts are likely to include a significant amount of unfamiliar Tier 3 vocabulary (subject-specific words). Challenging texts are also rich in Tier 2 vocabulary (words which are uncommon in everyday, spoken language but often appear in academic texts), and pupils' security in this vocabulary greatly affects their ability to read texts. Pupils need to be familiar with most of this vocabulary if they are to get the gist of the text.

Background knowledge
Academic texts often assume a high level of 'background' knowledge. To understand what they are reading, pupils therefore need to already have a strong sense of period and rich contextual knowledge.

Form
Pupils need a secure understanding of the form/structures/conventions of a type of text.

Motivation
Pupils are more likely to persist with a challenging text if they have confidence in their own ability to read and a desire to read.

Figure 9.2 The main factors that influence pupils' experience of reading, taken from Jenner (2019).

reason to not expose pupils to challenging texts, as Carroll explains in Chapter 14 we have to try and create writers from readers. Jenner (2019) in his article *Making Reading Routine* shows how work with interpretations, especially the work of historians, needs to be carefully planned for to support pupils to overcome the linguistic hurdles. He identifies and explains the main factors that influence pupils' experience of reading, shown in Figure 9.2. Interpretations work requires careful planning to pre-empt potential difficulties to be encountered by pupils. In class it is best that interpretations containing complex language are read expertly aloud by the teacher. Space can be provided around the interpretation to explain context and vocabulary, as well as answer questions designed to guide pupil understanding. What has come to be known as **guided reading**, often with the use of a visualiser, can support and scaffold pupils to access challenging historical texts.

My own article on interpretations of Cromwell (Keates, 2020) detailed our department's journey to building an effective interpretations enquiry. In it we used the CV Wedgwood quote in Figure 9.3, taken from her 1973 book *Cromwell*. We had to refine and develop our approach over time to support pupils to engage with it successfully. Before pupils begin to understand why an interpretation has been created, they must have a firm understanding of what the message is.

> 'Yet the personality of Cromwell remains enigmatic and his reputation changes – as it will continue to change – with the moral and political climate of the living world.... His actions in crisis, whether on the battlefield, in Parliament or at the Council table, show a clear and bold judgement; but he was not good at analysing or presenting the reasons behind his actions. Prayer helped him towards all his considered decisions. In his years of power there is no evidence of any personal pleasure at his own greatness. Can this be taken as evidence that personal ambition was never a motive with him? I am inclined to think so. As Protector he appeared, in spite of his power at home and prestige abroad, a sad and heavily burdened man.'
>
> C.V. Wedgwood, *Oliver Cromwell*, 1973

Figure 9.3 Extract from C.V. Wedgwood's *Oliver Cromwell*, 1973, used in the classroom.

> **Activity 9.1**
>
> Look at the interpretation by C.V. Wedgwood.
>
> (a) Highlight all the vocabulary which pupils might find difficult to understand and consider how you would explain these words to pupils.
> (b) Detail the historical knowledge that is needed for pupils to understand what Wedgwood is referring to in each of these points:
>
>   i. '… whether on the battlefield …'
>   ii. '… in Parliament or at the Council table …'
>   iii. '… his power and prestige at home and abroad …'
>
> (c) Where does Wedgwood imply the historical evidence is not sufficient to form strong conclusions on Cromwell and his character?
> (d) What is the overall message of Wedgwood's argument in describing Cromwell as 'an enigma'?

Hazard Two: Insufficient Knowledge

Hammond (2014) shows the importance of secure knowledge of the past to support high-quality writing, and such knowledge also supports the reading of academic texts or interpretations. However, for an interpretation this often means knowledge of two periods. This can be a challenge for pupils as they are asked to hold an understanding of two historical periods in their heads at the same time. Card (2004) described this as 'seeing double'. Essentially this means recognising the importance of the historical context in which an interpretation has been produced and asking pupils to 'see double' as they engage with two historical periods at the same time to visualise both the period being depicted and the period of the interpreter. Thus, the study of an interpretation could usefully come not just after the period being interpreted but also after the period in which the interpretation has been created. For example, an enquiry question 'Why did Shakespeare write plays about the Medieval past?' would come on the curriculum after studying events in Medieval England and Tudor England (Snelson, 2019). The idea is that once pupils are secure in their knowledge of both periods, they can really get their teeth into the interpretations (Counsell, 2014). Often, under careful scrutiny, an interpretation may tell us more about the world of the creator than the history being depicted.

Getting this 'double vision' right requires careful thought. Smith (2016) recognises the difficulties of 'pupils juggling knowledge of the period being interpreted as well as the period in which the interpretation was constructed' but showcases his work in getting 'students to hypothesise about patterns in changing interpretations' of the First World War throughout the 20th century. One of his main conclusions is that studying changing interpretations has been shown to be a 'knowledge-rich pursuit'. This reinforces the conclusion that if pupils are to successfully engage with an interpretation of the past, they need to have deep and secure knowledge of both periods.

Hazard Three: Oversimplification

As we can see, history teachers have increasingly used interpretations to provide an insight into the trends and ideas of a period overall. This can clearly be a powerful way to support pupil understanding of changing views. Whether it is views of the Battle of Rorke's Drift as shown by Fullard and Wheeley (2011) or changing views of the First World War as shown by Smith (2016), these can all be excellent ways to support pupil understanding of how interpretations are created in a particular context, and how any view of the past is heavily influenced by events in the present.

There is a note of caution here, outlined by Howells (2005), as he urges us to be wary of giving pupils too simplistic a view of how and why historians construct interpretations. He asks some important questions about how we approach historians' interpretations in the classroom and shows we need to be careful not to oversimplify the past and so produce our own skewed interpretation. For example, he challenges us, 'Are we happy saying that the Victorians admired Cromwell? And if we are to say that what type of Victorians and for what reasons?' His antidote to this is to ensure we are careful in our approach, guiding pupils towards focused questions on specific interpretations like 'Why are popular historical views of Charles II so different from those of academic historians?' He recommends trying to keep a tight focus on one area of how and why specific interpretations of the past are formed, to minimise the risk of too much oversimplification. What this means is that while a certain amount of oversimplification is unavoidable, and probably even desirable in the history classroom to make sense of the past, we can mitigate against spreading misinformation by focusing our enquiries on specific interpretations rather than using one to represent a whole period.

PRINCIPLES OF TEACHING INTERPRETATIONS

Thankfully, the work of history teachers helps us not only avoid some of the hazards in the teaching of historical interpretations but also develop some principles for their effective teaching in the history classroom.

Subsequentness

By definition an interpretation is something that has been produced subsequent to the period under study. It is important for pupils to see this 'subsequentness' and thus a study of the Bayeux Tapestry as an interpretation of the Battle of Hastings may cause confusion as it was created so close to the events being studied. However, Marc Morris (2013) and Simon Schama (2009) have crafted their interpretations of the Norman Conquest; the language used, detail selected and omitted, and the overall tone would certainly meet the criteria of subsequentness first described by McAleavy (1993).

Changing Interpretations

There have been some much-loved textbooks which have featured activities to support pupils' understanding of how and why interpretations have changed over time. The two main examples would be the Hodder *King Cromwell?* book (Dawson and Harmsworth, 2002) and the King John textbook (Banham and Dawson, 2000). In both books, this aspect of the enquiry comes towards the end once pupils are fully conversant with the lives of these two figures. We have already looked at the challenges of teaching pupils to 'see double'. Carroll (2017) tackles this issue as he plans for his A Level pupils to write about changing interpretations of Nazi Germany. He shows how subject knowledge is vitally important to place interpretations in context and these need to be organised within a chronological framework over time, thus moving from Card's 'double vision' to a panoramic view of events between the original event and the subsequent interpretations. Carroll talks about how his pupils needed to understand the 'event space' between the event being interpreted and the context of the interpreter. The example he gives is Victorian historian James Froude's writing about Mary I. In conversation with his mentor, he realises the obstacle his pupils had to understanding the interpretation was the broad knowledge that he himself had, but had taken for granted: 'I had grossly underestimated the importance of my own internalised knowledge of developments in Catholic-Protestant relations in England post-1558, and how these pertained to my understanding of Froude's interpretation of Mary'. It is good for us as teachers to remember this in our teaching; everything in between has helped to shape the subsequent interpretation, and at times we might forget how this could prove an additional obstacle to pupil understanding.

RANGE OF INTERPRETATIONS

Interpretations can take many forms, and much of this chapter so far has been discussing the work of historians. Looking again at Figure 9.1, we can see that a broader appreciation of this area could prove fruitful in the classroom. The following section provides a series of examples.

Museum Exhibits

The choices that are made in museums to select, design and present exhibits is valuable work to do with pupils. Wrenn (1999) designed an enquiry to support Year 9 pupils to not just understand the slavery exhibition in the Bristol City Museum as an interpretation but also the responses of the visitors themselves as interpretations of the past. This enquiry feels more relevant than ever to the lives of children in schools in England, as debates continue to rage in the public sphere over how Britain should remember its role in the Transatlantic Slave Trade.

Children's Books

The ever-growing market of children's books dealing with history provides an opportunity to the history teacher. Fordham (2014) shows the potential benefits of using both academic and non-academic interpretations with pupils. The enquiry he lays out looks at using the Dr Seuss book *The Butter Battle* as an interpretation of the Cold War. He is clear about the pitfalls of pupils taking children's books as accurate accounts and not recognising the simplifications, but clearly this is central to the role of any analysis of an interpretation. Second, he recognises that as this book was produced in 1984, we have to be aware that it might not be as subsequent to the events of the Cold War as we would want for some of our interpretations. However, the study of children's books as a way into interpretations is a potentially powerful tool in the classroom. The Ladybird Adventures from History books are an excellent way to engage pupils in this kind of analysis. They provide a clearly accessible interpretation of people and events in the past, often full of loaded language or choosing to embellish or omit certain details. The Cromwell enquiry mentioned previously compares the Laydbird book on Cromwell (Peach, 1963) with the Wedgwood interpretation (1973) and the Pogues song *Ned of the Hill*. The key here is a comparison of the intended audience, purpose and context in which the interpretation was created. This is all part of helping pupils to understand how and why the past is constructed.

Films

Extracts from films have provided excellent interpretations of the past for history teachers over the years. Whether this is the Battle of Rorke's Drift in *Zulu*, the execution of Charles I in *Cromwell* or the depiction of Wilberforce's contribution to the abolition of slavery in *Amazing Grace*. Banham and Hall (2003) unpack some strategies to analyse films as interpretations, focusing on the Oliver Stone film *JFK*. They show how we can work 'to encourage pupils to think about films at a deeper level and to apply the same critical thinking to a film as they would a written text'. The first thing to remember when showing any age-appropriate clip to pupils in the classroom is to have them thinking about the intended audience, purpose and context of the creator. The opening sequence of the *Cromwell* film has always been a powerful way to get pupils to think about what kind of man the director is trying to introduce the audience to.

Paintings

While historic paintings can seem to provide a powerful and accessible interpretation of the past, they must still be decoded and understood in detail. A spotlight can be a useful way to do this, blacking out much of the image to draw pupil attention to one small detail. This can be used as a 'hook' or lesson starter to build interest through mystery. Card (2004) shows how the portrait of Lady Jane Grey can be used to understand Victorian attitudes to religion and monarchy in the nineteenth century just as much as the sixteenth.

Historical Reconstructions

Historical reconstructions are detailed drawings or paintings which aim to inform and show a particular place, aspect or event in the past. They are often informed by the work of historians and archaeologists. Snelson (2019) shows how one particularly powerful activity might be to place a picture of an archaeological excavation alongside a historical reconstruction. This could be done on Sutton Hoo, which has inspired many historical reconstructions, which a quick search online can unearth (no pun intended). An activity like this can be an accessible way for all pupils to build an understanding of the relationship between evidence and interpretations.

Documentaries

While many history documentaries are invaluable sources of information, they can, and should at times, be analysed as interpretations themselves. One example of this might be the opening of the *Empire* series by Niall Ferguson (2016) charting the evolution of the British Empire. The episodes are available online, and in the opening episode his narration provides a summary of his positive interpretation of the British Empire and its legacy.

> Nowadays of course the phrase 'British Empire' conjures up images of chaps with stiff upper lips and pith helmets being waited on hand and foot by poor exploited natives. At best it's around a corny joke, at worst it's something we should say a collective sorry for. The Empire's sins tend to be better remembered than its achievements. Yet traveling the world today you keep on encountering the living legacies of Britain's age of empire. It was British traders who united the world in a single capitalist economy, while British migration changed the

face of whole continents. Protestant Christianity spread from Clapham to Cape Town. English became the world language. Western norms of law, order and government were exported - and parliamentary democracy became the yardstick by which all political systems are judged. These are the pillars of the modern world and if you like the modern world, you can't deny its debt to the British Empire.

Empire: How Britain Made the Modern World, Niall Ferguson, 2016

Activity 9.2

Look at the interpretation by Niall Ferguson.

(a) List how many achievements Niall Ferguson attributes to the legacy of the British Empire.
(b) Highlight where he implies he is responding to the interpretations of others.
(c) How does the purpose of the interpretation dictate the selection of information?
(d) What has Ferguson omitted from his interpretation and why?

Graphic Novels

Turner and Chapman (2023) show how pupils can be taken inside the process of creating an interpretation. They ask the pupils to engage with the process by which the graphic novel Peterloo Massacre was created. The questions they provided in their Teaching History article provide a useful framework for helping pupils think about other similar interpretations.

- From what perspective/s is the story told (and what perspectives are not present)? [Perspective]
- What does the story-telling focus on in detail (and what does it not focus on)? [Focus]
- What aspects of the story are told in detail (as it were, in 'real time')? [Scene]
- What aspects are cut, skimmed over or narrated in outline only? [Summary]

INTERPRETATION ENQUIRIES

Part of the role of interpretations within the history curriculum is to educate pupils in the idea of history as a living subject, constructed by others and shifting with the moods of the time, part of a conversation between historians and public memory. The power here lies in the reality that this conversation is not just between stuffy old academics (although plenty are neither old nor stuffy!) but exists in the public realm as well, within communities and their shared histories, and myths.

There are lots of questions that can be asked about historical interpretations in the classroom. It is worth starting by stating that while interpretations can be the main focus of an enquiry, they also can and should weave throughout our lessons and enquiries which are mainly focused on other historical concepts. We have already looked at how interpretations are crucial to a significance enquiry on Becket or can form part of an enquiry into change and continuity. Figure 9.4 organises some possible question stems, for not just writing and planning enquiry questions, but the kind of questions we can ask on interpretations in the classroom. This can also help us to

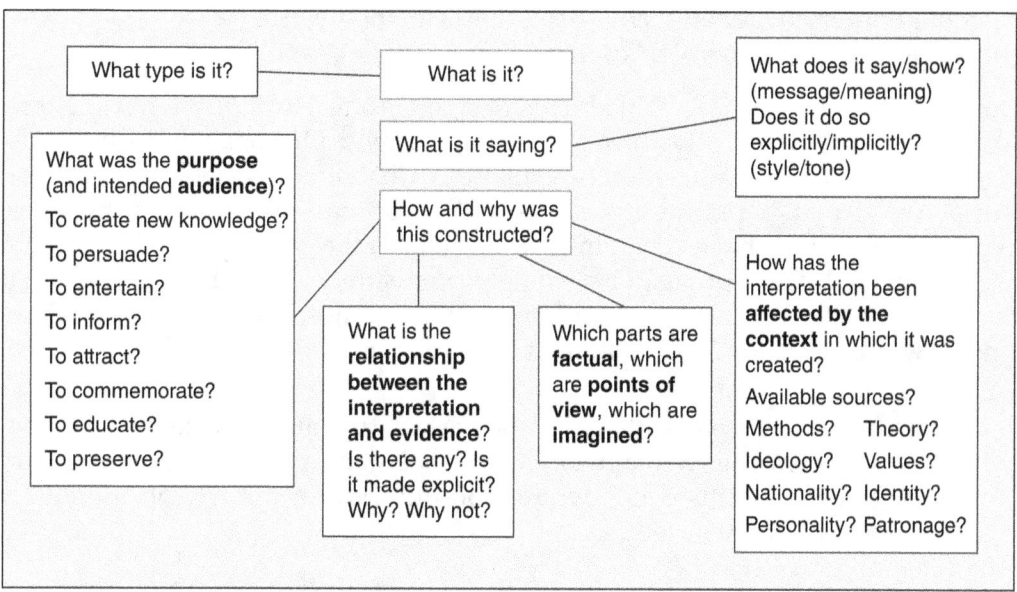

Figure 9.4 A guide to shaping questions in the study of interpretations, taken from 'What's the Wisdom On … Interpretations of the past?' in Teaching History, 177, and based on the 2004 HMI Conference on interpretations, Bristol.

think about a broad, but not rigid, hierarchy of thinking around interpretations. It is important for pupils to think about the type of interpretation first. Is it a film? Is it the work of a historian, and so making claims about accuracy and truth? Is it a painting, and perhaps trying to invoke an emotional response in the viewer? All of this then has a bearing on our understanding of what it says. What is the overall message, and is this communicated explicitly and clearly or is there a more subtle approach? Finally, we might guide pupils to think about why these decisions have been made, and the context in which the interpretation was produced. Crucially, this includes thinking carefully about the relationship to the evidence.

Relationship Between Evidence and Interpretation

Ford describes in Chapter 11 how we can think of historical evidence as 'traces of the past'. Interpretations are using those traces, directly or indirectly, as well as explicitly and implicitly. Pupils can be supported to think deeply about the evidence being used in the construction of a particular interpretation. This includes what has and what has not been selected to include, the order in which the evidence has been structured to tell a particular story, the way the evidence is made clear and equally where the creator is transparent about the absence of evidence or areas of uncertainty. Often it may be historians who are more confident and able to embrace uncertainty, while interpretations for other audiences will usually be inclined to smooth over these areas to cater for a particular audience or purpose. Hibbert and Patel (2019) show how this approach can be used with pupils in their article on their enquiry question *'How does the historian Yasmin Khan use evidence to reach conclusions about experiences of the Second World War?'* By recording Khan and integrating her explanation of her process into their lessons, they attempt to give pupils an 'explicit model of how an historian works'. They conclude that teachers need to 'consider evidential thinking and historical interpretations in a holistic and interconnected way', showing how pupils need to be introduced to different models of historical methodologies.

Example Enquiry: How and Why Did David Olusoga Write about the 'Forgotten Armies' of World War I?

The following enquiry (see Table 9.1) is designed to teach pupils about the First World War, but specifically through historian David Olusoga's 2014 book *The World's War*. As Lyndon and Garry explain in Chapter 12, school history has a crucial role to play in putting the voices of the marginalised back into the narrative from which they have been omitted. The aim of the enquiry is ambitious and relevant to the lives of pupils. First, to help pupils understand **how** Olusoga has created his work, selected, used and arranged evidence. Second, to think about **why** he wrote **this** book in 2014. In the words of Olusoga:

> More words have been written over the past century about the few dozen middle class officers who wrote their war memoirs and penned their war poetry than about the 4 million non-white, non-European soldiers who fought for Britain, France and their allies.

Table 9.1 An interpretations enquiry on the First World War

Lesson	Lesson Title	Lesson Summary
1	How did two shots in 1914 trigger a World War?	The first two lessons are asking pupils to engage with the causes of the war and the different sides in 1914. This is important background knowledge for not just this unit, but later learning on the rise of Hitler.
2	Who was most responsible for the outbreak of World War I?	
3.	A traditional interpretation of World War I	If pupils are to understand why Olusoga has created his work, they need to be introduced to the idea of history as a conversation. Olusoga sees his own book as a **response** to the work of previous historians so pupils need a simplified grasp of what he is responding to.
4.	Why did David Olusoga write about the Forgotten Armies?	In this lesson, pupils engage with the **purpose** and **context** in which Olusoga created his book.
5.	How does David Olusoga use evidence to write about the Forgotten Indian Army?	In these lessons, pupils engage directly with Olusoga's writing on the Indian and Algerian armies. They think about the stories he has chosen to show and some of the evidence he may have used.
6.	How does David Olusoga write about the Forgotten Algerian Army?	
7.	How might David Olusoga write about the Forgotten Native Canadian Army?	In this lesson, pupils are given the evidence that Olusoga may have used to tell the story of Mike Mountain Horse. Here they have the opportunity to imitate how Olusoga has written about this story. This is distinct from asking pupils to produce their own 'free-floating' interpretations, as pupils instead work in the style of Olusoga in order to understand his methods and approach.
8.	Assessment preparation	The assessment brings pupils back to the original enquiry question and asks them to write about *How and why did David Olusoga write about the 'Forgotten Armies' of World War I?*

SUMMARY OF KEY POINTS

- The study of historical interpretations is not asking pupils to produce their own 'free-floating' interpretations.
- The study of historical interpretations is asking pupils to analyse and understand interpretations, where they have come from and how and why they have been constructed.
- The study of historical interpretations is distinct, although closely related to the study of historical significance.
- Use challenging texts and the work of historians in sufficient length, in context and with plenty of support and preparation for pupils.
- Working with historical interpretations is asking pupils to 'see double' and requires sufficient historical knowledge of both the period being interpreted and the period the interpretation was created in.
- Be wary of oversimplifying historical interpretations or claiming they speak for the views of everyone at a particular time. Focusing enquiries on specific interpretations rather than using one interpretation to represent a whole period can mitigate against this.
- Vary the range of different types of interpretations in the classroom, not just academic ones, to show pupils how the past is always being used to make points in the present.

RESOURCES AND FURTHER READING

Banham, Dale, & Dawson, Ian. This Is History! King John: A Key Stage 3 Investigation into Medieval Monarchy. London: Hodder Education 2000.

Byrom, Jamie, Counsell, Christine, & Riley, Michael. 'Interpretations of History' [Paper Presentation], HMI Conference on Interpretations, Bristol, (2004).

Card, Jane. 'Seeing Double: How One Period Visualises another' in Teaching History, 117, Dealing with Distance Edition, (2004): 6–11. London: Historical Association.

Card, Jane. 'Should We Choose It and How can We Use It? Exploring the Relationship between Historical Significance and Historical interpretation' in Teaching History, 190, Ascribing Significance Edition, (2023): 31–43. London: Historical Association.

Carroll, James Edward. 'From 'double vision' to Panorama: Using History of Memory to Bridge 'event space' When Exploring Interpretations of Nazi Popularity With Year 13' in Teaching History 168, Re-examining History edition, (2017): 24–36. London: Historical Association.

Chapman, Arthur. 'Historical Interpretations' in Davies, Ian (ed.). Debates in History Teaching. London: Routledge 2017: 100–112.

Coffin, Caroline. Historical Discourse: the language of time, cause and evaluation. Continuum 2009: 167.

Counsell, Christine. 'On being guardians of an 's': who will polish and protect the curriculum jewel of interpretation(s) plural?' [Paper Presentation], Schools History Project Conference, (2014).

Dawson, Ian, & Harmsworth, Andy. This Is History! 'King' Cromwell? A Key Stage 3 Depth Study. London: Hodder Education 2002.

Department for Education. History Programmes of Study: Key Stage 3, National Curriculum in England. 2013: 1. It is also available here: https://assets.publishing.service.gov.uk/media/5a7c66d740f0b626628abcdd/SECONDARY_national_curriculum_-_History.pdf

Eliot, T. S. Murder in the Cathedral. London: Faber and Faber 1935.

Ferguson, Niall. Empire: How Britain Made the Modern World [TV Documentary], (2016).

Fordham, Michael. "'But Why Then?' Chronological Context and Historical interpretations' in Teaching History, 156, Chronology Edition, (2014): 32–39. London: Historical Association.

Banham, Dale, & Hall, Russell. 'JFK: the Medium, the Message and the myth' in Teaching History, 113, Creating Progress Edition, (2003): 6–12. London: Historical Association.

Hammond, Kate. 'The Knowledge That "flavours" a Claim: Towards Building and Assessing Historical Knowledge on Three scales' in Teaching History, 157, Assessment Edition, (2014): 18–25. London: Historical Association.

Harris, Richard. 'Disciplinary Knowledge Denied' in Chapman, Arthur (ed.). Knowing History in Schools. London: UCL Press 2021: 123.

Hibbert, David, & Patel, Zaiba. 'Modelling the Discipline: How can Yasmin Khan's Use of Evidence Enable Us to Teach a More Global World War II?' in Teaching History, 177, Building Knowledge Edition, (2019): 8–15. London: Historical Association.

Howells, Gary. 'Interpretations and History Teaching: Why Ronald Hutton's Debates in Stuart History matters' in Teaching History, 121, Transitions Edition, (2005): 29–35. London: Historical Association.

Jenner, Tim. 'Making reading Routine: Helping Key Stage 3 Pupils to Become Regular Readers of Historical scholarship' in Teaching History, 174, Structure Edition, (2019): 42–49. London: Historical Association.

Keates, Dan. 'Unpicking the Threads of Interpretations: Tangling up Year 8 in the Messy World of Views on Oliver Cromwell' in Teaching History 179, Culture in Conversation Edition, (2020): 36–43. London: Historical Association.

McAleavy, Tony. 'Using the Attainment Targets in Key Stage 3: AT2, 'Interpretations of History' in Teaching History, 72, (1993): 14–17. London: Historical Association.

Morris, Marc. The Norman Conquest. London: Windmill Books 2013.

Olusoga, David. The World's War: Forgotten Soldiers of Empire. London: Head of Zeus 2014.

Peach, L. du Garde. Oliver Cromwell: An Adventure from History, (A Ladybird Book 561). Loughborough: Wills and Hepworth (1963).

Riley, Michael. 'Into the Key Stage 3 History Garden: Choosing and Planting Your Enquiry questions' in Teaching History, 99, Curriculum Planning Edition, (2000): 8–13. London: Historical Association.

Schama, Simon. A History of Britain: At the Edge of the World? 3000BC-AD1603. London: The Bodley Head 2009.

Lee, Peter, & Shemilt, Dennis. 'I Just Wish We Could Go Back in the Past and Find Out What Really happened': Progression in Understanding About Historical accounts' in Teaching History, 117, Dealing with Distance Edition, (2004): 25–31. London: Historical Association.

Smith, Dan. 'How One Period Casts Shadows on Another: Exploring Year 8 Encounters With Multiple Interpretations of the First World War' in Teaching History, 162, Scales of Planning Edition, (2016): 46–55. London: Historical Association.

Snelson, Helen. 'Historical Interpretations CPD' [Paper Presentation], Historical Association Conference, (2019).

The Editorial Board. 'What's the Wisdom On... Interpretations of the Past?' in Teaching History, 177, Building Knowledge Edition, (2019): 23–27. London: Historical Association.

Turner, Jen, & Chapman, Arthur. "'It Does Duty for Any Amount of mayhem': Helping Year 8 to Understand historians' Narrative Decision-making' in Teaching History, 190, Ascribing Significance Edition, (2023): 80–91. London: Historical Association.

Wedgwood, C. V. Oliver Cromwell. London: Duckworth 1973.

Fullard, Giles, & Wheeley, Tom. 'Cunning Plan: Why Do Historical Interpretations Change Over Time?' in Teaching History, 142, Experiencing History Edition, (2011): 48–49. London: Historical Association.

Wrenn, Andrew. 'Substantial Sculptures or Sad Little Plaques? Making 'interpretations' Matter to Year 9' in Teaching History, 97, Visual History Edition (1999): 21–28. London: Historical Association.

Chapter 10   Historical Significance

Helen Snelson

BACKGROUND

Historical significance has been described as a meta-concept (Hunt, 2000). Indeed, as Keith Barton asserts 'All historical research and all historical education depends on some conception of significance' (Barton, 2005). That is, something integral to all history teaching, something that permeates all we do in the history classroom. It shapes what we teach. Whether or not we acknowledge it and make it explicit, everything we teach has involved a choice. A choice that someone has made, more or less consciously, about what is historically significant enough for young people to learn. By implication, choices have also been made about what from the past is not thought to be significant enough to make it onto the school history curriculum. The same can be said, of course, about other choices about the past: which aspects of the past an academic historian chooses to study, what parts of the historic environment are preserved, the focus chosen for history documentaries and podcasts, and the selections made for political speeches. Decisions about historical significance shape all of these choices.

The way we teach can maintain a silence over these choices. But teaching historical significance as a disciplinary concept in the history classroom involves making the choices, and the process of choosing, explicit. That is, making clear the choices that create school history curricula and the choices that shape the parts of the past that we choose to research and remember. It also involves investigating who makes the choices, using what criteria and how they are influenced by wider ideas and beliefs in society. What we regard as historically significant is shaped by where we are geographically located, by the groups with whom we identify and by the time periods in which we live. Making this explicit in the history classroom is both exciting and challenging: exciting because it is enabling pupils to take part in big conversations that shape society; challenging because it takes us into contested territory. Human beings dispute what is and what is not historically significant (Barton, 2005). They also dispute how particular things are judged to be historically significant.

This chapter will consider how historical significance at school history level is defined. It will discuss what we are trying to achieve when teaching about historical significance, the ethical dimension, the pupil perspective, the blocks to learning we may encounter and what progress may look like. The second part will suggest how enquiry questions, teacher talk and pupil activities can be used to secure progress in pupils' knowledge and understanding of the concept.

> **Activity 10.1**
>
> Snelson claims that historical significance is a 'meta-concept'. What does she mean by this?

A WORKING DEFINITION

Historical significance first became a curricular entitlement for Key Stage 3 pupils in England when it was written into the 1995 revision of the National Curriculum. Pupils were 'to consider the significance of the main events, people and changes studied'. The concept has also developed as part of history teaching in schools in other parts of the world. For example, as part of the Canadian Historical Thinking Project written about by Peter Seixas and Tom Morton (2013), who identify historical significance as one of six historical thinking concepts. But what is meant by the phrase?

Over the course of the last thirty years, the concept has been practically theorised in different educational settings. History teachers, history teacher educators and history education researchers have debated and developed its meaning and how pupils reason with it. They continue to do so. While there are many points of agreement, including that it is a complex and tricky concept (Worth 2023), there are also divergences. For example, Terry Haydn (2022) seems to take a broader definition of historical significance than Counsell (2004). However, *Teaching History's* 'What's the Wisdom on Historical Significance?' (2020) is a good place to start for a summary of the thinking in the context of the history curriculum in England. Beyond England, there has been a greater focus on what pupils themselves regard as historically significant (Barton, 2005), and this point will be developed further in a later section. Wide reading about the concept and people's thinking about it is recommended in order to join the debate, as is an appreciation that definitions of disciplinary concepts are not fixed and uncontestable. What is given here is a working definition of something that is not easily distilled into simple soundbites.

Historical significance, as defined for school history, is about what gets remembered and valued from the past by, for example, communities, nations and historians. This is not to say that historical significance can only be found in the stories of world-changing events and people. 'A historical person or event can acquire significance if we, the historians, can link it to larger trends and stories that reveal something important for us today' (The Historical Thinking Project). That is, if societal meaning can be made from it. Understanding the concept of historical significance therefore involves curiosity about the questions that are asked, and about how people imagine the past in order to make meaning from it.

If historical significance is concerned with what gets remembered and valued, it is also concerned with what gets ignored or forgotten and the questions that remain unasked. Pupils therefore need to learn about the process of forgetting as well as that of remembering. That is, why and how both happen and with what results.

What is regarded as historically significant varies within a time period and over time. That is, an event may be regarded as more or less historically significant in different places and at different times. Historical significance is something that is attributed to the past by people who came later. It is also possible that a person or event may continue to be regarded as historically significant, but for different reasons. For example, in England Guy Fawkes, the Gunpowder Plotter arrested at the House of Commons in 1605, was historically significant in the 18th century as part of an anti-Catholicism narrative but in our own times is written about in the context of terrorism (Pearson, 2022).

In school history a distinction is drawn between personal significance and historical significance. That is, a pupil's grandfather might be significant to the story of their family's past and therefore of personal significance to the pupil, but this is not what is meant by historical significance. Historical significance, as conceptualised in school history, requires that a person or event has a broader salience for a society's understanding of the past.

Activity 10.2

Try and make a list of historical events that represent the different ways in which things can be seen as historically significant from the discussion above.

- Something remembered and valued from the past by a nation;
- Something remembered and valued from the past by a community;
- Something remembered and valued by historians;
- Something that is (frequently) ignored or forgotten;
- Something whose significance has endured over time;
- Something whose significance has changed over time;
- Something that can 'link to larger trends and stories that reveal something important for us today'.

IMPLICATIONS FOR THE CLASSROOM

History teachers need to read and think about the concept before they can plan for learning about historical significance in their history classrooms.

Lomas (1990) wrote for the Historical Association about the thinking that pupils need to do in relation to historical significance. His ideas make clear that attribution of historical significance is problematic and has movement. It is never simple or fixed. His list (cited in Counsell, 2004) remains a useful guide for teachers as to what pupils need to be able to do if they are to identify the attribution of historical significance at work and to make their own judgements about what should be regarded as historically significant.

1. To understand that history operates on the basis that some events are more important than others.
2. To establish criteria for assessing the significance of events, people and issues in the past.
3. To understand that some events, which may have seemed significant at the time, were not, while the significance of other events is only recognised later.
4. To understand that different people will have different ideas about which people, events, changes and issues are significant.

5. To be able to understand why people may hold different ideas about what has been significant.
6. To understand that the significance of an event is determined by the nature of the historical enquiry.
7. To understand that relatively minor events can be highly significant (e.g. they have symbolic significance).
8. To be able to distinguish between the consequences of an event and its significance.
9. To understand that an event or change usually becomes significant because of its connection with other events.

The study of the attribution of historical significance is as much about the society, group or person doing the attributing as it is about the event or person itself. Counsell (2017) makes the point that pupils' work with the concept of historical significance rapidly becomes formulaic if they do not have enough substantive knowledge to frame their thinking. This substantive knowledge requires the same sort of 'double vision' that Card (2004) refers to when discussing the related disciplinary concept of historical interpretations.

Although historical interpretations and historical significance are related disciplinary concepts as theorised for school history, they are also distinct. A lively discussion would ensue if we gathered a group of history teachers together to talk about the similarities and differences between the two. Both involve dialogue between past and present and dialogue about the past. In Chapter 9, Keates defines the study of interpretations as the study of the material output created about the past (such as historians' accounts, children's books, films and museums). As a working distinction, we can define historical interpretations as a concept concerned primarily with how and why these views and representations of the past have been constructed, whereas the concept of historical significance is focused on the meaning that is attributed to the past and what something signifies.

THE PROBLEM OF TAXONOMIES

Classroom history teachers are time-poor and are continually needing to update their subject knowledge. It is therefore completely understandable that simple solutions can seem attractive. However, the reduction of a concept as complex as historical significance to an adopted taxonomy is problematic and will not result in secure learning for pupils.

In 2002, Phillips wrote about work specifically in relation to the historical significance of the First World War. He developed a set of criteria that his pupils could work with and understand in order to discuss the topic. He defined the First World War as follows:

Groundbreaking
Remembered by all
Events that were far reaching
Affected the future
Terrifying

This was not meant to be a taxonomy to apply to other topics. Counsell (2004) was also concerned that GREAT did not enable pupils to move beyond consequences and sought to develop criteria that made explicit that historical significance is attributed, rather than fixed. Her 5 Rs have been much written about, discussed and used in history classrooms:

- Remarkable – the event/development was remarked upon by people at the time and/or since.
- Remembered – the event/development was important at some stage in history within the collective memory of a group or groups.
- Resonant – people like to make analogies with it; it is possible to connect with experiences, beliefs or situations across time and space
- Resulting in change – it had consequences for the future
- Revealing – of some other aspect of the past

Counsell was concerned to include the making of meaning and the process of creating history, in addition to the consequential aspects of historical significance. On the one hand, her taxonomy is more widely applicable; on the other hand, it opens up the possibility that pupils will be given the 5Rs and simply asked to apply them to decide what is historically significant. As Worth (2019) reflected, applying criteria can become a tick box exercise that removes the excitement and puzzle that is part of studying history. Counsell (2004) warned against this tick box approach to applying the 5Rs: 'Perhaps we need to go back to the drawing board **and think through for ourselves** [this author's emphasis] what kinds of things cause people to attribute historical significance in the first place'.

The 5Rs might best be thought of as criteria for history teachers to discuss. For example, Brown and Woodcock (2009) shared the results of departmental reflection on, and discussion of, the 5Rs. That is, they used the criteria as a springboard for a continuing professional development discussion that enabled colleagues to better understand the concept and therefore to plan to teach it so that pupil learning would be secure. They thought deeply about the concept for themselves, using the 5Rs as a guide.

Activity 10.3

Reflecting on taxonomies.

Snelson gives us taxonomies written by Rob Phillips and Christine Counsell. However, she also points out that Counsell urges us to, 'think through for ourselves what kinds of things cause people to attribute historical significance', instead of simply applying her taxonomy.

- What problems might be caused by explicitly using these taxonomies with pupils?
- Does this mean that Phillips and Counsell's taxonomies are not helpful to us?

THE ETHICAL DIMENSION

Historical significance should be a concept that is exciting and challenging to teach and to learn. It should lead us to puzzle and to question. It is the stuff of debate and is contestable and contested. History is a messy business, and tidy answers are usually either so simplistic as to be ahistorical and/or silencing parts of the narrative that need to be heard.

There are important questions to be asked about who makes decisions, and how decisions are made, about the attribution of historical significance. These questions quickly lead us to questions about power. Who has the power to make decisions about collective memory, about the research questions that are asked, about the events from the past that are commemorated and so on?

The work of Trouillot (2015) has suggested to history teachers that historical silence is the opposite of historical significance. He talks of four crucial moments when power is exercised in a way that can shape the historical record.

> 'Silences enter the process of historical production at four crucial moments: the moment of fact creation (the making of sources), the moment of fact assembly (the making of archives), the moment of fact retrieval (the making of narratives), and the moment of retrospective significance (the making of history in the final instance)'.

While Trouillot only refers to significance in his final point, it is clear that all four points involve decisions about what is historically significant. Who has the power to make these decisions, and how that power is wielded, leads us into the ethical dimension of the concept. This can and should be discussed with pupils.

In addition, to return to the quote at the start of this chapter: 'All historical research and all historical education depends on some conception of significance' (Barton, 2005). It is our responsibility as history teachers to explore all the processes that attribute significance, including in our own curriculum choices. Inadequate reasoning for school history curriculum choices include the following:

- It must be significant because it is in the history textbook or curriculum materials we have been given.
- It is significant because we are interested in it.
- It has always been a school history topic (Historical Thinking Project).

History curriculum makers are powerful and need to wield their power responsibly. What a child learns in schools, alongside other societal influences, will shape what they come to regard as historically significant.

THE PUPIL PERSPECTIVE

High-quality history teaching pays close attention to pupils. It starts with the pupils' current knowledge to inform the next steps of knowledge building. Bergman (2020) researched the views of 11-year-olds in Sweden who had had no prior formal teaching of the concept of historical significance. She found that the pupils equated historical significance with 'the great men of the past, and the thrilling, entertaining parts of the past'. Significance was also attributed to positive change. Her findings concurred with the view of Wineburg (1999) that thinking historically needs to be explicitly taught and does not come naturally to young minds. It follows that historical significance needs to be explicitly taught if Lomas' list is to be known and understood by pupils.

Priggs (2020) is one example of many colleagues who have involved pupils in curriculum planning. Pupils are one group of stakeholders in the process of making and assessing the outcomes of decisions about curriculum planning. They do not arrive in history classrooms as blank slates. They have opinions about what is historically significant. Barton (2005) makes the point that teaching will be less effective unless teachers pay attention to these frameworks of knowledge that pupils already have. Put more simply, some history matters to pupils more than other history and this will shape what they are interested in and remember. Barton synthesises research from various studies that have shown that pupils draw upon community and popular, as well as more formal histories, to attribute historical significance. His own work with pupils from the Protestant and Catholic communities in Northern Ireland concurred with these findings. Levstik (Levstik & Barton, 2008) cautions that unless history teachers pay attention to community and popular histories then pupils who make meaning from them will be left cynical and disempowered by school history and ill equipped to engage with historical significance as a historical concept. By implication, they already have internalised criteria for assessing historical significance before they arrive in secondary history classrooms. History teachers need to start with pupils' pre-existing perspectives on historical significance and what is historically significant and seek to widen their frameworks of knowledge. They need to find out what meaning the children in front of them already make from the past in order to, as Barton (2005) states:

> 'expand students' ideas about significance ... including how ideas about significance vary across time, place, and account. When a topic does not relate to students' prior ideas, that is, educators need to help them understand which criteria of significance have been applied to it—why the event is considered important enough to include in the curriculum.

BLOCKS TO LEARNING ABOUT HISTORICAL SIGNIFICANCE

While historical significance has been theorised as a distinct disciplinary concept, it cannot be treated in isolation. There are ways of thinking and dispositions that will act as blocks to learning historical significance if they are not appreciated and addressed by the teacher. Not all of these are specifically about historical significance.

1. **History = the past.** Pupils are going to struggle with the concept of historical significance if they think that history and the past are the same thing. History is created and constructed when historical questions and research strategies are applied to a selection of what remains of the past in the context of what is already known and has been argued about the past. Pupils need to learn that the past is too vast to be known, and that the majority of people and events from the past are forgotten, if they are going to be able to work with the idea that history involves decisions about what is significant to remember.
2. **Right or wrong.** If pupils think that history is about binary answers, that there is simply right or wrong, then they will struggle with the concept of historical significance. Pupils need to know that there can be more than one possible answer to historical questions, that there are historical truths and not one historical truth. If pupils are still thinking in terms of right and wrong, then they are going to struggle to accept as valid different opinions about what is historically significant both across time and within time periods.
3. **Memory is accurate.** Humans have psychological defences that lead them to deny, project and repress memories (Llewellyn & Snelson, 2014). All humans do this to some degree, including historians. If pupils think that humans, whether they be eyewitnesses or historians, are able to be totally neutral and accurate witnesses, then they will not be able to understand why there are so many different ideas about historical significance.

4. **Records are neutral.** This block returns to Trouillot's point (2015) that the creation and preservation of records of the past is not a neutral process. Pupils need to be taught that an exercise of power is happening when decisions are made about what records to create and to preserve. What is regarded as historically significant can be shaped by these decisions as they shape what survives and is accessible.
5. **History as one thing after another.** If history is presented as a long narrative of facts and happenings, then pupils will also struggle with historical significance as a concept. Conversely, if pupils conceptualise history as a subject with purpose that leads us to consider how the world of today got to how it is, then it is easier to understand the idea of historical significance as meaning-making about the past.
6. **Significance is inherent.** This block is specifically about historical significance. Teachers need to tackle directly the naive idea that an event or a person is inherently significant. The idea that significance is not intrinsic and fixed, but attributed and changeable, is fundamental to thinking and learning about the concept.
7. **Community vs. school history.** To restate Levstik's point (2008), if school history simply ignores the history that pupils learn from their own community (whatever that may be) then it is unlikely that conceptual learning about historical significance will happen in the history classroom. That is because what matters to pupils and how they have thus far made meaning is being ignored.

GETTING BETTER AT HISTORICAL SIGNIFICANCE

Defining how pupils make progress with disciplinary concepts in history is not easy. First, history is not learnt in a linear way. It is not as simple as step one: apply criteria and then step two: develop your own. That is because of a second point, that the concepts are not learnt in isolation. It is not possible to learn historical significance separately from substantive topics and from other disciplinary processes, such as evidential thinking and communicating historically. Nevertheless, although it is not easy, we must try to define what getting better at historical significance means. Colleagues Cercadillo (2006) and Bradshaw (2006) both suggest models of progression, presented here.

Cercadillo's model

1. No allusion to any type of significance.
2. Intrinsic significance – it is inherent and simple.
3. Fixed contextual significance – in a specific time period and connected to causation.
4. Fixed contextual significance – but with recognition of different types of significance (e.g. symbolic or revealing).
5. Relative contextual significance – considers how different types of significance can change over time.

Bradshaw's model

1. Substantive knowledge about significant events
2. Learning about criteria for historical significance.
3. Applying criteria given to them.
4. Identifying how significance has been ascribed.
5. Develop and use criteria on their own.

Worth (2023) has turned the ideas of Bradshaw around and suggested that lower-attaining pupils may make progress more quickly if they first identify how significance has been ascribed before applying criteria given to them.

It is clear that there are quite different progression models for the same disciplinary concept. The best way for teachers to use them is not to take one and apply it directly. Instead, they, and the implications of using them, should be discussed as a departmental team in the context of the particular curriculum in a school. This will enable colleagues to explore the thinking behind the models and to reflect on how to apply this to a particular school setting and particular pupils' learning.

> **Activity 10.4**
>
> Think about an enquiry question that you teach that addresses or could address historical significance.
>
> - How far do the lessons and activities you teach allow your pupils to access the different levels of Bradshaw and Cercadillo's progression models?
> - Are you happy with the result?
> - What would you need to do to help pupils reach further?
> - Is this something that could be done within that enquiry? Or, would there need to be enquiries before, or after, that one in order to help pupils develop their understanding?

ENQUIRY QUESTIONS

A school history curriculum for secure learning is constructed so that pupils revisit the disciplinary concepts and work with them in relation to different substantive topics and different time periods. While historical significance should feature frequently in historical learning, teachers will sometimes make it the main disciplinary focus of a sequence of learning. The historical enquiry question has been practically theorised for many years, since the work of Riley (2000), and Worth in Chapter 3 shows how an enquiry question gives purpose to a sequence of lessons by combining a particular substantive and disciplinary focus for pupils and enabling them to answer a demanding and rigorous historical question.

Examples of enquiry questions which could be used to frame a sequence of lessons on aspects of historical significance:

- What was the most historically significant development of the 19th century?
- Why do British people remember the Holocaust?
- Why is the British Empire remembered differently?
- What does the story of the Banda Islands reveal?
- Why did so many people write about the Bolsheviks' capture of the Winter Palace?
- How has the historical significance of the Storming of the Bastille changed over time?
- Why does Britain still mark Remembrance Day?
- Why were the Victorians so interested in the Middle Ages?
- How does World War Two still define modern Britain?

- Why did early historians of the abolition of the British transatlantic slave trade ignore the contribution of enslaved people?
- Why do people disagree about the historical significance of Martin Luther King Junior?
- Why did historians become much more interested in women's history in the 1960s and 70s?
- How have new sources changed views about historical significance?

AN EXAMPLE OF A SIGNIFICANCE ENQUIRY

Worth discusses the enquiry outlined here in her 2023 Teaching History article and provides the resources for colleagues via her history education blog (Worth, 2020). The question that frames the enquiry is: 'What do the stories of the "often forgotten armies" reveal about the Western Front?'

Worth constructed four narratives about four different soldiers who fought in the First World War using the work of the historian David Olusoga (2014). She introduced these after a first lesson teaching the outline chronology and geography of the Western Front. Over the course of the next two lessons, Worth read and discussed the narratives with her pupils, enabling them to capture notes about each. She used the analogy of nesting dolls and focused pupils' thinking on what aspects of the past were opened up (revealed) by each story. Some aspects were revealed more than others. Pupils made notes in the image of a larger doll if more was revealed, and in a smaller doll if less was revealed, about an aspect from a story.

The reading, discussion and note-taking activity identified these individual stories as historically significant because of what they reveal about the Western Front. Until recently these stories were hidden, the historical narrative was silent. The enquiry gives agency to the four different soldiers by revealing the impact they had as well as how they were impacted by what happened to them. It is thus an example of an enquiry planned with consideration of both the conceptual and the ethical.

TEACHER TALK AND QUESTIONING

While the previous section suggested different enquiry questions that could be adapted to frame a sequence of learning focused specifically on an aspect of historical significance, learning about the concept should also be a part of most history lessons. It permeates all we do in the history classroom. Teachers need to pepper their teacher talk with it and use their questions to encourage pupils to think about it.

To do this effectively, teachers need to have a thorough understanding of the concept themselves, and so reading this chapter and the texts referred to is helpful. They also need to both plan interventions that make thinking about historical significance explicit and be prepared to respond to pupils in the moment. That is, to make decisions to focus pupils on matters of historical significance during lessons in response to pupils' thinking and responses.

Using the Language of Significance

Teachers need to explicitly, deliberately and frequently use the language associated with historical significance if pupils are to become familiar with it. For example, words such as meaning-making, signify, resonate, attribute, should pepper teacher talk and be explained in the course of it. Pupils should be encouraged to use the language themselves in classroom talk, with corrections from the teacher when it is used incorrectly.

Preparing Questions

For beginning teachers, it is helpful to pre-plan questions to encourage pupils to think about historical significance. Here are some examples of questions that will be useful:

- Why did people at the time think this was so remarkable?
- Why did people at the time not talk about this?
- How has this been remembered?
- Who has remembered this?
- Why has this been remembered?
- How has the memory of this changed?
- Why have we forgotten…?
- Who/what is missed out of this story?
- What resonance does this have for us today?
- How did X resonate for people (in a later time)?
- What did this change?
- How did this mean that things could not be the same again?
- What does this reveal to us?
- How is this revealing of…?
- Why are we studying this now?
- Why should we be interested in…?
- Why is the significance of this painful?
- Why do ideas about the significance of this vary so much?

Using Analogies

Colleagues in departments can create a useful set of analogies to explain the concept of historical significance. Here are two examples:

Things people are talking about at the time are not necessarily of historical significance.

Pupils might think that things that make news headlines must be historically significant. An analogy that can challenge this thinking is the example of snow. When it snows, the news tends to be full of pictures and stories of people stuck in traffic, sledging, etc. And yet the snow is usually gone very quickly and snow (at least in the UK) is rarely something that becomes historically significant.

Things that are historically significant may not be remarked on by people at the time.

Pupils might think that something historically significant must have been obvious and 'in the news' at the time. In his book on the causes of the First World War, Christopher Clark (2013) notes that Prime Minister Herbert Asquith's letters in the summer of 1914 are much more concerned with the question of Irish Home Rule than about the rising tensions between Austria and Serbia. Likewise, it is now known that Sars-CoV-2 clusters of infection were happening across the UK due to international travel before the headline impact of the first two lab-confirmed cases in the UK at the end of January 2020 (Du Plessis et al., 2021). Similarly, the arrival of the first plague-carrying rat fleas in Britain in 1347 would have gone entirely unrecorded until it was already far too late to stop the terror that was to unfold.

PUPIL ACTIVITIES

In this final section are a range of activities to help pupils learn about historical significance. They can all be adapted to specific topics and slotted into existing schemes of work. Notice that they all:

- Have the common theme of making thinking about historical significance explicit and giving pupils space and time to develop their own ideas.
- Require pupils to use their substantive historical knowledge.
- Require the teacher to have a really sound understanding of the concept themselves.

Activities will be successful if the purpose of the learning is clear, the activity is clearly linked to that purpose and the teacher has a clear sense of the key takeaways from the learning in terms of the progress that pupils are expected to make.

'Between Tube Stops' Persuasion

Taking a topic that pupils have studied, ask them to imagine they have the duration of a ride between London Tube stops (say 90–120 seconds) to persuade their partner why the topic is historically significant. Pupils then work in a pair to improve the persuasions. Share a few as a class and draw out the criteria that pupils are using to argue for historical significance. Challenge them with other possible criteria that could be used. Is their event still so historically significant?

Balloon Debate

Pupils are asked to imagine that a hot-air balloon is sinking. It has too much luggage on board, and their luggage will be thrown overboard unless they can argue persuasively. After studying a topic, such as Britain in the 19th century, pupils can be given a change, event or development and asked to justify its historical significance (in this case its place in the balloon). This works well if pupils are given their topic and then there is a class discussion to agree on the criteria that will be used by everyone to make judgements. With these criteria written on the board, the pupils then prepare their short justifications. They present to each other and are judged by their peers as to how well they meet the criteria, using a scoring system. The presentations with the highest scores then get to keep their luggage in the balloon. Depending on the nature of a class and on time available, you can organise this into rounds with more direct head-to-head debating and refutation.

Engaging with Historians

Introductions to history books, TV documentaries and short film clips are places where historians justify why the focus of their study is historically significant. Historians also talk about their revised perspectives on topics. By reading and watching these as part of studying a topic, pupils can identify the criteria that historians use to argue for historical significance. Worth (2023) suggests 'that inferring criteria [from the writing of historians] first, before applying given criteria, [helps] pupils to see that determining significance is relative and problematic'. In addition, comparing the work of historians also helps pupils to learn how and why perspectives on significance can change. They can also compare historians' views with those of others. For example, the populist political claims that the Battle of

Manzikert of 1071 was a major turning point, with the contextualisation of the battle by the historian Peter Frankopan (2012).

Uncovering the Curriculum

Pupils can review the Key Stage 3 history curriculum they have studied, or a textbook they have used, and be asked to work out what assumptions of historical significance lie behind the choices of topics. They can identify the criteria for selection that have been used. They can be asked to suggest how they would decide what to put into the history curriculum and why. They can also be asked to consider how the curriculum topics would be different if they had been at school in different places. An extension of this is to get hold of an example of an older curriculum, say from the 1950s. Pupils can discuss what it suggests about ideas of what was historically significant at a different point in time and then compare and contrast it to what they have learnt.

Exploring Resonance

Political speeches can be an interesting way for pupils to explore how past events resonate across time. For example, pupils who have studied the struggle for civil rights in America could identify how Barack Obama drew upon the civil rights era to highlight the historical significance of his election in his speech on 4 November 2008. Alternatively, how parallels were drawn between Winston Churchill and President Zelensky at the time of Zelensky's speech to the US Congress in December 2022. Zelensky arrived from a war-assaulted country, as did Churchill, and he drew parallels between the fighting around Bakhmut and the Battle of the Bulge in 1944.

Contested Places and Spaces

Contested places and spaces are useful for revealing the ways that historical significance can be differently attributed by different people and also in different time periods. There are many examples of such places and spaces, for example Hagia Sophia in Istanbul, the city of Lviv, the Mosque–Cathedral of Córdoba, the memorialisation of the site of the assassination in Sarajevo in 1914, and Lombok district in Utrecht. Finding examples that connect with curriculum topics and/or investigating local history examples, perhaps of streets and squares that have been renamed, can enable pupils to investigate how the concept of historical significance connects with contested history. Changes in the attribution of significance can be captured in diagrammatic form.

Local Identity

A study of who or what street names signify, or of statues erected, or of plaques put up, or of building use, can open windows into historical significance. Both what is regarded as historically significant in a community today and also what was historically significant to the people who created the environment that remains. Asking pupils to reflect on the places that are cherished in their local area can enable them to reflect on their significance. Walking tours for home learning, or presentations with images and text in class, including the use of maps, is a good way to make this learning accessible.

Popular Culture

Allsop (2010) used Billy Joel's 'We Didn't Start the Fire' to explore another person's thoughts about significance. Pupils researched the events mentioned in the song, and then careful work took place to draw out ideas about why Joel might have included them in 1989. Pupils were able to identify and classify the criteria. They were then challenged to write an updated version for their own age group. A similar activity could be developed around the 2012 London Olympic opening ceremony.

Curating an Exhibition

Pupils can be asked to curate an exhibition (or to create a documentary) on a topic that they have studied. The teacher as commissioner of the exhibition (or documentary) sets certain parameters. For example, the exhibition might be on the topic of the British Empire for the local museum and might need to include five elements. The pupils are asked to suggest the most historically significant elements of the topic and to justify their choices. At some point, the teacher changes the parameters. For example, by announcing that the exhibition is going on tour to five other Commonwealth countries. Pupils then need to reflect on how their suggestions need to change, and what can stay the same, in order to remain historically significant for the audience.

Activity 10.5

Choose three of the suggested activities to try yourself. Before teaching them consider:

- Which topic or enquiry would be most suitable for each activity?
- When would they best fit within the sequence of lessons?
- What would you want your pupils to learn from each activity?
- What are the things that you would need to be mindful of when running these activities?

Afterwards, evaluate the three activities and consider:

- What did pupils learn? How did these activities progress their understanding of historical significance?
- What limitations or gaps in your pupils' understanding did you notice?
- Which activity worked the best?
- What might you do differently next time?

SUMMARY OF KEY POINTS

- Historical significance is a disciplinary concept with many facets and is a curricular entitlement in school history.
- Teaching and learning historical significance should be exciting and challenging as it is about how humans make meaning from the past.
- Historical significance is part of the process of human dialogue with the past and is always attributed and never fixed.

- The concept is one that history teachers continue to debate and puzzle over. There is a conversation to join in order to continue to develop one's professional thinking.
- Avoid adopting others' mnemonics, use the work of historians and keep the focus on the problem and the puzzle of attributing meaning.
- Pay attention to pupils' existing ideas about historical significance in order to engage and motivate them to want to study the past and to think about it more deeply.
- Seek to expand pupils' range of what can be regarded as historically significant and why.

RESOURCES AND FURTHER READING

Allsop, Scott. "We Didn't Start the Fire': Using 1980s Popular Music to Explore Historical Significance by stealth' in Teaching History, 137, Marking Time Edition, (2010): 52–59. London: Historical Association.

Anand, Anita, Dalrymple, William, & Frankopan, Peter. 'Byzantium and the Rise of the Turks' [Podcast], Empire (2022). https://podcast24.co.uk/episodes/empire/21-byzantium-and-the-rise-of-the-turks-LnvX5O61Tq

Barton, Keith C. '"Best Not to Forget Them": Secondary Students' Judgments of Historical Significance in Northern Ireland' in Theory & Research in Social Education, 33:1, (2005): 9–44, 10.

Bergman, Karin. 'How Younger Students Perceive and Identify Historical significance' in History Education Research Journal, 17:2, (2020): 164–78, 176. https://journals.uclpress.co.uk/herj/article/id/69/

Bradshaw, Matthew. 'Creating Controversy in the Classroom: Making Progress With Historical significance' in Teaching History, 125, Significance Edition, (2006): 18–25. London: Historical Association.

Brown, Geraint, & Woodcock, James. 'Relevant, Rigorous and Revisited: Using Local History to Make Meaning of Historical significance' in Teaching History, 134, Local Voices Edition, (2009): 10–11. London: Historical Association.

Card, Jane. 'Seeing Double: How One Period Visualises another' in Teaching History, 117, Dealing with Distance Edition, (2004): 6–11. London: Historical Association.

Cercadillo, Lis. "Maybe They haven't Decided Yet What Is Right:' English and Spanish Perspectives on Teaching Historical significance' in Teaching History, 125, Significance Edition, (2006): 6–9. London: Historical Association.

Clark, Christopher. The Sleepwalkers: How Europe Went to War in 1914. London: Allen Lane (2012): 490.

Counsell, Christine. 'Looking Through a Josephine-Butler Shaped Window: Focusing pupils' Thinking on Historical significance' in Teaching History, 114, Making History Personal Edition, (2004): 30–33. London: Historical Association.

Counsell, Christine. 'The Fertility of Substantive Knowledge - in Search of Its Hidden, Generative power' in Davies, Ian (ed.). Debates in History Teaching. London: Routledge 2017: 89. https://doi.org/10.4324/9781315642864

Department for Education and Skills/Qualifications and Curriculum Authority. The National Curriculum: Handbook for secondary teachers in England Key stages 3 and 4, (2004): 94. https://education-uk.org/documents/pdfs/2004-nc-secondary-handbook.pdf

Du Plessis, Louis, McCrone, John T, Zarebski, Alexander E, Hill, Verity, Ruis, Christopher, Gutierrez, Bernardo, Raghwani, Jayna, Ashworth, Jordan,

Colquhoun, Rachel, Connor, Thomas R, & Faria, Nuno R. 'Establishment and Lineage Dynamics of the SARS-CoV-2 Epidemic in the UK' in Science, 371, 6530, (2021): 708–12.

Frankopan, Peter. The First Crusade: The Call from the East, London: The Bodley Head 2012.

Haydn, Terry, & Stephen, Alison. Learning to Teach History in the Secondary School: A Companion to School Experience (5th ed.). Routledge 2022: 172–77. https://doi.org/10.4324/9780429060885

Hunt, Martin. 'Teaching Historical Significance' in Arthur, James, & Phillips, Robert (eds.). Issues in History Teaching. London: Routledge 2000: 39–53.

Levstik, Linda. S, & Barton, Keith C. Researching History Education: Theory, Method, and Context (1st ed.). Routledge 2008: 286. https://doi.org/10.4324/9781315088815

Llewellyn, Anne, & Snelson, Helen. 'Bringing Psychology into History: Why Do Some Stories Disappear?' In Teaching History, 135, To They or Not to They Edition, (2014): 30–38. London: Historical Association.

Lomas, Tim (1990) cited in Counsell, Christine. 'Looking Through a Josephine-Butler Shaped Window: Focusing pupils' Thinking on Historical significance' in Teaching History, 114, Making History Personal Edition, (2004): 30–33. London: Historical Association.

Obama, Barack. 'Transcript of Barack Obama's Victory Speech' [Speech], NPR, (2008). https://www.npr.org/2008/11/05/96624326/transcript-of-barack-obamas-victory-speech

Olusoga, David. The World's War: Forgotten Soldiers of Empire. London: Head of Zeus 2014.

Pearson, Elizabeth. 'Guy Fawkes: Remembering Terrorism and Its Victims 400 Years On' [Online Article], Royal Holloway University of London, (2022). https://royalholloway.ac.uk/research-and-teaching/departments-and-schools/law-and-criminology/news/dr-elizabeth-pearson-wrote-for-the-international-centre-for-countering-terrorism-icct-on-reassure-report-findings-harms-to-extremism-researchers-1/

Phillips, Robert. 'Historical Significance: the Forgotten "Key Element?"' in Teaching History, 106, Citizens and Communities Edition, (2002): 14–19. London: Historical Association.

Priggs, Catherine. 'No More 'doing' Diversity: How One Department Used Year 8 Input to Reform Curricular Thinking About Content choice' in Teaching History, 179, Culture in Conversation Edition, (2020): 10–19. London: Historical Association.

Riley, Michael. 'Into the Key Stage 3 History Garden: Choosing and Planting Your Enquiry questions' in Teaching History, 99, Curriculum Planning Edition, (2000): 8–13. London: Historical Association.

Seixas, Peter, & Morton, Tom. The Big Six: Historical Thinking Concepts. Nelson Education 2013. Also available at: https://historicalthinking.ca/sites/default/files/files/docs/Guideposts.pdf

The Editorial Board. 'What's the Wisdom On… Historical Significance' in Teaching History, 181, Handling Sources Edition, (2020): 50–54. London: Historical Association.

The Historical Thinking Project. 'Historical Significance' https://historicalthinking.ca/historical-significance

Trouillot, Michel-Rolph. Silencing the Past: Power and the Production of History. Beacon Press 2015: 35.

Wineburg, Sam. 'Historical Thinking and Other Unnatural Acts' in The Phi Delta Kappan, 80:7, (1999): 488–99. http://www.jstor.org/stable/20439490

Worth, Paula. "Do we have to write an essay on this, Miss?' Reflecting on what we want pupils to do with historical significance – and when' [Blog Post], Lobworth, (2019). https://lobworth.com/2019/01/14/do-we-have-to-write-an-essay-on-this-miss-reflecting-on-what-we-want-pupils-to-do-with-historical-significance-and-when/

Worth, Paula. 'What do the stories of the 'often forgotten armies' reveal about the Western Front?' [Blog post], Lobworth, (2020). https://lobworth.com/2020/05/14/what-do-the-stories-of-the-often-forgotten-armies-reveal-about-the-western-front/

Worth, Paula. 'Falling Forward: Three Strategies to Support pupils' Study of Historical significance' in Teaching History, 190, Ascribing Significance Edition, (2023): 8–21. London: Historical Association.

Zelensky, Volodymyr. 'Ukrainian President Volodymyr Zelensky's remarks to Congress' [Speech], CNN (2022). https://edition.cnn.com/2022/12/22/politics/zelensky-congress-address-transcript/index.html

Chapter 11   Sources and Evidence

Alex Ford

BACKGROUND

In 1941, as the Nazi regime was busy occupying France and other parts of Europe, the Jewish historian Marc Bloch was secretly writing his last great work: *The Historian's Craft*. In it, he attempted to define the nature of historical study, and the importance of its continued study in understanding the present. He asserted that, 'It is a scandal that in our own age, which is more than ever exposed to the poisons of fraud and false rumour, the critical method is so completely absent from our school programs' (Bloch, 1992). Bloch argued history was ultimately the study of 'men *(sic)* in time'. More accurately, he reflected that it was in fact, 'the knowledge of their tracks'. This definition has always resonated with me as it strikes at the heart of history as a discipline. First, that history is a body of knowledge about the real and lived experiences of people in the past. Second, that this knowledge is reliant on the processes by which historians make claims based on the 'historical sources' or 'tracks' which are left behind by those people. History is therefore both fixed – it happened; and provisional – we can only theorise about it.

History as a school subject is challenging for precisely the same reason (Ashby, 2017). Young people are asked to develop their substantive knowledge of the past while always being aware that this knowledge is provisional. Alongside this they need to understand the disciplinary processes by which historians have sought to generate claims about the past and the evidence upon which these claims are based.

Despite the centrality of the concept of historical evidence to the discipline of history, the engagement of pupils with historical evidence in English schools was patchy until the advent of the National Curriculum in 1988. The fact that working with 'sources' has moved into the mainstream has been largely thanks to the pioneering work of the Schools History Project (SHP). SHP's Principles focus expressly on the importance of giving young people opportunities to understand, through participation, how historical interpretations are formed. This approach has been so influential that it can still be found in the current National Curriculum, as well as GCSE and A-Level specifications.

Although there is a long, and very rich, tradition of history educators seeking to better engage young people with the concept of historical evidence, 'source work' remains an area of history which many teachers and pupils regard as excessively challenging, or even dull. This is not helped by the ways in which 'source' questions have been framed in many examination specifications. It is therefore important to note that the acts of engaging with historical sources and wrestling with historical evidence are not an add-on to historical study. What is chilling, when reading Bloch's (1992) definition of history as a knowledge of people's 'tracks' is that, as he wrote those words, the Nazi regime was busy destroying the tracks of whole civilisations, not to mention the tracks of their own atrocities. For Bloch, engaging with historical evidence is a vital, ethical endeavour in seeking truth. By engaging with historical evidence pupils are asked to engage with and evaluate claims, not based on their own preconceptions, but by reference to the historical 'tracks' upon which they are based.

When Bloch wrote *The Historian's Craft* in the early 1940s, he noted that the Western world seemed to have 'lost the very taste for verification'. In the second decade of the 21st century, in an age which is often dubbed 'post truth', the importance of understanding the relationship between claims and evidence cannot be overstated. As Reisman and Wineburg (2012) argue 'the ability to read competing truth claims; and the ability to temper one's rush to judgement in the face of competing worldviews, constitute the heart of participatory democracy'. For school teachers to engage their pupils with the concept of historical evidence is therefore a key part of doing justice to both the past and the present. This is not just a matter of training young people in a set of skills. It is about enabling young people to adopt an historical mindset which empowers them to think critically, creatively and ethically about the historical claims they encounter in school, and which permeate into their everyday lives beyond the classroom.

Activity 11.1

Reflect on why sources are currently used, or not used, in your classroom.
What factors play a part in your decision to use them or not use them?
Are you persuaded by Bloch's argument that there is an ethical duty to engage with sources?
What more day-to-day reasons affect your decisions about how and why sources are used?

CHALLENGES FOR HISTORY TEACHERS

There are three fundamental issues which act as barriers for history teachers seeking to develop pupils' evidential thinking.

1. Being clear about definitions. What exactly is historical evidence and how can teachers define the role it plays in understanding history as a form of knowledge?
2. Working with historical evidence can feel overly complex or dry. How can pupils be encouraged to engage meaningfully with historical 'sources' in the classroom?
3. To appreciate how claims are made, young people need to be given opportunities to think critically about the nature of historical evidence. How can this complex process be made accessible in every school?

This chapter aims to address each of these challenges and to suggest ways in which history teachers can help to build young people's understanding of historical evidence.

The Importance of Definitions

One of the great challenges of history is that many of its core concepts and ideas seem to defy clear definitions. The terms 'source' and 'evidence' both have meanings in a variety of school contexts as well as in everyday life. Sometimes these connections can be helpful, for example, drawing connections between 'evidence' and the processes of a criminal investigation. However, analogies can also obscure subject-specific meanings. The police investigator may well need to work carefully with the evidential traces, but the hope is that a single truth is established by the end of the process. As Ian Dawson argues, one of the key aspects of historical study which pupils often struggle with is that it embraces messy uncertainty (Dawson, 2021). Historians almost always finish their research with more questions and possibilities opened up than they have closed down.

This section aims to provide four key definitions which will underpin the remainder of the chapter.

Historical Sources and Historical Evidence

For many, the term 'historical sources' brings to mind a textbook page of documentary extracts. For those educated in the early years of the National Curriculum, a 'source task' was almost inevitably a challenge to extract relevant information from these sources as a form of information retrieval or to practise 'source skills', as demanded by the National Curriculum. The prevalence of this approach in the 1990s and early 2000s led Counsell to label it 'death by sources A-F' (Counsell, 2000).

But beyond being dull, the 'source work' approach was particularly problematic as it encouraged young people to develop significant misconceptions. 'Historical sources' are not simple windows through which pupils can look to find relevant information, nor are they neat collections of information arranged, clipped and ready to be used. 'Historical sources' cannot speak for themselves. They require careful questioning and an appreciation of the mindsets of those who created them. Twenty years on, the baggage of the 'source work' approach still colours how many teachers think about historical evidence in the classroom.

One way to move our thinking forwards is to utilise language more carefully and precisely. Rather than referring to 'historical sources' it might be better to adopt the term historical 'tracks', like Bloch (1992), or historical 'traces'. Where 'sources' might be extracts from documents, or occasionally images, or political cartoons, 'traces' encompasses 'bones immured in Syrian fortifications, a word whose form reveals a custom, a narrative written by the witness of some scene ...' (Bloch, 1992) or any number of other residues of human action created deliberately or otherwise. Suddenly history is liberated from being stored solely in libraries or archives and becomes a living, breathing part of the world in which pupils live. The traces of people's experiences of migration to England in the 20th century can be just as easily found in the oral histories passed down through families, or the demographic makeup of a Bradford suburb, as they might in the reports of immigration officials, or newspaper articles. Similarly, 'traces' places the human element back at the heart of history by forcing us to consider the ways in which these 'traces' might have been formed.

If we have reframed 'sources' as 'traces', then what is the distinction between these traces of the past and the concept of historical evidence? To put things simply, historical traces become historical evidence when they are applied to specific historical questions. As Seixas and Morton (2013) note, the fundamental process of historical construction is an interplay between historians asking good questions, analysing historical traces and considering the historical contexts in which those traces were created. It is this asking of questions that guides historians to seek and utilise particular traces of the past. And it is in this process of selecting relevant traces that historical traces transform into a new conceptual category: historical evidence. Ultimately the questions historians seek to pursue guide what will form useful evidence, as well as what might be considered reliable for these purposes.

Historical Processes

Historical traces and historical evidence only make sense if pupils have a knowledge of the ways in which historians make claims about the past. At this point, it is helpful to look at an extract from an historian doing just that. The following extract comes from Caroline Dodds Pennock's, *On Savage Shores* (2023). Here she is exploring the treatment of Indigenous peoples transported to Spain in the mid-16th century, and the actions of specific individuals. As you read, consider the questions she is asking and how she makes use of her evidence cautiously in making claims.

The Iberian peninsula ... quickly saw an influx of enslaved Indigenous people, compelled to labour in the homes and businesses across the region. Fragments of their lives become increasingly visible to us ... [as] enslaved people realised their ability to challenge their oppressors through the courts...

After 1542, hundreds of Indigenous people from across Spain appear in the archives appealing for their freedom...The records of such appeals offer us a window onto the complex, diverse and often horrifying experiences of Indigenous people who were enslaved. They provide a rare chance to glimpse their lives and to hear their voices, though at times muffled by legal formulas ...

A young Guatemalan couple...Francisco and Juana – pleaded for their freedom on the grounds that they had been illegally enslaved as children ... [They] were declared free on 13 May 1549. Wasting no time, they appealed to the Crown to pay their passage home, and that summer Francisco, his wife Juana, and their daughter, took a ship at the Crown's expense, and vanish from the historical record. Assuming they survived the journey, it must have been quite a shock for the little family to return 'home'... During their time away the great cocoliztli epidemic had swept the region, killing millions of people ... so – even if they made their way back home, Francisco and Juana would have found their families and communities desolated.

This extract reveals a number of key aspects about the ways in which evidential thinking is central to historians' work. These aspects are summarised below and explored more fully in Table 11.1.

- Historians ask questions about the past, either implicitly or explicitly.
- Historians analyse historical traces and use them as evidence to make cautious claims in relation to their questions.
- Historians make sense of historical traces by using their knowledge of historical context.
- Historians sometimes need to engage in empathetic thinking.

Figure 11.1 attempts to summarise the process of making historical claims as outlined in Table 11.1. It is adapted from Husbands' *What is History Teaching?* (1996). As Husbands notes, this process is 'an active dialogue between ourselves, in the present, and the evidence in whatever form which the past has left behind'.

Table 11.1 Ways in which historians work

Historians ask questions	Dodds Pennock does not state her questions explicitly in this extract but she is clearly addressing a number of key historical questions: 'How were Indigenous people treated by Europeans?' and 'Did Indigenous people resist their captivity in Europe?' These questions fundamentally shape the historical traces Dodds Pennock chooses to explore and transforms them into an evidence base to address these questions.
Historians analyse historical traces and use them as evidence to pursue their questions cautiously	Dodds Pennock clearly notes the limits of the traces she is able to access in relation to Indigenous experiences and attitudes in Spain at this time. She therefore draws on a variety of court records and other official documents, reading them 'against the grain' to shed light on Indigenous people's experiences and actions. In doing this, she turns her traces into an evidence base to answer specific questions. She also makes her claims cautiously, cross-referencing and corroborating her evidence. She considers aspects of usefulness, reliability and typicality almost implicitly. She notes the limits of the provenance of her specific traces and the 'muffling' effect of the legal formulas. The language of certainty also makes an appearance, we are told that Francisco and Juana 'must have' found their return home a shock, but with the caveat that this assumes they 'survived the journey'.
Historians make sense of historical traces by using the historical context	Dodds Pennock connects her evidential reasoning to wider contextual knowledge throughout to ground her claims. For instance, she draws on contextual knowledge of the issuing of the New Laws and the impact of the cocoliztli epidemic. Here again, the language of certainty is brought into play. Knowledge of the epidemic allows Dodds Pennock to make the claim that, 'if' they managed to return home, they 'would have' found their communities decimated.
Historians sometimes need to engage in empathetic thinking	At points Dodds Pennock is forced to consider the mindsets or mentalities of the historical actors appearing in her evidence base. This involves historians in a careful exploration of evidence and context to make claims about thoughts or even feelings. In this example, Dodds Pennock asks us to consider the shock Francisco and Juana must have felt had they arrived home again. As Nelson puts it, making historical claims sometimes involves, 'sailing close to the imaginative wind, and certainly into the eye of the speculative storm, to make the acquaintance of my subject as a person, to guess plausibly, if no more, at what made him tick' (Nelson, 2006). Although there is not space to explore it in this chapter, this kind of empathetic work is important because, if done carefully, it humanises the past.

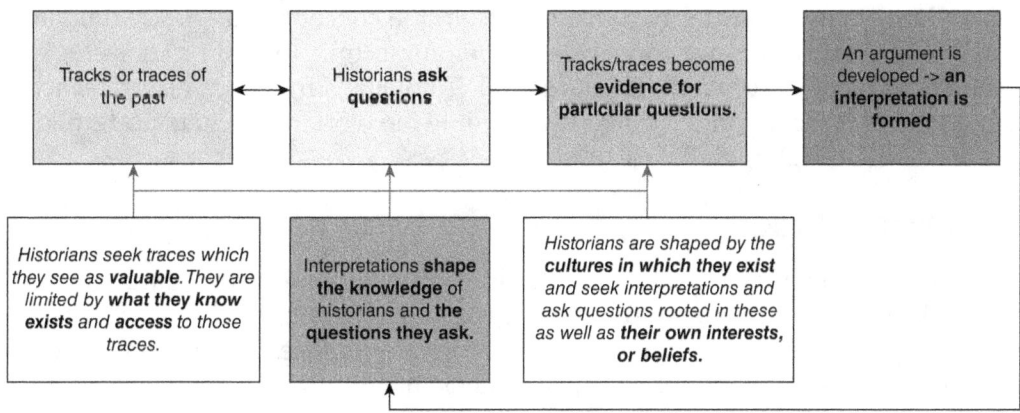

Figure 11.1 'The Historical Process' adapted from Husbands (1996).

Therefore, historians are always asking questions which are shaped both by existing historical interpretations, as well as historians' own knowledge, backgrounds, beliefs, prejudices and of course the times in which they live.

But there is another layer yet. Bloch (1992) often complained that the academic structures of French history limited the diversity and progress of the wider discipline. He consciously referred to the body of academic historians as 'the Guild', conjuring up those same images of petty self-interest and control. Similarly, in his *Silencing the Past*, Trouillot (2015) shows how history itself is often interpreted through an intensely white, Western, colonial lens. Trouillot argues that silences exist in the production of history and that these silences occur due to the power structures which shape and control the wider discipline. This in turn has created a tradition of history in which particular voices have been heard more readily and therefore shaped the questions historians have been asking. Trouillot identifies four key points at which silences in history arise:

- At the moment of fact creation – some people have greater opportunities to leave traces behind.
- At the point of fact assembly – the process of preserving and archiving itself involves human choices and selection which will eliminate some traces from view.
- At the moment of ascribing significance to events – historians choose what questions to ask and these questions are shaped by the factors already noted.
- At the moment of narrative construction – historians draw on the traces they see to be relevant to the questions they are asking from the archives or other locations they can access.

Each of these four silences has direct implications for the ways in which we think about historical evidence in the classroom. As Blackbird and Dodds Pennock (2021) explain in relation to indigenous histories, 'oral histories are often dismissed as "anecdote" and indigenous elders as "storytellers", as if this were different from being historians'. For historians to disrupt this cycle requires a significant effort in terms of breaking new ground, accessing new traces, seeing value in different types of traces, and battling to de-centre powerful voices. This begins in the classroom by broadening what we demonstrate to young people as history.

Mohamud and Whitburn (2016) characterise the roles teachers need to play in regard to overcoming silences in the history classroom as: pugilists, diggers and choreographers. Pugilists make the case for why overcoming silences in history is vital; diggers search for the traces and interpretations which are not being heard; and choreographers bring everything together in meaningful classroom experiences. Because of its centrality to history itself, the concept of evidence demands teachers take on all three of these roles in helping pupils to build a more holistic understanding of history and its issues. This is not just a matter of historical accuracy, but one of social justice. Wherever possible the work of teachers undertaking this task will be highlighted.

EVIDENTIAL THINKING

Attempting to define what evidential thinking involves and how this might manifest itself in pupils' understanding are a necessary part of enabling teachers to engage young people with the concept of historical evidence (Lee & Shemilt, 2003). Over the last 50 years and more, history teachers have sought to develop evidence-based models of how young people engage in evidential thinking. The model in Table 11.2 is adapted from work done by Tom Morton and Peter Seixas (2013),

Table 11.2 A model for evidential thinking, adapted from work done by Tom Morton and Peter Seixas (2013), Peter Lee and Denis Shemilt (2003), and Arthur Chapman (2015)

Signpost	Powerful Understanding	Potential Misconceptions
Signpost 1: Historical interpretations are responses to historical questions and based on evidence drawn from diverse traces of the past.	Pupils are able to ask relevant historical questions of historical traces. They are aware that traces come in a wide variety of forms.	Historical traces are seen as simple sources of information or 'facts'. There is limited awareness of what constitutes a 'trace' of the past.
Signpost 2: Silences and gaps in records of the past impact the availability of some historical traces. Some traces may need to be read against the grain.	Pupils are aware that not everything in history is recorded and that some groups are less likely to appear in the historical record. They are aware of ways to find hidden presences within historical traces.	The traces of the past are seen as a complete record. The absence of written records of some groups or people is not recognised or seen as in need of recognition.
Signpost 3: Historical traces are not windows on the past. Historians need to draw inferences related to the questions they have asked.	Pupils are able to draw inferences from source materials which go beyond a surface reading, to address historical questions.	Historical traces are treated as simple 'windows' on the past. The value of an historical trace is seen in relation to its surface features only.
Signpost 4: Historical claims are based on connections between multiple pieces of evidence.	Pupils are able to cross reference inferences drawn from various historical traces to act as evidence in pursuing specific questions. Pupils use language of certainty in expressing their claims.	Claims about the past are often shaky or unwarranted. The value of corroborating historical evidence is not recognised.
Signpost 5: The value of historical evidence must be considered critically in relation to the questions being asked.	Pupils are aware that the value of historical traces depends on the way they are being used in pursuit of specific historical questions. The value of a set of evidence might vary depending on the question.	Historical traces are seen as having a fixed value. For example, propaganda posters are seen as inherently un-useful based only on their nature or content and with no reference to the questions being pursued.
Signpost 6: Working with historical evidence involves critical consideration of the provenance of historical traces and how this impacts their weight as evidence for specific questions.	Pupils understand that the author, intended audience, and purpose of historical traces are important. They can explain the potential impact of a source's provenance on its reliability or utility for a particular enquiry.	The provenance of evidence is not questioned or seen as important.
Signpost 7: Historical traces need to be connected to the context in which they were created.	Pupils are able to connect historical traces to their wider context when making claims, e.g., by commenting on typicality. Pupils are also able to think about historical traces with appreciation for the mentalities of the time period.	Historical evidence is not connected with the wider context, impacting on the quality of claims made. Historical inferences are drawn from a modern mindset, rather than attempting to consider the mentalities of the time.

Peter Lee and Denis Shemilt (2003) and Arthur Chapman (2015). It identifies seven core signposts of powerful historical thinking in relation to the concept of historical evidence. It also identifies potential misconceptions which have been seen in pupils' thinking and which might act as barriers to evidential thinking in relation to any given substantive topic area.

Using these signposts, it is possible to see how a teacher might begin to plan specific opportunities during lessons, or across sequences of lessons, to encourage pupils to think in more powerful ways about historical evidence. However, it is important to say that these thought processes do not exist in isolation from the substantive content of history, they need to be brought into conversation with specific historical studies via particular historical questions. Different signposts will be more or less relevant depending on the nature of these questions. A constant revisiting of these ideas across multiple historical contexts is a core part of the learning process.

Activity 11.2

For each of the signposts, come up with an example of something that could be used in your classroom that might help elicit powerful understanding in your pupils.

For Signpost 1, can you identify a historical interpretation where the author is explicit about their evidence base? Have you read books or articles which are explicitly based on a particular source such as the records of a parish priest, personal diaries, records of court proceedings? Would it be possible to introduce these into lessons in school?

For Signpost 2, can you identify a person from history whose story is known but only from traces that were not created by them? For example, records of colonisation that are exclusively from the point of view of the coloniser? Official records that indicate the presence of people but do not record their voices? How might these be useful in the classroom for introducing the idea of silences?

For Signpost 3, can you think of a historical trace that lends itself to deeper reading? For example, in accounts or confessions, what is being said and what is unsaid? In official records, what is revealed as being important to the record-keeper and what is regarded as extraneous? What might that tell pupils about the people of the past?

For Signpost 4, can you think of an example of a historical work where the author is explicit about the ways in which he or she has used multiple pieces of evidence to corroborate their claims? How might you highlight this process to pupils?

For Signpost 5, can you think of a historical trace that is used in your classroom about which different historical questions might be asked? How might you ask pupils to reflect on these differences?

For Signpost 6, can you think of a historical trace whose meaning would be radically changed were it to have a different provenance? Or one where there is more sense to be made when thought is given to the author's intended audience?

For Signpost 7, can you think of a historical trace that could be brought into your classroom that is either very typical of its historical context or very unusual in its historical context?

PRACTICAL CONSIDERATIONS FOR WORKING WITH HISTORICAL TRACES AND EVIDENCE

This section will explore the various ways history teachers might engage pupils with historical traces and the concept of historical evidence in the classroom.

Any opportunity to engage with evidential thinking needs to be driven by a clear sense of purpose. These purposes might range from embedding knowledge or a sense of period, to empowering pupils to draw their own tentative conclusions in relation to an historical question. In either of these cases, or anywhere in between, teachers need to think carefully about the kinds of evidential thinking required for success.

Table 11.3 provides some potential uses of historical traces in the classroom, the conceptual justifications for these and the kinds of evidential thinking which might be developed. Three of the purposes shown are then explored in more detail.

Table 11.3 Potential uses of historical traces in the classroom

Purpose	Justification	Evidential Thinking
Providing Initial Simulus Material	Historical traces are used to provide a 'hook' into a period or topic area for study. Traces are provided without context to encourage pupils to question or seek to look more deeply at these traces. The focus is placed on asking good questions and drawing inferences to challenge an idea.	Signpost 1: History requires the asking of good questions. Signpost 3: Historians draw inferences from historical traces to address their questions.
Developing a Sense of Period	Traces are used to build a sense of period. This might be through images, texts, oral recounts, music, or other means. The aim is to help build broad generalisations to ground a future study.	Signpost 3: Historians draw inferences from historical traces to address their questions. Signpost 4: Historical claims are based on multiple pieces of evidence.
Embedding Understanding	Pupils are asked to make sense of historical traces using their existing knowledge. This helps student to consolidate knowledge and understanding by drawing on long term memory to make meaning of the traces. This is closest to how inference questions at GCSE work.	Signpost 1: History requires the asking of good questions. Signpost 3: Historians draw inferences from historical traces to address their questions. Signpost 7: Historical evidence needs to be understood in its own context.
Revealing the Basis for Historical Claims	Traces are used in illustrating historical claims, or pupils are asked to engage with traces and find their connections to specific historical claims. This may lead into critical evaluation.	Signpost 1: History requires the asking of good questions. Signpost 3: Historians draw inferences from historical traces to address their questions. Signpost 4: Historical claims are based on multiple pieces of evidence.

(Continued)

Table 11.3 Potential uses of historical traces in the classroom (Continued)

Purpose	Justification	Evidential Thinking
Forming Historical Arguments	Pupils engage with a range of historical traces and are asked to use them critically and cautiously as evidence to build their own claims about a question or set of questions. These questions could focus on any number of second-order concepts from causation to change and continuity.	Signpost 1: History requires the asking of good questions. Signpost 2: There are silences in the traces available to historians. Signpost 3: Historians draw inferences from historical traces to address their questions. Signpost 4: Historical claims are based on multiple pieces of evidence. Signpost 5: The value of historical evidence is tied to the question being asked. Signpost 6: Provenance can impact the value of evidence for specific questions. Signpost 7: Historical evidence needs to be understood in its own context.
Considering Evidence as a Concept	Pupils engage with the nature of evidence in relation to specific historical issues or questions. They are asked to consider issues including historical methods, archiving, the production of traces, the voices we hear, the provisional nature of utility and reliability, typicality, etc.	Signpost 2: There are silences in the traces available to historians. Signpost 4: Historical claims are based on multiple pieces of evidence. Signpost 5: The value of historical evidence is tied to the question being asked. Signpost 6: Provenance can impact the value of evidence for specific questions. Signpost 7: Historical evidence needs to be understood in its own context.

Initial Stimulus Material

One key use of historical traces in the classroom is to provide pupils with Initial Stimulus Material (ISM): an access point or 'hook' into a particular historical period or enquiry (Phillips, 2001). When used as ISM, historical traces can provide a low-risk entry point into evidential thinking. As Wineburg notes, pupils tend to want to rush to judgement when presented with historical traces. Activities which involve finding information or a rush to find evidence of 'bias' lead to pupils accepting or rejecting historical traces based on surface features. For evidential thinking to occur, pupils need to temper their 'rush to judgement' and allow themselves to occupy 'the heart of the historical problem space' (Reisman & Wineburg, 2012). The use of historical traces as ISM encourages this slowing down. An ISM approach, done well, establishes historical traces as something to puzzle over, something requiring close reading and deeper thought. ISM approaches also encourage pupils to attempt to comprehend historical traces before attempting to critically analyse or evaluate them – the point at which accusations of 'bias' begin.

One of the best ways to use ISM is to choose an historical trace which appears to be strange, startling or unusual. As White (1998) explains, 'Any good history begins in strangeness. The past should not be comfortable. The past should not be a familiar echo of the present ... The past should be so strange that you wonder how you and the people you know, and love could come from such a time ... When you have traced this trajectory, you have learnt something'. For White, the strangeness is the launching point for slowing down thinking – it forces us to think deeply about what we are encountering. Leaning into this strangeness also reduces the need for pupils to have significant prior knowledge when working with traces as ISM, again reducing the barriers to entry. Here is an example of this:

A Strange Outing

Look at the image and the brief context provided in Figure 11.2. This is an image I have used many times with pupils in Year 9. What happens immediately in your mind? As a history teacher, your brain is probably already heading down thought paths which have been developed through your own exposure to history. You have probably already begun to ask questions: Who took this photo? When was it taken? Who are the people? Why are they all sat together? You have also most likely begun to look for the clues to answer your own questions. You might have noticed the rough date and location, clocked the clothing, or the gender balance in the image.

As history teachers, this curiosity can come very naturally. However, many pupils will need to be trained to see this puzzle. If we want pupils to be curious, it helps to make evident the thought processes we have internalised. Here are three stages I use when working with unseen historical traces like this one in order to build pupils' curiosity. Note in particular how this process begins with a basic attempt to comprehend the photograph and becomes more complex.

1. First, I ask pupils: 'What can you see in this photograph?' I ask them to annotate and pick out any details which interest them. Following this I take feedback, scribbling on a large version of the photograph projected on the white board. The aim here is just to spark that curiosity – to encourage close observation and to slow down their thinking.

Figure 11.2 A photograph taken in the United States of America in the mid-19th century.

2. Next, I ask pupils to list four questions, the answers to which might help them better understand the photograph. Usually, I ask them to provide me with good question words, and model an example together. This stage is vital as it brings in the idea of historical enquiry and the importance of asking questions. In a few minutes we have a shared list of questions. I might point out that each question will require the use of the photograph in slightly different ways, or indeed require other traces.
3. In the final stage, I ask pupils to draw some inferences in an attempt to answer each of the questions they have asked. I encourage them to go back to their original observations and to look for new things as they do. Again, I like to model some examples of tentative language here, for example saying aloud: 'I think the people might be on a church outing because they all seem to be wearing formal clothes and the group is mixed'. Again, I take feedback and allow some discussion.

Crucially, through these three stages, pupils are encouraged to want to find out more about the photograph, its context, even its provenance. This leads nicely into issues of how historical traces come to exist in the first place.

However, this is not the final point of this ISM. For this photograph to really hit home, pupils need to know more about the context in which it was taken. At this point I encourage them to consider how we might be more definite in answering some of our questions. This leads to the introduction of more historical traces. In this instance, I bring in the following newspaper extract, contemporaneous to the photo.

> 'They came in all manner of ways, some in stylish carriages, others in city hacks, and still others in buggies, horseback and even on foot ... It was Sunday and everybody seemed to have taken a general holiday ... All manner of people were represented in this crowd, from the most grave and noble senators to hotel waiters ... The spectators were all excited, and a lady with an opera glass who was near me was quite beside herself – 'That is splendid, Oh my! Is not that first rate?'

Again, we work through the extract, this time looking for textual clues in the language and tone of the newspaper. Finally, it is revealed that the spectators have come to watch the Battle of Bull Run, which opened the American Civil War in 1861, and during which over 2000 soldiers were killed or went missing. The shock of this reveal then leads pupils into a whole new set of questions, now related to the Civil War itself. This in turn leads us onto the enquiry question for our lesson sequence: 'Why was America so divided by 1861?' Just as important as the connection between the ISM and the key question, however, is the historical processes pupils have engaged in to build that interest. This kind of activity suddenly makes what could be a seemingly remote topic seem vivid and real.

It is worth noting that, while the example I have given here uses a photograph, similar approaches can be used with text, music or audio traces, but with more focus on tone, language choice, timbre or mood. There are also other ways to approach the process of moving to inferences. For instance, photographs or images can be slowly revealed like jigsaw pieces, with pupils making observations, asking or refining questions and drawing inferences after each reveal.

> **Activity 11.3**
>
> Can you think of any historical traces that would make good ISMs? Which topics could they be used to introduce?

Embedding Understanding

The use of historical traces to embed understanding is extremely common in GCSE classrooms. Pupils are often asked to consider an historical trace and connect it to their wider knowledge. There are several ways to do this effectively; however, the two most common are as follows:

1. To teach a set of content and then ask pupils to connect this to an extract or image contemporary to the period being studied.
2. To use an extract or image contemporary to the period being studied as ISM and then revisit it later in the sequence of lessons with greater understanding for comment or analysis.

To give an example, look at the following extract from a GCSE question paper on Weimar and Nazi Germany:

> An extract from a poster published by the Weimar government in March 1920
> Workers, Party comrades! The military putsch has started. The Freikorps, fearing they will be disbanded, are trying to remove the Republic and to form a military dictatorship. Kapp is at their head. Everything is at stake. No factory must work while the military dictatorship rules! Therefore down tools! Come out on strike! Down with the counter-revolution.

This extract might be used to embed a range of substantive knowledge about Weimar Germany, as well as encouraging evidential thinking. Table 11.4 provides a list of questions teachers might ask, along with the understanding they might seek to embed.

However, just as in our previous example, for pupils to embed any of the understandings outlined in Table 11.4, they first need to comprehend the historical trace in question. The following questions provide some ways teachers can encourage this close reading and comprehension of historical traces. Many of the examples could be enacted as simple highlighting or annotation exercises, but could also be adapted for auditory materials. For example, pupils might raise a hand when they hear something relevant or important.

Table 11.4 Potential uses of historical traces in embedding understanding

Question	Substantive Understanding Embedded	Evidential Thinking
How useful is source A for an enquiry into problems in Germany 1919-23?	Pupils would be prompted to identify the Kapp Putsch and explain its role as an issue in Germany. They would also need to draw on wider contextual knowledge to discuss other problems in the era: hyperinflation, attempted communist revolutions, the Munich Putsch and note the limited use of the source for these purposes. This would also test knowledge of substantive concepts, e.g., 'Workers', 'comrades', 'dictatorship', 'strike' and 'counter-revolution'.	Pupils would be reinforcing the idea that utility can only be discussed in relation to a given purpose. (Signpost 5) There is potential to embed the concept that provenance will have an impact on how useful Source A is for revealing communist and socialist threats to the Weimar Republic. (Signpost 6)
How reliable is Source A for an enquiry into why the Kapp Putsch failed?	Pupils would need to look at the methods suggested in Source A and compare these to their wider knowledge of the methods involved in breaking the Kapp Putsch. They would also need to draw on knowledge of the position of the Weimar government in 1920 and its political makeup to establish a meaningful understanding of the provenance.	Again, pupils would be reinforcing the idea that reliability can only be discussed in relation to the question being asked. (Signpost 4) Pupils would need to consider the role of source provenance in impacting upon reliability and connect this with wider contextual knowledge. (Signpost 6)
Why do you think Source A was published by the Weimar government in 1920?	Pupils would need to establish that the extract is referring specifically to the Kapp Putsch and that it is addressed to the largely left-leaning workers of Germany. They would also need to read quite closely to spot the tone, purpose and intended audience of the extract. They would need to connect their knowledge of events in Germany around 1920 to establish why the source might have been published.	Pupils would need to understand that historical traces are not simply windows into the past but need to be read closely and connected to context so that inferences might be drawn about their purposes. (Signpost 3, Signpost 7)

Encouraging Comprehension of Historical Traces

- Ask pupils to pick out details which show something specific. E.g., 'Find two examples which show you who was the target audience for this poster'.
- Ask pupils to explain a particular word or phrase (or choice of symbol). E.g., 'What do you think the poster means when it says 'everything is at stake'?'
- Ask pupils to establish the perspective of the piece. E.g., 'Find two examples which show the Weimar government did not support Kapp'.
- Ask pupils to reflect on what might be revealed through the content. E.g., 'What can this poster reveal about how powerful the Weimar government were in 1920?'
- Ask pupils to listen carefully for tone (written or oral). E.g., 'How can you tell the Weimar government was desperate?'
- Ask pupils to compare the content to other content. E.g., 'How similar is the message of this poster to Ebert's speech we looked at earlier?'
- Ask pupils to consider what they could use the content for. E.g., 'What questions could you answer about Weimar Germany using this extract? What else would you want to know?'

Encouraging Critical Thinking About the Provenance of Historical Traces

- Ask pupils to connect specific words/phrases/images/symbols to their contextual knowledge. *E.g., 'What do you think the poster means by 'the counter-revolution'?'*
- Ask pupils to consider the date carefully. *E.g., 'What was happening in 1920 which might help explain why this poster was published?'*
- Ask pupils to critically consider the impact of the author and their purposes. *E.g., 'What might the government have been hoping to achieve through this poster?'*
- Ask pupils to be aware of the audience. *E.g., 'Who was meant to see this poster and how might that impact what was included?'*

Forming Historical Arguments

As a final example, pupils might be asked to use a body of historical traces as evidence to answer their own, meaningful historical questions. This kind of work can be extremely powerful as it involves pupils in the majority of the historical thought processes outlined in Table 11.2. More than this however, forming historical arguments involves pupils in the creative act of breathing life into their study of history. In the words of former SHP Director, David Sylvester (1976), history is 'a perpetual act of resurrection in which pupils, teachers and historians reconstruct the past and so make it become real and "present" to them'.

If we want pupils to develop meaningful historical arguments which enable this process of resurrection, then having an historical question to answer is paramount. Just like historians, pupils need to be engaged in a process of asking questions and making claims about the past. Unlike historians however, pupils often need a little more guidance in choosing their questions for more detailed study. There is a long tradition in history teaching in England of using carefully crafted 'enquiry questions' to this end (Riley, 2000). As Worth explains in Chapter 3, an enquiry question holds together the disciplinary and substantive aims of a sequence of lessons, while also modelling the processes of the discipline of history.

Table 11.5 contains a range of enquiry questions which ask pupils to develop historical arguments rooted in historical evidence. For each one, clear links have been made to the desired evidential thinking. In all of the examples given, the use of historical traces as evidence is central to making the necessary arguments. Many of the examples have been written up in *Teaching History*, should you wish to find out more about a particular enquiry.

Table 11.5 Examples of evidential enquiry questions

Enquiry Question	Focus	Evidential Thinking/Misconceptions
How did the peasants' leader actually die? (Byrom, 1998)	Pupils use a range of conflicting chronicles critically to construct an account of the death of Wat Tyler.	Signpost 1: History requires the asking of good questions. Signpost 2: There are silences in the traces available to historians. Signpost 3: Historians draw inferences from historical traces to address their questions. Signpost 4: Historical claims are based on multiple pieces of evidence. Signpost 7: Historical evidence needs to be understood in its own context.

(Continued)

Table 11.5 Examples of evidential enquiry questions (Continued)

Enquiry Question	Focus	Evidential Thinking/Misconceptions
'How might a skeleton end up in a field near Reading?' (Podesta, 2013)	Pupils investigate the archaeological remains of a skeleton found in Reading in conjunction with other artefacts to suggest tentative connections between the locality and the Roman past.	Signpost 1: History requires the asking of good questions. Signpost 3: Historians draw inferences from historical traces to address their questions. Signpost 4: Historical claims are based on multiple pieces of evidence. Signpost 7: Historical evidence needs to be understood in its own context.
When was 'race' invented? (Apps, 2021)	In this enquiry pupils are asked to engage in a range of smaller evidential studies, including an exploration of 16th century European accounts relating to Africa and people of African descent, from which pupils build generalisations. This is followed by studies of materials from the 17th century, exploring the hardening of racial attitudes.	Signpost 1: History requires the asking of good questions. Signpost 2: There are silences in the traces available to historians. Signpost 3: Historians draw inferences from historical traces to address their questions. Signpost 4: Historical claims are based on multiple pieces of evidence. Signpost 7: Historical evidence needs to be understood in its own context.
How can historians investigate connections between religions and Africa? (Mohamud & Whitburn, 2020)	Pupils use a wide variety of historical traces to address a range of historical questions about religion and rulers of Lalibela, Axum and Mali, e.g., 'What was King Lalibela's project all about?' They are encouraged to turn a variety of traces into evidence to answer these questions and to draw tentative conclusions from this evidence base and wider historical input.	Signpost 1: History requires the asking of good questions. Signpost 2: There are silences in the traces available to historians. Signpost 3: Historians draw inferences from historical traces to address their questions. Signpost 4: Historical claims are based on multiple pieces of evidence. Signpost 5: The value of historical evidence is tied to the question being asked. Signpost 6: Provenance can impact the value of evidence for specific questions. Signpost 7: Historical evidence needs to be understood in its own context.
How does the historian Yasmin Khan use evidence to reach conclusions about experiences of the Second World War? (Hibbert & Patel, 2019)	This question has a wider focus, however several lesson questions ask pupils directly to engage with a body of evidence and draw tentative conclusions in relation to specific questions. Two good examples are: 'Was Britain alone?' and 'Was the Indian Army truly voluntary?'	Signpost 1: History requires the asking of good questions. Signpost 2: There are silences in the traces available to historians. Signpost 3: Historians draw inferences from historical traces to address their questions. Signpost 4: Historical claims are based on multiple pieces of evidence. Signpost 5: The value of historical evidence is tied to the question being asked. Signpost 6: Provenance can impact the value of evidence for specific questions. Signpost 7: Historical evidence needs to be understood in its own context.
What is the story of the skeletons of Maiden Castle? (Dawson & Wilson, 2008)	Pupils develop their own questions about some skeletons found at Maiden Castle and use a range of traces to provide a tentative explanation in relation to who they were and what happened to them.	Signpost 1: History requires the asking of good questions. Signpost 3: Historians draw inferences from historical traces to address their questions. Signpost 4: Historical claims are based on multiple pieces of evidence. Signpost 5: The value of historical evidence is tied to the question being asked. Signpost 7: Historical evidence needs to be understood in its own context.

It is helpful to unpack one of these examples a little further to establish the kinds of evidential thinking pupils are being engaged in. In Mohamud and Whitburn's (2020) enquiry for instance, pupils are encouraged to engage with a diverse range of historical traces from the outset. The summary of the first four lessons of their sequence in Table 11.6 illustrates how pupils use historical interpretations and wider resources to reflect upon and make sense of their historical traces, which in turn are used to explore a range of historical questions.

One of the most important aspects of this lesson sequence is providing pupils with a language toolkit to express degrees of certainty in relation to historical traces and their evidence base. As mentioned previously, history is not about answers but to explore possibilities and their plausibility. Pupils are encouraged to find links and connections between pieces of evidence and their wider knowledge and to draw tentative conclusions based on the strength of these links. This language of certainty is then woven into the writing prompts. In the first lesson for instance, pupils are asked to make statements from their evidence base to address the question 'what kind of ruler was King Ezana?' However, they are also asked to cite their

Table 11.6 A summary of four lessons from Mohamud and Whitburn's enquiry, taken from Mohamud and Whitburn (2020)

Lesson	Focus	Questions and activities
1	Setting up the enquiry into the history of religion and Africa. Sources from the past: the wonders of Lalibela. The coins from Axum.	• What, where and when is the mystery building? • What historical questions should we ask about religion and Africa? • How can historians investigate connections between religion and Africa? • What can we learn from historians Henry Louis Gates and Abebaw Gela about the religions of Axum from the two coins?
2	Time and place in the study of history: chronology and maps. The Axumite Empire, trade and religion in the fourth century CE.	• How can we show events across time? The meaning of chronology and the use of a timeline to show the passage of time. Setting the timeline for use during the enquiry. • Where did all this happen? The location of the Axumite Empire in Africa and its connections with the Middle East. Setting the map for use during the enquiry. • The significance of the Axumite Empire in the fourth century CE, using a Greek text. What could be the connection between trade and the arrival of Christianity in Axum?
3	King Ezana of Axum and his conversion to Christianity. Using sources to support statements about the past.	• Exploring who was responsible for bringing Christianity to Axum. What is the mix of myth and history in the conversion of King Ezana? • What can we learn about the complexity of their religion from the memorials of the stellae of the kings of Axum? • Looking for evidence from sources to support statements about King Ezana and Axum.
4	The churches at Lalibela and their significance. Gus Casely-Hayford's exploration of the churches.	• What was the significance of the names of the Lalibela churches? What was King Lalibela's project all about? • How does an historian explore Lalibela? The awe of the churches for Casely-Hayford, and the significance of cosmopolitan influences from Judaism and Byzantium. • Exploring links between the Lalibela church buildings and the stellae of Axum.

supporting evidence, comment on how strong the evidence is in support of their claim, and to make use of hedging language in their responses, for example 'Ezana was probably a very religious ruler. This is supported strongly by several pieces of evidence. For instance...'

It is worth noting here that enquiry questions which expressly deal with certainty can be very powerful in developing pupils' thinking. For instance, pupils might ask 'How certain can we be about what happened at Maiden Castle?' rather than the example cited in Table 11.5. Dawson (2021) makes the case that this kind of work is vital in school history: 'One of the potential reasons for teaching history is to help pupils become more comfortable with uncertainty in their lives and in the world around them and that they don't always expect neat, simple solutions to local, national and international problems'.

Although 'forming historical arguments' has been the final part of this section, it should not be implied that pupils should not engage with this kind of work from the outset. At least three of the examples given in Table 11.5 are designed for use at the beginning of Year 7 as a meaningful and grounded introduction to history and the methods of historians.

ENGAGING WITH HISTORICAL EVIDENCE AS A CONCEPT

So far, this chapter has focused on enabling pupils to critically engage with historical traces to build understanding, embed knowledge, or form their own tentative arguments. However, historical evidence can also be considered as a conceptual focus of an entire enquiry. The difference is subtle but important. A focus on evidence as a concept is not just about engaging in the historical process but critically thinking about the process itself. This is especially important in the light of Trouillot's (2015) work on silences in history. Recognising the silences in the historical record requires young people to be critically aware of the processes by which historical traces come into being, are assembled, are ascribed significance by historians and ultimately utilised as evidence for their enquiries.

Understanding Evidence as a Concept

A focus on historical evidence as a concept requires us to shift the focus away from the creation of arguments about causes, consequences, change, continuity, or other second-order concepts. Instead, the focus needs to be placed on the evidence itself.

In the left-hand column of the table in Table 11.7 are two enquiry questions. These both make extensive use of evidential thinking but are not enquiries focused on evidence as a concept in its own right. The third column of the table contains a version of each question which has been revised to shift the focus onto the concept of historical evidence.

This shift from using historical traces as evidence to considering the nature of that evidence is especially difficult. However, understanding evidence as a concept is foundational if we want young people to really grasp the provisional nature of historical claims and what makes some claims to historical truth well, or indeed poorly grounded. This kind of thinking is especially important when even mainstream 'history' books seem to be so littered with partial and inaccurate uses of historical evidence. Nigel Biggar's *Colonialism: A Moral Reckoning* has for instance been criticised for cherry picking its evidence to such a degree that he created the impression that the Métis leader Louis Riel was acknowledging the British right to take Métis lands, when in fact he was doing the exact opposite (Lester, 2023). This failure might be attributed to Biggar's background as a theologian, rather

Table 11.7 Shifting the focus onto historical evidence as a concept

Original Question	Original Focus		Revised Question	Revised Focus
'**How** did the peasants' leader actually die?'	Requires pupils to carefully connect and consider historical evidence in relation to building a specific **causal** argument.	→	'Why is it so **hard to find out** how Wat Tyler died?'	Requires pupils to explore the **evidence base** for claims about Tyler's death – covering issues related to the historical traces, their agreement and disagreement, their preservation and their transmission.
'**When** was 'race' invented?'	Requires pupils to deploy a range of historical evidence in an argument about **change and continuity**.	→	'What can C16th and C17th **paintings reveal** about changing attitudes to race?'	Requires pupils to think carefully about a **particular type of historical trace**, weighing up its contributions to understanding as a **form of evidence**.

than an historian, but the power of publication gives his claims significant weight. Enabling pupils to critically reflect on the basis for the claims made in books such as these, and of course in the wider media, is therefore a vital part of doing justice to history.

Critically Engaging with Historical Evidence as a Concept

Here are five useful questions stems which encourage pupils to think about evidence as a concept. The first one especially is well suited to explorations of hidden or silenced histories.

- **Why is it so hard to find out…?** E.g., Why is it so hard to find out about black Tudors?
- **Why is it hard to be certain about…?** E.g., Why is it hard to be certain about who led the Match Women's strike?
- **What can we learn from… about…?** E.g., What can we learn from Ivor Gurney's poems about the Western Front?
- **What kinds of sources reveal most about…?** E.g., What kinds of sources reveal most about Indigenous resistance to US colonialism 1850-1930?
- **How can we make sense of sources about…?** E.g., How can we make sense of sources about the society of medieval Mali?

To give a recent example, Davies, Rakib and Zakaria (2022) posed their Year 9 groups the evidential question: 'Why have some stories of 1971 been so difficult to tell?' when studying the Bangladesh Liberation War. This enquiry is particularly powerful as it involves pupils engaging with oral recounts as well as more traditional sources. In the enquiry, pupils are encouraged to compare and contrast official and personal recounts of the creation of Bangladesh, and to assess the potential impact of trauma upon the oral recounts. A brief summary of the lesson sequence is provided in Table 11.8.

Despite the conceptual complexity of what Davies et al. were attempting in this enquiry, they note that 'All pupils understood and could explain in detail why some stories from the past could be difficult to tell'. They also found that lower attaining pupils especially were captivated by the enquiry.

Table 11.8 A summary of Davies, Rakib and Zakaria's lesson sequence, taken from Davies, Rakib and Zakaria (2022)

Lesson 1 What are the state interpretations of 1971?	After some ISM, pupils are given a basic outline of the events leading up to the Bangladesh Liberation War. Pupils analyse aspects of two official interpretations told by parts of the contemporary Pakistani and Bangladeshi states – connecting this to the enquiry question.
Lesson 2 Why have Meghna, Ferdousi and Shafiqul's stories of 1971 been so difficult to tell? **Lesson 3 Why have Ahmad, Tariq and Khalid's stories been so difficult to tell?** **Lesson 4 Why have 'Ansar' and Jinnah's stories been told selectively?**	In lessons 2–4, pupils explore a range of differing accounts of events before, during and after 1971. They are asked to explore the tone and content of the interviews initially before moving on compare and contrast accounts, and to consider issues related to provenance. Each new story adds a layer of complexity and allows pupils to consider why the story of 1971 is so difficult to tell.
Lesson 5 Why have some stories of 1971 been so difficult to tell?	Pupils address the enquiry question in an open piece of writing. Key words for concepts and context are provided but no other structure.

CONCLUSIONS

This chapter has aimed to provide a rationale for engaging pupils with evidential thinking, to provide a framework for teachers to think about what this might look like, and to offer suggestions for how this may be enabled. Encouraging young people to develop their evidential thinking is by no means an easy task. Human beings are pre-programmed to seek simple answers and to reinforce our own ideas and preconceptions (Wineburg, 1999). Working with traces of the past and thinking about historical evidence as a concept forces us to step outside these comfort zones. However, as Wineburg (2007) suggests, evidential thinking is unnatural, but essential – it builds modes of thinking which help us better navigate the world around us.

Throughout his life, Marc Bloch campaigned to place evidential rigour at the heart of the discipline of history. In 1940s France, Bloch wrote of being surrounded by a society 'corrupted by dogma and myth' (Bloch, 1992). Eighty years on, those words seem worryingly prescient. In the end Bloch made the ultimate sacrifice in the pursuit of truth. He was executed as a member of the French resistance in June 1944. Even to the end however he believed in the power of history to liberate. In *The Historians Craft he* claimed that 'history may reckon among its most certain glories that, by this elaboration of its technique, it has pioneered for mankind a new path to truth and, hence, to justice'. And at the very core of this historical technique is the evidential thinking which has been the subject of this chapter. It is something all history teachers need to nurture in our continuing fight against injustice.

SUMMARY OF KEY POINTS

- Studying the concept of historical evidence is central to pupils' understanding of the discipline of history, and the provisional nature of its claims.
- History teachers need to be careful in their use of the terms 'sources' and 'evidence'.
- The term 'traces' of the past might be a more helpful term than sources, as it naturally encompasses all that remains from the past, as opposed to just the documentary record.

- Traces of the past become 'evidence' when they are used to answer certain historical questions.
- Traces can be used in many different ways in the history classroom: as an ISM, to embed understanding and as evidence for pupils to form their own arguments about the past.
- Pupils should also tackle the concept of evidence head-on. This involves pupils not only using traces as evidence for their own argument but reflecting on the process of evidence-collection itself.
- The study of historical evidence ultimately has an ethical dimension; it involves pupils in the pursuit of truth and the study of people whose history has been overlooked.

RESOURCES AND FURTHER READING

Apps, Kerry. 'Inventing Race? Year 8 Use Early Modern Primary Sources to Investigate the Complex Origins of Racial Thinking in the past' in Teaching History, 183, Race Edition, (2021): 8–19. London: Historical Association.

Ashby, Rosalyn, 'Understanding Historical Evidence: Teaching and Learning Challenges', in Davies, Ian (ed.). Debates in History Teaching. London: Routledge 2017: 144–54. https://doi.org/10.4324/9781315642864

Blackbird, Leila K, & Dodds Pennock, Caroline. 'How Making Space for Indigenous Peoples Changes History', in Carr, Helen, & Lipscomb, Suzannah (eds.). What Is History, Now? How the Past and Present Speak to Each Other. London: Weidenfeld & Nicolson 2021: 251.

Bloch, Marc. The Historian's Craft, ed. Peter Burke, trans. Peter Putnam. Manchester: Manchester University Press 1992: 23, 45, 113.

Byrom, Jamie. 'Working With sources' in Teaching History, 91, Evidence and Interpretation Edition, (1998). London: Historical Association.

Chapman, Arthur. Historical Thinking Progression Map. Oxford: Pearsons 2015.

Counsell, Christine. '"Didn't We Do That in Year 7?" Planning for Progress in Evidential Understanding' in Teaching History, 99, Curriculum Planning Edition, (2000): 36–41. London: Historical Association.

Davies, Nathanael, Rakib, Taslima, & Zakaria, Anam. 'Telling Difficult Stories about the Creation of Bangladesh' in Teaching History, 188, Representing History Edition, (2022): 28–39. London: Historical Association.

Dawson, Ian. 'What Do We Want Students to Understand about the Process of "Doing History"?' in Exploring and Teaching Medieval History in Schools, (2018): 109–12. London: Historical Association. Available here: https://www.history.org.uk/secondary/resource/9290/exploring-and-teaching-medieval-history-in-schools

Dawson, Ian. 'Why We Should Frame Questions That Explicitly Suggest Answers Will Be Uncertain' [Blog Post], Thinking History, (2021). https://thinkinghistory.co.uk/Issues/QuestionsWithUncertainty.html

Dawson, Ian, & Wilson, Maggie. SHP History Year 7 Pupil's Book. London: Hodder Education 2008.

Husbands, Chris. What Is History Teaching?: Language, Ideas, and Meaning in Learning About the Past. Buckingham and Philadelphia: Open University Press 1996: 13.

Lee, Peter, & Shemilt, Dennis. 'A Scaffold, Not a Cage: Progression and Progression Models in History' in Teaching History, 113, Creating Progress Edition (2003): 13–23. London: Historical Association.

Lester, Alan. 'The British Empire Rehabilitated?' [Online Book Review], Bella Caledonia, (2023). https://bellacaledonia.org.uk/2023/03/07/the-british-empire-rehabilitated/

Mohamud, Abdul, & Whitburn, Robin. Doing Justice to History: Transforming Black History in Secondary Schools. London: Trentham Books 2016.

Nelson, Janet L. 'Did Charlemagne Have a Private Life?' in Bates, David, & Crick, Julia, & Hamilton, Sarah (eds.). Writing Medieval Biography, 750-1250: Essays in Honour of Frank Barlow. London: Boydell & Brewer 2006.

Hibbert, David, & Patel, Zaiba. 'Modelling the Discipline: How can Yasmin Khan's Use of Evidence Enable Us to Teach a More Global World War II?' in Teaching History, 177, Building Knowledge Edition, (2019): 8–15. London: Historical Association.

Dodds Pennock, Caroline. 'On Savage Shores: How Indigenous Americans Discovered Europe' in Weidenfeld & Nicolson, (2023): 56–58.

Phillips, Robert. 'Making History Curious: Using Initial Stimulus Material (ISM) to Promote Enquiry, Thinking and literacy' in Teaching History, 105, Talking History Edition, (2001): 19–25. London: Historical Association.

Podesta, Ed. 'Helping Year 7 Put Some Flesh on Roman bones' in Teaching History, 149, In Search of the Question Edition, (2013): 8–17. London: Historical Association.

Reisman, Abby, & Wineburg, Sam. 'Ways of Knowing and the History Classroom: Supporting Disciplinary Discussion and Reasoning About Texts' in Carretero, Mario, & Asensio, Mikel, & Rodríguez Moneo, Maria (eds.). History Education and the Construction of National Identities, International Review of History Education. Charlotte: Information Age Publishing 2012: 172, 175.

Riley, Michael. 'Into the Key Stage 3 History Garden: Choosing and Planting Your Enquiry questions' in Teaching History, 99, Curriculum Planning Edition, (2000): 8–13. London: Historical Association.

Seixas, Peter, & Morton, Tom. The Big Six: Historical Thinking Concepts. Nelson Education 2013. Also available at: https://historicalthinking.ca/sites/default/files/files/docs/Guideposts.pdf

Sylvester, David (ed.). A New Look at History, Schools Council History 13 - 16 Project. Edinburgh: Holmes McDougall 1976: 36.

Trouillot, Michel-Rolph. Silencing the Past: Power and the Production of History. Beacon Press 2015: 35.

Mohamud, Abdul, & Whitburn, Robin. "What Is history': Africa and the Excitement of Sources With Year 7' in Teaching History, 181, Handling Sources Edition, (2020): 17–25. London: Historical Association.

White, Richard. 'Remembering Ahanagran: Storytelling in a Family's Past' in Hill & Wang, (1998): 13.

Wineburg, Sam. 'Historical Thinking and Other Unnatural Acts' in The Phi Delta Kappan, 80:7, (1999): 488–99. http://www.jstor.org/stable/20439490

Wineburg, Sam. 'Unnatural and Essential: The Nature of Historical Thinking' in Teaching History, 129, Disciplined Minds Edition, (2007): 6–12. London: Historical Association.

Chapter 12
'Decolonising' the History Curriculum in Schools

Dan Lyndon-Cohen and Josh Preye Garry

BACKGROUND

Decolonisation is a contested term that has multiple meanings, ranging from the ongoing struggles against colonial rule, particularly in the 20th century, to the desire to challenge dominant narratives and the construction of history, typically based on a Eurocentric disciplinary tradition. This chapter will start by exploring the changing meaning of 'decolonisation' and then examine a number of ways in which one school has started to revise content, assessment practice and pedagogy, in order to bring about substantive change in the ways in which history is taught and learnt. At different points in the chapter, the reader will be able to reflect on these approaches and consider how they might choose to apply them.

WHAT DOES 'DECOLONISATION' MEAN?

The meaning of decolonisation has changed over time. Does the term represent the creation of new flags and constitutions, or something that happens in the minds of the colonised and the coloniser? Is the process political, cultural or both? (Webb, 2020). The term decolonisation has been credited to M.J. Bonn, a German-Jewish academic who fled Nazi persecution and moved to London, teaching at the London School of Economics (Klose, 2016). However, this has been challenged by those who argue that the process of decolonisation was first discussed in 1900 during the First Pan-African Conference in London. Notable black intellectuals, including W. E. B. Dubois, the American historian and civil rights activist, and Dadabhai Naoroji, the first British-Indian Member of Parliament, held discussions aiming to overturn the existing imperial political order and its enforcement of white supremacist ideologies (Richards, 2020). After the Second World War, decolonisation took on a more practical meaning when waves of independence movements across Africa and Asia brought European colonial rule closer to an end. This was in line with Bonn's argument that 'All over the world a period of counter colonization began, and decolonization is rapidly proceeding' (Klose, 2016): decolonisation was the moment of removing colonial power from former colonies, an explicit political act.

However, the Maori academic Linda Tuhiwai Smith (Ngati Awa and Ngati Porou, 1999) describes decolonisation as a process that centres around the different ways in which indigenous peoples have struggled to recover histories, lands, languages and basic human dignity. Tuhiwai Smith argues that indigenous communities have had to overcome an education system designed to destroy indigenous cultures, value systems and appearances, and raises a very pertinent question:

> Why then has revisiting history been a significant part of decolonization? The answer, I suggest, lies in the intersection of indigenous approaches to the past, of the modernist history project itself and of the resistance strategies which have been employed. Coming to know the past has been part of the critical pedagogy of decolonisation. To hold alternative histories is to hold alternative knowledges. The pedagogical implication of this access to alternative knowledges is that they can form the basis of alternative ways of doing things. Transforming our colonized views of our own history (as written by the West), however, requires us to revisit, site by site, our history under Western eyes. This in turn requires a theory or approach which helps us to engage with, understand and then act upon history.

Tuhiwai Smith's work is supported by Frantz Fanon, a psychiatrist and political philosopher from Martinique. For Fanon (1963), decolonisation involved 'a whole social structure' being changed from the bottom up through the mobilisation of the universal proletariat of 'natives'. Fanon essentially calls for a dramatic change in power relations between the coloniser and the colonised. Michel-Ralph Trouillot's book *The Power of Silence* (2015) is very important in understanding the concept of decolonisation in the context of the discipline of history. Although Trouillot does not mention the term directly, he successfully builds on Fanon's argument of a 'bottom-up' approach in exploring the importance of power in the construction of history. He argues that the 'exercise of power (can) make some narratives possible and silence others' and states that there are four 'moments' in which silences are created: there is the moment of fact creation (the making of sources); the moment of fact assembly (the making of archives); the moment of fact retrieval (the making of narratives); and the moment of retrospective significance (the making of history in the final instance). Here, Trouillot's definition of decolonisation corresponds with Fanon's, where power becomes central to the creation of a narrative. This has two important implications in tying down the definition of decolonisation further. Firstly, the process of the creation of a narrative must be addressed. There needs to be a clear understanding of who, why and how narratives are being constructed. If it derives from those already in a position of power, then by Trouillot's logic, a colonised form of history will occur. Secondly, this contributes to the nature of the narrative. If the process of history being created is not interrogated, then the narratives that follow will focus on those with power and the alternative narratives of the marginalised will continue to be silenced and may even disappear altogether. Emma Dabiri, in her book *Don't Touch My Hair* (2020) captures this very effectively:

> The historical records present significant challenges when our interest is in black lives. Black life has not been archived or documented in the same way that white life has. There are no oil paintings that display our wealth and power. We are present, but you have to look for us elsewhere, perhaps in the language you use, in the way you dance, in the food you eat, in the computers you use, in the art you make or the music that is the soundtrack to your life. Black people are there, although recognition is scarce.

'DECOLONISING' THE HISTORY CURRICULUM IN SCHOOLS

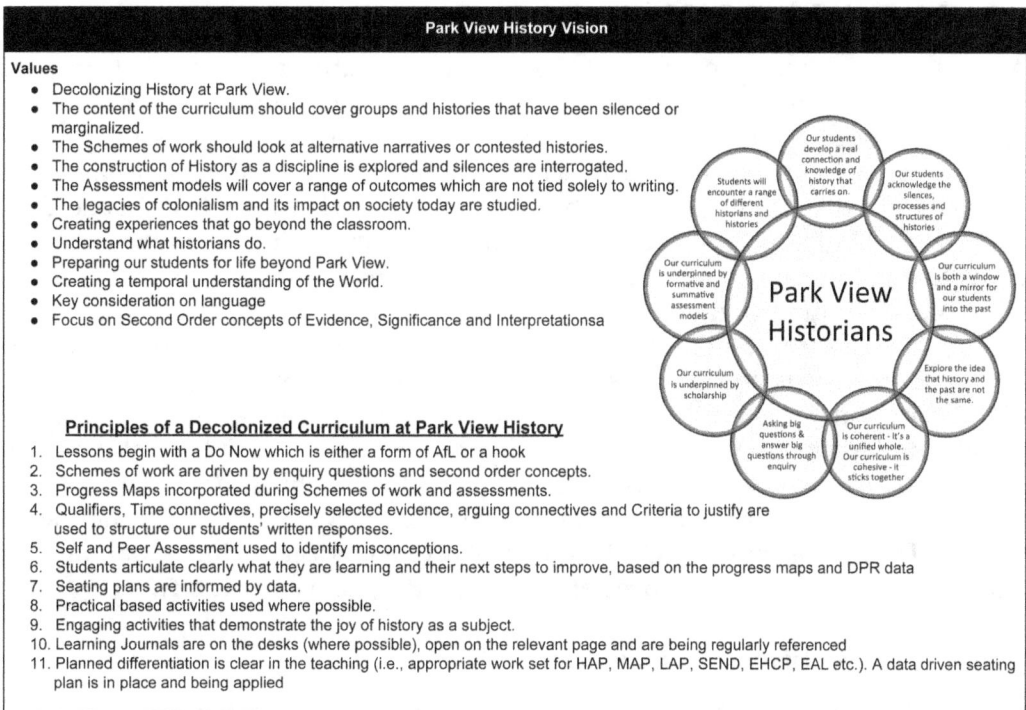

Figure 12.1 Vision of the Park View History Department.

In this context, Dabiri is specifically referring to Black History, but the arguments put forward by her apply to all groups within society who do not belong to the elite classes or those groups with power. This can be people of colour, women, people from the LGTBQ community and people with disabilities. Dabiri captures Fanon's and Trouillot's arguments here for a clear definition of 'Decolonisation'. This is that the construction of history must be explored and interrogated so that the stories of the 'bottom up' are told. If there is only a focus on sources such as 'paintings' and 'letters', then only those people with power will ever have their stories told. By interrogating the construction of history through the lens of power, those groups who have been marginalised and silenced can have their histories explored.

Collectively, Tuhiwai Smith, Fanon, Trouillot and Dabiri provide the basis for a working definition of decolonisation, the challenge for school history teachers is to translate this into a practical application of the decolonisation processes. Our first step in the history department at Park View School was to use these writings to inform our curriculum planning. After much discussion, we were able to come up with a set of guiding principles that underpin our approaches to the construction of our Key Stage 3 curriculum, as shown in Figure 12.1.

Activity 12.1

Read the extract from Linda Tuhiwai Smith and think about:

1. What does she mean by decolonisation?
2. What are the practical implications for the history classroom that she raises?

DECOLONISING THE CURRICULUM IN PRACTICE

At Park View School, we acknowledge Trouillot's (2015) assertion that 'power' is central to the construction of history. As a consequence, we have attempted to find a variety of ways to engage pupils in dialogue about, and facilitate practical experience of, alternative approaches that challenge the dominant narrative. We recognise that there is a diversity of communities that have been silenced or marginalised but hope that our pupils can also find commonalities in these experiences and understand how resistance and survivance continues to inspire those still engaged in the struggle for equity. As Abigail Echo-Hawk (2019) wrote in her description of Native Americans, 'We are not a "historically" underserved population. My history is one of ancestors who survived so I could thrive. My history didn't start with "western civilization". I am colonially underserved. I am institutionally underserved. And I am historically resilient'. The examples that we share in this chapter cover a range of topics that can be taught in both primary and secondary sectors, but typically may occur in Key Stage 3, for which they were written. They focus on LGBTQ+ histories, Native American histories, and an oral history unit about the experiences of the British-Pakistani community.

Opening the Archive with a Suitcase

Pupils at Park View are introduced to the power dynamics of the archive in the first few weeks of their Year 7 curriculum. The department was fortunate to be given access to a wonderful resource that provides pupils with an insight into the history of the school's local community: a suitcase, crammed full of ephemera dating back to the late 19th century, found in the attic of a local resident. After many hours of sorting through knitting patterns and pictures of cats, which sadly ended up in the recycling bin, what remained was pure gold: Naturalisation papers from 1907 showing how the Swiss owner of the suitcase became a British citizen; a dog-eared but lovingly preserved advert from a local newspaper desperately seeking support to find their son who was missing in action at the Somme; an invitation to the opening of the Cenotaph in 1921. All this and more became the centre pieces of the activity to construct a narrative about the owner of the suitcase, and their connection to our world. This task enabled pupils to engage with the work of the historian and the tools at their disposal. However, underpinning this, and explicit in the teaching of these lessons is the recognition that their teachers held the power to construct the archive, curating the narrative and erasing other aspects of the story.

> **Activity 12.2**
>
> 1. Can you think of a similar opportunity that you can use to expose pupils to the power of the archivist?
> 2. Can you think of ways that pupils can practically experience the construction of an archive which is relevant to your curriculum?

Fred Oxby (2023), in his dissertation 'All eyes on me: Racism, Diversity and Decoloniality in the Secondary School History Classroom', argues that one of the most potent forms of decolonisation occurs when pupils are empowered to participate in the process of curriculum development, 'to deliver lessons that are transformative, teachers must be prepared to enter into dialogue and collaboration with students to develop a perception of reality and history that is both critical and humanising'. As referenced by Helen Snelson in Chapter 10, Catherine Priggs (2020) has shared the ways in which her pupils changed the curriculum at her school to widen the representation within it. The Key Stage 3 history curriculum at Park View comes full circle when the power of the archivist is placed into the hands of the pupils, in their final unit at the end of Year 9. Inspired by the work of Dr Samantha Cutrara, a Canadian history teacher and teacher-trainer, pupils have an opportunity to 'decolonise' the archive and navigate their own way through the construction of a digital archive on LGBTQ+ history. In her article *The subjectivity of archives*, Cutrara (2019) states that the work that her postgraduate pupils were completing in their digital archive …

> … was a (re)construction of a moment or moments in time though the (re) valuation and (re)presentation of materials. More specifically, their archive was a (re)construction not because they were putting the original meaning back together again – where, perhaps, some of their hesitation lay – but a (re)construction because they were constructing meaning again (and again and again) through the organization, publication, and ultimate use of these materials.

The LGBTQ+ history unit at Park View challenges pupils to answer the enquiry question 'Parliament, Protest or Pop Culture', which did more to change the position of LGBTQ+ people in Britain?. Each lesson was designed to expose pupils to a wide range of material culture that was present throughout key moments of LGBTQ+ British history since the 1930s, such as the legalisation of homosexuality, Section 28, the AIDS Crisis, and recent legislation to improve civil rights. Every lesson starts with a song that relates to the time period and events being studied and includes filmed interviews, produced by the department, from a wide range of contributors who were asked to select an artefact for a digital archive on LGBTQ+ history. Pupils are invited to hashtag (an accessible form of metadata) a selection of source materials as a precursor to their own decision-making later in the unit. The final outcome of the unit empowers pupils to answer the enquiry question through the construction of their own digital archive, selecting five sources that best support their response, and justifying their choices in a reflective piece of writing. As the responses in Figure 12.2 reveal, the pupils were able to engage in a

---

Image chosen: Marriage (Same Sex Couples) Act, passed on July 17th 2013

Tags: #SameSexMarriageAct #2013 #Legislation #LGBTQ+ #Rights #Government #MariaMiller #QueerRights

I chose this act as it was a massive stepping stone in the history of the LGBT community. This piece of legislation is highly significant to us LGBTQ+ individuals as it allows us to engage in marriage with a partner of the same sex. Not only is it allowing us of the rights we deserve but it also ensures lawful protection against discrimination and harassment. Maria Miller is the one who introduced this law/act.

Image chosen: The trailer image for the hit Netflix series, Heartstopper

Tags: #LGBTQ+ #Netflix #Series #Raisingawareness

I have chosen this image from the Netflix show Heartstopper because it shows how far people have come with accepting that people can be openly gay. Heartstopper is a teen-drama with most of the cast and characters being members of the LGBTQ+ community. It was the number 1 watched show on Netflix for three whole weeks. If content like this was released 10 years ago, it would have been reported, mocked and eventually taken down.

Figure 12.2 Samples of student responses to the creation of a digital archive on the history of the British LGBTQ+ community.

process which allowed them to navigate through the archive in meaningful ways. The first example demonstrates the personal impact of the learning experience, with the pupil feeling so empowered that they are able to publicly acknowledge their identity through their response.

Centring Indigenous Voices

In her aforementioned article, Cutrara (2019) cites the influence of Tuhiwai Smith when she argues that 'the historical method, the standards of reason and logic, and much of how we come to understand the past and present in the Western world come from traditions of Western liberalism situated within genealogies of colonialism, imperialism, capitalism and patriarchy'. Accordingly, an essential aspect of decolonising a curriculum is recognising that there has to be a substantive and substantial shift in both the content and the pedagogy taught in the history classroom. Ned Blackhawk (2023) in his book *The Rediscovery of America* argues that 'It is time to put down the interpretive tools of the previous century and take up new ones'. Heather McGregor (2017) from the University of Ottowa has identified a number of ways in which indigenous approaches to the construction of history differ from the traditional disciplinary approach. For example, she states 'Indigenous knowledge relies on openness to, and the credibility of, orality for a continual (re)making of meaning in the present, including sharing memories, testimony and story'. In addition, indigenous historians use 'Temporal arrangements (which) are not necessarily chronological, linear or progressive, but rather emphasise cycles or circles' or recognise 'Relationships (including with animals) are embedded in an ecological web, where humans are not necessarily dominant, frequently mediated by spiritual understandings'. If we are to take on Blackhawk's challenge of finding new 'tools' then we need to actively participate in the process, with openness and curiosity.

Activity 12.3

1. What are the challenges for teachers that have been trained in the Western European model for working with indigenous voices in the classroom?
2. Are there any 'easy wins' that can help to get started with bringing indigenous voices into the classroom?
3. For which aspects of your current curriculum could you bring in different lenses to view the past?

As the Park View history department values and principles (Figure 12.1) state, we are committed to exploring alternative narratives and teach histories that have previously been marginalised or actively silenced. Throughout the Key Stage 3 curriculum, there are multiple opportunities for pupils to engage with these histories, but in this section, we will focus on the teaching of Native American history to show how we have recentred Indigenous voices.

> Indigenous absence has been a long tradition of American historical analysis… A full telling of American history must account for the dynamics of struggle, survival, and resurgence that frame America's Indigenous past … Existing paradigms of U.S. history remain incomplete when they fail to engage the field. We need to build a more inclusive narrative, and this cannot be accomplished simply by adding new cast members to the dramas of the past. Our history

must reckon with the fact that Indigenous peoples, African Americans, and millions of other non-white citizens have not enjoyed the self-evident truths of equality, life, liberty and the pursuit of happiness.

(Blackhawk, 2023)

In light of Blackhawk's quote, the assessment question for the Year 8 unit on Native American history has undergone a substantial amount of revision over the last five years. The original question was 'What was the most important factor in the destruction of the Native American way of life?'. This was highly problematic because, as Blackhawk argues, this approach 'often foregrounds Indigenous "elimination" as the defining aspect of Native American history and minimises the extent of Indigenous power and agency'. As a result, our pupils were (poorly) taught about the different factors that led to this destruction, including war, technology and the impact of reservations, and were encouraged to analyse which factor was the most significant. The revised assessment question 'Explain how Native Americans were able to resist and survive the attempts to destroy their way of life' represents a substantial shift to acknowledge the 'power and agency' of Native American communities in bringing about sustained resistance and survivance.

The revised teaching started by immediately acknowledging the continued and growing presence of Native Americans in what is today called the United States of America (note the language that is being used here, to acknowledge the impact of settler colonialism on the landform of the Americas). Pupils were introduced to a range of images of Native American traditions and people, deliberately including Deb Haaland, the first Native American to serve in the American Cabinet, as the current Secretary of the Interior in the Biden administration. The revised first lesson also amplified Indigenous voices by including a video from Michael Spears (2014), a well-known actor from the Lakota tribe, talking about the importance of the Tipi for the nomadic tribes on the northern Plains. Further changes were made to the second lesson on the importance of the buffalo, which had previously focused largely on practical aspects such as tipi making. By bringing in the story of the Buffalo Dance from the Aamsskaapipkani (Blackfoot) tribe, pupils were now able to understand the cultural significance of the buffalo, which later supported their understanding of why the deliberate policy to destroy the buffalo herds, had such a devastating impact on Native American communities. The revised third lesson focused on the importance of the natural world and was able to bring in Indigenous voices from the 19th century as well as contemporary writers to show the centrality of the land and how it can 'be positioned as source of knowledge' (McGregor, 2017). Extracts from Black Elk (Oglala Lakota) and Standing Bear (Ponca) described ways in which the natural world informs so much of Native American culture and tradition. The pupils then looked at extracts from a children's picture book, *We are Water Protectors*, by Carole Lindstrom (Ojibwe, 2020) an allegorical tale about the Dakota Access Pipeline protests, demonstrating the continued symbiosis between the natural world and Indigenous cultures, and the ongoing struggles for social and environmental justice.

The fourth lesson was about the early contact between European settlers and the Native American tribes that lived on the east coast. The first iteration relied solely on accounts from Europeans, and completely erased the voices of communities like the Wampanoag and Narraganset. The updated lesson used contemporary scholarship from historian Roxanne Dunbar-Ortiz (2019) in her book *An Indigenous People's History of the United States for Young People*, shown in Figure 12.3, and Lisa Brook's (Missisquoi Abenaki, 2019) *Our Beloved Kin*, to redress this imbalance. Figure 12.3 also invites pupils to use a critical eye on the representation of Native Americans from the settler perspective.

Seal
This seal, from 1629 was used for important documents in Massachusetts where English settlers lived. What is the Native American man saying? Why?

Extract from An Indigenous People's History of the United States for Young People, 2019

To Native American peoples, these colonisers (who were taking over their land) sometimes seemed – and often were – incompetent and virtually helpless. But it soon became clear that they felt entitled to take Native American land and resources for the king or for themselves. They were driven by greed and willing to do just about anything to get what they wanted. This included acts of genocide (mass murder).

Figure 12.3 Extracts from the lesson on settler colonialism in the United States.

The lesson on the Gold Rush shifted the focus away from the practicalities of gold mining and the migration of 'panners' to the west coast, towards the devastating impact on the Native American tribes that had been living in the region. However, whilst pupils were able to learn about what has now been termed the California genocide, with the Native population declining by nearly 90%, they were also shown examples of resistance and survivance in extreme circumstances. A similar focus was brought into the lesson about the forced migrations and the Trail of Tears, where pupils were given the opportunity to explore why the 'Five Civilised Tribes' made a conscious choice to assimilate and adapt their traditional customs and practices in order to survive, and whether this trade-off was worthwhile. Resistance against the US Army was also taught, from the perspective of the Lakota warriors involved in the Battle of the Greasy Grass (Custer's Last Stand), using the artwork of One Bull (Hunkpapa Lakota), who had fought in the battle. The final content that was taught in the unit focused on the Reservations, and particularly the Reservation schools. This was again revised in order to show how relevant this episode is to contemporary America with the recent discovery of mass graves in Canada and the United States. Pupils watched a video clip from Deb Haaland describing the resilience of survivors of the schools.

As a result of this decolonised approach to teaching the history of Native Americans, the pupils were able to respond far more effectively to Blackhawk's (2023) challenge to create a 'full telling of American history (that) must account for the dynamics of struggle, survival, and resurgence that frame America's Indigenous past'.

Activity 12.4

1. Can you identify opportunities in your curriculum where you can amplify voices that have been marginalised or silenced?
2. Can you identify opportunities in your curriculum where you can 'flip the narrative' by looking at examples of resistance and survivance?

Tape Letters

The final case study of decolonisation in practice comes from our introduction of oral history at Parkview, thus bringing voices of the British-Pakistani community directly into the classroom to explore issues around migration, empire and the partition of India and Pakistan. The Tape Letters Project, housed at the Bishopsgate Library in East London, is 'an oral history project aiming to identify, collect and archive messages sent on cassette tape in the 1960s through to the 1980s by families who migrated to the UK from Pakistan between 1950 and 1970' (Bishopsgate Institute, 2024). Working with the founder of the project, Wajid Yaseen, the department produced a scheme of work that draws heavily on source material directly from the cassette tapes and interviews that were carried out with families involved in the practice of using 'Tape Letters' to communicate with their families. Being mindful of Toby Green's warning (2020) of the 'tyranny of the written word' the lessons were largely constructed with the understanding that pupils would be exposed to the historical content of the lessons through listening to oral extracts either as a whole class through the interactive whiteboard, or independently using their phones or laptops. In this way, we were explicitly acknowledging the validity of oral history as an important disciplinary tool, which can also act as a decolonising agent. Alongside the historical content, pupils were also introduced to a range of skills that they would utilise at the end of the unit, when they were asked to conduct their own oral history interview.

The first three lessons of the enquiry focused on the migration experience of the British-Pakistani community, based around the key questions: 'Why did Pakistani people migrate to Britain?', 'What were their experiences?' and 'What was the emotional impact of the Tape Letters?'. By listening to extracts such as those transcribed in Figure 12.4, the pupils were able to engage at a much deeper emotional level than if they had just read the transcripts. Wajid was able to participate in many of the lessons and 'sensed the children experienced a more tangible sort of history' (Lyndon-Cohen, 2023).

The second half of the unit focused on the British Empire in India and Partition. In the first lesson on empire, pupils had the opportunity to listen to an extract

Abda Khan

My mom really struggled when she got here, because she didn't know anybody, she didn't speak any English, um, she had all these children to bring up and uh, you know, we grew up in a poverty really. Uh, we definitely grew up in poverty. I mean, uh, I remember my mom used to get our clothes from like jumble sales and, um, salvation army used to do a jumble sale. I remember I used to go down with her to that. And, um, she used to make all our winter clothes, like our jumpers and everything. She used to knit them herself. Uh, and then she got an allotment and she used to work really hard to grow her own fruit and veg because it's too expensive to buy, all that kind of thing. So my mom was an amazing woman, very entrepreneurial. Um, no education, but she was bright, she was sharp.

Asma Mirza

I used to wait for his cassette, or postman, I used to wait for the postman, like when would postman come and when he will give me the cassette. So, I was waiting, I was waiting then postman came and then he it's like a registry, it's like a big parcel, So, I opened and I just straight away listened to it, and it was just the feeling, it's just, ummm... I can't, I can't describe those feelings, it's just, ummm... it's just like I am listening to him for the first time, it's like I am listening what is in his heart for the first time, and what he thinks about me, and it's just amazing feeling, I can't describe right now what I felt when I listened to his cassette first time. So, I thought that there is somebody else who loves me that much. It's just I couldn't believe that there is person who loves me that much. So, this was his first cassette, So, this thing didn't stop there and it just going on and on and on, for I think, for a year, two years or three years, I don't know, I am not sure for how long, but it continued for So, many years.

Figure 12.4 Extracts pupils listened to from The Tape Letters Project.

from an interview with Wajid's mother, who only speaks Potwari, an oral-only language from the Pakistani Punjab region. Despite hearing the audio clip in a language which none of the pupils spoke, they were easily able to identify the emotion (anger) that was behind her comments as she described the British as 'snakes in the grass, waiting to strike'. In the lesson on Partition, pupils watched an interview between Wajid and Masooma Malik and then responded to the following questions, drawing on their prior knowledge of Trouillot's work: 'Why have some people found it hard to talk about Partition?' and 'Why might there be silences about the Partition experiences of Indian and Pakistani people?'. The final task was for pupils to conduct their own oral history interviews with a member of their family with a focus on their own migration history. Pupils were encouraged to use a range of open and closed questions, and to conduct their interviews using an AI recording app on their phones which transcribed their interviews.

Decolonising the Mainstream Curriculum

Here are some suggested alternatives to typical enquiry questions or topics that might appear in many schools across the UK:

- How different were medieval ideas of love and relationships from our own?
- How can Black Tudors help us to understand how historians construct the past?
- What can you learn from the letters of Walter Tull about the experiences of soldiers during WWI?
- Explain how Native Americans were able to resist and survive the attempts to destroy their way of life.

CONCLUSIONS

The case studies shared in this chapter represent the opening foray into constructing a decolonised history curriculum at Park View School. This is not something that can be achieved in the short term, but instead involves a long-term commitment to redesigning and redrafting a curriculum that reflects not just a more diverse representation within the history classroom, but also acknowledges the power relations that have resided in the discipline. The combination of evidential material that derives from the experience of both the 'coloniser' and the 'colonised' with the 'alternative knowledges' signposted by Tuhiwai Smith, informing our pedagogy, has started to deliver a curriculum that 'is both critical and humanising'.

SUMMARY OF KEY POINTS

- Decolonisation is a contested term, but the work of the academics Tuhiwai Smith, Fanon, Trouillot and Dabiri helps provide us with a working definition.
- Decolonisation involves interrogating the construction of history, so that the stories of the 'bottom up' are told.
- Academics such as Tuhiwai Smith, Trouillot, Dabiri and Cutrara offer a range of approaches that can widen the lens within the history curriculum and de-centre the Eurocentric approach to the content and construction of history.
- Decolonising the content of the history curriculum involves studying communities who have been silenced or marginalised, and placing their stories at the centre of enquiries.

- When studying the histories of indigenous communities, it is important for pupils to learn how they have resisted and survived settler colonialism to give them back their power and agency.
- Decolonising the construction of history involves pupils using new approaches and non-traditional sources to study the past. Oral history and archiving can provide ways for pupils to navigate and challenge the dominant narratives.

RESOURCES AND FURTHER READING

Ahlberg Yohe, Jill, & Zucker, Steven. 'Custer's Last Stand — from the Lakota perspective' [YouTube Video], 2018. https://www.youtube.com/watch?v=OtDT_WcIEgo

Bishopsgate Institute. 'Tape Letters Project', [Online Article], Bishopsgate Institute, 2024. https://www.bishopsgate.org.uk/collections/tape-letters-project

Blackhawk, Ned. The Rediscovery of America: Native Peoples and the Unmaking of U.S. History. New Haven and London: Yale University Press 2023: 2–5.

Bonn, M. J. 'Imperialism' in Encyclopaedia of the Social Sciences, (1932): 612. Quoted in Klose, Fabian. 'Decolonization and Revolution' [Blog Post], Brewminate: A Bold Blend of News and Ideas, (2016). https://brewminate.com/decolonization-and-revolution/

Brooks, Lisa. Our Beloved Kin: A New History of King Philip's War. New Haven and London: Yale University Press 2019.

'California Genocide', Wikipedia. https://en.wikipedia.org/wiki/California_genocide

Cutrara, S. 'The Subjectivity of Archives: Learning from, With, and Resisting Archives and Archival Sources in Teaching and Learning history' in Historical Encounters, 6:1, (2019): 117–132. Available here: https://www.hej-hermes.net/_files/ugd/f067ea_284bebadace64843b1fc715fe2ed449a.pdf#page=120

Dabiri, Emma. Don't Touch My Hair. London: Penguin 2020.

Dunbar-Ortiz, Roxanne. An Indigenous People's History of the United States for Young People. Boston: Beacon Press 2019.

Echo-Hawk, Abigail (2019) on Twitter. https://twitter.com/echohawkd3/status/1170371608894046208?lang=en

Fanon, Frantz. The Wretched of the Earth. New York: Grove Press 1963: 35.

Green, Toby. 'What Have Historians Been Arguing About… African History in the Precolonial Period?' in Teaching History, 181, Handling Sources Edition, (2020): 26–27. London: Historical Association.

Klose, Fabian. 'Decolonization and Revolution' [Blog Post], Brewminate: A Bold Blend of News and Ideas, (2016). https://brewminate.com/decolonization-and-revolution/

Lindstrom, Carole. We Are Water Protectors. New York: Roaring Book Press 2020.

Lyndon-Cohen, Dan. 'Oral History' in Fairlamb, Alex, & Ball, Rachel. (eds.). What Is History Teaching, Now?. Woodbridge: John Catt 2023: 123.

McGregor, Heather Elizabeth. 'One Classroom, Two Teachers? Historical Thinking and Indigenous Education in Canada' in Critical Education, 8(14), (2017): 1–18.

Oxby, Fred. '"All eyes on me": Racism, Diversity and Decoloniality in the Secondary School History Classroom' [Dissertation], Decolonial Curriculum, (2023). https://decolonial-curriculum.pubpub.org/pub/1chsznkr

Priggs, Catherine. 'No More 'doing' Diversity: How One Department Used Year 8 Input to Reform Curricular Thinking About Content choice' in Teaching History, 179, Culture in Conversation Edition, (2020): 10–19. London: Historical Association.

Richards, Elizabeth. 'The First Pan-African Conference' [Online Article], Black History Month, (2020). https://www.blackhistorymonth.org.uk/article/section/history-of-politics/first-pan-african-conference/

Spears, Michael. 'Telling story about the tipi' [YouTube Video], (2014). https://www.youtube.com/watch?v=pH2vmzDusgA&t=3s

Trouillot, Michel-Rolph. Silencing the Past: Power and the Production of History. Beacon Press 2015: 35–36.

Tuhiwai Smith, Linda. Decolonizing Methodologies: Research and Indigenous Peoples. Dunedin: University of Otago Press 1999: 34.

Webb, Edward. 'What Have Historians Been Arguing About … … Decolonisation and the British Empire?' in Teaching History, 178, Constructing Accounts Edition, (2020): 42–43. London: Historical Association.

Chapter 13 Progress and Assessment in History

Victoria Barnett

BACKGROUND

If you have been working your way through each of the preceding chapters, then you have already done some real grappling with curriculum and lesson design. You've already explored the importance of a strong enquiry question, what it means to teach each of the disciplinary concepts and how to support pupils in wrestling with these. The next thorny question is 'how do pupils get better and make progress in history?' and the next logical step, 'how can we tell?'.

Before we look at the 'how', it is worth discussing the 'what'. Consider the following questions:

- What is historical knowledge?
- How might historical knowledge differ from other subject knowledge, such as mathematical knowledge? What impact does this have on assessment?

Historical knowledge can be understood as a combination of substantive knowledge and disciplinary knowledge. Whilst substantive knowledge is knowledge about the past (the 'what' of history), disciplinary knowledge is 'knowledge about how historians and others study the past, and how they construct historical claims, arguments and accounts' (the 'how' of history). This is 'not a set of generic skills, but a complex body of knowledge' (Ofsted subject review of history, 2023). See Chapter 4 for further analysis of substantive and disciplinary knowledge in history, and examples of what they both involve.

Historical knowledge is also cumulative in nature, compared with a hierarchical subject such as maths: this means that there are fewer threshold concepts in history that require one component to be taught before another (Howard & Hill, 2020). In maths, pupils have to begin by learning their numbers and how to count before they can progress any further, whilst in history pupils could begin by studying any time period (even if there are reasons for choosing one over another). This doesn't mean that each unit should be taught in isolation however – key concepts, ideas and themes run throughout history that can be used to help build pupil knowledge and understanding over time. These ideas surrounding historical knowledge throw up further questions: How do we **create** assessments that capture the nuances of historical study? And how do we encapsulate all of this in a **measurable** way?

THE PROBLEM WITH LEVEL DESCRIPTORS AND GCSE MARK SCHEMES

The history-teaching community have been grappling with these issues for decades. Following the introduction of national curriculum levels in 1988, various history teachers were critical of how these levels, designed to provide best-fit descriptions of pupils' progress across a key stage, were being used to assess individual pieces of work. Burnham and Brown (2009) presented an approach to 'Assessment without Level Descriptors' which spoke of the irrelevance of level descriptors for measuring progress. A real opportunity was presented in 2014 when Michael Gove, then Secretary of State for Education, announced that the National Curriculum reforms would include the removal of the heavily criticised 'attainment levels'. All schools were left with the same question: 'What could life after levels look like?'

In the immediate aftermath, for many schools, assessment involved recreating their own level descriptors that mirrored those just removed to demonstrate pupil progress, or looking at GCSE mark schemes and creating a GCSE style grading system across Key Stage 3 and Key Stage 4. Progress could be demonstrated through pupils remaining on the same GCSE 'number' whilst the domain expanded. There were many problems with these approaches; namely that all the issues seen with levels were just rebranded and that the reliance on GCSE style assessments led to incorrect inferences about attainment. Progress was seen as something that needed to be mapped and tracked on a linear scale, that looked like a mark scheme or progression ladder.

Kate Hammond's hugely influential article (2014) in Teaching History encapsulated the problems with this approach to assessment and progress and demonstrated the beginnings of the change in thinking. Hammond wanted to interrogate what led to stronger historical analysis in pupil essays. She found that pupils with stronger analysis drew on a range of substantive knowledge including 'period knowledge' and 'wider historical knowledge' that went far beyond that taught for the particular essay question. When turning to the grading of this pupil work however, Hammond identified that generic GCSE mark schemes didn't fully capture the 'layers of knowledge' that differentiated exceptional pupil responses from those that had a more surface level understanding, instead rewarding specific details and precision of substantive material. This was clear through Hammond's examination of two pupils' work, both of whom were awarded an A grade on an essay question concerning the role of propaganda in Hitler's rise to Chancellor in January 1933. Both pupils demonstrated 'sustained focus' and 'accurate and relevant material' when crafting their arguments – however, one pupil based their line of argument solely within the realms of topic knowledge whilst the other pupil used period and wider historical knowledge to craft a more nuanced and sophisticated argument.

Bjork's work (2012) on cognitive science and performance similarly supports the issues with over reliance on mark schemes and grades for understanding progress. He explains the difference between performance and learning and states '... performance is often fleeting' with short-term performance on assessments often being a misnomer to long-term learning (2013). Pupils being able to achieve the often vague descriptors on mark schemes is therefore a poor proxy for making judgements on genuine progress in history. Their knowledge may be surface level, may have been crammed for the purposes of the assessment and then not retained in the long term, or not show the deeper, nuanced historical understanding we want our pupils to have.

WHAT ARE WE TRYING TO ASSESS?

Christine Counsell and Michael Fordham (2020) built on the work of Kate Hammond, pioneering the idea of the 'curriculum as the progression model'. In this instance, progress is not about meeting arbitrary descriptors of performance, but instead the journey a pupil takes through a well sequenced curriculum which becomes more complex over time. The reforms to Ofsted inspections in 2019 also adopted this approach to evaluating the curriculum: '[Inspectors] will also look at how leaders have broken down the content into components and sequenced that content in a logical progression, systematically and explicitly, for all pupils to acquire the intended knowledge and skills'. History deep dives during inspections now interrogate the curriculum, asking subject leads to explain the rationale for curriculum sequencing and how this aids pupils to progress in the subject.

But what does 'curriculum as the progression model' mean? Quite literally it means that pupils make progress through their experience of the substantive and disciplinary knowledge embedded in the curriculum. This curriculum won't be one made up of standalone historical enquiries that might be interesting in their own merit. This curriculum instead relies on a carefully planned sequence of enquiry questions, treated as building blocks that allow pupils to build both their substantive knowledge of the past and their disciplinary knowledge of how historians have studied it. As Kate Hammond (2014) asked in her article, 'What tactics are we employing to ensure this week's topic knowledge becomes next week's period knowledge and next year's wider historical knowledge?'

Figure 13.1 shows my Key Stage 3 curriculum with key enquiries highlighted to show how pupils' understanding of disciplinary history builds across the three years. We have several enquiries that look at *how* history is constructed, focusing on the use of sources and what they tell us about the period. This is the first unit we do with Year 7 through examining Britain after the Romans left, and the last unit they study in Year 9 where they use contemporary sources to construct different narratives about the 1960s. Similarly, we build pupils' exposure to interpretations across the three years, with pupils engaging with Schama's opinion on the Norman Conquest through to pupils writing how far they agree with Richard Overy's reason for the outcome of World War II in Year 9. The curriculum also allows for key substantive concepts to build: one example is the theme of power which pupils study through different lenses and in different time periods so they can develop a strong schema of 'power' as a concept in history.

This approach to curriculum design and progress is also supported by recent developments in cognitive science and how pupils learn. For our pupils to write those confident, well-developed answers, they need to be able to remember different types of information – facts, concepts and norms. However, as stated by Yana Weinstein and Megan Sumeracki (otherwise known as the Learning Scientists, 2019) 'as soon as we learn something, we immediately start to forget it'. The key to remembering as much information as possible is for our pupils to move their knowledge from their short-term memory to their long-term memory, and an important way in ensuring that happens is for information to be encoded in a meaningful way (Craik & Lockhart, 1972). This can happen when pupils integrate new information with pre-existing knowledge that helps develop schema, an over-arching structure of knowledge which makes it easier to remember new information later and creates security in understanding. Designing a curriculum that builds upon prior knowledge through recall and retrieval, and through doing so allows knowledge to be developed and changed, ensures that pupils make progress through their study of the curriculum and become more confident historians.

Year 7: Enquiries	Year 8: Enquiries	Year 9: Enquiries
How can we find out about who lived in Britain after the Romans?	Why did Henry VIII break from Rome?	Why did World War I begin in 1914?
Why was King Alfred known as the Great?	In what ways did the Reformation matter to ordinary people?	Who fought on the Western Front?
How did William of Normandy become King of England?	Why did the Civil War break out in 1642?	Why did World War I come to an end in 1918?
How did England change during the Norman Conquest?	In what ways was Britain turned upside down in the seventeenth century?	What did Communism look like in the Soviet Union?
Which sources reveal the most about medieval peasants?	What were the causes and consequences of the American Revolution?	How did Stalin control the people of the USSR?
How was Baghdad connected to the wider world?	What were the causes and consequences of the French Revolution?	What was the turning point of World War II?
Why did Europeans go on Crusade?	Were events in eighteenth century America and France more revolutionary than events in seventeenth century Britain?	Holocaust Unit: How did life change for European Jews by 1939?
Who lived in the Crusader states?	Was the British Empire a force for good?	Holocaust Unit: What was the Holocaust?
What does the life of Eleanor of Aquitaine tell us about who held power in the Middle Ages?	Why was the slave trade abolished in the British Empire in 1807?	What was the impact of the World Wars on migration to Britain?
Why did Kings struggle to rule England?	Why do historians disagree about the impact of the Industrial Revolution?	What stories can be told about the 1960s?
Why have the Mongols been remembered as violent?	How did Britain become a democracy?	
How big a threat was the Peasants' Revolt to the power of the monarchs?		

Figure 13.1 My Key Stage 3 curriculum.

'Curriculum as the progression model' therefore encourages curriculum design that allows for pupils to return to key substantive and disciplinary knowledge, adding greater depth and understanding to this each time. The model can also be used to help teachers identify key areas of content to be assessed across the curriculum. It is important, however, that assessment design in this model does assess the curriculum being delivered and doesn't go beyond these parameters. The developments in cognitive science for learning outlined in the previous paragraph can also complement and aid these decisions about assessment.

HOW CAN WE ASSESS?

To ensure that pupils are grasping the curriculum and making progress, we need to embed routine formative [informal] assessment into our lessons, as well as looking for opportunities for summative [formal] assessment too. Formative or 'informal' assessment is a method of assessing whilst learning is happening, as opposed to a summative or 'formal' assessment which takes place at the end of a topic or sequence of learning. When considering which type of assessment to use when, one important thing to consider is that there is no perfect assessment. Dylan Wiliam (2020) explains this when writing that 'every assessment system involves trade-offs…'. No one assessment will be able to provide all the information we want to acquire about our curriculums and how well pupils have grasped it. Michael Fordham's idea (2014) of a 'mixed constitution' of assessment captures this. He argues that different forms of assessment, such as low-stakes knowledge tests, end-of-enquiry outcome tasks and end-of-year assessments, all play a different role in helping us to assess pupils' overall progress in history. This 'mixed constitution' approach to assessment avoids one method dominating teacher inferences on progress, as well as preventing the pitfalls that predictable assessments can create for a teacher's analysis of progress (Wiliam, 2020). A multi-faceted approach to assessment in the history classroom reflects the multi-faceted nature of the subject and allows for greater teacher understanding about how well pupils are moving through the curriculum.

How Do I Use Informal Assessment?

Informal assessments give us instant feedback on our teaching and how pupils are responding to the curriculum. In turn, they help guide us in what we need to do in response to prevent the development of misconceptions and to unpick errors and confusion in pupil thinking. Informal assessment therefore needs to be carefully embedded into your sequenced lessons at an appropriate time to give you timely feedback that can be responded to. The remainder of this section provides a variety of informal assessments which can be used and adapted to provide a broad set of insights as to how pupils are developing both their substantive and disciplinary knowledge.

Lesson Quizzes

Teachers can devise simple quizzes to check pupils remember essentials from previous lessons. These will often be simple recall questions to check factual understanding, such as 'When was the Battle of Hastings?'. Displaying the answers whilst pupils check, and then asking pupils to raise their hand if they got question 1 correct very quickly gives the teacher invaluable information about which content pupils got correct and which will need revisiting. These knowledge quizzes can also be used to check the security of core knowledge needed across an enquiry, such as vocabulary, dates and chronology, and can be retested throughout an enquiry (and beyond) to check that pupils have a solid understanding before moving on (Donaghy, 2014). Varying the wording of the question will check that pupils have fully grasped the knowledge rather than just remembering the predictability of the assessment.

Multiple Choice Questions

Teachers can devise a multiple choice 'hinge' question, which provides plausible distractors that encourage pupils to really think about the correct answer as opposed to it being obvious. The creation of these are very difficult to get right – the teacher needs to think about what they want the 'incorrect' answers to show and what this would mean for their reteaching. For example:

> What is a **citizen**?
>
> A person who has rights because they are from a certain place
> The richer people of Rome
> The poorer people of Rome
> A person who is allowed to vote for their leader

This multiple choice question focuses on a particular substantive concept in Ancient Rome. The question is concise to avoid cognitive overload, whilst the distractors are all plausible. Each 'incorrect answer' reveals something to me about pupil understanding and thinking, allowing me to unpick and reteach accordingly.

Daisy Christodoulou (2017) writes a very compelling argument for the benefits of well-crafted multiple choice questions (MCQs) and the information they can provide teachers. Well-chosen 'distractors' can provide insight into misconceptions that longer, open-ended written pieces of work wouldn't necessarily pick up. Across a set of 10 MCQs teachers could track the number of pupils who got the right or wrong answer, but also the distractor that was chosen. This allows teachers to provide meaningful feedback – not just 'here is the correct answer' but 'this is why the others are incorrect'. A later round of similar questions helps to see if the pupils have understood. MCQs take a long time to create, but once done are invaluable for checking conceptual, factual and chronological understanding.

Timelines

Teachers can use a quick timeline assessment to see if pupils are secure in the narrative of events just studied. These assessments help give pupils a sense of time and place as well as helping to develop teacher explanations on cause and consequence. They can be used to support and check for disciplinary understanding based on how historians develop narratives, as well as being used to check for pupils' understanding of a series of events stretching over a broader chronological period. Elizabeth Carr and Christine Counsell (2014) trialled this approach in their respective settings and wrote about how it was utilised to assess understanding of historical periods.

Answering the Enquiry Question

Pupils can demonstrate their knowledge and thinking from a sequence of lessons by answering the enquiry question. In my previous role as Head of History when I was designing the Key Stage 3 curriculum along with my department, we planned our enquiry questions and their duration with this model in mind. With our enquiry questions lasting anywhere between 4 and 6 lessons, it meant pupils were writing a response to the question every 2–3 weeks. This wasn't always an essay – sometimes they were responding to a historian's interpretations of events such as Simon Schama's take on the impact of the Norman Conquest. Sometimes pupils were examining how a source helped someone who was studying that topic, such as understanding responses to appeasement. Circulating and live marking during the task itself helped identify misconceptions in the moment and sample marking allowed for a more in depth look at their work to provide feedback on what to develop next. The carefully sequenced curriculum which built in enquiry questions on causation, and change and continuity meant that pupils were responding to a different focus each time, giving us a greater insight into their developing understanding of the substantive and disciplinary domains.

Class Discussion

Creating an opportunity for pupil discussion surrounding a key substantive concept or term allows for a non-written form of formative assessment to take place in the classroom. The example created by Burnham and Brown (2009) where spoken tasks were created around the term 'imperialism' allowed for teachers to hear which pupils had an uncertain understanding of the term, which pupils had grasped the basic premise but had a limited idea of what the term encompassed, and which pupils were ready to be stretched with additional or challenging examples.

The great news about these informal assessments is not only that it gives you as the teacher some key information to inform what you do next. Testing by its very nature encourages the recall of information from memory, which research shows when done frequently helps strengthen the memory itself (Weinstein & Sumeracki, 2019). For teachers then, informal assessment helps measure understanding, whilst for pupils, it actually helps develop understanding. This is called the Testing Effect and was an idea first put forward by Roediger and Karpicke (2006). In their study, they identified that testing not only measured knowledge, but also had a positive impact on future retention of that knowledge. In fact, testing had a greater impact on retention of knowledge than the equal time restudying the material.

> **Activity 13.1**
>
> Consider a series of lessons you have planned:
>
> - What do you want to find out about what pupils have learned from this enquiry? Do you want to check for security of the knowledge acquired, or try to find the misconceptions they have developed?
> - Based on your answers to these questions, which of the examples of informal assessment would give you the most helpful information on what pupils have learned from this enquiry? Remember – whilst a varied approach is key, if you have followed the principles of a good enquiry the lesson sequence won't be that long so be realistic about how much informal assessment you can realistically complete.
> - Now you have considered the tasks, whereabouts in the lesson sequences should they take place?

Responding to Informal Assessment

All of this information should influence what you do next as a teacher. This action will occur on different timescales depending on the findings that you have gathered and when you gathered them within the enquiry. Before deciding the appropriate time frame, I like to ask myself the following questions to help make the decision about the most appropriate action:

- Have the vast majority understood? A re-teach in these scenarios isn't always going to be the best use of lesson time. Speaking individually to the few may be a more effective targeted approach.

- Have over half understood? Whilst there is no definitive number for what decides a re-teach, I tend to work with 50% as my base. If over 50% of them have got the answer correct but it isn't the vast majority, I would plan for a quick reteach. As a teacher you will get a sense of the level of reteach needed – is this a quick reminder of a concept to jog the memory, or does your questioning demonstrate a lack of deeper understanding? This will help determine the timeframe of the action.
- I generally consider scenarios where more than 50% pupils are getting the incorrect answer or are showing misconceptions in their written work worthy of a full re-teach.

An important note at this stage – a reteach doesn't necessarily mean replanning and delivering the knowledge in an entirely different way to how it was done the first-time round. Cognitive science shows us that forgetting is a natural part of how the brain functions. Ebbinghaus' forgetting curve shows that even if pupils have previously learnt something it can still be forgotten (Lemov, 2021). Reteaching doesn't necessarily mean reinvention – it can sometimes just mean revisiting.

Your informal assessment will have given you some key findings. The above questions will hopefully have helped you consider the actions required. The next crucial part is the timeframe. When should the action be taken?

You might remedy the issue immediately. A lot of evidence suggests the most effective time is to deal with it in the moment. For example, a recap quiz has shown that two Year 7 pupils have incorrectly identified that the Vikings came from Germany. An effective way of tackling this would be to talk to these two specific pupils during the lesson to unpick and correct the misconception. This can be done verbally. The teacher may then revisit these pupils when the question comes up again later in the enquiry to check that they now have the correct answer. Similarly, during circulating you may notice that a significant proportion of pupils have misunderstood hyperinflation. Rather than let this develop further, you could pause the lesson and revisit the concept. Use cold calling of pupils who have understood to help develop pupil understanding alongside your re-explanation. Then ask pupils to revisit their written answer and edit it accordingly. Check in on three of those pupils who had misconceptions earlier in the lesson to see what their edits look like now.

Alternatively, you might re-plan the next lesson. It is possible that the findings lend itself to something that needs to be revisited in the next lesson rather than something that needs to be unpicked immediately. If pupils have demonstrated narrative confusion, it may be that you start the next lesson with a retelling of a story from an earlier lesson for them to attach the new content too. A visual source may help add detail to the period where pupils are lacking to recall the multifaceted nature of the period – think the World Turned Upside cartoon to encourage pupils to consider the multitude of reasons for instability in the 17th century. Sources can also be used to add additional period detail. If pupils are struggling to fully demonstrate their understanding of a period, getting them to grapple with a source from the time and analyse its content is another way of encouraging them to use their contextual understanding to place it within the enquiry (see Chapter 11 for further discussion of the use of historical sources to embed understanding).

Finally, you might re-think part of your curriculum. When I was Head of Department, I would build in department time to run 'MOTs' of our enquiry questions and lessons. Part of that included teachers bringing their findings from informal assessment for that question and the department discussing these. Were these findings apparent across all six classes? What were the common misconceptions? Were the lessons leading up to pupils reading Bede detailed enough for pupils to have the knowledge to grapple with his account of England? Do we need to change the order of our lessons in Year 8 to help pupils gain a greater sense of the connections between empire, industry and slavery?

These are decisions that are best made with colleagues in your department but that are important to regularly grapple with. A bit like the painting of the San Francisco bridge, the curriculum is never done. Make notes of your findings from informal assessments and bring them to department meetings so that the curriculum is constantly developing to ensure pupils make the greatest progress.

This responsive approach to teaching in history is part of what makes good teaching in the subject. The use of regular informal assessment allows you to regularly investigate and interrogate pupils' knowledge of the past and how historians work. It can prevent misconceptions from embedding, it allows you to spot opportunities for developing understanding into the strong understanding seen by Kate Hammond in her Year 11 assessments, as well as providing opportunities to build on the work of cognitive science to develop those moments to build fluency and retain knowledge. This in turn helps pupils make progress across the curriculum.

THE 'MIXED CONSTITUTION'

All of the informal assessments mentioned in the previous section can together provide a 'mixed constitution' of assessment, as advocated by Fordham (2014). Individually, they are isolated components of what it means to make progress in history. Recap quizzes based around recall of information can help us confirm who is secure in their understanding of key dates, names and events. Timelines can help teachers understand who has a strong grasp of the chronology of the immediate topic but also the wider period. A carefully created multiple choice hinge question will help teachers identify and unpick any misconceptions. However, a pupil who regularly gets 5/5 on recap quizzes may not know how to turn these facts into an argument to answer a broader question. A pupil who is able to create a detailed timeline of a period may not be able to create a narrative of cause or causation from these details. A MCQ only identifies that pupils perhaps haven't developed this misconception – they may have others. It is only when we take these components together, from knowledge quizzes to extended writing, that we get a clearer picture of pupils' overall progress in history.

Dylan Wiliam (2020) writes about this when he talks about how 'assessment can be valid in some circumstances but not in others'. Whilst the informal assessments mentioned allow us to make inferences, they only provide us with information about that particular task. As teachers we shouldn't be placing additional weight onto what this information tells us as it can lead us to make poor conclusions about what pupils can and cannot do. Similarly, we need to be careful about using these informal assessments to measure progress.

Consider the following situation. Pupil A completes 4 recap quizzes, and the teacher records the following marks:

	Recap Quiz 1 (/20)	RQ2	RQ3	RQ4
	End of WWI/Treaty of Versailles	Treaty of Versailles/ Weimar Germany up to 1924	Weimar Germany 1924-1929	Rise of the Nazis 1929-1932
Pupil A	6	6	7	8

The teacher is thrilled! Pupil A is making good progress in history! Or are they?

Whilst the data seems to suggest progress because the mark is increasing each time, the conclusion drawn is a false one. The questions asked focus on a different area of historical knowledge each time – the pupil isn't necessarily making progress but is instead stronger in one area of the topic than the others. The pupil has performed differently on each assessment due to this rather than making progress in history. Drawing conclusions based on the change between scores can also create a false sense of security too – we could assume that a pupil has made progress because their knowledge quiz scores have changed, or that pupils haven't made progress because the data shows that their second knowledge quiz is the same as the first. However, given everything we have looked at about the isolated components and subject domain focus there needs to be caution in drawing any conclusions from this 'change data' and what it tells us about pupil progress in history (Wiliam, 2020).

These informal assessment points can be used throughout an enquiry to get a sense of pupils' knowledge as they build towards an end of enquiry task. As you have read in Chapter 3 on planning enquiries by Paula Worth, enquiry questions frame a sequence of lessons around a meaningful and intriguing historical question, focused on a disciplinary concept. These enquiry questions and end of enquiry tasks can allow teachers to assess a wide variety of types of historical thinking. In a key article looking at 'Assessment after Levels', Geraint Brown and Sally Burnham (2014) surmised the significance of these when they wrote 'These enquiry-based tasks ensure that assessment is integral to the teaching, bringing together the learning that has taken place rather than being bolted on at the end of a topic'.

These end of enquiry activities can vary and focus on different aspects of substantive and disciplinary knowledge. My department and I worked on the opening Year 7 enquiry of the year where at the end of six lessons they answer the question 'How can we find out who lived in Britain after the Romans?'. The sequence of lessons looks at a variety of sources from the period including extracts from Gildas and Bede, artefacts from the Sutton Hoo hoard, surviving 'buildings' such as the Saxon 'Wayland Smithy temple' and Pope Gregory's letter to his priests. The lessons encouraged pupils to engage with the disciplinary nature of the subject by examining the sources historians interrogate for evidence alongside learning the narrative of the 'Dark Ages' through a differing lens. Within this enquiry pupils complete informal assessment in the form of recap quizzes focused on key dates and individuals they need to know for this unit. MCQs such as those shown in Figure 13.2 identify any misconceptions arising from the narrative of the unit. The write up to this question however goes beyond this factual recall and instead showed teachers how well pupils were able to use varying source types as evidence to support their inferences, alongside their grasp of the 'difference' of this world before moving onto the next enquiry. This varied approach to assessment across the unit gives our Year 7 teachers insight into the cohort's comprehension of the significant events from this time frame and their chronological understanding of what happened after the Romans left, alongside the pupils developing conceptual understanding of the formation of England as well as their ability to use evidence to formulate an argument.

FORMAL ASSESSMENTS

The 'mixed constitution' approach outlined can also be applied when designing formal (summative) assessments. As Daisy Christodoulou (2017) writes, 'We cannot rely on just one assessment or one style of assessment for all the assessment

1. Which of the following was a kingdom formed by the Angles?
    a. Northumbria
    b. Essex
    c. Kent
    d. Wessex
    e. Sussex
2. Where did the Jutes settle?
    a. Northumbria
    b. Essex
    c. Kent
    d. Wessex
    e. Sussex
3. From what part of Europe did the Anglo-Saxons migrate to Britain?
    a. Spain
    b. Ireland
    c. Norway
    d. Germany
    e. Normandy
4. Paganism was a polytheistic religion. What does this mean?
    a. They believed in one god.
    b. They believed in many gods.
    c. They did not believe in any gods.
5. Which empire abandoned Britain around 410?
    a. Byzantine
    b. Scandinavian
    c. Anglo-Saxon
    d. French
    e. Roman
6. Who was sent by Pope Gregory to convert the Angles in 597?
    a. Alfred
    b. Offa
    c. Bede
    d. Augustine
    e. Edward
7. What was the first Anglo-Saxon kingdom to convert to Christianity?
    a. Mercia
    b. Essex
    c. Kent
    d. Wessex
    e. Sussex
8. What was the *wergeld*?
    a. The Anglo-Saxon army
    b. The value placed on someone's life
    c. Money paid to the Vikings
    d. The home of the pagan gods
    e. An illuminated manuscript
9. Which monastery was sacked by the Vikings in 793?
    a. Lindisfarne
    b. Rome
    c. London
    d. Iona
    e. Winchester
10. The Vikings originally came from which part of Europe?
    a. Germany
    b. Ireland
    c. France
    d. Scandinavia
    e. Britain

Figure 13.2 Example multiple choice questions from an enquiry on the 'Dark Ages'.

information we need'. These formal assessments usually take place at various points across the academic year and will vary from school to school – in some places formal assessment can take place three times a year and, in some schools, it is once a year.

Working out what should be tested in these summative assessments can sometimes be very difficult to establish and will again look different from school to school. The assessment should focus on what the key takeaway knowledge is that you want pupils to be able to recall from the last unit, the last term, since the last assessment point, and possibly even from last year. Consider the model of building a curriculum from different building blocks that adds to a secure understanding for our pupils from the beginning of this chapter – using a similar approach to designing assessment is a good starting place.

For example, take the scenario of an end of Year 9 formal assessment. For some pupils, this may be the last history assessment they do if they haven't chosen the subject for GCSE. So, what do you want to see if pupils know? What could you include to find that knowledge? And what do you want to find out from your pupils who are continuing onto Key Stage 4? A blend of different types of questions will work here to test the range of knowledge these pupils have:

- Incorporate some quick recall questions: a series of quick responses on key years, events and individuals can be effective for assessing pupils' substantive knowledge of what they have been taught.
- Multiple choice questions from a broader time frame with well-constructed distractors will allow pupils to demonstrate some broader conceptual understanding from across enquiry questions.
- A timeline activity will allow pupils to demonstrate their narrative understanding of a unit or two. Extensions here can include picking two events and asking pupils to explain how one led to another.
- Providing pupils with a written source from one of the time periods being examined and asking them to identify some key details from it, or to explain which event it is connected to and how they know, can give some insight into their ability to tackle primary sources. It is worth remembering that pupils' ability to tackle the language of the source and their ability to decode unfamiliar language, particularly if it is an unseen source, may impact their success with this task, and so inferences from this type of activity should be cautious.
- A piece of historical scholarship where pupils read and summarise the opinion being put forward can give insight into how pupils grapple with the work of historians (again, some caution needed based on pupils' reading ability).
- Some essay questions focused on different disciplinary thinking that draw on but don't use the exact same enquiry questions that the pupils have come across in lessons. These can be topic focused or perhaps pose broader questions.

Here are some example essay questions for Year 8:

- Why did the English Civil War break out in 1642?
- How had the power of monarchs changed by the end of the 17th century?
- Were events in 18th-century France more revolutionary than events in 17th-century Britain?

The first essay question encourages pupils to focus on one unit they had previously studied. The second essay question is broader in scope and encourages pupils to recall information from the power of monarchs unit they studied in Year 7, and compare this to the power of monarchs they studied at the beginning of Year 8. Pupils will demonstrate their understanding of what monarchical power looks like and how it changes and why through this question. The third essay question interrogates pupil understanding of revolution as a substantive concept, and how that can look different in different countries. They should then use their understanding of that to compare two different nations from two different time periods to reach a decision.

Teachers can not only make inferences based on what the pupils write but also on what questions they choose – if Year 8 predominantly choose Essay Question 1, what does that tell us about them as historians? Are they confident enough to be tackling these other trickier questions? Is their knowledge secure enough to be able to compare two time periods? What does that mean for our curriculum? Should we look for more opportunities for pupils to do this?

A combination of these tasks in a formal assessment can provide teachers with a wealth of information. However, it can also lead to some incorrect inferences.

It is easy to use formal assessments at any level to establish gaps in pupil understanding. Year 11 mock exams may show gaps in understanding about Weimar Germany's economic problems. Year 13 formal assessments may demonstrate a gap in understanding the differences between Communism and Capitalism. Year 7 assessment may show a gap in understanding about the religious reasons Henry VIII broke away from the Catholic Church. There is a temptation to want to plug these gaps with interventions, revision sessions, booklets, and heavy reteaching. However, everything we now know about cognitive science can help us as teachers to understand some of the reasons for these gaps – it could be a natural part of the Ebbinghaus forgetting curve for example, or it may be something pupils just left out of their answer as they didn't deem it crucial but they still know it. A formal assessment is a poor guide to the true gaps pupils have as despite the 'mixed constitution' approach, you are only ever going to be able to sample a small part of the domain. You therefore shouldn't rely too heavily on the inferences produced by these assessments and instead should focus on the techniques provided in all the previous chapters to ensure that pupils have a strong sense of security in their knowledge in the first place.

SUMMARY OF KEY POINTS

- Teachers should avoid relying on formal grades and their descriptors as a measure of pupil progress.
- A carefully sequenced curriculum focused on building upon prior substantive and disciplinary knowledge naturally creates opportunities for pupils to make progress in history.
- No one type of assessment is perfect – a 'mixed constitution' is important to get a holistic picture of pupil understanding.
- Don't be blinded by data that seems to suggest progress – question what the context and content is sitting behind it, before drawing conclusions.
- Cognitive science and understanding how pupils learn can help with assessment design and inferences from assessment outcomes.
- Use findings from assessments proactively and ask yourself: What (if anything) needs to be done next?

RESOURCES AND FURTHER READING

Bjork, Robert A. 'Disassociating Learning from Performance,' [YouTube video], Go Cognitive, 2012. https://www.youtube.com/watch?v=MMixjUDJVlwube

Bjork, Robert A, & Soderstrom, Nicholas C. 'Learning Versus performance' in Dunn, Dana S. (ed.). Oxford Bibliographies in Psychology. Oxford and New York: Oxford University Press 2013.

Burnham, Sally, & Brown, Geraint. 'Assessment Without Level Descriptions', in Teaching History, 115, Assessment without Levels? Edition, (2009): 5–15. London: Historical Association.

Brown, Geraint, & Burnham, Sally. 'Assessment after Levels' in Teaching History, 157' in (eds.). Assessment Edition, (2014): 8–17. London: Historical Association.

Christodoulou, Daisy. Making Good Progress?: The Future of Assessment for Leaning. Oxford: Oxford University Press 2017: 141, 169

Carr, Elizabeth, & Counsell, Christine. (2014) 'Using Timelines in Assessment' in Teaching History, 157, Assessment Edition, (2014): 54–62. London: Historical Association.

Craik, Fergus I.M, & Lockhart, Robert S. 'Levels of Processing: A Framework for Memory Research' in Journal of Verbal Learning and Verbal Behaviour, 11:6, (1972): 671–684.

Donaghy, Lee. 'Using Regular, Low-Stakes Tests to Secure pupils' Contextual Knowledge in Year 10' in Teaching History, 157' in Assessment Edition, (2014): 44–53. London: Historical Association.

Fordham, M., 'What did I mean by 'the curriculum is the progression model'?' [Blog Post], Clioetcetera, (2020). https://clioetcetera.com/2020/02/08/what-did-i-mean-by-the-curriculum-is-the-progression-model/

Fordham, Michael. 'Levels: Where It All Went Wrong' [Blog Post], Clioetcetera, (2014). https://clioetcetera.com/2014/02/08/levels-where-is-all-went-wrong/

Fordham, Michael. 'O Brave New World, Without Those Levels in't: Where Now for Key Stage 3 Assessment in History?' in Teaching History, 153, Curriculum Evolution Supplement, (2014). London: Historical Association.

Hammond, Kate. 'The Knowledge That 'flavours' a Claim: Towards Building and Assessing Historical Knowledge on Three scales' in Teaching History, 157, Assessment Edition, (2014): 18–25. London: Historical Association.

Howard, Kat, & Hill, Claire. Symbiosis – the Curriculum and the Classroom. Woodbridge: John Catt Educational 2020.

Lemov, Doug. 'An Annotated Forgetting Curve' [Blog Post], Teach Like a Champion, (2021). https://teachlikeachampion.org/blog/an-annotated-forgetting-curve/

Ofsted. School Inspection Handbook. 2019, updated 2024: point 235. https://www.gov.uk/government/publications/school-inspection-handbook-eif/

Ofsted. Rich encounters with the past: history subject report. 2023. https://www.gov.uk/government/publications/subject-report-series-history/rich-encounters-with-the-past-history-subject-report

Roediger, Henry L, & Karpicke, Jeffrey D. 'The Power of Testing Memory: Basic Research and Implications for Educational Practice' in Perspectives on Psychological Science, 1 (3), (2006): 181–210.

Weinstein, Yana, & Sumeracki, Megan. Understanding How We Learn: A Visual Guide. London: Routledge 2019: 64–67.

Wiliam, Dylan. 'How to Think About Assessment' in Donarski, Sarah, & Bennett, Tom (eds.). The researchED Guide to Assessment: An Evidence-Informed Guide for Teachers. Woodbridge: John Catt Publishers 2020: 21–27, 35.

Chapter 14
Teaching Extended Writing in History

Jim Carroll

BACKGROUND

As I struggle to make the deadline for this chapter, I'm starkly reminded that extended writing is hard! This also applies to history pupils at secondary school when they write their arguments. The stakes regarding extended historical writing are high. In some cases, concerns regarding 'lower-attainers' ability to handle the 'writing demands' of GSCE and A Level are used to prevent pupils studying history beyond the compulsory stage (Ward, 2006). Even at ages 11–14, such worries might mean pupils are denied their entitlement of constructing their *own* written arguments. A 'strategy of avoidance' regarding extended historical writing might be employed where extended writing is side-stepped altogether (Counsell, 2004). Alternatively, pupils might be provided with overly rigid scaffolds that bypass – or even misrepresent – the complexity of historical thinking that underpins written argument. Such a strategy may mean pupils write seemingly impressive one-off products, but the responses are near-identical to their classmates and their teacher's model. Consequently, many of those pupils will struggle in the future to produce their own arguments once the scaffolds are removed – such as when answering unseen examination questions.

As Christine Counsell (1997) notes, recognising something is difficult is not the same as dismissing it as impossible. Since the 1990s, history teachers in England have developed their own answers to the challenges of teaching extended historical writing. Elaborating on, challenging, and refining each other's work, their cumulative body of knowledge has led to them being dubbed the 'extended writing movement' (Counsell, 2011). What has united these teachers' work has been a commitment to improving standards of written historical arguments for pupils of *all* prior-attainment levels through history-specific approaches to literacy. To this end, a sustained focus on written argument from the start of Key Stage 3 is the surest way to ensure pupils of all abilities can achieve at GCSE and A Level.

These teachers aim to make clear to pupils the intrinsic purpose, empowering quality and joy of committing one's own argument to writing. The extended writing movement has generally focused on what pupils find difficult about extended historical writing – the disciplinary underpinnings of argument – rather than avoiding the challenge. Their approach depends on creating a culture of extended writing that embraces and foregrounds the puzzles of historical argument. For these teachers, therefore, the 'history' and the 'literacy' are indivisible: the planning and writing of essays developing historical thinking, rather than simply capturing a pupil's thoughts at the point of writing. A comprehensive summary of these history teachers' collective wisdom is beyond the scope of this chapter. Instead, I will outline some of their key ideas which have directly inspired my own teaching, using two of my enquiries as examples.

> **Activity 14.1**
>
> Reflect on the curriculum in your school.
>
> - How many opportunities do pupils have to undertake extended writing?
> - What do these look like? How are they different from other writing tasks you ask them to do?
> - At what length do pupils have to write in order to do 'extended' writing? Are your expectations the same at Key Stages 3, 4 and 5?

PRINCIPLE 1: USE ENQUIRY QUESTIONS TO CREATE HISTORICAL PUZZLES

To achieve the higher levels of attainment in history, pupils are required to construct their *own* convincing written arguments. Simply memorising and regurgitating pre-prepared responses will not cut it. Historical questions explore events that are unique and unrepeatable; rely on incomplete evidential bases; involve trying to determine the thought processes behind people's actions; and cover long-lasting, complex, social scenarios. Historical writing, therefore, can never be categorical; it invariably involves taking a position and trying to *persuade* the reader. In my experience, few things are as likely to elicit groans from pupils than the announcement of a PEEL paragraph or examination-question 'practice' – decontextualised and atomised tasks divorced from argument – arbitrarily tacked onto the end of a lesson. What motivates young people to write *at length* is a genuine historical puzzle, sufficient substantive and disciplinary knowledge to write something meaningful, and the opportunity to have their own argumentative voice.

If you haven't read Chapter 3 by Paula Worth already, do so now. Well-crafted enquiry questions are crucial in laying the groundwork – both in terms of knowledge and motivation – for extended historical writing. As Michael Riley (2000) noted, a strong enquiry question should capture pupil imaginations. Pupils should want to investigate it and, by implication, write in response to it. First, the question should clearly focus on a particular type of disciplinary thinking, usually a 'second-order concept'. Second-order concepts relate to the types of questions historians typically ask; historical methodologies; how historical claims are made and challenged; and how information about the past is structured into historical knowledge. In short, they give the teacher a handle on what historians routinely argue about. Second, an enquiry question should facilitate genuine debate, allowing multiple plausible interpretations. Third, the question's wording ought to be pithy, engaging, and intriguing for young people. In summary, the enquiry question should represent a historical puzzle – an issue that can be genuinely and satisfyingly argued over in writing. To ensure the indivisibility of the 'history' and 'literacy', the enquiry question also acts as a crucial reference point for the teacher – does this resource I'm creating help pupils not only write but think about the question they are answering? In this way, precious contact time with classes is saved: the pupils are learning literacy and history *at the same time*.

> **Activity 14.2**
>
> Reflect on the questions your curriculum asks pupils to answer.
>
> - How many of the questions in your curriculum are 'genuine historical puzzle[s]' using Jim's description of a good enquiry question?

As discussed in Chapter 15 by Victoria Crooks, historical scholarship is critical in informing our planning, and this also applies to enquiry questions that generate argument. Historians' book introductions, for example, often outline the existing debates on a topic and how the author's work will contribute to that public knowledge. When I was planning an enquiry with Year 13 on the Salem witch trials (Carroll, 2018, 2022), I knew there was mileage in causal enquiry when I read Benjamin C. Ray's (2015) introduction. In it, Ray noted 'historians have repeatedly asked why Salem's witch hunt became so widespread, lasted so long, and spiralled so dangerously out of control'. This reading helped me settle on a question – 'Why was there a witch crisis in Salem in 1692?' – that I was confident could facilitate pupils' arguments just as it had driven debate amongst generations of academic and popular historians (see Table 14.1 for an overview of the enquiry).

An extended writing task can act as the outcome activity that the class know they are working towards over a sequence of lessons. This allows the teacher to guide them on this journey, curating and building their knowledge cumulatively and attending to pupils' working memory. As Mark King (2015) demonstrated with his Year 7 pupils, substantive knowledge security in the pupils' long-term memory frees their working memory to concentrate on the complexities of extended writing: determining their own argument; challenging counterarguments; selecting relevant evidence; organising evidence into paragraphs; and so on. A sequence of lessons also means pupils can encounter a variety of competing interpretations on the issue, with enough time to meaningfully evaluate these interpretations' relative strengths. It is hard to enter into an argument without an awareness of the existing claims, and impossible to do so persuasively without the requisite knowledge to apprise those viewpoints.

Without such foundations, pupils' motivation and performance in extended writing will suffer. They will fail to see why the question being answered demands a considered response. Their working memory will be overloaded when they come to write. What they do write will be replete with inane, unsubstantiated judgements. There will be no sense of debate because they have no competing viewpoints to contrast, corroborate or kick back against. The pupils won't *argue* at all.

PRINCIPLE 2: CREATE WRITERS FROM THE READERS

Given historical written argument requires convincing the reader, argumentative texts should include expressions of judgement and persuasive emphases. Authors must also interweave references to the evidential bases of their claims, which often involves hedges indicating speculations. Textbooks, by contrast, often

Table 14.1 Example enquiry 'Why was there a witch crisis in Salem in 1692' (Year 13) including scholarship and linguistic focuses

Lesson No.	Lesson Question	Scholarship Read in Class	Linguistic Focus
1	Did Native American raids create a 'tinder box' for the Salem witch crisis?	Norton, M.B. (2002). *In the Devil's Snare: The Salem Witchcraft Crisis of 1692*, pp. 296–297. Ray, B.C. (2015). *Satan & Salem: The Witch-hunt Crisis of 1692*, pp. 4 & 198–201.	Nouns, verbs and prepositional phrases including metaphorical language for longer-term conditions
2	Did political instability in New England 'provide fertile ground' for the Salem witch crisis?	Baker, E. W. (2015). *A Storm of Witchcraft: The Salem Trials and the American Experience*, pp.54 & 64–67. Ray p. 3 Rosenthal, B. (1993). *Salem Story: Reading the Witch Trials of 1692* pp.3-4.	
3	Was the Puritan worldview the 'foundation' of the Salem witch crisis?	Baker p. 126. Ray p. 5. Hansen, C. (1970). *Witchcraft at Salem* pp. 145–146.	
4	Did village tensions 'underlie' the Salem witch crisis?	Boyer, P. & Nissenbaum, S. (1976). *Salem Possessed*. pp. 50–52 & 68–69. Ray pp. 3–4 & 188–200. Rosenthal p. 3.	
5	Did Cotton Mather 'lay the groundwork' for the Salem witch crisis?	Hansen pp. 84–85 & 204.	
6	Did societal gatekeepers 'legitimise' the Salem witch crisis?	Baker pp. 183–186. Norton p. 72. Ray pp. 35, 46, 66–67, 94–96, 144–145 & 149–150. Rosenthal pp. 193–195.	Nouns, verbs and prepositional phrases including metaphorical language for shorter-term and exacerbating causes
7	Why did the Salem crisis 'spiral so dangerously out of control'?	Baker pp. 31 & 127. Ray pp. 7–8, 33–34, 40–41, 89–90, 116–117 & 136–137 Starkey, M. (1949). *The Devil in Massachusetts*, p. 183	
8	Why was Salem so different from previous witchcraft episodes in New England?	Norton pp. 8, 34–36, 77–78 & 296–297 Ray p. 29 Rosenthal pp. 3–7	Counterfactual conditional clauses
9	So why was there a witch crisis in Salem in 1692?		Nominalisation

leave the language indicating such interpretative processes out. Instead, history is presented – seemingly and misleadingly – as objective, unelaborated and straightforward, all emanating from an anonymous, 'truth'-giving author (Counsell, 2004). But that is precisely how we do not want pupils to write!

For many history teachers, therefore, historical scholarship is the best quarry for argumentative language: both for informing their planning and as models for pupils' writing. Rachel Ward (2006), for example, recommended teachers create 'writers from the readers'. Ward introduced her Year 13 pupils to Eamon Duffy's 'devices' – his use of adjectives and superlatives – to exemplify the persuasive emphases in a historian's argument. Similarly, Counsell (1997) wanted her Year 7 pupils to consider grading and indicating the strength of their inferences to the reader. In Eileen Power's *Medieval Women*, Counsell found an explicit example of a historian highlighting their uncertainties through modal verbs (e.g., 'must have'; 'might have'; or 'could not have'); distancing verbs (e.g., 'seem' or 'appear'); or qualifiers (e.g., 'probably' or 'perhaps'). Counsell asked her pupils to concentrate on Power's speculative language and in each case determine whether Power was 'very certain', 'moderately certain', or 'not very certain' about her claim.

It is unrealistic, of course, to present historical scholarship to pupils – especially at Key Stage 3 – and simply expect them to read it. Pupils need to be prepared: not only in terms of accessing the text but *wanting* to read it. Teachers such as Rachel Foster (2011) and Tim Jenner (2019) have identified strategies for building enquiries from Year 7 onward around reading historical scholarship by historians such as Mary Beard, John Hatcher and Christopher Browning. First, selected extracts should be clearly argumentative. This means the text should be clearly relevant to the enquiry question. Pupils can then situate the text within the overall puzzle they are exploring, and teachers can ensure in prior lessons they have attended to the critical mass of knowledge pupils require to navigate it. But even more importantly, the historian should be clearly trying to persuade the reader. A gripping argument from a named and visible historian compels engagement and motivates the pupil to overcome the challenges of the text.

Second, allow the pupils to 'hear' the historian's voice. Initially, the pupils might only listen to the teacher reading the text out loud, immersing them in the argument. The teacher's intonation can emphasise the argumentative flow and tone, and pupils will not trip over vocabulary they are unfamiliar with. After this initial reading, the teacher can take feedback to ensure pupils have understood the gist. Now, having seen their teacher model scholarly interest with their voice, confident they understand the essence of the argument, and having not seen the text themselves, the pupils will be more motivated to explore what they might have initially missed. Third, once the pupils have the text in front of them the tasks set should be clear, limited and manageable. Such tasks mean the pupil can see they do not need to understand every single word to successfully *read* it. If the objective is modelling historians' argumentative language, this might mean activities such as those by Ward and Counsell described previously.

In my Year 13 Salem enquiry (Carroll 2022), each lesson included the reading of scholarship with the pupils encountering arguments by historians regarding the relative importance of different causes of the witch crisis (see Table 14.1). In my planning, I had noted these historians often used metaphorical language – such as references to plants, diseases, theatres, buildings and fires – to characterise the roles of causes (see Figure 14.1). Having read the arguments in class we discussed such language, for example how references to 'fertile soil', 'atmospheres' or 'foundations' might indicate the historian is describing longer-term conditions – circumstances that do not directly cause an event but make it possible (see Figures 14.2–14.4).

In all of these examples, the teachers sought to improve pupils' written arguments from the weakest to the highest achievers. If pupils only encounter 'simplified' texts which hide the language of argument, the teacher might inadvertently be making it *harder* for the pupil to grasp what is expected of them in writing. Reading scholarship provides pupils with arguments on which to latch. They can

> When 'Salem witchcraft', like some **exotic cut flower**, is **plucked from the soil which nurtured it** – or, to change the image, when **the roles assigned to the actors** of 1692 are shaped by **a script not of their own making** – then this terrible event cannot rise above the level of **gripping melodrama**. It is only as we come to sense how deeply the witchcraft **outbreak** was **rooted** in the prosaic, everyday lives of obscure and inarticulate men and women, and how profoundly those lives were being shaped by powerful forces of historical change that the **melodrama** begins to take on the harsher contours of **tragedy**.
>
> Boyer, P. and Nissenbaum, S. (1976), *Salem Possessed*, p.12

- plant
- theatre
- disease

Figure 14.1 A pronounced example of academic historians employing causal metaphors, taken from Carroll (2022).

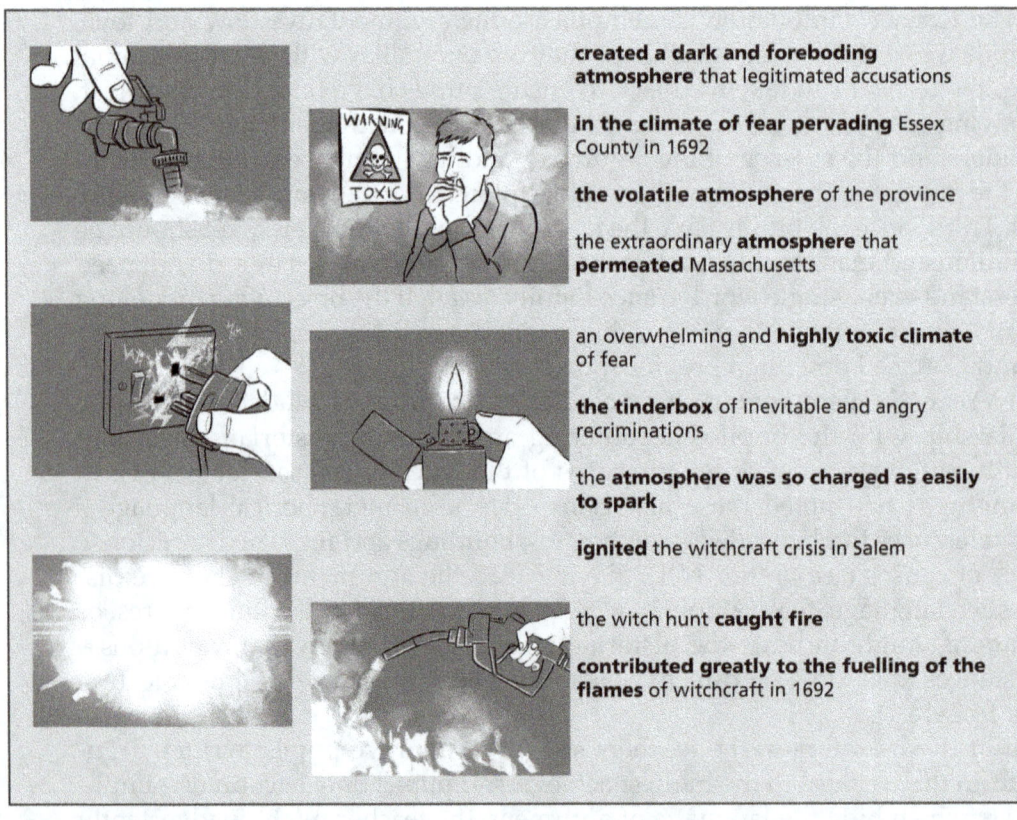

Figure 14.2 Historians' use of metaphor to argue causal conditions (fire), taken from Carroll (2022).

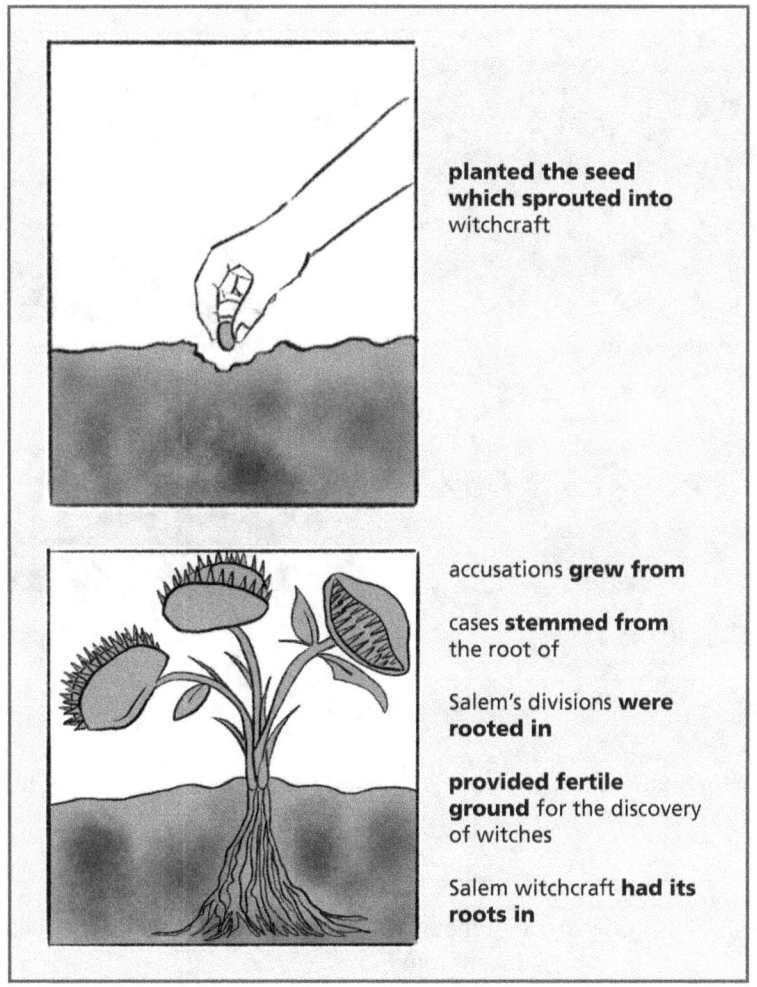

Figure 14.3 Historians' use of metaphor to argue causal conditions (plants), taken from Carroll (2022).

orient their own arguments in relation to what they have encountered and, if appropriate, react against it. Pupils can also encounter the linguistic devices for argument in their natural habitat. Without reading authentic historical argument, some pupils may never realise they have to argue in their own writing at all (Carroll, 2017).

Activity 14.3

Find a history book that you have enjoyed or admired recently and re-read the introduction.

- Is it possible to summarise the historian's argument from what is written in the introduction?
- Can you find examples of metaphor in that historian's writing? How similar or different are these from the examples given in Figures 14.2–14.4?
- How might you use this text in a classroom to show pupils how metaphors can be used in historical writing? What might you need to do to support pupils' understanding?

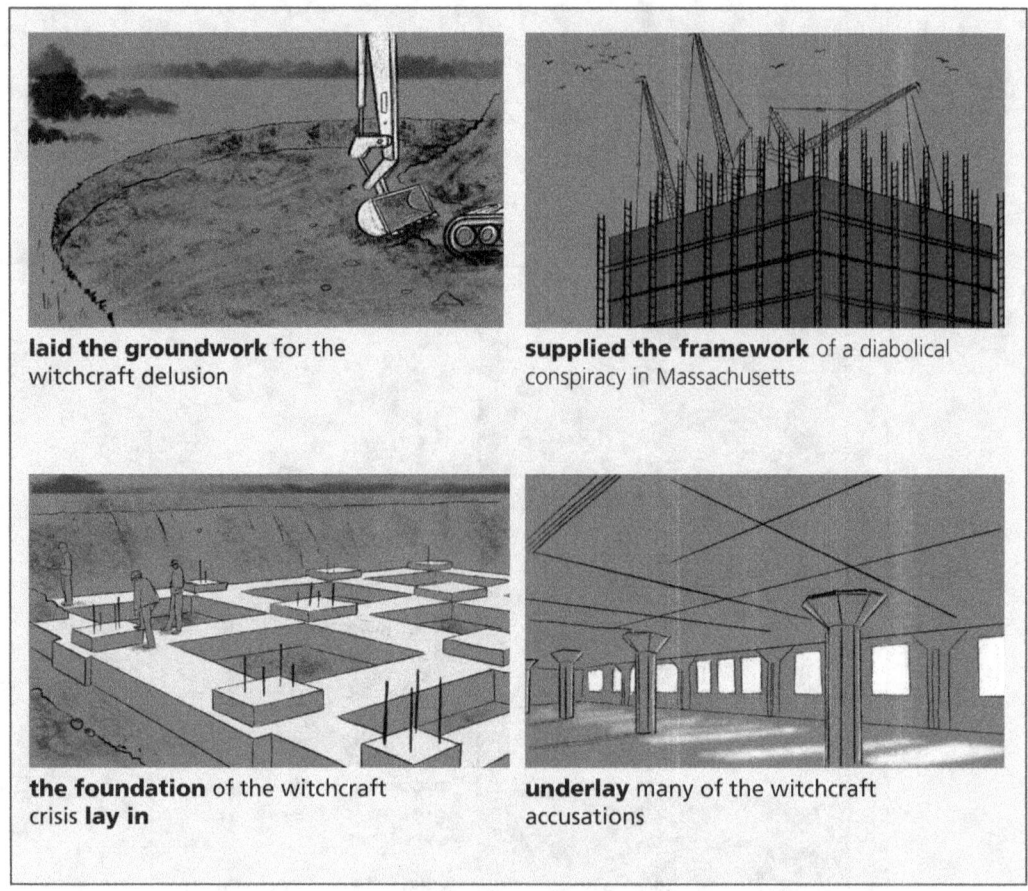

Figure 14.4 Historians' use of metaphor to argue causal conditions (buildings), taken from Carroll (2022).

PRINCIPLE 3: FOCUS ON VOCABULARY SO THE LINGUISTIC RELEASES THE CONCEPTUAL

Historical writing has its own conventions in terms of vocabulary. Its substantive terms which be topic-specific or technical: for example, 'sepoy', 'doctrine of lapse' or 'zamindar' if pupils are arguing about the Indian Rebellion of 1857. Different vocabulary is also required depending on the second-order concept being argued about. For instance, change and continuity arguments require language to describe the nature, extent and rate of change such as nouns or adjectives like 'transformation', 'escalation' or 'imperceptible' (Foster, 2013). Such language would be of less value, however, for enquiries focused on other forms of disciplinary thinking such as similarity and difference.

In 2002, the Department for Education and Skills released the *Key Stage 3 National Strategy – Literacy in History*. Despite its title, this publication pushed a generic approach to the writing of history. Teachers were instructed to teach pupils to produce strictly separated 'non-fiction genres', often involving similarly generic 'writing frames' of doubtful applicability in history. History teachers soon began to react against the stifling genericism of such resources. They quickly recognised that general non-fiction genres were far too blunt an instrument in helping pupils write arguments centred on history's different second-order concepts that the government's own National Curriculum required.

In this respect, work by teachers such as James Woodcock (2005) on vocabulary has been highly influential. Woodcock wanted his Year 10 pupils to write arguments with a specific conceptual focus, in his case causation. The *National Strategy* advised pupils use highly limiting 'causal connectives' such as 'because' and 'so' to write about the relationship between historical causes and consequences. Turning to scholarship, Woodcock realised such recommendations were problematic. Historians instead tend to position nouns (e.g., 'foundation', 'origin' or 'spark') and verbs (e.g., 'underpin', 'allow' or 'incite') within the clause to argue causally. Unlike connectives such as 'because', these words allow the historian to 'fine-tune' their causal arguments regarding the role, inter-connectedness, and relative importance of causes (Martin, 2007). If Woodcock had followed the *National Strategy's* guidance, his pupils would not have been able to move beyond producing dry lists of 'x happened because of y' relationships.

Woodcock's work exemplifies a healthy scepticism from history teachers about 'bolting on' generic literacy approaches that have not been designed specifically for history (Counsell, 2004). Woodcock's insight has been particularly impactful, becoming the most widely cited article related to pupils' extended writing in the practitioner journal *Teaching History* (Fordham, 2015). Other teachers have adopted similar approaches focusing on other second-order concepts from Year 7 to Year 13: for example, Foster (2013) on change and continuity, Worth (2018) on interpretations and Matthew Bradshaw (2009) on similarity and difference.

Like Woodcock, I wanted my pupils to think about the language required to write causal arguments. In an enquiry on Hitler's rise to the chancellorship titled 'Why did Hitler come out on top?', the pupils read extracts by Richard Evans and Ian Kershaw and as a class we noted some of the language they used in their causal arguments (see Figure 14.5, Carroll 2016). In other words, the pupils had come across the language in its fuller context – both in the historians' original texts but also in the broader sense of the overall enquiry the pupils were investigating.

Reducing Woodcock's argument to the slogan 'the linguistic releases the conceptual' robs his suggestions of much of their nuance. Providing vocabulary is not equivalent to teaching the underlying concepts the language signifies. As Woodcock noted, in the strictest sense the linguistic cannot 'release the conceptual' because any new language shorn from context – for example in a decontextualised wall display or bookmark – has

allowed	(consequence) **arose from** (cause)	the basis for (consequence) **was** (cause)	breakthrough	in the climate of (cause), (consequence)
(cause) **dealt a mortal blow to**…	(cause) **significantly contributed to** (consequence)	(cause) **compelled**	(cause) **convinced**	develop
to (consequence) it **was essential to** (cause)	(cause) **established** (consequence)	**exploited** (cause)	(cause) **guaranteed** (consequence)	Had (cause) (not) **happened** (consequence) may/might/would (not) have happened
(cause) **helped** (consequence)	(cause) **was a prerequisite for** (consequence)	(cause) **was rooted in** (cause)	(consequence) **was more of a consequence of** (cause) **than** (cause)	(cause) **laid the platform for** (consequence)
(cause) **was the inspiration behind** (consequence)	(cause) **was the necessary prelude to** (consequence)	(cause) **played a vital part in** (consequence)	(cause) **opened up the way for/the possibility of** (consequence)	(cause) **was the onset of** (consequence)
(cause) **provoked** (consequence)	(cause) **was of only secondary importance in** (consequence)	(consequence) **required** (cause)	(consequence) **would not have been possible without** (cause)	**weakened in the aftermath of** (cause)
in the wake of (cause), (consequence)	(cause) **undermined**	**underlying** (cause)	(cause) **triggered** (consequence)	(cause) **had** (not) **proved/was** (not) **sufficient**

Figure 14.5 Examples of Richard Evans's and Ian Kershaw's causal vocabulary, taken from Carroll (2016).

no meaning (conceptual or otherwise) for the pupil. Woodcock's assertion, which we sometimes forget, is that explicit linguistic instruction depends on pupils having at least vague pre-familiarities with the language if the historical meaning behind it is to be unlocked. Otherwise, pupils may produce scatter-gun essays where words are indiscriminately thrown at the page in the hope that some will stick.

Woodcock got teachers considering how the introduction of new language could liberate pupils' conceptual thinking. Overreliance on poorly selected scaffolds can, in Jennifer Evans and Gemma Pate's (2007) phrase, 'make pupils fall' by actively concealing – or indeed distorting – the type of historical thinking we hope to encourage. Simplified language we well-meaningly intend as an introductory leg-up for the pupil all too quickly becomes a shackle tethering them to the floor. A pupil who comes across a verb such as 'underpin', however, might consider – possibly for the first time – that their writing about causation requires argument regarding the role, importance and linkage of causes.

> **Activity 14.4**
>
> Look at the vocabulary used by Evans and Kershaw in Figure 14.5. Choose one and write a sentence including it.
>
> - How would the meaning of the sentence be changed if that word were substituted by another?
> - How might you use a word-substitution activity in a lesson to help pupils focus on a historian's argument?

PRINCIPLE 4: GO BEYOND THE WORD WITH GRAMMAR

Historical writing has its own grammatical conventions. Most obviously, a pupil who does not have command of the different past tenses will almost certainly struggle to write history. While not as developed as thinking about vocabulary, increasingly history teachers have thought about how pupils might construct historical argument at the level of a clause (Counsell, 2004; Foster, 2015).

Understandably, tackling grammar in the classroom can make history teachers feel uneasy. We may not feel comfortable with its 'metalanguage' (the language we use to talk about language) such as 'counterfactual conditional', 'modal verb' or 'prepositional phrase'. But Key Stage 3 pupils now arrive from primary school having encountered some metalanguage and a history teacher can build on this for historical ends. Additionally, while the terminology is technical, it has been developed precisely because it is the most pithy and effective way of talking about complex ideas that you might want to convey to pupils to improve their writing. Most crucially, historical argument does not only operate at the level of the word; pupils who are not supported beyond vocabulary struggle to write confident, sophisticated, intelligible prose. If you lack confidence in your metalanguage, then a focus on grammar might be the focus of an interdisciplinary project with your English department to build your and your pupils' knowledge.

I was motivated to focus on grammatical instruction in my teaching after reading my pupils' essays. Like many history teachers, during causal enquiries I often encouraged my pupils to reason counterfactually – 'if x had (not) happened, would y have (not) happened?' – to characterise necessary preconditions and prioritise causes. Pupils often use this type of conditional in speech ('I wouldn't have been late sir if my bus hadn't been delayed!') and were happy to counterfactually reason in classroom discussion. I often encountered, however, spoken informalities bleeding into my pupils' formal writing, with even my strongest Year 13 writers struggling with the complicated grammar of the counterfactual conditional. Some would incorrectly use 'of' when 'have' was required, for example:

> The Haitian Revolution might not of [sic] been so successful if Toussaint L'Oueverture had not been the leader.

Others would unnecessarily add an extra 'have':

> The Haitian Revolution might not have been so successful if Toussaint L'Oueverture had not've [sic] been the leader'.

Here was an example of historical argument that I was encouraging pupils to use that could *only* be expressed at the level of the clause, but I was failing to provide them the grammatical support they clearly needed. Instead of taking my class on a decontextualised tangent where I clarified conditional clauses – immensely valuable though explicit focus on grammar in itself can be – I judged this as an opportunity to simultaneously develop the historical thinking my pupils were struggling to communicate grammatically. For example, in my aforementioned enquiries pupils read extracts by historians where they counterfactually reasoned, and I asked the pupils to consider how the historian used the language to ascribe causal importance and necessity (for example, Figure 14.6, Carroll, 2016). I then took care to model the grammar, often using a historian's example (for example,

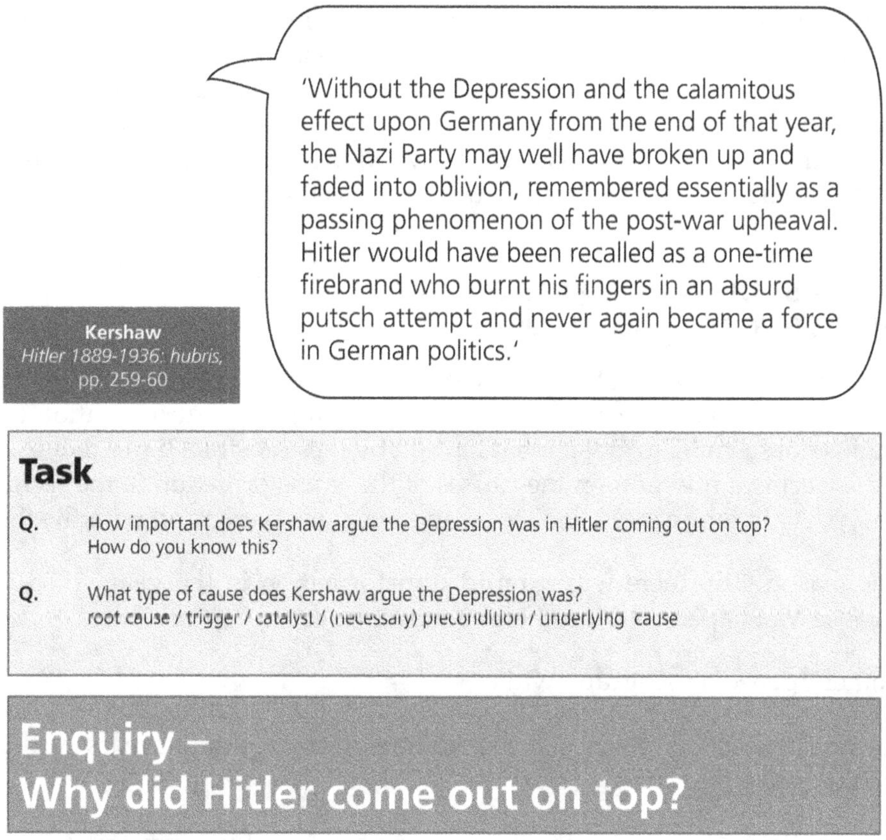

Kershaw
Hitler 1889-1936: hubris, pp. 259-60

'Without the Depression and the calamitous effect upon Germany from the end of that year, the Nazi Party may well have broken up and faded into oblivion, remembered essentially as a passing phenomenon of the post-war upheaval. Hitler would have been recalled as a one-time firebrand who burnt his fingers in an absurd putsch attempt and never again became a force in German politics.'

Task

Q. How important does Kershaw argue the Depression was in Hitler coming out on top? How do you know this?

Q. What type of cause does Kershaw argue the Depression was?
root cause / trigger / catalyst / (necessary) precondition / underlying cause

**Enquiry –
Why did Hitler come out on top?**

Figure 14.6 Example of task asking pupils to consider how Ian Kershaw (2001) used a counterfactual to ascribe importance and characterise necessary preconditions, taken from Carroll (2016).

> **Language for counterfactual reasoning**
>
> Would/modal + have + past participle   had   + past participle
> 'One wonders **what** <u>would</u> **have** <u>happened</u> **had** Parris and the judges **not coerced**
>
> Would/modal + have + past participle
> Tituba into confessing. The Salem witchcraft outbreak **might** conceivably <u>have been</u>
>
> limited to three people – a fairly typical case of no particular note, and certainly not a
>
> pivotal moment in American history.'
>
> ## So what did make Salem in 1692 unique?

Figure 14.7 Modelling of Emerson W. Baker's (2015) counterfactual conditional for pupils, taken from Carroll (2018).

Figure 14.7). Finally, I gave the pupils a low-stake opportunity to practise the grammar while also developing their own arguments, for instance by posing a number of 'what if?' questions that they answered in writing (e.g., 'what if the magistrates in the Salem trials had not accepted spectral evidence?') (Carroll, 2018).

Success in extended historical writing involves the history teacher taking responsibility for literacy in their classes, including at the level of the clause. Although cross-institutional literacy co-ordinators and initiatives can be vital for addressing universally applicable literacy concerns, the history teacher is accountable for historical discourse. If pupils are encountering difficulties with the grammar of historical reasoning, it seems unrealistic (and unreasonable) to expect colleagues not trained in the discipline of history to address the issue. The division of 'grammar' and 'meaning' in history is a false dualism. There are some aspects of historical argumentation that are only constructed beyond the word, and, if so identified and presented to pupils as such, may also help 'release the conceptual'.

PRINCIPLE 5: SHOW HOW PARAGRAPHS SHAPE HISTORICAL KNOWLEDGE

The teaching of paragraphs often involves the use of heuristics emphasising 'Points', 'Evidence' and so on. Marking my pupils' essays, a persistent frustration of mine was pupils not seeming to grasp what I meant by these abstract terms. For example, when answering a question on the causes of the 'transformation in the fortunes of the Nazi party in the years 1930-33' one pupil began a paragraph with the 'Point':

> One reason why there was a rapid transformation in the years 1930-33 was because Van Papen convinced Hindenburg he could control Hitler.

Another opened a paragraph with:

> The final reason why there was a rapid transformation in the years 1930-33 was politics.

These points are not without their redeeming features. They focus on the question (or at least parrot its wording). They also provide some thematic organisation for the paragraph. But there was very little argument. In the first, the pupil seems not to understand the relationship between the general point and particular evidence.

Papen's persuasion of Hindenburg exemplifies a broader trend: for example, the underestimation of the Nazi threat by the conservatives. The second has no analytical power. Every society in the history of humanity has had 'politics' of some form, but only one has elected and appointed Adolf Hitler to the chancellorship.

Counsell (1997) noted her Year 7 pupils' difficulty distinguishing between 'big points' (the generalisation that acts at the overall point of a paragraph) and 'little points' (lower-level generalisations and supporting evidence). Abstraction and its relationship to specific examples can be challenging for pupils. In everyday life, they experience individual, local and short-term events. Geographically broad, longer-term, collective events are therefore harder to conceptualise. Furthermore, abstract points require pupils to use language in unintuitive ways (Martin, 2007). In conversation and non-academic writing, language tends to behave in the ways we are taught to expect: verbs for actions, nouns for things, conjunctions for logical relations, and adjectives for qualities. So, a pupil might presume a historical sentence will read:

> Stalin was ruthless [adjective/quality] about increasing [verb/action] his power, therefore [conjunction/logical relation] he put [verb/action] Zinoviev and Kamenev on show trial.

This sentence might be appropriate within a paragraph, but it is too specific to act as a general point because it limits the pupil's scope to consider further examples. An essay that only uses paragraph points such as this will in all likelihood have too narrow a focus. In academic writing therefore – particularly when the author needs to densely summarise such as in paragraph points, introductions, and conclusions – language often behaves differently. Actions and qualities might be expressed as nouns, and logical relations as verbs and nouns. This increased use of nouns is called 'nominalisation', and a sentence involving it might read:

> Stalin's ruthless elimination of his opponents [noun/quality and actions] enabled [verb/logical relation] his consolidation of power [noun/action].

Nominalisation partly explains why academic writing can read densely. The increased use of nouns allows broad generalisations that can package many individual events under one umbrella term, thematically organising historical knowledge. For example, this paragraph point allows the pupil to explore a number of examples in their paragraph: Stalin's purging of the Congress of Victors, Bukharin's trial and execution, Trotsky's enforced exile and execution, and so on. Shuttling between abstract generalisation and substantiating examples in this way is essential in historical paragraphs.

Activity 14.5

Write a sentence about the causes of a historical event that you are familiar with using a nominalisation.

- To do this, remember what Jim says; that 'actions and qualities might be expressed as nouns'. So, instead of 'The tribes of Arabia were united by Islam, this made them effective at taking more land'. 'The unity of the Arabian tribes provided by Islam, made them effective at taking more land'.
- How might you model this in a classroom?

I encountered similar frustrations when I implored pupils to include 'evidence' in their arguments. An argument, by definition, is an answer to a question and therefore requires pupils not only recalling *information* about a topic but winnowing that information down to relevant *evidence* (Counsell, 2004, Foster & Gadd, 2013). Pupils often find making this distinction difficult, leading to essays replete with irrelevance. Even if a pupil manages to reduce their information to evidence, they must still 'shape' their jumble of facts into structured paragraphs according to thematic similarity, or the reader will be confronted with a disorganised splurge.

I wanted to make these abstract ideas which underpin successful paragraph construction concrete to my pupils. Adapting activities Counsell (2004) used with her Year 7 pupils, during my enquiry 'Why did Hitler come out on top?' I designed a card sort-activity (see Figure 14.8). A card sort helps pupils to concentrate on thinking about the argumentative complexity of distilling, shaping, and naming their information – the foundational thinking of a historical paragraph. First, to make the pupils consider the difference between 'topic information' and 'question relevance' I asked them to place any information cards they considered irrelevant to the question outside of their A3-sized 'zone of relevance'. With their remaining evidence, I instructed the pupils to organise their cards according to thematic similarity. With both tasks, debating and justifying their decisions in groups opened the pupils' eyes to the problem of selecting the most relevant evidence and organising it in paragraphs in the most appropriate way.

I then asked the pupils to debate how best to 'name' their points with a particular focus on whether the name captured the thematic similarity of the evidence; was general enough to encapsulate more than one piece of evidence; and whether the named point helped to answer the question. If pupils resorted to 'off-the-shelf' points such as 'politics', 'the economy' or 'society' I asked them to hone their points further. This allowed pupils to construct paragraph points with greater analytical power: such as 'Anti-Communist fear in Germany was a necessary prelude to Hitler coming to power'. The pupils had now shaped their information into paragraphs; they had their essay plans.

A historical paragraph does not only organise information; it also should drive argument. Allowing pupils to puzzle over the paragraph's underlying argumentative thinking allows them to see more clearly what terms such as 'Point' or 'Evidence'

Hitler was an exceptionally charismatic public speaker. Contemporaries spoke of his 'hypnotic' effect. He presented himself as an alternative to the 'traditional' politicians who he said had failed Germany.	Hitler managed to put down Stennes' SA rebellion in 1931. This suggested to some conservatives that Hitler was prepared to rein in the more extreme sections of his party.	The KPD refused to join the SPD in a 'united front' against Nazism because they still resented Ebert's actions in 1919-1920.	The elites were concerned by Schleicher's plan to build a coalition with the SPD and the Strasserite Nazis, believing it was too left-wing an approach.
The Nazis' policies emphasised volkspartei, were anti-Communist, and promised to save Germany from the shame and failures of Weimar.	Some industrialists wanted authoritarian government. They disliked the power of trade unions and feared the spread of communism. Individual industrialists such as Fritz Thyssen did contribute large amounts of money to support the Nazis.	Hindenburg was upset that Bruning couldn't convince the Reichstag to reappoint him President without an election in March 1932. Hindenburg beat Hitler in the election, but the conservatives voted for Hitler and Hindenburg had to rely on Centre and SPD votes to win, which infuriated him.	In July 1932, elections took place, as promised by von Schleicher. These were a triumph for the Nazi Party who won 37% of the vote, giving them 230 seats in the Reichstag and making them the largest party. Hitler refused to join von Papen's cabinet unless he was made Chancellor. Hindenburg disliked Hitler and refused his demand.

Figure 14.8 Example cards for the card sort, taken from Carroll (2016).

actually mean in historical writing. While heuristics may have their place, as with any proxy if they substitute the underlying thinking they are supposed to summarise their potential effectiveness will almost certainly be lost in transit. Pupils might be left scratching their heads wondering: 'but what is *the point*?'.

PRINCIPLE 6: REHEARSE ARGUMENTS IN SPEECH

A genuine historical question should encourage argument; it should allow several – but not infinite – plausible answers. For a pupil to be successful, therefore, they do not only have to consider their *own* argument. Different possible interpretations need to be pre-empted, acknowledged and counter-argued in relation to the author's own. Furthermore, justifications of why the author's argument is *most* convincing are required. In this sense, written historical argument is 'multi-voiced', which pupils can find difficult (Coffin, 2006).

There are activities we might set pupils to make them aware of historical argument's multi-voicedness. Spoken debates can act a bridge to writing that includes multiple perspectives. While obviously there are differences, in many ways written argument is closer to speech than other genres. Both share an immediate sense of audience, require an audience to be convinced, include multiple voices, and so on. In this sense, speech – for example in preparatory debates – can act as a crucial 'oral rehearsal' for writing.

Oral rehearsal can make clearer to a pupil the importance of *convincing* an audience. For example, Kate Hammond (2002) was frustrated when reading her Year 10 pupils' unevidenced claims in their essays, and wanted her pupils to *experience* why having precise evidence was crucial for persuasive argument. She therefore organised a 'boxing match' debate with her class. In this activity, small groups of pupils prepared a presentation arguing a case in answer to an overall question (in Hammond's example, each group was assigned a different cause of Hitler's rise to the Chancellorship in 1933). Members from two opposing groups presented their arguments to the class, and the other pupils decided which group had been most convincing according to specific criteria for successful argument (e.g., precise, factual evidence). The winners then took on a new challenger, and the process repeated. Before 'Round 2', the groups reconvened to redress the weaknesses in their own arguments and to prepare attacks on the flaws of other's. Hammond found the activity benefitted her pupils' writing because it forced them to confront how emergent argument fails to convince unless substantiated by detail. In other words, her pupils became critical of their own and other's employment of evidence which was manifested in their writing.

Oral rehearsal can also be achieved in smaller pair- and group-work. While teaching my enquiry 'Why did Hitler come out on top?' I wanted to encourage my pupils to hear multi-voicedness (Carroll, 2017). In the final lesson, I organised small group debates of three or four pupils revolving around the enquiry question. For a number of pupils such as Lucia, the debate appeared to allow them to see other plausible counterarguments existed, and the need to argue against them was apparent in their essays (see Figure 14.9).

> ### Activity 14.6
>
> Rehearsing arguments in speech.
>
> - What activities could you devise that would allow pupils to rehearse historical arguments in speech?

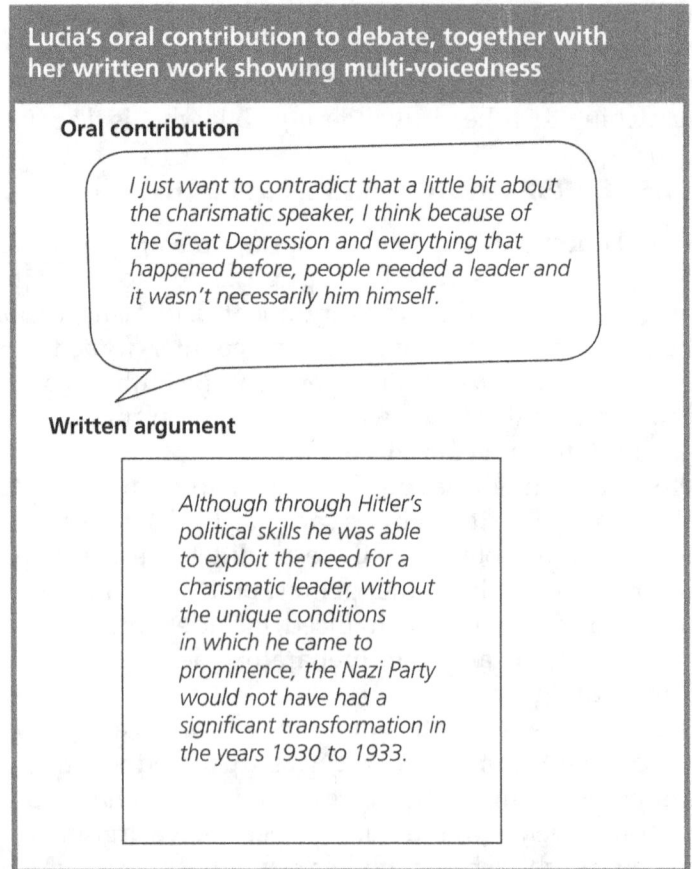

Figure 14.9 Example of one pupil's 'oral rehearsal' and subsequent 'multi-voiced' work, taken from Carroll (2017).

Speech, in the form of preparatory debates, helps make argument explicit to pupils. First, it allows pupils' emergent arguments to be critiqued in a low-stakes manner before being committed to writing in a higher-stakes essay. Public scrutiny means the pupil can improve, modify or discard unconvincing aspects of their initial argument. Speech also makes clearer to pupils that multiple plausible interpretations can exist and that this needs to be acknowledged in writing. In fact, this is the very lifeblood of academic history. Historians develop their arguments in response to existing interpretations, release them into the public domain where they add to cumulative knowledge, and therefore invite critique themselves. Spoken debates therefore help pupils imagine themselves a wider historical community – including the historians they read, examiners, teachers and fellow pupils – as an audience to engage with and to position oneself in relation to. This is crucial because interactions with public knowledge make historical argument possible; argument presupposes an audience that needs to be *convinced* (Fordham, 2007).

Extended written argument is how most historical knowledge is constructed. If we take the discipline of history seriously, and if we view the business of school history as inducting young people – at a developmentally appropriate level – into that discipline, what are the implications of making written argument the preserve of older, higher-attaining pupils? For the pupil who finishes their compulsory history education at 14 without having learnt to construct their own extended argument, without experiencing the liberating power of expressing their *own* academic voice in the discipline, can we say that pupil has actually studied 'history' at all?

SUMMARY OF KEY POINTS

- Extended writing is an entitlement for all pupils in their study of history.
- Use enquiry questions to direct learning across a sequence of lessons and provide pupils with an intriguing and worthwhile puzzle they want to address in extended writing.
- Create writers from the readers, by introducing pupils to carefully chosen extracts of historical scholarship.
- Focus on vocabulary so pupils can argue in a way specific to history and each of its second-order concepts, as the linguistic releases the conceptual.
- Go beyond the word and teach pupils the grammar needed for historical reasoning.
- Show how the paragraph shapes historical knowledge through the use of card sorts and nominalisation to create more effective points.
- Rehearse arguments through class debate and group discussion, so pupils can see the argument their writing responds to.

RESOURCES AND FURTHER READING

Baker, Emerson W. A Storm of Author: Please provide the publisher location. Witchcraft: The Salem Trials and the American Experience. Oxford University Press 2015.

Boyer, Paul, & Nissenbaum, Stephen. Salem Possessed: The Social Origins of Witchcraft. Cambridge: Harvard University Press 1976.

Bradshaw, Matthew. 'Drilling Down: How One History Department Is Working Towards Progression in pupils' Thinking About Diversity Across Years 7, 8 and 9' in Teaching History, 135, To They or Not to They Edition, (2009): 4–12. London: Historical Association.

Carroll, James Edward. 'The Whole Point of the Thing: How Nominalisation Might Develop students' Written Causal arguments' in Teaching History, 162, Scales of Planning Edition, (2016): 16–25. London: Historical Association.

Carroll, James Edward. 'Grammar. Nazis. Does the Grammatical 'release the conceptual'?' in Teaching History, 163, Get Excited & Carry On Edition, (2016): 8–16. London: Historical Association.

Carroll, James Edward. "I Feel Like If I Say This in My Essay it's Not Going to Be as strong': Multi-Voicedness, 'oral rehearsal' and Year 13 students' Written arguments' in Teaching History, 167, Complicating Narratives Edition, (2017): 8–17. London: Historical Association.

Carroll, James Edward. 'Couching Counterfactuals in Knowledge When Explaining the Salem Witch Trials With Year 13' in Teaching History, 172, Cause and Consequence Edition, (2018): 18–29. London: Historical Association.

Carroll, James Edward. 'Terms and Conditions: Using Metaphor to Highlight Causal Processes With Year 13' in Teaching History, 187, Widening the World Lens Edition, (2022): 40–49. London: Historical Association.

Coffin, Caroline. Historical Discourse: The Language of Time, Cause and Evaluation. London and New York: Continuum 2006: 85.

Counsell, C. Building the Lesson Around the Text, History and Literacy in Year 7. London: Hodder Education 2004: 4, 41, 111.

Counsell, Christine. Analytic and Discursive Writing at Key Stage 3. London: Historical Association 1997.

Counsell, Christine. 'History Teachers as Curriculum Makers: Professional Problem-Solving in Secondary School History in England' in Schüllerqvist, Bengt (ed.). Patterns of Research in Civics, History, Geography and Religious Education: Key Presentations and Responses from an International Conference at Karlstad University, Sweden. Karlstad University Press 2011: 53–88.

Department for Education and Skills. Key Stage 3 National Strategy – Literacy in History. London: DfEaS 2002: 19–20.

Evans, Jennifer, & Pate, Gemma. 'Does Scaffolding Make Them Fall? Reflecting on Strategies for Developing Causal Argument in Years 8 and 11' in Teaching History, 128, Beyond the Exam Edition, (2007): 18–29. London: Historical Association.

Fordham, Michael. 'Realising and Extending Stenhouse's Vision of Teacher Research: the Case of English History Teachers' in British Educational Research Journal, 42(1), (2015): 135–150.

Fordham, Michael. 'Slaying Dragons and Sorcerers in Year 12: in Search of Historical argument' in Teaching History, 129, Disciplined Minds Edition, (2007): 31–38. London: Historical Association.

Foster, Rachel. 'Using Academic History in the classroom' in Davies, Ian (ed.). Debates in History Teaching. London: Routledge 2011: 199–211.

Foster, Rachel. 'The More Things Change, the More They Stay the Same: Developing pupils' Thinking About Change and continuity' in Teaching History, 151, Continuity Edition, (2013): 8–17. London: Historical Association.

Foster, Rachel. 'Pipes's Punctuation and Making Complex Historical Claims: How the Direct Teaching of Punctuation can Improve pupils' Historical Thinking and Written argument' in Teaching History, 159, Underneath the essay edition, (2015): 8–13. London: Historical Association.

Foster, Rachel, & Gadd, Sarah. 'Let's Play Supermarket 'Evidential' Sweep: Developing students' Awareness of the Need to Select evidence' in Teaching History, 152, Putting it all Together Edition, (2013): 24–29. London: Historical Association.

Hammond, Kate. 'Getting Year 10 to Understand the Value of Precise Factual knowledge' in Teaching History, 109, Examining History Edition, (2002): 10–15. London: Historical Association.

Hansen, Chadwick. Witchcraft at Salem. New York: Braziller Books 1970.

Jenner, Tim. 'Making Reading Routine: Helping Key Stage 3 Pupils to Become Regular Readers of Historical Scholarship' in Teaching History, 174, Structure Edition, (2019): 42–49. London: Historical Association.

Kershaw, Ian. Hitler 1889- 1936: Hubris. London: Penguin 2001: 259–260.

King, Mark. 'The Role of Secure Knowledge in Enabling Year 7 Pupils to Write Essays on Magna Carta' in Teaching History, 159, Underneath the essay edition, (2015): 18–24. London: Historical Association.

Martin, J. R. 'Construing Knowledge: a Functional Linguistic perspective' in Christie, Frances, & Martin, J. R., (eds.). Language, Knowledge and Pedagogy. London and New York: Continuum 2007: 34–64.

Norton, Mary Beth. In the Devil's Snare: The Salem Witchcraft Crisis of 1692. New York: Knopf Doubleday Publishing Group 2002.

Ray, Benjamin. C. Satan and Salem: the Witch-Hunt Crisis of 1692. Charlottesville: University of Virginia Press 2015: 2.

Riley, Michael. 'Into the Key Stage 3 History Garden: Choosing and Planting Your Enquiry questions' in Teaching History, 99, Curriculum Planning Edition, (2000): 8–13. London: Historical Association.

Rosenthal, Bernard. Salem Story: Reading the Witch Trials of 1692. Cambridge: Cambridge University Press 1993.

Starkey, Marion L. The Devil in Massachusetts: A Modern Enquiry into the Salem Witch Trials. Garden City, New York: Anchor Books 1949.

Ward, Rachel. 'Duffy's Devices: Teaching Year 13 to Read and write' in Teaching History, 124, Teaching the most able Edition, (2006): 9–16. London: Historical Association.

Woodcock, James. 'Does the Linguistic Release the Conceptual? Helping Year 10 to Improve Their Causal reasoning' in Teaching History, 119, Language Edition, (2005): 5–23. London: Historical Association.

Worth, Paula. "This Extract Is No Good, Miss!': Helping Post-16 Students to Make Judgements About an historian's Construction of argument' in Teaching History, 170, Historians Edition, (2018): 16–21. London: Historical Association.

Chapter 15
Teaching Using Historical Scholarship

Victoria Crooks

BACKGROUND

I often find myself in conversation with prospective PGCE students about their views on using academic historical scholarship in the classroom. The most common view, firmly expressed by these potential history teachers, is that historical scholarship doesn't really have a place in the classroom because it is too complex or impenetrable for children to access. Occasionally, they may concede that engagement with academic history is important at Key Stage 5, but only by way of preparing pupils for degree level study. Invariably, as I begin to probe the reasons for them holding this position with such conviction, their certainty begins to dissipate. They reflect on their own experiences as a pupil of school history and the many ways in which they directly or indirectly engaged with historical scholarship in the classroom. Suddenly, the penny drops, and they are brimming with ideas for the ways in which pupils can be introduced to academic history. Engagement with historical scholarship is, after all, an essential element of effective history teaching.

Learning history means engaging with an evolving discipline, not simply to learn a static body of factual information about the past. Consequently, engagement with recent historical scholarship cannot be an optional extra. Understanding the conditional and changeable nature of how history is made, shaped by, and results in, different interpretations of the past, plays a vital role in the education of teachers preparing to teach history and pupils beginning to understand the nature of history making.

> **Activity 15.1 Initial reflection**
>
> - What is your view of the value and purpose of historical scholarship in the classroom?
> - How are the roles of academic historians and history teachers different?
> - When and where in the curriculum do you think it is most appropriate for pupils to encounter historical scholarship?
> - What would you say are the main challenges for using historical scholarship in school history?

This chapter will set out three principles for using academic historical scholarship in the classroom.

Principle 1: Engagement with academic historical scholarship is critical for the ongoing subject knowledge enhancement of teachers, curriculum design and planning.

Principle 2: The work of historians can enrich and stimulate the historical writing of pupils.

Principle 3: The work of historians helps pupils to see and engage with the interpretative nature of the discipline.

PRINCIPLE 1: ENGAGEMENT WITH ACADEMIC HISTORICAL SCHOLARSHIP IS CRITICAL FOR THE ONGOING SUBJECT KNOWLEDGE ENHANCEMENT OF TEACHERS, CURRICULUM DESIGN AND PLANNING

I have the privilege of observing many lessons each year. Without fail, the common factor linking those lessons that truly 'fly' is the depth of the teacher's own subject knowledge – substantive knowledge about the historical moment, its wider context and the historical debate surrounding the lesson focus. Engagement with academic historical scholarship is vitally important for history teachers' personal ongoing subject knowledge development. Teachers who read academic scholarship, or engage with the work of historians through podcasts, documentaries or presentations, are involved in a process of subject knowledge enhancement at the substantive level (strengthening their own particular topic knowledge, their broader sense of period and conceptual understanding in context) and from a disciplinary perspective (developing their appreciation of the second-order conceptual lenses through which historians are examining the past). In doing so, they are inevitably strengthening their subject knowledge to inform their planning and teaching.

Scholarship for Lesson Planning

An accessible place to begin using and integrating historical scholarship into the classroom is within lessons at a micro level. Teachers who possess secure and confident subject knowledge are able to communicate precise and engaging exposition, develop agile questioning phases and know exactly where to pause and place emphasis. Best of all, engagement beyond the textbook provides those small but perfectly judged historical anecdotes which, when woven into a lesson, build genuine intrigue.

Examples of how scholarship can encourage engagement can be found in texts such as Boyd's *Travellers in the Third Reich* (2017), and her sequel with Patel, *A Village in the Third Reich* (2023), which gathers the experiences of a wide range of ordinary people visiting and living in Nazi Germany. Many teachers have found these vignettes or small encounters to be useful for moving pupils beyond generalised understandings of the past disconnected from the people these events impacted. Instead, they have used Boyd's accounts and quoted source material to illuminate the motivations and experiences of real people and bring the period to life (see Activity 15.2). Meanwhile, texts like *Femina* by the historian Ramirez (2022) have helped to give voice to medieval women, providing rich examples of women, such as a tenth century Birka warrior and the 15th-century Christian mystic

Margery Kempe, through whom teachers have built a more complex, nuanced and representative medieval world for their pupils.

> ### Activity 15.2 Small stories
>
> This example of an extract from Boyd's *Traveller's in the Third Reich* (2017) helps to world build for pupils by revealing the wider context of the historical events they are studying. In this vignette, the discrimination experienced by Jesse Owens at the 1936 Olympics is thrown into relief by providing context through the experience of Black Americans at the hand of Jim Crow laws in their own home-nation.
>
> > Although American journalists did their best to unearth stories of discrimination against black and Jewish members of the US team, they received little cooperation from either group. Hitler may have refused to shake hands with Jesse Owens, winner of four gold medals, but the German people took the great black athlete to their hearts, chanting 'Oh-vens! Oh-vens' whenever he appeared... Archie Williams, the African-American 400 metres gold medallist, made plain the underlying point in an interview with the San Francisco Chronicle. 'When I came home, somebody asked me "How did those dirty Nazis treat you?" I replied that I didn't see any dirty Nazis, just a lot of nice German people. And I didn't have to ride in the back of the bus.
> >
> > Boyd, Julia. Travellers in the Third Reich: The Rise of Fascism Through the Eyes of Everyday People.
> >
> > (2017), p. 169
>
> Having used this vignette in your teaching, pupils could be asked:
>
> - Is there anything that surprises you about this extract?
> - What does this extract reveal about 1930s Germany?
> - What does this extract reveal about 1930s America?

Scholarship for Enquiry Planning

Drawing on historical scholarship to inform curriculum design at a macro level is well established. Many history teachers have been inspired by scholarship to develop enquiries for the classroom (such as Foster, 2011a; Carr, 2017), refocusing pupils onto the historically worthwhile questions historians themselves are asking (see Chapter 3 by Paula Worth for more on devising effective and rigorous enquiry questions). Schama's interpretation (2009) that the Norman Conquest was 'decisive, bloody, traumatic ... wiping out everything that gives a culture its bearings' has led teachers to move beyond the well-trodden path of 'Why did William win the Battle of Hastings?' to embrace enquiries such as 'Did William bring a 'truckload of trouble' to England in 1066?' (Historical Association, 2021). The work of Foster and Goudie (2016) also demonstrates how historical scholarship can provide a way for teachers to marshal and structure a manageable and accessible enquiry, solving the planning dilemmas that arise when the depth and breadth of the history feels too overwhelming to be contained in the school curriculum.

Scholarship can also provide stimulus to reconsider the history curriculum through a new lens. In recent years, popular historical scholarship has had a transformative effect upon school curricula. Worth (2019) reveals how this process of engagement with historical scholarship, including Frankopan's *Silk Roads* (2016), Olusoga's *Black and British: A Forgotten History* (2017), and Yerxa's edited volume of *Recent Themes in The History of Africa and the Atlantic World: Historians in Conversation* (2008), helped her to decide the most meaningful way to incorporate Medieval Mali into the established, relatively Eurocentric, curriculum. Worth was concerned with improving the 'scope and rigour' of the curriculum, to 'shine a light on other cultures and empires way beyond the Williams, Edwards and Richards of England'. For many teachers (Cusworth, 2021; Garry, 2021; Woods, 2021, provide superb examples), it is scholarship that provides the impetus or the means to re-evaluate their schemes of learning, to ask whose voices are heard in their curriculum and whether the lenses they have applied in the past are still authentic to the evolving discipline of history. The enquiries that have resulted from this engagement have broadened the conversation and encouraged teachers to include marginalised voices (exemplified in Table 15.1).

Table 15.1 Examples of enquiries reframed by engagement with recent scholarship

Scholarship	Key Themes	Examples of Enquiry Questions Developed in Response to Scholarship
Cat Jarman, River Kings (2021)	An archaeologist's exploration of how a carnelian bead, found during a dig in Repton, Derbyshire, came to be found in that location. It traces the links between the Viking world, eighth-century Baghdad and India, revealing the connections that existed between the Eastern and Western worlds via the Silk Road.	What can a carnelian bead tell us about the Vikings? (Sally Burnham)
Peter Frankopan, The Silk Roads (2016)	Frankopan provides a new lens for considering the history of the world by exploring ancient trading corridors to reveal the relationship between the East and the West, moving beyond the traditional narrative of Western Christendom's inexorable rise.	How did the Silk Roads shape the world? (Pattison, 2021)
Toby Green, A Fistful of Shells (2020)	Green explores the trade of equals that existed between Europe and the sophisticated kingdoms of West and West-Central Africa prior to the 17th century. It examines how over time the shift in this relationship, to one revolving around the trade in enslaved peoples, led to a growing political and economic power imbalance in Europe's favour.	How far did the transatlantic slave trade under develop the kingdom of Benin 1500-1897? (Garry, 2021)
Miranda Kauffman, Black Tudors, (2017)	Telling the stories of ten Africans living in Britain during the Tudor and Stuart eras, Kauffman demonstrates that black Tudors were part of Tudor society and that religion, rather than race, was the more significant aspect of social identity.	What was life like in Tudor England? (Lewis, 2018)

(Continued)

Table 15.1 Examples of enquiries reframed by engagement with recent scholarship (Continued)

Scholarship	Key Themes	Examples of Enquiry Questions Developed in Response to Scholarship
Sathnam Sanghera, Empireland (2021)	Sanghera critiques the history of the British Empire, its continuing impact on British society and its contemporary significance for the nation.	How has Imperialism shaped modern Britain?
Hallie Rubenhold, The Five (2019)	Rubenhold shifts the focus of the Whitechapel murders onto the working-class women who fell victim to both these crimes and the social and economic conditions of the Victorian age. It addresses the ethics of centring this historical moment around misogyny and male violence towards women.	How has Hallie Rubenhold rewritten the story of the Whitechapel murders? (Burney, 2023)
Fern Riddell, Death in Ten Minutes (2018)	Riddell asks whether the Suffragettes' more violent acts of protests were in fact equivalent to acts of domestic terrorism, raising the question of why the history of the women's suffrage movement has been sanitised.	Why do historians have different views of the suffrage movement? (Holliss, n.d.)
David Olugsoga, The World's War (2014)	Olusoga reveals the forgotten stories of soldiers from the colonial armies who fought on the Western Front in World War One alongside their white British counterparts.	What do the stories of the 'often forgotten armies' reveal about the Western Front? (Worth, 2020)

Scholarship for Big Picture Curriculum Planning

Of course, there is always the potential for history teachers to get carried away with their enthusiasm for a new history book that has captured their imagination. Designing a new enquiry around your most recent scholarship reading can seem an obvious response to reading an exciting new piece of historical scholarship. However, shoehorning your latest historical passion into the curriculum does not always result in a successful outcome for pupils. Olivey (2021) helpfully shared his own reflections of how his initial excitement at constructing an enquiry around Frankopan's *The Silk Roads* fell away when he realised the lessons were 'prohibitively difficult for most pupils' due to the 'sheer number of 'new' peoples and places in the enquiry'. He latterly recognised that the inspiration he had drawn from engaging with Frankopan's scholarly work could not be translated for use in the classroom as a stand-alone enquiry. Instead, it demanded a more significant curricula approach; to meet his ambition of a 'culturally diverse *and* more substantively coherent Year 7 curriculum' required the reconceptualization of the curriculum into eight linked enquiries that showed the 'connections between past societies'.

Not all departments will plan in this way but, where historical scholarship is used to inform curriculum planning, we can see how it:

- provides key reference texts for teachers' subject knowledge enhancement.
- contributes interpretations, narrative vignettes, and references to historical source material for lesson activities.

- informs enquiry construction, including identifying the conceptual foci of enquiries.
- inspires curriculum development.

PRINCIPLE 2: THE WORK OF HISTORIANS CAN ENRICH AND STIMULATE THE HISTORICAL WRITING OF PUPILS

Independently building an analytical and discursive historical argument is a challenging skill for pupils to acquire (Banham, 1998). It requires pupils to develop procedural and epistemic knowledge *and* an understanding of the form historical arguments take by drawing on knowledge claims based in evidence (Chapman, 2021). This cannot be achieved quickly. It is a longer-term work, requiring a more 'systematic and holistic approach to progression in historical communication' (Counsell, 1997).

A range of approaches have been developed for integrating historians' texts within enquiries to meaningfully enhance pupils' historical thinking and communication. Counsell (1997) introduced Key Stage 3 pupils to the writing of the historian Eileen Power with the three-fold intention of enabling pupils to 'to enjoy historical argument written by real historians... explore the lively personality in one example of such writing; and... replicate some of its conventions, features and energy in their own writing'. Foster (2011b) meanwhile built on Counsell's (1997) notion that 'historians reveal their puzzling through their prose' by introducing pupils to historical scholarship so they could see historical argument in context to understand what it is and how it is formed. Foster (2015) illustrated this potential by showing that A Level pupils could be supported to identify how historians carefully craft their opening sentences, considering the role of punctuation and clausal structure, to 'delineate an argument'. Meanwhile, Foster and Gadd (2013) have also demonstrated how scaffolded use of historical scholarship can lay bare the degree to which historians select and synthesise specific substantive examples and source material as evidence to support their historical claims. Likewise, Laffin (2012) has shown how introducing pupils to historical scholarship allows them to see and then adopt for themselves the vocabulary and language forms used by historians in their writing. Her pupils were surprised to find that historians' judgements were 'were tentative and cautious in nature' and that they frequently used vocabulary enabling them to communicate the voracity of their claims and the strength of their evidential basis to convey 'weighing up', change over time and relative importance'.

Writing frames, providing scaffolding for pupils in the form of pre-determined structures, have become a mainstay of the history classroom – a pragmatic, quick fix to the challenge of getting pupils writing. However, most history teachers will have had experiences echoing those of Foster and Gadd (2013) who asserted that 'over-reliance on writing frames in particular, or the application of them in too rigid a way risks *hindering* students'. Communicating historically involves historical thinking, not just organisational literacy, and this is something that writing frames and structure mnemonics, such as the all-pervasive PEE/PEEL, cannot help. Drawing on historical texts in the classroom therefore allows pupils to develop their awareness of how historians write to reveal this thinking, while activities (such as the example offered in Activity 15.3) can be designed to allow them to practise translating this learning into their own historical writing. As Laffin (2012) eloquently expressed, 'our students are fledgling historians. They need to become good historical writers and immersing themselves in historical prose is the best way to do that, however challenging, complicated and confusing it is. No wonder their own writing tends to be banal and repetitive if they do not engage with fluent, logical and expressive historical writing in their own studies'.

See Chapter 14 by Jim Carroll for further examples of teachers using historical scholarship to develop pupils' extended writing, as well as other activities which can be used to improve pupils' historical writing.

> **Activity 15.3 Beat the textbook**
>
> A 'beat the textbook' task can be used to scaffold pupils into writing in more scholarly historical ways.
>
> - Analyse an extract of relevant historical scholarship with your pupils, noting in particular the sentence construction and hedging language used by the historian to qualify their claims.
> - Select a textbook, or webpage, extract written for young people which conveys your chosen historical topic with certainty and little explicit reference to the evidential basis upon which it has been constructed.
> - Ask the pupils to rewrite the textbook extract using their understanding of scholarly modes of writing to see if they can 'beat the textbook'.

PRINCIPLE 3: THE WORK OF HISTORIANS HELPS PUPILS TO SEE AND ENGAGE WITH THE INTERPRETATIVE NATURE OF THE DISCIPLINE

'Powerful Knowledge' in History Requires Engagement with Academic Historical Scholarship

English education in the 2010s was marked by a movement which has come to be known as the 'knowledge turn' (Chapman, 2021). Young's (2009) notion of 'powerful knowledge' has underpinned much of the curriculum reform that has resulted from this movement and has provided an opportunity for subject teachers to reengage with curriculum making. It has necessitated the re-examination of 'the relationships between the school subject (aligned to educational goals and purposes) and the wider academic discipline (aligned to research and knowledge creation)' (Lambert, 2014). However, long before powerful knowledge became a watch word in our educational discourse, Seixas (1993) suggested that the specialised teacher knowledge of the history teacher was to be found in the provision of 'a bridge between communities [the scholarly community and classroom community], extending outward to historians in one direction and to students in another'. For the history teacher, this poses an enormous challenge. If teachers are to claim their history curriculum has power, it needs to engage pupils with the discipline of history, not simply 'subscribe to populist and mythic constructions of the past' (Shemilt, 2000). As Burn (2021) has discussed, this 'raises important questions about the kind of relationship that should exist between academic practitioners and classroom teachers'.

Counsell (2011) asserted that 'the most explicit exploration by history teachers of the boundary between disciplinary and 'everyday' knowledge lies in "Interpretations of history"'. Consequently, if the history classroom is to be a locus of rich and powerful knowledge, as opposed to offering pupils 'inert information about the past' far removed from the academic discipline, it must involve opportunities to engage with the scholarly community of practice – 'in which historians form questions and interpretations are responding to current concerns' (Burn, 2021). Opportunities for pupils to read, analyse and interrogate academic scholarship is an important aspect of bringing history to life. While history teachers are not usually involved in history making themselves, they are still engaged in the scholarly work of generating interpretations (Dawson, 2023a). This necessarily involves both revealing to pupils that the discipline of history is 'provisional and tentative... an ongoing dialogue within a community of scholars' (Seixas, 1993), and supporting pupils in beginning to generate their own in a scaffolded and appropriate way.

Narratives have long since been a feature of the history classroom, whether conveyed through a teacher's oral retellings, textbooks or the more recent (and increasingly influential) phenomenon of teacher-authored curriculum booklets. So integral is the role played by narrative in history teaching, that Counsell (2023) has asserted 'History's chief mode of accounting is narrative. Without narrative, nothing is stated other than free-floating fact'. Narrative is undoubtedly an incredibly useful pedagogical approach – one which helps pupils to world-build in their imaginations the substantive knowledge and sense of period necessary to develop a rich understanding of the past – often providing pupils with a bridge via which to engage with historical scholarship. However, the use of school-history focused narrative designed exclusively for the classroom does not remove the need for pupils to engage with academic history.

Wineburg (2001) has written extensively about the 'unnatural act' that is historical thinking, and the need for teachers to plan systematically for this in their teaching. While much historical scholarship is a form of narrative, in academic historical scholarship there is often more explicit reference to the process that led to its creation. As Carr (1961) said:

> When you read a work of history, always listen out for the buzzing. If you can detect none, either you are tone deaf or your historian is a dull dog. The facts are really not at all like fish on the fishmonger's slab. They are like fish swimming about in a vast and sometimes inaccessible ocean; and what the historian catches will depend partly on chance, but mainly on what part of the ocean he chooses to fish in and what tackle he chooses to use-these two factors being, of course, determined by the kind of fish he wants to catch. By and large, the historian will get the kind of facts he wants. History means interpretation.

A key responsibility of the history teacher must therefore be to convey to pupils that all history is an interpretation and to be transparent about the status of any historical account as a construction; a history which has been made, rather than objectively recorded (Activity 15.4 provides an example of an activity which begins to reveal this to pupils).

Narrative devoid of explicit reference to the processes which led to its creation will not provide pupils with the crucial insight they need into the provenance of that text. Crismore's (1984) study of 'The Rhetoric of Textbooks' revealed that, 'non-textbook writers use more hedges [the language of uncertainty] perhaps because they keep in mind that history is memory of the past rather than a record of the past and that many historians often disagree about issues. The textbook writers more often use flat assertions'. Dawson (2023b), drawing on his extensive experience as a textbook author and editor, is clear that 'presenting text in schoolbooks as the unchallengeable 'word of authority' runs counter to the reasons why we develop students' understanding of the processes of studying the past. Consequently, if pupils are to grasp both the purpose of learning history and the complexity involved in constructing historical arguments, they need to encounter historical texts beyond textbooks and teacher created booklets, a form which Schrag (1991) has described as writing history 'as if their authors did not exist at all, as if they were simply the instruments of a heavenly intelligence transcribing official truths'. Historical scholarship is therefore an important component of a history classroom seeking to disrupt prevailing narratives and develop pupils' epistemic understanding of history.

More about historical interpretations, including helping pupils analyse the work of a historian as an interpretation, can be found in Chapter 9.

Activity 15.4 Understanding construction

Judging a book by its cover

Exploring history book titles, blurbs and front covers with pupils can be a helpful task for illuminating the different questions historians ask about the same historical moment and the differing interpretations they form as a result. Pupils can be presented the book jacket information and asked questions such as:

- What is the focus of the historian's study?
- Can you tell anything about the nature of the evidence they are drawing upon?
- Are there any clues that this book might be advancing a new interpretation or is it building on previous interpretations?
- Can you identify what the interpretation offered by this book might be?

One possible outcome task could be to ask pupils to design their own book cover at the end of the enquiry to reflect their understanding of the historical scholarship and key takeaways from the enquiry.

As illustrated in Figure 15.1, Hiscox (2021) has developed an excellent contextualised example of this kind of activity.

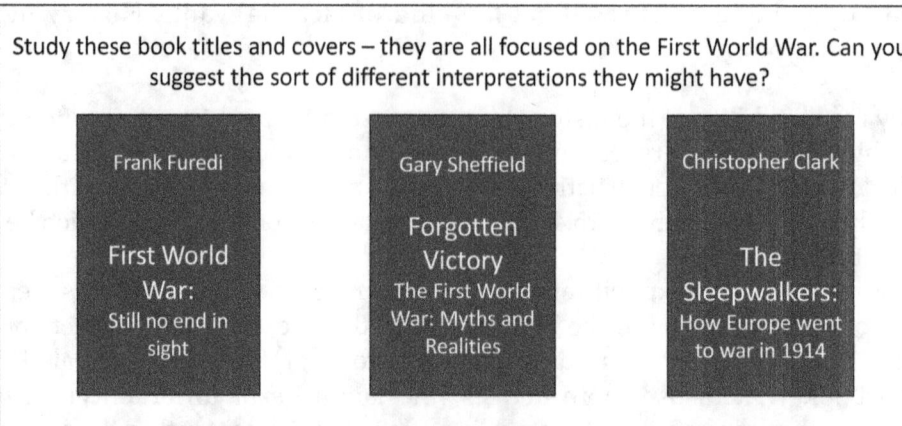

Figure 15.1 Book title task, taken from Hiscox (2021).

Historical Scholarship can Enliven Pupils' Rigorous Historical Thinking

History is a heuristic discipline. As Colby (2020) has explored, 'the multilayered cognitions typically used by historians can be difficult for teachers to teach and for students to learn'. We do, however, need to find ways to teach pupils to understand the 'habits of mind and rules of thumbs' (Nokes, 2011) employed by historians to make sense of the past. Lee and Shemilt's Project Chata research explored the role historical accounts can play in developing pupils' historical consciousness (Lee & Shemilt, 2004). It provides an insight into the contribution historical scholarship can play in changing pupils' ideas about history as a discipline – most importantly, that history is consciously constructed. Encounters with historical scholarship help pupils to progress in their understanding that, because of the ways they have been constructed, historical accounts may differ in the focus and conviction of their argument (Activity 15.5 explores an approach for introducing this idea to the classroom). It helps pupils to develop more nuanced understandings of the discipline and to move beyond the notion that differences within historical accounts are simply due to differing opinions. As Colby (2020) has asserted, 'wise teachers, who acknowledge that adolescents read and think differently from experienced historians, intentionally expose students to experts who think in action, especially about primary sources'.

Familiarity with historical scholarship also allows pupils to see how historical narrative or argumentation requires the interplay of different forms of knowledge. Hammond (2014) showed how the most historically convincing GCSE examination responses produced by her Year 11 pupils came from pupils who were able to securely and confidently draw upon different layers of knowledge to 'flavour the construction of a claim' and develop a more sophisticated historical analysis. Exposing pupils to historical scholarship also allows them to observe how second-order conceptual thinking provides a framework for that substantive knowledge. It enables them to see in action the 'dynamic textures of history, its dance of general and particular, in other words, the way in which we come to assimilate historical knowledge and to move about within it' (Counsell, 2023). It reveals the possibility of complex, rather than formulaic historical communication.

> **Activity 15.5 Revealing historians' methods of historical construction**
>
> Hiscox's (2021) article explains how she invited historians into the classroom to explore their methods of construction with pupils. Increasingly, historians are making this aspect of their work more visible via podcasts or webinars, meaning it's possible to explore these themes with pupils in classrooms on a more regular basis.
>
> The Historical Association and BeBold history network host podcasts and webinars from historians who generously share both their work and their process. Dr. Sarah Longair (2022) is an excellent example of a historian who seeks to make her own historical process visible, sharing how material culture is used by historians as historical evidence.
>
> Rebecca Hall's book *Wake* (2021) is a fascinating graphic history which, as well as focusing on the forgotten histories of women-led slave revolts, also depicts the efforts required to research and assemble this historical account.
>
> - Identify an enquiry in your curriculum where you could integrate the scholarship and voice of an historian into the enquiry and use this as a springboard for:
>   - exploring what questions historians are asking about the period/topic focus.

- identifying the sources historians draw upon as evidence.
- examining how historians leverage their evidence to develop a line of argument.
- comparing the works of different historians to identify how and why they might differ in the interpretations they offer.

RECOGNISING THE LITERACY CHALLENGE

As Jenner (2019) clearly articulated, while 'the value of academic texts inheres in their complexity… this complexity is also what makes their use in the classroom challenging'. Any activity we use in the classroom needs to be thought about carefully, and this is equally true of historical scholarship. We therefore need to be clear on the purpose behind integrating historical scholarship into a particular lesson and provide appropriate scaffolding to support pupils to access the text and work with it in meaningful ways to develop 'disciplinary literacy' (Quigley, 2020). Scaffolding is likely to be required before, during and after engaging with historical scholarship in the classroom, for example:

- Pre-reading – establishing the context and making connections with pupils' established schema.
- During reading – reading with a purpose, reading with fluency (this may require the teacher to read aloud to add colour and emphasis to the text), modelling interaction with the text, summarising key themes, defining vocabulary and checking for understanding through questioning.
- Post-reading – working with the text (to analyse or critically engage with the interpretation) to achieve the historical purpose which led to its inclusion in the lesson.

The selection of the text is also key. Popular history texts often offer up passages which can be extracted as focused gobbets. More recently, there has been a trend for publishers to produce young adult or children's versions of popular historical texts. Olusoga's *Black and British* (2017, 2020) and Frankopan's *The Silk Roads* (2016, 2018) are excellent examples of this, providing history teachers with a more accessible version of the historian's work for use in the classroom (as illustrated in Figure 15.2).

However, even carefully selected passages from historians' work may pose literacy challenges for pupils, and so appropriate scaffolding will be required. Reading aloud together, for example, allows a teacher to 'nurture the motivation of pupils as they grapple with the frustrations of their slow, effortful reading … while modelling the strategies a more mature reader undertakes with seeming effortlessness' (Quigley, 2020). Similarly, a method such as guided reading using DARTs (Directed Activities Related to Text) can be highly beneficial for building pupils' confidence to engage with historical scholarship, support their ability to read for meaning, while developing their own historical-literacy toolkit (see Figure 15.3).

SUMMARY OF KEY POINTS

- The use of historical scholarship should be a mainstay of the history classroom, introduced to pupils in meaningful ways that both broaden and deepen their historical experience.

> **Extract from the adult version of *The Silk Roads***
>
> While such countries may seem wild to us, these are no back waters, no obscure wastelands. In fact the bridge between east and west is the very crossroads of civilisation. Far from being on the fringe of global affairs, these countries lie at its very centre – as they have done since the beginning of history. It was here that Civilisation was born, and where many believed Mankind had been created – in the Garden of Eden, 'planted by the Lord God' with 'every tree that is pleasant to the sight and good for food', which was widely thought to be located in the rich fields between the Tigris and Euphrates.
>
> It was in this bridge between east and west that great metropolises were established nearly 5,000 years ago, where the cities of Harappa and Mohenjo-daro in the Indus valley were wonders of the ancient world, with populations numbering in the tens of thousands and streets connecting into a sophisticated sewage system that would not be rivalled in Europe for thousands of years. Other great centres of civilisation such as Babylon, Nineveh, Uruk and Akkad in Mesopotamia were famed for their grandeur and architectural innovation. One Chinese geographer, meanwhile, writing more than two millennia ago, noted that the inhabitants of Bactria, centred on the Oxus river and now located in northern Afghanistan, were legendary negotiators and traders; its capital city was home to a market where a huge range of products were bought and sold, carried from far and wide.

> **Extract from the children's version of *The Silk Roads*, recommended for readers aged 11+**
>
> The heart of Asia is where civilisation was born. In ancient Mesopotamia along the banks of the mighty Tigris and Euphrates rivers and steeped in the Indus Valley stood the very first towns and cities known to mankind. The abundance of water oozing from the banks was vital for the inhabitants of the cities built there; citizens of Babylon, Nineveh and Uruk in Mesopotamia and Harappa, Mohenjo-Daro and Dholavira in the Indus Valley would be able to go about their business refreshed, clean and healthy. Water was also important to help crops grow in the fertile fields along the riverbanks. Little wonder that many believed mankind itself was created in the fertile fields of Mesopotamia (literally 'the land between the rivers').
>
> This is where it was widely believed that the Garden of Eden was located, 'planted by the Lord God' with 'every tree that is pleasant to the sight and good for food'. Control of the thriving fields and cities allowed kings to reign and empires to be built.

Figure 15.2 Comparable extracts from Frankopan's *The Silk Roads* written for an adult- and then child-audience, taken from Frankopan (2016) and Frankopan and Packer (2018).

- History teachers need to continue developing their subject knowledge throughout their careers and therefore need to engage with historical scholarship.
- 'Powerful knowledge' in history requires engagement with academic historical scholarship so that pupils can see the interpretative nature of the discipline.
- The work of historians can enrich, enliven and stimulate rigorous historical thinking by pupils and the historical writing of pupils.
- There are many ways that historical scholarship can be introduced meaningfully into the classroom at the level of curriculum design and through lesson activities.
- Using historical scholarship in the classroom will require careful selection, planning and scaffolding to enable pupils to access complex texts.

Activity 15.6 Final Reflection

- If you were going to identify some companion texts for your history curriculum, what would they be? How can you use this to inform your next department planning opportunity? How could you make opportunities to engage with historical scholarship more accessible for the department (e.g., set up a small departmental lending-library or a departmental book club)?
- How will you make the most of the expertise that already exists in your department/ links with your local university to enhance engagement with historical scholarship in your school?
- What historical scholarship will you personally read next? Will this be a text to inform your current curriculum plan or one to challenge it?
- It is impossible to do everything at once, so where will you focus your development efforts and engagement with scholarship as a department to make the most impact?

Give each paragraph a title and answer the linked questions	Extract from Toby Green's *A Fistful of* Shells (2020), Chapter 6.	Key word definitions
	Find and highlight the key word definitions in the extract. *<u>Underline</u> any other words you'd like to discuss*	
Title: What factors were involved in bringing about slavery?	The key to understanding slavery as it emerged in West and West-Central Africa from the fifteenth to the nineteenth centuries is not just its economic function, but its relationship to warfare, kinship and honour. Just as among Native American peoples, warfare often shaped how slavery was seen in many parts of Africa. Successful wars helped a society grow in size and strength. War captives could be incorporated as new members of an expanding society, with dependent status….	**economic** = money **kinship** = family relationships **society** = community of people
Title: What does Toby Green think about the view that 'it was 'Africans' who sold 'Africans' into the slave trade'? How does this expand your understanding of the factors leading to the Transatlantic trade in enslaved people?	This fundamental relationship of dependence and warfare did, however, change over time. As the slave trade expanded hugely in the eighteenth century, so, too, did the capture of enslaved persons by warfare… That enslaved persons were most often outsiders is important, as it shows up the fallacy in the idea often put forward that it was 'Africans' who sold 'Africans' into the slave trade. This argument is usually developed as a way of alleviating discourses of Euro-American guilt, discourses that themselves emerge from the history of abolitionism. But it completely misunderstands identities in the seventeenth and eighteenth centuries, when, as noted in the Introduction, people did not see themselves as 'African' but rather as belonging to a specific lineage, kingdom and ritual community – just as people did not see themselves as 'Europeans' at the outset of this time, but rather defined themselves according to the style of Christian belief and nation.	**enslaved person** = a person who has their freedom taken away, who is forced to work for no pay and be treated like a possession. **fallacy** = mistaken belief **discourses** = debates **lineage** = being part of a particular family

Figure 15.3 An example of a guided reading passage to support pupils engaging with historical scholarship.

RESOURCES AND FURTHER READING

It can be difficult to know where to start when seeking to source appropriate historical scholarship for use in the history classroom. Fortunately, there are a number of helpful resources to point you in the right direction.

- **A history teacher subject knowledge reading list can be found at** The Historical Association's One Big History Department website: https://onebighistorydepartment.com/2020/02/26/new-reading-list-with-reviews/
- The Historical Association webpage includes a number of helpful resources for history teachers seeking to engage with historical scholarship.
  - Book and publications reviews: https://www.history.org.uk/historian/categories/reviews

- Podcasts: https://www.history.org.uk/podcasts
- 'What historians have been arguing about …' (formerly Polychronicon) feature in Teaching history: https://www.history.org.uk/publications/module/8697/teaching-history-regular-features/9163/what-historians-have-been-arguing-about

REFERENCES

Banham, Dale. 'Getting Ready for the Grand Prix: Learning How to Build a Substantiated Argument in Year 7' in Teaching History, 92, Explanation and Argument Edition, (1998): 15. London: Historical Association.

Boyd, Julia. Travellers in the Third Reich: The Rise of Fascism Through the Eyes of Everyday People. London: Elliott and Thompson 2017: 169.

Boyd, Julia, & Patel, Angelika. A. Village in the Third Reich: How Ordinary Lives Were Transformed by the Rise of Fascism. London: Pegasus Books 2023.

Burn, Katharine. 'The Power of Knowledge: The Impact on History Teachers of Sustained Subject-Rich Professional development' in Chapman, Arthur (ed.). Knowing History in Schools: Powerful Knowledge and the Powers of Knowledge. London: UCL Press 2021: 129–131.

Burney, Rachel. 'Harnessing the power of historical scholarship in the mixed ability classroom' [Paper Presentation], L.E.A.D Teaching School Hub Secondary History Conference, (2023).

Carr, E. H. What Is History? London: Macmillan 1961: 23.

Carr, Elizabeth. 'Cunning Plan: Complicating Industrial change' in Teaching History, 167, Complicating Narratives Edition, (2017): 38–40. London: Historical Association.

Chapman, Arthur. 'Introduction: Historical Knowing and the 'knowledge turn'' in Chapman, Arthur (ed.). Knowing History in Schools: Powerful Knowledge and the Powers of Knowledge. London: UCL Press 2021: 1–31.

Colby, Sherri Rae. 'Enacting Historical Thinking With Heuristic Organizers' in The History Teacher, 53:2, (2020): 354, 364. Society for History Education.

Counsell, Christine. 'Analytic and Discursive Writing at Key Stage 3' in Historical Association, 7, (1997): 101.

Counsell, Christine. 'Disciplinary Knowledge for All, the Secondary History Curriculum and History Teachers' Achievement' in Curriculum Journal, 22(2), (2011): 212.

Counsell, Christine. 'Laughing Muppets, Lost Memories and Lethal Mutations: Rescuing Assessment from 'knowledge-Rich Gone wrong' in Teaching History, 193, Mediating History Edition, (2023): 8–25. London: Historical Association.

Crismore, Avon. 'The Rhetoric of Textbooks: Metadiscourse' in Journal of Curriculum Studies, 16(3), (1984): 293.

Cusworth, Hannah. 'Putting Black into the Union Jack: Weaving Black History into the Year 7 to 9 Curriculum' in Teaching History, 183, Race Edition, (2021): 20–26. London: Historical Association.

Dawson, Ian. 'Building A level students' confidence and ability as learners: Writing and Editing A level books 1990-2015' [Blog Post], Thinking History, (2023a). https://www.thinkinghistory.co.uk/Writings/downloads/Writing_ALevel.pdf

Dawson, Ian. 'CPD in a Textbook? From teaching about concepts to challenging misconceptions' [Blog Post], Thinking History, (2023b). https://www.thinkinghistory.co.uk/Writings/downloads/Writing_KS3.pdf.

Foster, Rachel. 'Passive Receivers or Constructive Readers? Pupils' Experiences of an Encounter With Academic History' in Teaching History, 142, Experiencing History Edition, (2011a): 4–13. London: Historical Association.

Foster, Rachel. 'Using Academic History in the Classroom' in Davies, Ian (ed.). Debates in History Teaching. Oxon: Routledge 2011b: 199–211.

Foster, Rachel. 'Pipes's Punctuation and Making Complex Historical Claims: How the Direct Teaching of Punctuation can Improve pupils' Historical Thinking and Written argument' in Teaching History, 159, Underneath the essay edition, (2015): 8–13. London: Historical Association.

Frankopan, Peter. The Silk Roads: A New History of the World. Bloomsbury Paperbacks 2016: xv.

Frankopan, Peter, & Packer, Neil. The Silk Roads: A New History of the World. London: Bloomsbury Children's Books 2018: 15.

Foster, Rachel, & Gadd, Sarah. 'Let's Play Supermarket 'Evidential' Sweep: Developing students' Awareness of the Need to Select evidence' in Teaching History, 152, Putting it all Together Edition, (2013): 24–29. London: Historical Association.

Garry, Josh. 'The Underdevelopment of Africa: Broadening and Deepening Narratives of Benin for Year 8' in Teaching History, 183, Race Edition, (2021): 32–43. London: Historical Association.

Foster, Rachel, & Goudie, Kath. 'Shaping the Debate: Why Historians Matter More than Ever at GCSE' in Teaching History, 163, Get Excited & Carry On Edition, (2016): 17–24. London: Historical Association.

Green, Toby. A Fistful of Shells: West Africa from the Rise of the Slave Trade to the Age of Revolution. Penguin Books 2020: 267–268.

Hall, Rebecca, & Martinez, Hugo. Wake: The Hidden History of Women-Led Slave Revolts. Particular Books 2021.

Hammond, Kate. 'The Knowledge That Flavours a claim' in Teaching History, 157, Assessment Edition, (2014): 18–25. London: Historical Association.

Hiscox, Holly. 'The Mechanics of History: Helping A-Level Students to Uncover the Processes of Claim Construction That Underpin Different Interpretations' in (eds.). Teaching History, 182, A Sense of Period Edition, (2021): 64–75. London: Historical Association.

Historical Association. 'Lesson Sequence: The Normans' [Teaching Unit], Historical Association, (2021). https://www.history.org.uk/secondary/resource/10043/lesson-sequence-the-normans

Holliss, C. 'Why do historians have different views of the suffrage movement?' [Teaching Unit}, Women's Suffrage: History and citizenship resources for schools, (n.d.). https://www.suffrageresources.org.uk/activity/3211/why-do-historians-have-different-views-of-the-suffrage-movement

Jarman, Cat. River Kings: The Vikings from Scandinavia to the Silk Roads. London: Harper Collins 2021.

Jenner, Tim. 'Making reading Routine: Helping Key Stage 3 Pupils to Become Regular Readers of Historical scholarship' in Teaching History, 174, Structure Edition, (2019): 42–49. London: Historical Association.

Kauffman, Miranda. Black Tudors: The Untold Story. London: Oneworld 2017.

Laffin, Diana. 'Marr: Magpie or Marsh Harrier? The Quest for the Common Characteristics of the Genus 'historians' With 16-19-Year-olds' in Teaching History, 149, In Search of the Question Edition, (2012): 18–25. London: Historical Association.

Lambert, David. 'Subject Teachers in Knowledge-Led schools' in Young, Michael, & Lambert, David (eds.). Knowledge and the Future School: Curriculum and Social Justice. London: Bloomsbury 2014: 161.

Lee, Peter, & Shemilt, Dennis. "I Just Wish We Could Go Back in the Past and Find Out What Really happened': Progression in Understanding About Historical Accounts' in Teaching History, 117, Dealing with Distance Edition, (2004): 31. London: Historical Association.

Lewis, Chris. 'Cunning Plan 173: Using Black Tudors as a Window into Tudor England' in Teaching History, 173, Opening Doors Edition, (2018): 23. London: Historical Association.

Longair, Sarah. 'Teaching with things: History Through Material Culture' [YouTube Video], BeBold History Network, (2022). https://www.youtube.com/watch?v=WECmFL2yqx4

Nokes, Jeffery D. 'Recognizing and Addressing the Barriers to Adolescents' "Reading Like Historians"'in The History Teacher, 44(3), (2011): 382. Society for History Education.

Olivey, Jacob. 'They Sometimes Clashed, and Ultimately Blended: Planning a More Diverse and Coherent Year 7 Curriculum' n Teaching History, 184, Different Lenses Edition, (2021): 22–31. London: Historical Association.

Olusoga, David. The World's War: Forgotten Soldiers of Empire. London: Head of Zeus 2014.

Olusoga, David. Black and British: A Forgotten History. London: Pan Books 2017.

Olusoga, David. Black and British: A Short, Essential History. London: Macmillan Children's Books 2020.

Pattison, Tom. 'From The Silk Roads to Essex: Bringing Scholarship into the Classroom' [Online Article], Practical Histories, (2021). https://practicalhistories.com/2021/04/from-the-silk-roads-to-essex-bringing-scholarship-into-the-classroom

Quigley, Alex. Closing the Reading Gap. Oxon: Routledge 2020: 44, 58–59.

Ramirez, Janina. Femina: A New History of the Middle Ages, Through the Women Written Out of It. London: WH Allen 2022.

Riddell, Fern. Death in Ten Minutes: The Forgotten Life of Radical Suffragette Kitty Marion. London: Hodder & Stoughton 2018.

Rubenhold, Hallie. The Five: The Untold Lives of the Women Killed by Jack the Ripper. Boston: Houghton Mifflin Harcourt: 2019.

Sanghera, Sathnam. Empireland: How Imperialism Has Shaped Modern Britain. London: Penguin Books Limited 2021.

Schama, Simon. A History of Britain: At the Edge of the World? 3000BC-AD1603. London: Bodley Head 2009.

Schrag, Peter quoted in Wineburg, Samuel. 'On the Reading of Historical Texts: Notes on the Breach between School and Academy' in American Educational Research Journal, 28(3), (1991): 511.

Seixas, Peter. 'The Community of Inquiry as a Basis for Knowledge and Learning: The Case of History' in American Educational Research Journal, 30:2, (1993): 313, 31616

Shemilt, Dennis. 'The Caliph's Coin: The Currency of Narrative Frameworks in History Teaching' in Stearns, Peter N., Seixas, Peter, & Wineburg, Samuel (eds.). Knowing, Teaching and Learning History: National and International Perspectives. New York: New York University Press 2000: 100.

Wineburg, Samuel. Historical Thinking and Other Unnatural Acts: Charting the Future of Teaching the Past. Philadelphia: Temple University Press 2001.

Woods, Theo. 'Diversifying the Curriculum: One Department's Holistic Approach' in Teaching History, 183, Race Edition, (2021): 62–71. London: Historical Association.

Worth, Paula. 'What do the stories of the 'often forgotten armies' reveal about the Western Front?' [Blog Post], Lobworth, (2020). https://lobworth.com/2020/05/14/what-do-the-stories-of-the-often-forgotten-armies-reveal-about-the-western-front/

Worth, Paula. 'Are you a 'lumper' or a 'splitter'? Deciding how to incorporate the history of medieval Mali into our Year 7 history curriculum' [Blog Post], Lobworth (2019). https://lobworth.com/2019/09/08/are-you-a-lumper-or-a-splitter-deciding-how-to-incorporate-the-history-of-medieval-mali-into-our-history-curriculum/

Yerxa, Donald A. ed.. Recent Themes in The History of Africa and the Atlantic World: Historians in Conversation. South Carolina: University of South Carolina Press 2008.

Young, Michael. 'Education, Globalisation and the "voice of Knowledge"' in Journal of Education and Work, 22 (3), (2009): 193–204.

Chapter 16 Teaching Local History

Luke Mayhew

BACKGROUND

For many people interested in history, a visit to a local castle, museum or site as a child was their first real interaction with history, which kindled a lifelong interest in the mythical distant past and the people that lived there. As a child, visiting the Suffolk Regimental Museum with my grandparents was always a highlight of my time with them. Often the only visitors, I remember fondly the curator being a mine of information, who was plagued by this small child asking a million questions about the uniforms, equipment and weapons! For many of the pupils I teach, they will get the bus home with Norwich Castle looming above them, but do many of them really think about the history of this location; they see the 'big grey box' and are aware of the castle, but do they pause to consider whether it has always been this way? Many pupils think of Norwich and Norfolk as a sleepy, slow-paced location where nothing really happens or happened, whereas the reality is very different. Historically incredibly important, a hotbed of radicalism and rebellion, there are various figures and events jumping out at us *if* we look, and it is our role as teachers to ensure that our pupils are able to see these rich and varied histories. Local history can grab pupils, whilst at the same time challenging sometimes deeply embedded misconceptions, and so it is our duty to do local history justice.

LOCAL HISTORY IN SCHOOLS – THE CURRENT SITUATION

Despite being a requirement of the National Curriculum and recognised by Ofsted as good practice, local history was for years an afterthought in many schools. Although this has improved over the past decade, local history is often the first area to suffer in curriculum time. A survey I carried out via what was then Twitter and social media at the end of July 2023 found that 65% of secondary schools surveyed included a specific local history study/unit in their Key Stage 3 provision, though sadly 35% said that they did not. Reasons for not teaching a specific site study included lack of curriculum time and not knowing what to remove, lack of detailed local knowledge as well as lack of time to research and develop a local study. Following on, 87% of secondary schools incorporate local history throughout their schemes of work where possible; including information about local soldiers when looking at the First World War, the local Domesday entry and local involvement in the Civil Wars. At Key Stage 4, the inclusion of local history becomes more challenging due to time and specification constraints, with 54% of surveyed schools incorporating some local history, with 46% currently not doing so. At Key Stage 5, the picture becomes even bleaker with 79% of surveyed schools not including any local history in their teaching, with the majority of local history anecdotal, and only possible where an event marries up with the specification. It is important to recognise the pressures that schools and history departments are under in terms of exam results, but it is imperative that we allow our pupils the opportunity to investigate their own rich and varied local history, making greater sense of the world around them. As stated by Jenner, 'Local histories enable pupils to identify, challenge and move beyond generalisations and to consider similarity and difference in experiences' (Ofsted Research review series, 2021).

> **Activity 16.1**
>
> Reflect on the inclusion of local history within your school's history curriculum.
>
> - What local history is included and how? Are there separate local history units or is it included through other units?
> - What are the reasons behind local history's inclusion or omission from your history curriculum?
> - What rationale does Mayhew offer for the inclusion of local history?

INCORPORATING LOCAL HISTORY

The easiest way for teachers to incorporate local history into their schemes of work is to build local examples, events and individuals into their existing provision. What can be incorporated will of course depend on the location and context of the school, but local history could be anything within a few hundred metres from the school, to something that is from the same county. Either approach will help pupils to make a more concrete connection with the events that they are studying.

Idea 1 – Domesday Book Year 7

When looking at the aftermath of the Norman conquest (as the majority of schools do), looking at a local Domesday entry can engage pupils in thinking about their own location. The website https://opendomesday.org/ offers teachers a quick and easy way to do this, showing digitised images of the original Domesday entries as well as accessible transcripts of the information (see Figures 16.1 and 16.2). When considering the transfer of power, wealth and land after the conquest, this is a great way to show (most commonly) the disappearance of the Saxon elite, emergence of Norman lords and the increased wealth and power of the King. By adding this local element, pupils can then begin to see how their own area was affected by the Norman Conquest, as well as how the significance of a site has changed over time. Support and scaffolding will obviously be needed to provide pupils with the understanding of different terms, allowing them to ask questions such as what a plough team was and represented, or how common was slavery at this point?

It is then possible to zoom out to the national picture, as each of the tenants is clickable, showing you how much other land they held, and (significantly) where this land was, Moving from the local level to the national picture allows pupils to

TEACHING LOCAL HISTORY

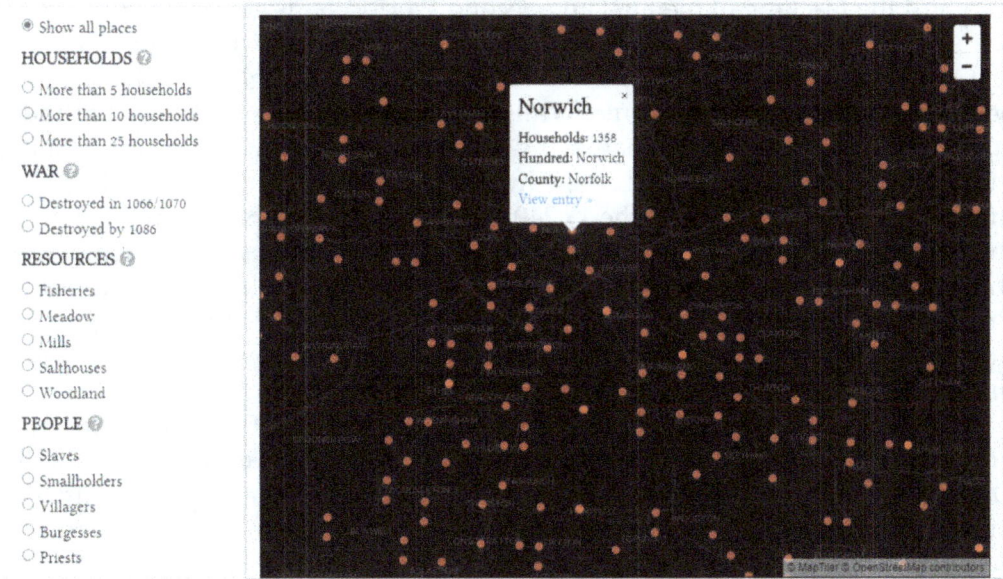

Figure 16.1 Screenshot from www.opendomesday.org showing the searchable map function on the website.

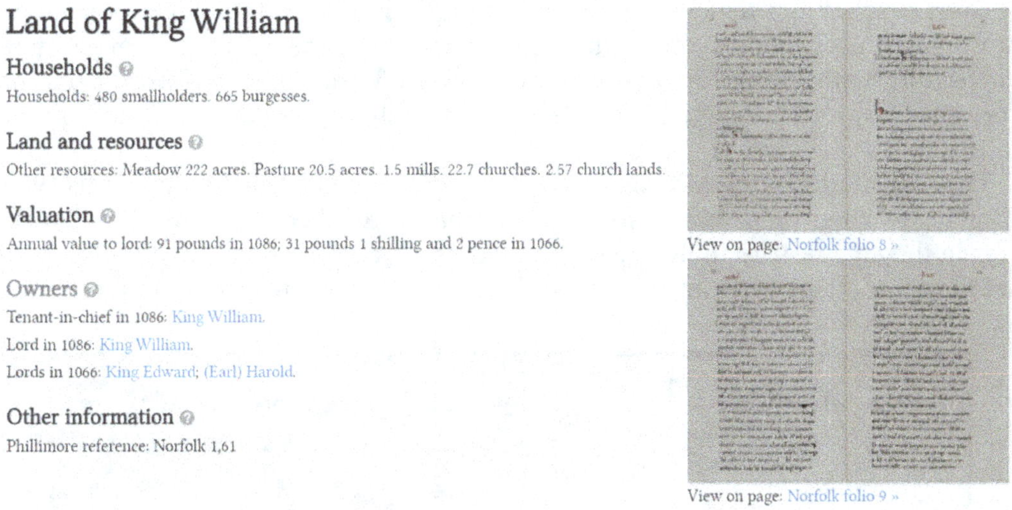

Figure 16.2 Screenshot from www.opendomesday.org showing the detail contained on individual sites and the images of the actual Domesday Book the information has been transcribed from.

consider the extent of change that occurred after 1066, showing how their local area was directly changed by this nationally significant event.

Idea 2 – 20th Century Conflict

A very powerful way that we can incorporate local history into our teaching is through the examination of local aspects of either the First or Second World War. In many communities, the local war memorial can provide an anchoring focal point when studying either conflict. Some prominent, with others far more hidden, these monuments can act as a local lens to focus in on individual stories embedded within the often-huge stories of these conflicts.

Whilst the teaching of the First and Second World War is generally done well in our schools, offering pupils clear narratives of the conflicts, these can sometimes feel distant and detached for pupils. A common topic taught in schools at Key Stage 3 is the Battle of the Somme. Whilst it is essential that pupils gain an understanding of the course of the battle and what the outcome was, this can result in pupils struggling to contextualise the human impact contained within the shocking statistics. When talking of the 19,240 men killed on the first day of the Battle of the Somme, or the 420,000 British and Commonwealth troops killed or injured by the end of the battle, some pupils struggle to understand what this really means. Presenting pupils with information about a local individual is therefore extremely powerful as it presents a human face to an otherwise incomprehensible statistic, linking a real life to the big picture.

The Thiepval exhibition 'Missing but not Forgotten' in 2012 showed 'the story of an individual recorded as missing on each of the 141 days of the Somme battle'. Over 600 biographies and photographs have been compiled by Ken and Pam Linge for the exhibition, with a selection included in the book 'Missing but Not Forgotten: Men of the Thiepval Memorial – Somme' (Linge, 2015). These biographies cover the stories of men from counties across the country and can help to humanise the story of the battle and conflict, avoiding the pitfall of pupils becoming focussed on the often-overwhelming statistics and instead allowing them to look at the events through a more personal, individual lens. Figure 16.3 shows one of these case studies that can be used to humanise the conflict. This information can then be used exclusively in the lesson examining the Somme, or even more powerfully, with a range of other stories, woven into the scheme of work from the very start, exploring the men from the local area who signed up and fought in the conflict.

The website https://astreetnearyou.org/ can be used effectively in this way, allowing teachers (or pupils) to look at those that were killed during the First World War in the area near to their school. Some of these records hold great amounts of detail, including pictures and (if you are lucky) letters or further details about their

Sapper, 21314, Walter Charles Fry, 15th Field Company, Royal Engineers, was killed on 23rd October 1916 aged 28.

Lieutenant Robert Miller Taylor of 15th Field Company wrote to the family:-

"Your son was killed by shell fire as 2.35 pm on the 23rd inst. His death was instantaneous, as the shell fell in the trench beside him and killed one of his comrades at the same time. He was buried on the battlefield close to the front trenches, and it is my intention to have the place of burial marked with a cross..."

Walter Charles Fry is commemorated on Pier and Face 8A of the Thiepval Memorial together with his comrade Sapper, 120714, Charles Henry Flower, 15th Field Company, Royal Engineers, also aged 28.

Figure 16.3 One of the case studies from the exhibition 'Missing but Not Forgotten: Men of the Thiepval Memorial – Somme'.

lives, including direct links to relevant sections from regimental diaries digitised by the National Archives.

Liaison with local history societies, museum services, archives and regimental museums can prove invaluable; these institutions and groups will, given time, be able to provide teachers with an incredibly rich range of sources, details and material that will allow our pupils to link major events to their local area. They will often have further details about the impact of the First and Second World Wars on the local community, and the local inhabitants. Building relationships with your local historical society can offer access to resources that may previously have been inaccessible.

> **Activity 16.2**
>
> Mayhew offers various resources you could use to introduce local history into your school's current teaching of either the Norman Conquest and the World Wars.
> Choose one resource to introduce with your pupils.
>
> - Which resource would you like to introduce to your pupils?
> - What would you like your pupils to learn?
> - When in the current scheme of work would be the best place to introduce it?
> - How could you introduce it? As an anecdote to tell the class? As an activity in its own right or perhaps a homework task?

STUDYING THE HISTORIC ENVIRONMENT

Another possible approach to incorporating local history is through studying the historic environment. Studying the historic environment is an extremely valuable activity for pupils and helps them to comprehend how a site or area changes over time. Currently, this component of the OCR B GCSE History course offers pupils the chance to study in great detail a local site of their school's choice. Through studying a site, pupils will be able to explore how its significance may have changed over time, consider importance on a local and national scale, explore how the use and appearance of the site have varied as well as a range of other questions.

When planning a study of an historic environment, it is essential we have considered the place and purpose of our study. As Burn and Todd (2018) state 'Given the range of possibilities inherent in any particular place, it is important in constructing any history curriculum (but particularly a Key Stage 3 curriculum of only two years' duration) to be clear about the specific rationale for its inclusion and the purposes that it is intended to serve'. So, after deciding on the actual site, our first stage of planning should be deciding on what the extent of the study will be, both in terms of size and time. Will you look at how an entire village changes or just focus on a single site within that area? Both options offer advantages and disadvantages; the study of a larger area can offer far more variety but can sometimes then lack coherence. The study of a single site is dependent on the availability of information and evidence that can be used. Local history societies, museum services and archives will be invaluable at this stage, allowing you to judge whether your proposed study is feasible or potentially has too much in terms of evidence. Though the latter point may seem a strange problem, we must be realistic in terms of the time that we can allocate to developing our site study.

A useful set of questions that can be asked when deciding on the feasibility of a site are outlined in the following list, which have been adapted from the OCR B

GCSE J411 specification (OCR, 2024). While not all may be relevant to your specific enquiry, they can help to focus your study, setting clear boundaries and parameters, and help you to establish what will be needed in terms of resources to deliver the unit effectively.

- What were the reasons for the location of the site within its surroundings?
- When was the site first created?
- Why was the site first created?
- What are the different ways in which the site has changed over time?
- How has the use of the site changed throughout its history?
- Why did changes to the site occur?
- How diverse are the activities and the people linked to the site throughout its history?
- Are there any significant periods in the site in terms of turning points, developments or the highest amount of use?
- Are there any specific features of significance that either remain at the site or previously existed?
- How significant has the site been locally and nationally throughout its history?
- How typical is the site in comparison to other similar sites?
- What can we learn about everyday life, attitudes and values in different periods through studying the site?
- How do historians use the physical remains at the site to prompt valid historical questions and enquiries?
- What sources of information have artistic reconstructions of the site used?
- What are the challenges and benefits of studying the historic environment, of this site and generally?

The Historical Association 2021–22 Teacher Fellowship Programme produced an incredible range of resources with the aim of 'integrating local history into the classroom through the stories of the people and places which make the history of your school's community exciting and unique'. These are all available from the Historical Association website (Historical Association, 2022), illustrating different ways that teachers have introduced a local study to their pupils.

Thanks to advances in technology, and the digitisation of various archives, we now have at our fingertips quick and easy ways to examine specific sites, examining how they have changed over time. One of the most useful when looking at the historic environment, is the collection of aerial photos held by Historic England. Historic England's Aerial Photo Explorer holds a collection of over 400,000 images (which is still being added to) which can be a superb way to show pupils how a particular site or area has changed over the past century. The image trail shown in Figures 16.4–16.6 could be used by pupils exploring how Norwich Castle and the area around it has changed over the past century. Though potentially time consuming in terms of selecting the best and most appropriate images from the archive, once done, this can offer an extremely valuable and accessible route for pupils to explore the changes to a site over time.

Activity 16.3

Visit Historic England's Aerial Photo Explorer online. Zoom in on your local area and see what historic photos you can find. Which photos stand out? Are there any you could share with your pupils?

TEACHING LOCAL HISTORY

Figure 16.4 Norwich Castle and Cattle market, Norwich, 1920, source: Historic England Archive – EPW001766

Figure 16.5 The Castle, Norwich, 1950, © Historic England Archive – BB91_03019

Figure 16.6 Norwich Castle, 2001, © Mr Peter Smee. Source: Historic England Archive – IOE01_03795_20

ORAL HISTORY

An often underutilised, but potentially incredibly powerful source of information, is that of oral history. Explored brilliantly by Toettcher and West (2021) in Teaching History, their article explores potential approaches as well as the challenges faced when using oral histories in the classroom. As the article outlines, one of the key opportunities oral history offers, is the ability for pupils to 'connect young people more readily to people from the past'. Toettcher and West also outline in simple, straightforward steps, how to plan for, carry out and consider pitfalls of carrying out oral history interviews.

There are also huge numbers of collections held across the country, by record offices, museums and universities that can be used with pupils with relative ease and without the need to carry out their own interviews. The British Library sound archive is an excellent starting point, covering a wide range of topics and time periods. There is also clear guidance and support available to help those looking to plan and carry out their own interview; for example, the Norfolk Record Office has produced an excellent guide outlining how to approach oral history interviews. Similarly, the Oral History Society (http://www.ohs.org.uk/) offers guidance to help get started, as well as demonstrating how much of an opportunity oral history projects can be for pupils, highlighted by the excellent Windrush Project film.

Oral history also allows us to ensure that a diversity of voices and narratives are heard as highlighted by Sarah Hartsmith and Andrew Sweet (2023). See Chapter 12 for how the Park View History Department have used oral history to bring the voices of the British-Pakistani community directly into the classroom. Managing our pupils' exploration, we could either allow them to explore a range of different voices, or provide them with a selection to ensure that this diversity is present. Using whichever approach works best for you and your pupils will help ensure that they are able to really benefit from the exercise.

SUMMARY OF KEY POINTS

- Local history is vital for pupils to make greater sense of the world around them, whilst also providing examples that can embellish, illuminate or even challenge the national picture.
- Local history can both be incorporated throughout the existing curriculum and made the focus of a local study.
- When establishing a local study, it is essential to establish clear criteria in terms of time, space and focus.
- Forge links with your local museum service and with local historical societies – they will want to help! Ensure this is not something rushed, but part of your long-term planning.
- Explore examples of work carried out by other schools – via the Historical Association and other professional bodies such as the British Association for Local History, or the Oral History Society.
- Ensure that your local study has a purpose and function; how does your local study contribute to your pupils' wider historical understanding?

RESOURCES AND FURTHER READING

A Street Near You. https://astreetnearyou.org/

Bates, Neil, & Bowry, Robert. "That's Next to My Gran's house': Building Local History into the curriculum' in Teaching History, 185, Missing Stories Edition, (2021): 34–43. London: Historical Association.

Burn, Katherine, & Todd, Jason. 'Right up My Street: the Knowledge Needed to Plan a Local History enquiry' in Teaching History, 170, Historians Edition, (2018): 50–63. London: Historical Association.

Hartsmith, Sarah, & Sweet, Andrew. 'Looking Through the Microhistory lens' in Fairlamb, Alex, & Ball, Rachel. What Is History Teaching, Now? A Practical Handbook for All History Teachers and Educators. Hodder Education 2023.

Historic England. 'Aerial Photo Explorer' [Online Resource]. https://historicengland.org.uk/images-books/archive/collections/aerial-photos/

Historical Association. 'Teacher Fellowship Programme: Local history' [Online Resources], (2022). https://www.history.org.uk/secondary/categories/8/module/8741/teacher-fellowship-programme-local-history

Ken, & Linge, Pam. Missing but Not Forgotten: Men of the Thiepval Memorial – Somme. Barnsley: Pen & Sword Military 2015.

OCR. GCSE (9-1) Specification: History B (Schools History Project). 2024. 47–48. https://ocr.org.uk/Images/207164-specification-accredited-gcse-history-b-.pdf

Ofsted. Research Review Series: History. 2021. https://www.gov.uk/government/publications/research-review-series-history/research-review-series-history

Powell-Smith, Anna. 'Open Domesday' [Website]. https://opendomesday.org/

The Editorial Board. 'Move Me On: Planning a Local History Enquiry' in Teaching History, 169, A Time and a Place Edition, (2017): 68–71. London: Historical Association.

Toettcher, Emily, & West, Eliza. 'Exploring the 'remembered': Using Oral History to Enhance a Local History partnership' in Teaching History, 182, A Sense of Period Edition, (2021): 8–15. London: Historical Association.

Wilkinson, Alf. A Local History Toolkit. London: Historical Association 2011.

Index

African history 10, 18, 20, 57, 150–1, 157, 205
Ashton, Rosemary 90, 92
assessment 171–81; and enquiry questions 178; formal 179–81; formative 172–3; informal 172–8; and lesson quizzes 173; level descriptors and GCSE markschemes 170; and a 'mixed constitution' 173, 177–8; and multiple-choice questions 173–4, 177, 179, 180; and Ofsted 171; summative 172–3, 178; and the 'testing effect' 175; and timelines 174, 177, 180
Austin, Amy 8

Bailey-Watson, Will 5, 8, 10, 13, 14
Bangladeshi history 21–3
Banham, Dale 6, 109, 111, 207
Barton, Keith C. 118, 119, 123–4
Bateman, Chloe 11–12
Beard, Mary 187
BeBold History Network 20, 211
Becket, Thomas 64, 106, 112
Benger, Alexander 94–5
Bergman, Karin 123
Biggar, Nigel 152–3
Bjork, Robert 170, 181
Black Death: as subject of change enquiry 27; as subject of consequences enquiry 81, 86, 87
Black Elk 163
Black pupils, and their experiences of history in English classrooms 8
Black history 8, 9, 47–8, 158–59
Black Tudors 153, 166, 205
Blackbird, Leila 140
Blackhawk, Ned 162–4
Bloch, Marc 135–6, 137, 140, 154
Bonn, M.J. 157
Boyd, Julia 95, 96, 203–4
Boyd, Susanna 8
Bradshaw, Matthew 125–6, 191
British-Pakistani community, bringing their voices into the classroom 164–6
Brown, Geraint 58, 122, 170, 175, 178
Browning, Christopher 187
Burke, Peter 92
Burn, Katharine 208–9, 223

Burney, Rachel 206
Burnham, Sally 58, 170, 175, 178, 205
Byrom, Jamie 5–8, 24, 149

Canadian Historical Thinking Project 119, 161
Canning, Pam 11
Card, Jane 106, 108, 110, 111, 121
Carr, Edward Hallett 57, 62, 209
Carr, Elizabeth 91, 174
Carroll, Jim 67, 73, 107, 109–10, 191
Caulfield, Mike 40
causation, second-order concept 57–70; is not change and continuity 43–44; and enquiry questions 59–62; progression in 58; and teaching activities 62–69
Cercadillo, Lis 125–6
change and continuity, second-order concept 43–55; and activities for teaching 49–53; is not causation 43; is not consequence 44; and enquiry questions 46–8; and thematic studies at GCSE 53–4
Changing Histories textbook series 18, 19
Chapman, Arthur 59, 66, 67, 104, 112, 141–2, 207, 208
Chase, Malcolm 96, 98, 100–1
Christodoulou, Daisy 174, 178–9
Clark, Christopher 40, 128
Coffin, Caroline 106, 197
Colby, Sherri Rae 211
colligatory concepts 44–5, 73–4, 77, 81
consequence, second-order concept 72–88; is not change and continuity 44, 75; is not causation 75–6; defined 76–7; enquiry questions 80–6; is not significance 121; and teaching activities 78–80, 86–8; and timelines 174
Cook, Rachael 62, 66
Counsell, Christine: on change and continuity 43, 46; and *Changing Histories* textbooks 18, 19, 25, 47; on curriculum 171; on enquiry questions 27; on extended writing 183, 186, 187, 191, 192, 195, 196, 207, 208; on interpretations 108, 207; on the role of knowledge 36, 38, 208, 211; on narrative 209; on second-order concepts 39; on

similarity and difference 91–92; on historical significance 119–22; on sourcework 137; and timelines 174; and zones of relevance exercises 64–65
Craik, Fergus 171
Cromwell, Oliver, as focus on interpretations enquiry 105, 107–9, 110, 111
Crooks, Victoria 61
cultural turn in history 92–3
Curricularium, the 9
curriculum as progression model 171–2
Cusworth, Hannah 9, 205
Cutrara, Samantha 161, 162, 166

Dabiri, Emma 158–9, 166
Davies, Nathaneal 21–3, 47–8, 153–4
Dawson, Ian 49, 58, 109, 137, 150, 152, 209
decolonisation 157–67; definition 157–9; and archives 160–1, and indigenous approaches to history 162–4
disability history 8
disciplinary knowledge 32–42; defined 34–5; and second-order concepts 38–9; and historians' methods 40; and progression 172
documentaries, as historical interpretations 111–2
Dodds Pennock, Caroline 138–40
Domesday Book, as source for local history 220–1
Donaghy, Lee 173
DuBois W.E.B. 157
Duffy, Eamon 23–4, 46–7, 187
Dunbar-Ortiz, Roxanne 163

Ebbinghaus' forgetting curve 176, 181
Echo-Hawk, Abigail 160
Eliot, T.S. 106
Elsdon, Kathryn 93–4
empathy 92–5, 98
enquiry questions 16–30; difference from enquiry learning 17; and historical scholarship 206–7; in Key Stage 3 planning 16–30; in Key Stage 4 and 5 planning 22; as puzzles 23; putting substantive concepts at the heart of 22–3
environmental history 8, 68, 163
Evans, Jennifer 192
Evans, Richard J. 51–2, 191
extended writing 183–98; and argumentative language 184, 186–7; and grammar 192–4; and historical scholarship 180, 185–7, 199; and paragraphs 194–7; and reading 185–9; and rehearsing arguments in speech 197–8; and vocabulary 190–2

Fanon, Frantz 158–9, 166
female suffrage campaign, as example of causation enquiry 60–1
Ferguson, Niall 111–2
films, as historical interpretations 111
Ford, Alex 10–2, 58
Fordham, Michael 110, 171, 173, 177, 191, 198
forgetting curve *see* Ebbinghaus' forgetting curve
Foster, Rachel 27, 40, 50, 93–4, 187, 190, 191, 192, 196, 204, 207
Frankopan, Peter 129–30, 205–6, 213
Fullard, Giles 109

Gadd, Sarah 196, 207–8
Goudie, Kath 204
Goullée, Corinne 46–7
Gove, Michael 8, 170
Graham, Helen 69
Grande, Jonathan 65, 66
Green, Toby 165, 205
Grey, Lady Jane; as subject of interpretations enquiry 111
Griffin, Emma 17–20, 22, 24, 75
Gypsy, Roma and Traveller (GRT) history 20

Haaland, Deb 163
Hackett, Eve 46
Hall, Rebecca 111
Hammond, Kate 32–3, 37, 108, 170–1, 177, 197, 211
Harmsworth, Andy 109
Harris, R. 8, 104
Hartsmith, Sarah 226
Hatcher, John 187
Hawkey, Kate 8, 68
Hayden, Terry 119
Hibbert, David 113, 150
Hill, Claire 169
Hiscox, Holly 210–1
Historic England Aerial Photo Explorer 224–6
historic environment; GCSE unit 223–4
Historical Association 1, 9, 21, 227; Teacher Fellowship Programme 224
historical fiction 12
historical perspective: case for inclusion as a second-order concept 90–102; defined 93; used to teach pupils about Chartism 95–102
historical scholarship 202–14; and big picture curriculum planning 206–7; and challenges of literacy 212, and enquiry examples 204–6, and historical thinking 211–2; and interpretations 208–10; and lesson planning 203–4; and narratives 211; and powerful knowledge 208
historical significance *see* significance
'history from the inside' 91–5, 102
Holliss, Claire 40, 206
Horrible Histories 52, 106
Howard, Hannah 93–4
Howard, Kat 169
Howells, Gary 109
Hunt, Martin 118
Husbands, Chris 13, 138–9

imperialism, British, as example of scholarship shaping an enquiry question 206
indigenous peoples 138–40, 158, 162–4, 167
Initial Stimulus Material (ISM) 144–5
interpretations, second-order concept 105–15; and children's books 110; defined 104–5; documentaries 111–2; and 'double vision' 108, 110, 121; and enquiries 20, 22, 112–4; and films 111; and museum exhibits 110; and paintings 111; and historical reconstructions 111; is not historical significance 121; and subsequentness 109, 110
Iranian Revolution, as subject of causation enquiry 60

Jackson-Buckley, Sarah 94
Jarman, Cat 72–4, 205
Jenner, Tim 107, 187, 212, 220
'Jew's House', Lincoln 53–4

INDEX

Karpicke, Jeffrey D. 175
Kaufmann, Miranda 205
Keates, Dan 107
Kennett, Rich 10–12, 13
Kerridge, Richard 20
Kershaw, Ian 191–3
Key Stage 3 planning 4–14; as 'cartography' 12–13; as 'conducting' 10–12; and historical scholarship 202–15; as 'architecture' 9–10; as 'professional wrestling' 5–7; as 'pugilism' 7–9; and progression 5, 29, 58–9, 125–6, 171–2, 207; as 'TV production' 11
Key Stage 3 National Strategy – Literacy in History 190
Klose, Fabian 157
knowledge 32–42; *see also* disciplinary knowledge; 'knowledge-rich' curricula; powerful knowledge; procedural knowledge; propositional knowledge; substantive knowledge
knowledge turn 208
'knowledge-rich' curricula 10, 108

Laffin, Diana 207
Lal, Ruby 25, 27–8
Lambert, David 208
Learning Scientists, the 171
Lee, Peter 45, 58, 93, 106, 140–2, 211
Lemov, Doug 176
Lester, Alan 152
Levstik, Linda 124–5
Lewis, Chris 205
LGBTQ+ history 8, 160–1
Lindstrom, Carole 163
Lingard, Ruth 8
local history 219–27; and an archive 160; and Roman history 150; and historical significance 130–1; a study of one street 94
Lockhart, Robert 171
Lomas, Tim 120–1, 123
London, Laura 61
Longair, Sarah 20, 211
Luff, Ian 91
Lyndon-Cohen, Dan 114, 165

Mary I, as subject of a consequences enquiry 87, 88
McAleavy, Tony 40, 104–5, 109
McGregor, Heather 162, 163
'Meanwhile, Elsewhere' 12–3
medicine, as GCSE thematic study 49, 53
migration 15, 53–4, 73, 76, 94, 111–2, 137, 164–6
Mohamud, Abdul 7–9, 10, 13, 24, 140, 151
Morris, Marc 46, 109
Morton, Tom 39, 58, 94, 119, 138, 140–1
Mughal India 24–8, 29, 37

Naoroji, Dadabhai 157
Narraganset people 163
National Curriculum: 1991 edition 76, 93, 105; 1995 edition 39, 119; 2000 edition 4, 8; 2013 draft 8; 2013 edition 105, 170; and requirement for local history 219
Ned of the Hill, song by The Pogues 110
Norman Conquest: as subject of changes enquiry 46; as subject of interpretations enquiry 109, 171, 174, 204; and local history 220–1

Oak National Academy 46
Ofsted: and curriculum 171; and local history 219; Research Review Series (2021) 220; History Subject Report (2023) 169
Ohlmeyer, Jane 21
Olusoga, David 32–3, 114, 127, 205–6, 212
oral history 160, 164–6, 167, 226, 227
Overy, Richard 171
Oxby, Fred 160

paintings, as historical interpretations 111
partition of India 165–6
Pate, Gemma 192
Patel, Zaiba 113, 150
Pattison, Tom 205
Phillips, Jessica 94
Phillips, Robert 11, 121–2, 144
political reform in the nineteenth century 50, 95–9
Power, Eileen 207
power, and the construction of history 125, 140, 153, 159, 160, 163, 166, 167
powerful knowledge 208; *see also* knowledge
Preye Garry, Josh 205
Priggs, Catherine 123, 161
procedural knowledge 34–41; defined 34
progression *see* Key Stage 3 planning
propositional knowledge 34–42; defined 34
Purvis, June 60

Quinn, Emmy 21, 30

Rakib, Taslima 21, 153–4
Ramirez, Janina 203
reform *see* political reform in the nineteenth century
reading challenging texts 107–8
reconstructions, as historical interpretations 111
Reformation, the 20, 23, 43, 45, 46–7
Reisman, Abby 136, 144
Reynolds, David 73–5, 81–4, 92
Riley, Michael 4–8, 13, 22–3, 24, 27, 29, 58–9, 81, 105, 126, 149, 184
Roediger, Henry L 175
Rorke's Drift, the Battle of, as subject of interpretations enquiry 109, 111
Rubenhold, Hallie 206
Rubin, Miri 92

Salem Witch Trials, as subject of A Level lessons 185–7, 194
Sanghera, Sathnam 206
Schama, Simon 46, 109, 171, 174, 204
scholarship *see* historical scholarship
Schools Council History Project *see* Schools History Project (SHP)
Schools History Project (SHP) 53, 135, 149
second-order concepts; and causation *see* causation *and* consequence; and change and continuity *see* change and continuity; and historical significance *see* significance; and interpretations *see* interpretations; and similarity and difference *see* similarity and difference; and use of evidence *see* sources and evidence
Second World War: and causation 62; and evidence 113, 150; and historical change 44, 81; and local history 221–3

Seixas, Peter 39, 58, 94, 119, 138, 140–1, 208–9
Shakespeare, William, as subject of interpretations enquiry 108
Shemilt, Denis 45, 93, 106, 140–1, 142, 208, 211
significance, second-order concept 118–32; activities to teach 127–3; defined 119–20; and enquiry questions 126–7; and ethical implications 122–3; as a meta-concept 118; misconceptions 124–5; progress in 125–6; and taxonomies 121–2
silences 123, 140, 141, 142, 144, 149, 150, 152, 153, 158–9, 160, 162, 164, 166
Silk Roads: and Frankopan's children's book about 213; as subject of KS3 enquiries 18, 205–6
similarity and difference, second-order concept 90–102; activities for teaching 91–2
sources and evidence, second-order concept 135–55; activities for teaching 143–52; and pupils' evidential thinking 140–2, 152–4; and relationship between evidence and interpretation 113; and sources and evidence 137–8; and 'traces' 113, 137–50; and 'tracks' 135; use by historians 138–40
Snelson, Helen *v*, 8, 20, 108, 111
Spanish Civil War, as subject of causation enquiry 60
Spears, Michael 163
Standing Bear 163
Stanford, Matt 29, 40, 59
studies in depth *see* thematic studies
substantive knowledge 32–42; simple facts 36; narratives and stories 37; sense of period 37; substantive concepts 37–8
Sumeracki, Megan *see* Learning Scientists, the
Sweet, Andrew 226
Sylvester, David 93, 149

Tape Letters Project, the 164–5
Taylor, Becky 20

testing effect, the 175
thematic studies at GCSE 53–4
Third Reich, the: and 'history from below' 95–6, 98; and scholarship for lesson planning 203–4; as subject of change enquiry 51–2
Thompson, E.P. 95
Todd, Jason 223
Toettcher, Emily 226
traces 137–50
Trail of Tears, the; in a Key Stage 3 enquiry 164
Trouillot, Michel-Rolph 123, 125, 140, 152, 158–9, 160, 166
Tuhiwai Smith, Linda 158–9 162, 166
Tull, Walter 166
Turner, Jen 112

Wampanoag people 163
Ward, Rachel 187
Wedgwood, C.V. 107–8, 110
Weimar Germany; as subject of change enquiry 49, 51–2; and sources at GCSE 147–8
West, Eliza 226
Wheeley, Tom 109
Whitburn, Robin 7–9, 10, 13, 24, 140, 151
White, Richard 144
Weinstein, Yana *see* Learning Scientists, the
Wiliam, Dylan 173, 177, 178
Wineberg, Sam 40, 123, 136, 144, 154, 209
women's history 8–9, 19–20, 25, 44, 60, 61, 96, 97, 127, 153, 159, 187, 203, 206, 211
Woodcock, James 50, 67, 122, 190–2
Worth, Paula Lobo 7, 78–80, 87, 88, 122, 126, 127, 129, 191, 205

Yaseen, Wajid 165
Yerxa, Donald A. 205

Zakaria, Anam 21–22, 153–4

For Product Safety Concerns and Information please contact our EU representative GPSR@taylorandfrancis.com
Taylor & Francis Verlag GmbH, Kaufingerstraße 24, 80331 München, Germany

www.ingramcontent.com/pod-product-compliance
Lightning Source LLC
Chambersburg PA
CBHW080849010526
44115CB00016B/2777